# Ben Graham Was a Quant

Founded in 1807, John Wiley & Sons is the oldest independent publishing company in the United States. With offices in North America, Europe, Australia, and Asia, Wiley is globally committed to developing and marketing print and electronic products and services for our customers' professional and personal knowledge and understanding.

The Wiley Finance series contains books written specifically for finance and investment professionals as well as sophisticated individual investors and their financial advisors. Book topics range from portfolio management to e-commerce, risk management, financial engineering, valuation and financial instrument analysis, as well as much more.

For a list of available titles, visit our web site at www.WileyFinance.com.

# Ben Graham Was a Quant

*Raising the IQ of the Intelligent Investor*

STEVEN P. GREINER, PhD

WILEY
John Wiley & Sons, Inc.

Published by John Wiley & Sons, Inc., Hoboken, New Jersey.
Published simultaneously in Canada.



For general information on our other products and services or for technical support, please contact our Customer Care Department within the United States at (800) 762-2974, outside the United States at (317) 572-3993 or fax (317) 572-4002.

Wiley also publishes its books in a variety of electronic formats. Some content that appears in print may not be available in electronic books. For more information about Wiley products, visit our web site at www.wiley.com.

***Library of Congress Cataloging-in-Publication Data:***

Greiner, Steven P.
Ben Graham was a quant : raising the IQ of the intelligent investor / Steven P. Greiner.
p. cm. – (Wiley finance series)
Includes bibliographical references and index.
ISBN 978-0-470-64207-8 (cloth); ISBN 978-1-118-01340-3 (ebk);
ISBN 978-1-118-01338-0 (ebk); ISBN 978-1-118-01339-7 (ebk)
1. Securities. 2. Investments. 3. Investment analysis. 4. Graham, Benjamin, 1894–1976. I. Title.
HG4521.G723 2011
332.63′2042–dc22

2010039909

Printed in the United States of America

10 9 8 7 6 5 4 3 2 1

*There are two groups I dedicate this book to. The first are those just entering the quant workforce, whether experienced scientists making a career change, or those graduating from some financial engineering curriculum. They should find the history in this book enabling. The second group are those people who helped me get started in this business, too numerous to mention individually. To both, I raise a hearty glass of burgundy and toast them, "to success in the markets." Cheers!*

# Contents

# Preface

*I earnestly ask that everything be read with an open mind and that the defects in a subject so difficult may be not so much reprehended as investigated, and kindly supplemented, by new endeavors of my readers.*

—Isaac Newton, *The Principia*[1]

The history of quantitative investing goes back farther than most people realize. You might even say it got its start long before the famous Black-Scholes option pricing equation was introduced.[2] You could even say it began before the advent of computers, and certainly before the PC revolution. The history of quantitative investing began when Ben Graham put his philosophy into easy-to-understand screens. Graham later wrote *The Intelligent Investor*, which Warren Buffett read in 1950 and used to develop his brilliant formula for investing.[3] Since then, quantitative investing has come from the impoverished backwater of investing to the forefront of today's asset management business.

So what is quantitative investing? What does it mean to be a quant? How can the average investor use the tools of this perhaps esoteric but benign field? Quantitative investing has grown widely over the past few years, due in part to its successful implementation during the years following the tech bubble until about 2006. Since then poorer years followed, in which algorithms all but replaced the fundamental investment manager. Then during the 2007–2009 credit crisis, quant investing got a bad rap when many criticized quantitative risk management as the cause of the crisis and even more said that, minimally, it did not help avoid losses. For these people, quant is a wasting asset and should be relegated to its backwater beginnings for it is indeed impoverishing. However, these criticisms come from a misunderstanding of what quant methods are and what it means to be a quantitative investment manager or what it means to use a quantitative process in building stock portfolios. We shall clarify these matters in the body of this work.

In reality, investment managers have a bias or an investment philosophy they adhere to. These investment philosophies can be value oriented like Ben Graham's, or they can be growth oriented, focusing on growing earnings, sales, or margins. Good managers adhere to their principles both in good times and in bad. That is precisely the message (not the only one) famed value investor Ben Graham advocates in *The Intelligent Investor*—that of adhering to your stock selection process come hell or high water, and it puts the onus on the individual investor to control your impulses to give in to primal urges or behaviors governed by fear. For instance, we are naturally disposed to not sell assets at prices below cost (i.e., the sunk-cost effect) because we expect price rebound and are subject to anchoring (we tend to remember the most recent history and act accordingly). This results in investors chasing historical returns rather than expected returns, so we constantly choose last year's winning mutual funds to invest in. However, if we design and implement mathematical models for predicting stock or market movements, then there can be no better way to remain objective than to turn your investment process over to algorithms, or quantitative investing!

This book is for you, the investor, who likes to sleep at night secure in the knowledge that the stocks you own are good bets, even if you have no way of knowing their daily share price. What is so good about quantitative investing is that it ultimately leads to disciplined investing. Codifying Ben Graham's value philosophy and marrying it with quantitative methods is a win-win for the investor and that is what this book is about.

This book will teach you how to:

- Create custom screens based on Graham's methods for security selection.
- Find the most influential factors in forecasting stock returns, focusing on the fundamental and financial factors used in selecting Graham stocks.
- Test these factors with software on the market today.
- Combine these factors into a quantitative model and become a disciplined intelligent investor.
- Build models for other style, size, and international strategies.

There is no reason you cannot benefit from the research of myriad PhD's, academics, and Wall Street whiz kids just because you did not take college calculus. This book is the essential how-to when it comes to building your own quantitative model and joining the ranks of the quants with the added benefit of maintaining the 3T's (i.e., tried, true, and trusted) fundamental approaches of Ben Graham. All this and very little mathematics! Nevertheless, we cannot forget that despite his investment methods, Graham himself suffered a harrowing loss of over 65 percent during the Crash of 1929–1932. The adage "past performance is not a predictor of future returns" must always apply.

This book is not about financial planning, estate planning, or tax planning. This book is part tutorial, part history lesson, part critique, and part future outlook. Though the prudent investor must remain aware of corporate bond yields, this book is mostly about investing in stocks. Also, it generally refers to investment of liquid investable securities and does not address emergency cash needs, household budgeting, or the like. You might also read this book before tackling Ben Graham's *The Intelligent Investor*, especially if you are approaching the investment field from an engineering background rather than a financial one, for the brevity of the financial terms in this book is far more understandable, approachable, and filtered down to those most relevant variables for you. Conversely, in Ben's Graham's book, an accounting background is more helpful than a degree in mechanical engineering.

Likewise, the investable universe in vogue today that includes stocks (equities), fixed income (government and corporate bonds), commodities, futures, options, and real estate are all part of an institutional asset allocation schema that is not addressed here either. This book is 99 percent about equities with a smidgen of corporate debt.

You will come away with a much better understanding of value, growth, relative value, quality, momentum, and various styles associated with equity investing. Certainly the Morningstar-style box, defined by small to large and value to growth, will be studied, and the differences among developed markets, global investing, international investing, and emerging markets will all be heavily defined. We will cover how the Graham method can be applied to markets outside the United States as well.

Generally, this book takes the perspective of the long-term investor talking about saving for retirement, so this constitutes the focus we have adopted, well in line with Graham's focus. In addition, we concentrate on mid- to large-cap equities in the United States and talk about how to apply the Graham method to global markets. Global markets allow for the universe of equities chosen. As written previously, the very first step is to define the investment area one wants to concentrate on and, from this, choose the universe of stocks on which the intelligent investor should concentrate.

This book is organized as follows: The introduction covers some history and identifies who the quants are, where they came from, and the types of quants that exist. Chapter 1 defines the search for alpha and explains what alpha is. Chapter 2 discusses risk; it is a "think chapter" filled with useful information and new perspectives. Chapter 2 also functions a bit as an apologetic for quants, but it comes down hard on those who criticize quant methods without also lauding their accomplishments. Chapter 3 moves on to discuss some inadequacies of modern portfolio theory and explains why easy approximations and assumptions are usually violated in finance. It is here that g-factor is introduced as a better method to measure stock volatility.

After the first three chapters, you will be armed to dig into Graham's method, which is outlined in Chapter 4. The chapter defines the Graham factors and shows examples of other factors, illustrating what they are and how they are measured and validated. Chapter 5 is an important chapter that teaches the relevant methods in building factor models, and it reviews important data considerations before modeling can commence. Chapter 6 is about the actual testing of factors; you will see exactly how to do so with live examples and data. Chapter 7 takes the output of the previous chapter and shows how to put factors together to form models, specifically several Graham models. Chapter 8 summarizes the issues for putting the Graham model to work and reviews consideration for building a portfolio.

Chapters 9 and 10 are more unusual. Chapter 9 breaks down stock returns by discussing new ways to describe them and introduces better, lesser known theories on stock behavior. This is not a finance chapter. However, it has its base in econophysics, but it is far easier to understand than material you would find elsewhere written by academics. Chapter 10 offers the future view. Anyone who cares to know what the world will be like in the near future as well as twenty years from now should read this chapter. It is based on broad trends that seem to have nothing to stop them from continuing. From here, get your latte or pour your favorite Bordeaux and jump in. You are about to get the keys to quantdom!

Steven P. Greiner
*Chicago, Illinois*
*November 2010*

INTRODUCTION

# The Birth of the Quant

Quantitative investing (quant) as we know it today began when computers became both small enough and fast enough to process data in real time. The start of quantitative investing is still in debate, but cannot claim usage widely enough until after the advent of the personal computer. This would obviously be after 1982, for in that year, the "Z-80" was still the programmer's basic system.[1] When DOS came into its own from its birth from under CP/M, the operating system of the time, the quant world began. This was the Big Bang for quant, for then investment houses and proprietary trading desks began hiring physicists and mathematicians, and it was when many quants began their careers.[2]

Going back further, many cite a paper written in 1952 by Harry Markowitz as giving birth to quant's modern beginnings.[3] His creativity also birthed Modern Portfolio Theory (MPT), which was later added to by Sharpe, Merton, Black, Litterman, and many others. That the theoretical gave way to the practical and the use of normal (sometimes referred to as Gaussian, for the name of the shape of the normal distribution) statistics came into use as tools of the quant was simply because computing power was small and normal statistics were easy to compute, sometimes even by hand with paper and pencil.

Initially, quant had the wind at its back because of people like John C. Bogle who, in launching Vanguard Funds in 1975, argued that active management was not worth it for two main reasons: first, the fees were too high, and second, investors could not beat the market in the long run. These two accusations launched a strong attack on fundamentally active managers. Sophisticated analytics were in their infancy at the time, and it was difficult to generate data to argue against John Bogle's viewpoint. Only the Capital Asset Pricing Model (CAPM) was around, having been published by William Sharpe in 1963, to allow Bogle support for his supposition that most active managers offered little "alpha" and that many of their supposed returns were from "beta" plays.[4,5]

In my attempt to offer a basic understanding of alpha and beta, I will throw away Joseph de Maistre's quote: "There is no easy method of learning difficult things. The method is to close the door, give out that you are not at home and work." In so doing, we offer a simple explanation of alpha and beta using a very plain analogy (though clearly incorrect). Think of the ninth-grade algebra equation $y = mx + b$. In the CAPM, $y$ is the excess return of the active manager's portfolio over cash, and $x$ is the market's return over cash. Then, $m$ is like beta and $b$ is like alpha. This is clearly wrong in the absolute sense, but makes the idea easy to grasp so it is only a little wrong.

Beginning in the 1960s, the Efficient Market Hypothesis (EMH) gained hold (believed and espoused by Bogle, for instance) and was being taught at schools like the University of Chicago. The EMH implied that all known information about a security was already in its market price. Eugene Fama, an EMH founder, along with Ken French began a search for a model to replace the outdated CAPM from William Sharpe, finally publishing a seminal paper outlining three main factors that do a better job explaining returns.[6] These were classic CAPM beta (the market beta), firm size (market capitalization), and book to market. The analogy for the Fama-French model, then, is an equation like $y = m_1x_1 + m_2x_2 + m_3x_3 + b$, so that now there are three betas ($m_1$, $m_2$ and $m_3$) but still only one alpha. This work motivated one of the largest concentrations of academic effort in finance, that of finding other equations made similarly using financial statement data as factors (balance sheet, income statement, or cash flow statement data), in a simple linear equation like the Fama-French.

Indeed, even more work was done (most of which remains unpublished) in the basements and halls of the large institutional asset managers, banks, and hedge funds, looking for the Holy-Grail equation to explain returns and offer the investor an advantage over the market. However, the intent of these efforts were meant to contradict the EMH in the sense that the researchers were out to build portfolios in which to outperform the market and seek alpha, whereas Fama-French were trying to describe the market, in support of the Efficient Market Hypothesis. So imagine if you were the researcher who came up with a model that showed a positive $b$ or alpha in the equation describing returns. This would indeed give you a competitive advantage over the market, if your equation held through time. The fact that most of these researchers utilized math and statistics, searching through the data looking for these relationships while rejecting the old-fashioned method of combing through the fundamental data manually, is what branded them as quants. Of course, to find such an anomalous equation was rare, but the promises of riches were enough to motivate far more than a few to the chore.

## CHARACTERIZING THE QUANT

The quant method can be defined as any method for security selection that comes from a systematic, disciplined, and repeated application of a process. When a computer program performs this process in the form of a mathematical algorithm, the computer, not the process, is the topic of conversation. If we change the topic of conversation from computers to process or methodology, then a working definition of a quant becomes: A quant designs and implements mathematical models for the pricing of derivatives, assessment of risk, or predicting market movements. There's nothing in that definition about the computer.

Back in 1949, when Benjamin Graham published *The Intelligent Investor*, he listed seven criteria that, in his opinion, defined "the quantitatively tested portfolio," consisting of (1) adequate size of the enterprise, (2) sufficiently strong financial condition, (3) earnings stability, (4) dividend record, (5) earnings growth, (6) moderate P/E ratio, and (7) moderate ratio of price to book.[7] He then goes on to show the application of these criteria to the list of stocks in the Dow Jones Industrial Average (DJIA) index. There cannot be any other interpretation than that of the author himself who concludes that the application of these criteria builds a quantitatively derived portfolio.

Thus begins quantitative asset management, its birth given to us by Benjamin Graham. Since that time there has been growth of assets and growth of the profession. Quants have roles to play and it appears their role can be categorized in three succinct ways. The first group of quants, which we call Type 1, still are beholden to the EMH.[8] In so doing, they employ their talents creating exchange traded funds (ETF) and index tracking portfolios. Thus the firms of Barclays Global, WisdomTree, PowerShares, Rydex, State Street Global, and Vanguard have many quants working for them designing, running, and essentially maintaining products that don't compete with the market but reproduce it for very low fees. They attend academic conferences; publish very esoteric pieces, if they publish at all; and tend to be stable, risk averse individuals who dress casually for work. Their time horizon for investing is typically years. These quants have PhDs but fewer CFAs. Of course, I'm generalizing, and many quants employed as Type 1 deviate from my simple characterization, but my description is more fun.

The second group of quants, Type 2, are those employed in active management; they attend meetings of the Chicago Quantitative Alliance, Society of Quantitative Analysts, and Quantitative Work Alliance for Applied Finance, Education, and Wisdom (QWAFAFEW). These people are those sifting through financial statement and economic data looking for relationships between returns and fundamental factors, many of the same factors that traditional fundamental analysts look at. Their time horizon of investing is a few months to a couple of years. Their portfolios typically have a value bias to them, similar to Ben Graham–style portfolios. Here you will find equal numbers of PhDs, MBAs, and CFAs. Typical companies employing these quants are First Quadrant, Numeric Investors, State Street Global, Acadian Asset Management, InTech, LSV, DFA (though with a caveat that DFA founders were EMH proponents), Batterymarch, GlobeFlex, Harris Investment Management, Geode Capital, and so forth. These quants are generally not traders, nor do they think of themselves as traders, as wrongly accused.[9] In fact, these quants actually don't want to trade. They want portfolios with low turnover, due to the costs of trading, because, in general, trading costs a portfolio alpha. These quants are investors in the same mode as traditional asset managers using fundamental approaches like Peter Lynch (formerly of Fidelity), Bill Miller (of Legg Mason), or Robert Rodriguez (of FPA). They tend to specialize mostly in equities and ordinary fixed income (not sophisticated structured products, distressed debt, real estate, derivatives, futures, or commodities).

I digress just for a moment to distinguish trading (more speculative in its nature) from investing, and Ben Graham makes a clear distinction in *The Intelligent Investor*'s first chapter where he says, "An investment is one which, upon thorough analysis, promises safety of principal and an adequate return. Operations not meeting these requirements are speculative." Later he says, "We must prevent our readers from accepting the common jargon which applies the term 'investor' to anybody and everybody in the stock market." Likewise, applying the term *trader* to everybody and anybody in the stock market is apportioning a very small part of what is involved in the activity of investing as an apt title for the activity as a whole. We don't call all the players of a baseball team catchers, though all of them catch baseballs, right? I make a point of this because, within the industry, traders, analysts, and portfolio managers are separate activities, and quants are hired into each of those activities with clearly distinct roles and job descriptions.

The last type of quant, the Type 3 quant, is probably the rocket-science type if ever there is any, and their activities mostly involve trading. These people are working in the bowels of the investment banks, hedge funds, and proprietary trading desks. Often they are considered traders rather than investors because their portfolios can consist of many asset classes simultaneously and have very high turnover with holding periods ranging from intradaily to days. They also encompass the flash traders and high-frequency traders. Their members are hard-core quants working on derivatives doing fancy finite element models, Black-Scholes option solvers, and working to solve complicated equations in finance. Firms like D.E. Shaw, Renaissance Technologies, Bluefin Trading, Two Sigma, and Citadel hire these positions. In the book *My Life as a Quant* by Emanuel Derman, these kinds of quants are described quite succinctly, and their history may be typical of Dr. Derman's.[10] They attend the International Association of Financial Engineers meetings and, occasionally, maybe, the Q-Group. They correspond with the scientists at the Sante Fe Institute (complexity and nonlinear research institute). Most of them have PhDs, but, more recently, they are obtaining Financial Engineering degrees, a new academic curriculum. For the most part, these types of quants are not employed as investors nor thought of as such. The kind of work they do and the applications of their work are more speculative in nature and heavily involved in trading. Their trading is very technology oriented, and without trading, these types of firms do not make money. In contrast, trading is an anathema to the process for the previous Type 2 quants. Type 3 quants work in all asset classes including equity, fixed income, CMOs, CDOs, CDS, MBS, CMBS, MUNIs, convertibles, currencies, futures, options, energy, and commodities. If you can trade it, they are into it.

Now, these three types articulate the basic operations and definitions of quants in what is known as the buy side, that is, quants who manage other people's money or capital. There are quants on the sell side as well, who would rather sell picks and shovels to the miners rather than do the mining. Firms such as CSFB, Bernstein Research, Nomura Securities, UBS, Leuthold Group, and various broker/dealers also have quants on their staff providing quantitative research to buy-side quants in lieu of trading dollars. Their clients are mostly Type 2 quants, those doing active management. Type 1 quants use less of this research because they aren't necessarily looking for a market advantage and Type 3 quants compete with the broker/dealers and sell side since they, too, are doing a lot of trading.

Next, there are many quants working for firms that provide data to the buy-side quants, too. They are separate from sell-side quants, however, in that they don't provide research per se; they provide research tools and data. Firms like FactSet, Clarifi, S&P, Reuters, and Bloomberg provide sophisticated tools and data for company or security analysis, charting, earnings release information, valuation, and, of course, pricing. They provide other content and value, too. For instance, FactSet offers portfolio optimization, risk modeling, portfolio attribution, and other analysis software. These firms either collect soft or hard dollars for their services.[11] Their clients are all three types of quants on the buy side.

The last group of quants resides in risk-management firms. These are rather unique in their service in that they are much more highly integrated into the investment process than other service providers. Their product is usually composed of two parts: part data and part model. Just like their buy-side brethren, these quants produce models, not to explain return, but to explain variance or the volatility of return. Firms like FinAnalytica, Northfield, MSCI-Barra, Axioma, ITG, SunGard-APT, and R-Squared Risk Management all provide quant investors risk models as well as optimizers or risk attribution software, enabling buy-side quants (mostly Type 2) to partition their portfolios by various risk attributes. These firms are filled with quants of all three types. They also get paid by hard or soft dollars. Algorithmics and MSCI-RiskMetrics are two firms noted for risk management, and they also hire quants, but these are mostly back-office quants whose clients need firm-wide risk management and are less directly involved in the management of assets. Many of their quants are actuaries and focus on liabilities, so they are not of the same color as the quants previously defined.

Now that you know the three types of quants, let's look at the three elements of a portfolio. These involve the return forecast (the alpha in the simplest sense), the volatility forecast (the risk), and lastly the weights of the security in the portfolio and how you can combine them. These three elements are essential and a necessary condition to have a portfolio, by definition. All three quant types need these three elements. From here on, however, I will be restraining my conversation to Type-2 quants on the buy side. These are the quants whose general outcome is most similar to the Ben Graham type of investor, that of constructing portfolios of stocks (or corporate bonds) with holding periods perhaps as short as three months to several years. The details of these three components of a portfolio will be examined in greater detail in the beginning chapters, but there remains one more topic of discussion in this introduction—that of the contrast between proponents of active management and those supporting the Efficient Market Hypothesis (EMH).

## ACTIVE VERSUS PASSIVE INVESTING

Ben Graham clearly was a believer in active management. There can be no doubt that he believed there were companies on the market that were available at a discount to their intrinsic price. On the other hand, the market is smart, as are the academics who founded Modern Portfolio Theory and the EMH, so how does the individual investor reconcile these differences? This is a very, very good question that I've been thinking about for years. I may not have the answer, but I will offer some reasonable explanations that allow you to sleep at night after having purchased a portfolio of individually selected stocks. First, what is the market? There are, at any one time, somewhere around 5,000 investable securities in the U.S. stock market for the average investor. Is this the market? What about securities in other countries? If we add the rest of the world's securities, there are maybe 35,000 that the average investor can invest in. Is this the market the efficient market theorists are talking about?

Generally, in the United States, we're talking about the S&P 500, which in its simplest sense are the 500 largest stocks in the country. Often people quote the DJIA, which is composed of only 30 stocks, so if we want to make a proxy for the market, the S&P is certainly a better choice than the DJIA. However, where does the S&P 500 come from? Well, it's produced by Standard & Poors taking into account liquidity, sector representation, public float of the security, domicile, financial viability, and other factors.[12] Well, wait a minute. That sure sounds like an actively managed portfolio to me, and, yes, it is. There is no doubt that the S&P 500 is not the market. It is a proxy, and the assumptions that make it a proxy aren't all bad. In fact, they are pretty good. But in reality, the S&P 500 is an actively managed portfolio produced by the company Standard & Poors. It is not passive; do not let anybody kid you. It has low turnover, but it is actively managed.

Moreover, the Wilshire 5000 is a better proxy than is the S&P because it contains 5,000 stocks, right? Do you get the picture? The market isn't so clearly defined as many people would have you believe. So when we say "efficient market," what exactly are we talking about? We are really saying that any publically traded stock has all the information that's fit to print and known, already in its current price, and it moves rapidly to reflect any change in known information, so that the market is efficient in its adjustment to new information.

The implication is that no investor can gain an advantage over any other because the stock moves too quickly to arbitrage the information. Hence, buy the market we are told, but as I have just illustrated, what is the market? This is the conundrum. It is not surprising that there's a correlation between the Wilshire 5000 and the S&P 500, but having a strong correlation doesn't mean their returns are equivalent. For instance, from their respective web sites, the returns ending 12/31/2009 for the Wilshire 5000 and the S&P 500 were:

| Index: | 1-Year | 3-Year | 5-Year |
|---|---|---|---|
| W-5000 | 28.30 | −5.25 | 0.93 |
| S&P 500 | 23.45 | −7.70 | −1.65 |

This comparison clearly distinguishes the performance of the two indexes, in which neither is really the market. So far, we have established that the market is a broad, inexact concept that is hard to define and that the

S&P 500 isn't the market. The financial engineers and quants of Type 1 pedigree have made plenty of "assive" (conjugation of active-passive) investment opportunities through ETFs and index tracking funds for anybody to purchase, given the information just disclosed.

Now, it is common knowledge that the majority of open-ended mutual funds have not beaten the S&P 500 over long time periods, which isn't the market, by the way. This is often taken as evidence in support of why you should buy the S&P 500, the supposed market. However, doing so is seldom seen as just poor investment management; rather, buying the S&P 500 is seen as supporting the efficient market. In other words, it could still be true that markets are inefficient, as Ben Graham would have us believe, and simultaneously it could be true that the majority of open-ended mutual funds have not beaten the S&P 500. It is not a proof that markets are efficient, that open-ended mutual funds mostly lose to the S&P 500, because the S&P 500 is really another managed portfolio. It might just mean that the managers of the S&P 500 are good managers.

Lastly, and here is a single example where subjectivity rules but I can only offer anecdotal evidence in support of inefficient markets, or shall we say semi-efficient markets. In 2008 and up to March of 2009 a flight to quality ensued from investors and away from any securities that had financial leverage. Essentially, securities that would have passed Ben Graham's screen (high quality stocks) maintained their value for no apparent reason, for little news appeared of idiosyncratic (stock specific) nature, only news of economic nature.

At the same time, stocks of high leverage got priced as if death (bankruptcy) was at their door, though there was no news to support that possibility, either. So high quality stocks (to be defined in greater detail in later chapters) held a margin of safety per Ben Graham's ideology and low quality stocks got progressively cheaper. However, once March 2009 came along, the reversal was enough to choke a mule! Suddenly the deep value stocks were all of low quality, highly leveraged companies, and they rose dramatically from depressed levels. High quality Ben Graham stocks could not keep up. What was happening? What was happening was nothing more than fear up until March 2009 and relief thereafter. Hence, behavior was driving the market. It had little to do with the underlying financial conditions of the companies, hence no news was required for the stocks to move. Phenomena like this have given rise to a competitive economic theory to MPT and EMH fostered by anomalous market action, termed "Behavioral Finance." The numerous observations of such anomalies keep the Type 2 quants in the game for the most part, and there are a litany of academic papers on the subject, with price momentum being one particular anomaly studied vigorously and being undeniably efficacious for stock selection.[13]

Ben Graham stated, "I deny emphatically that because the market has all the information it needs to establish a correct price, that the prices it actually registers are in fact correct."[14] He then gives an example of seemingly random pricing of Avon in 1973–1974, and, finally, he says, "The market may have had all the information it needed about Avon; what it has lacked is the right kind of judgment in evaluating its knowledge." Mohamed El-Erian, the very successful Harvard Endowment CIO now at PIMCO, put it this way: "Rather, it is whether predominantly rational market participants are occasionally impacted by distorted influences and as a result valuation and liquidity dislocations emerge as markets adapt slowly to the new realities."[15] The latter quotation is, of course, a modern interpretation of inefficient market causes, and it is an acceptable one, of course. Jeremy Grantham of GMO also stated, "The market is incredibly inefficient and people have a hard time getting their brains around that."[16] It is an interesting observation to me that many long-time practicing investors with healthy investment records stand on the side of inefficient markets, whereas inexperienced (from an investment management perspective) academics support the opposite view.

I myself have noticed similar behavior in some stocks that have more in common with mispricing than proper pricing. A common example is a stock that is selling for less than its break-apart price; that is, the stock price is less than the sum of its parts if they were sold for scrap. Even in a closed end fund, why does the portfolio sell for a premium or discount to the sum of the prices of their individually held securities? That is neither rational nor is it efficient, and investing in those closed end funds selling for a discount to their intrinsic value is one of Graham's easy money-making investment strategies.

In summary, the market is hard to define, and the S&P 500, a managed portfolio that is hard to beat because of its good management, is not it. Sometimes markets (and stocks) completely decouple from their underlying logical fundamentals and financial statement data due to human fear and greed. What we want to focus on, then, is how to beat the market, but with the stability that Ben Graham created for us and with the wide margin of safety his methods enable. We begin with the search for alpha.

# CHAPTER 1

# Desperately Seeking Alpha

*Thus, if the earth were viewed from the planets, it would doubtless shine with the light of its own clouds, and its solid body would be almost hidden beneath the clouds. Thus, the belts of Jupiter are formed in the clouds of that planet, since they change their situation relative to one another, and the solid body of Jupiter is seen with greater difficulty through those clouds. And the bodies of comets must be much more hidden beneath their atmospheres, which are both deeper and thicker.*

—Isaac Newton, *The Principia*[1]

Before there was a Hubble Space Telescope, humans looked at the heavens with the naked eye. In awe they stood, transfixed for a moment wondering where it all came from. On the shoulders of giants like Newton, God installed a mind able to breach the walls of their confines to offer a glimmer of how things worked. Alpha is both a symbol and a term used to describe a variety of tangible things or concepts, but it always refers to the first or most significant occurrence of something. Although the alpha that everyone was seeking in Newton's day was an understanding of the universe, the history of alpha seekers in the literal sense goes back millennia.

For instance, the Bible documents the Israelites' investing in land; certainly the early years of their inhabiting Palestine were all about building orchards and vineyards and turning the land from desert and fallow to productive tilling. And of course as evil as it was, slave-traders made investments in ships and the necessary accoutrements for transporting human capital across the ocean. Though these examples are not purely alpha as we think of it today, it was indeed about making an investment, with an expected return as its end point.

Shift to the Netherlands of the 1630s, when an economic bubble formed around the price of newly introduced tulip bulbs. The price of tulip bulbs escalated to dizzying heights before it collapsed, causing great shock to the economy. Alas, tulipmania demonstrates the human tendency to make an investment, with the idea of garnering a return.[2] I believe it's within the definition of being human that one wants to be able to trade labor, capital, or currency for a greater return. The only difference between any business activity and that of an investor purchasing a bundle of securities, representing pieces of a business, is that in the case of the investor, there is a benchmark. In a single business investment, in which the investor is the founder and all the capital is deployed in this business, the investor doesn't usually consider making money above and beyond that of a benchmark. The business owner investor just maximizes profit alone; profit isn't measured against a standard but is measured in an absolute sense.

In William Sharpe's ideas about capital asset pricing model (CAPM), the benchmark is the market. However, it comes with a murky definition, usually left for investors to define for themselves. Firms such as Morningstar and Lipper have made a business of measuring portfolio managers' returns versus their interpretation of what the appropriate benchmark, or market, is. People pay for this interpretation, and the evidence shows that, more than often, portfolio managers do not add value above that of their benchmark (Morningstar or Lipper's definition). However, the fund is often classified incorrectly and a very inappropriate market benchmark is applied against which to measure the portfolio manager's performance. For instance, commonly, the S&P 500 is the designated benchmark and the portfolio might be a large-cap growth fund while the S&P 500 is thought of as a core portfolio, showing neither growth nor value characteristics. Also, large-cap–value portfolios are often compared with the S&P 500. This puts the portfolio manager at a disadvantage, because the assigned Morningstar benchmark is not what the manager actually uses to measure risk against nor is it what the managers design their portfolios to outperform. Style matters. To say that portfolio managers do not add much value above the benchmark when one really means the S&P 500 is misleading, because it is entirely possible that professional managers are beating their benchmarks but not beating the S&P 500, because not every manager's benchmark is the S&P.

To give you an example of benchmark misclassification, here is a partial list of funds that have core benchmarks listed as their main benchmark at Morningstar, although they actually have clear style bias:

**LARGE-CAP VALUE**

| | |
|---|---|
| Valley Forge Fund: | VAFGX |
| Gabelli Equity Income: | GABEX |
| PNC Large Cap Value: | PLVAX |

**LARGE-CAP GROWTH**

| | |
|---|---|
| Fidelity Nasdaq Comp. Index: | FNCMX |
| ETF Market Opportunity: | ETFOX |

**SMALL-CAP VALUE**

| | |
|---|---|
| Fidelity Small Value: | FCPVX |
| PNC Multi-Factor SCValue: | PMRRX |

Now Morningstar will also offer other information. For instance, Table 1.1 lists some mutual funds that have several categories of benchmarks listed. In particular, the prospectuses for these funds indicate the managers all compare themselves to the S&P 500, whereas Morningstar preferred to compare them to another benchmark. Then, regressions of the funds' past 36-month returns were performed (month ending June 30, 2010) against a large group of benchmarks, and the subsequent $R^2$ of the regression is reported. The higher the $R^2$, the more variance of return is explained by the regression and the more alike the mutual fund's return behavior has been to the modern portfolio theory (MPT) benchmark used in the regression. This demonstrates higher correspondence of return for some other benchmark rather than the one the managers measure themselves against or the one assigned by Morningstar.

In truth, there is nothing technically wrong with the reported numbers. However, it is misleading to investors for a couple of reasons. The first reason is that it violates the law of large numbers. For instance, if you regress the S&P 100 index against a suite of benchmarks, say, 76 randomly selected indexes using the past 36-month returns, it is highly likely that, for any given three-year-return time series, at least one of those benchmarks will have a higher correlation (and $R^2$) than with the S&P 500, with which it shares the top 100 stocks. This would be true for other indexes, too. So, if in that period of time the better fit for the S&P 100 is with the Russell 1000 Growth index, you would believe that there is a style bias to the S&P 100. That would be a completely crazy notion, however.

Table 1.1 shows a real-world example in which Fidelity Magellan (FMR) has a higher $R^2$ to Russell Midcap Growth index rather than the S&P 500. Now, does anybody really believe that the Fidelity Magellan fund is anything other than a large-cap fund that disregards style? It has been run that way since Peter Lynch was its manager. The S&P or Russell 1000 are Magellan's benchmark simply by its claim in its prospectus that it "is not constrained by any particular investment style." At any given time, FMR may tend to buy growth stocks or value stocks or a combination of both types.[3] Hence, a fund's benchmark is defined by the methodology employed in its stock

**TABLE 1.1** Morningstar Listed Mutual Funds with Questionable Benchmark Assignments

| Fund Name | Ticker | Prospectus Benchmark | Morningstar Assigned Bench | MPT Benchmark | $R^2$ to S&P 500 | $R^2$ to best fit |
|---|---|---|---|---|---|---|
| Oakmark I | OAKMX | S&P 500 | Russell 1000 | Morningstar Mid Value | 96 | 93 |
| Amana Trust Income | AMANX | S&P 500 | Russell 1000 Value | MSCI World NR | 90 | 87 |
| American Funds New Eco. | ANEFX | S&P 500 | Russell 1000 Growth | Morningstar Lifetime Moderate 2050 | 95 | 92 |
| Yacktman Focused | YAFFX | S&P 500 | Russell 1000 Value | Morningstar Mid Value | 86 | 81 |
| Fidelity Magellan | FMAGX | S&P 500 | Russell 1000 Growth | Russell Midcap Growth | 91 | 97 |
| Sequoia | SEQUX | S&P 500 | Russell 1000 | S&P 1500 Cons Discretionary | 88 | 77 |

selection strategy and portfolio construction process, not by some simple regression vs. returns.

In addition, given that the Morningstar style boxes (large, mid, small, growth, core or blend, value) are their own design, one would think they should know better than to compare a value or growth manager with a core index or benchmark, which is their proxy for the market. Nevertheless, it seems to happen more than often.

The July 12, 2010 issue of *Barron's* pours more water on the subject of fund classification by Morningstar. *Barron's* reports that, of 248 funds carrying five-star ratings as of December 1999, just four had retained that status through December of 2009, 87 could no longer be found, and the rest had all been downgraded. The point is not to chastise Morningstar as much as it is to point out that critics and watchdogs of professional money managers do not often have such a stellar (pun intended) record. In this particular case, the star ratings have no predictive ability, and it is misleading to investors that they do. Yet the SEC does not have the authority to assess this concern for investors because Morningstar does not manage money.

Now, to qualify these comments, sometimes it does happen that unscrupulous managers pick a benchmark with a design in mind of picking something easier to beat than the proper bench. We would suppose companies like Morningstar and Lipper shine the spotlight on these kinds of behaviors, because, if a stated benchmark is the Russell Midcap Value index and the fund's past returns have an $R^2$ with the EAFE index (a large-cap international index), that is 20 points higher than the Mid Cap Value index. Clearly, there is something corrupt here, and one should be on guard against what the manager says the fund is doing versus what it is actually doing with its investment process. In general, regressing returns against various benchmarks in hopes of trying to better pick the benchmark than the one given in the fund's prospectus is very much like having a hammer and needing a nail. Sometimes it really is the case that the process acting like a consultant really has only one tool and they are looking for a problem to solve with it, rather than choosing the right tool for the problem.

The regression of returns with an eye toward rightly classifying a fund's investment objectives is called a returns-based approach. An alternative methodology involves analyzing the holdings of mutual funds rather than examining the returns. If, for instance, a large (by assets under management) mutual fund owns 234 positions, all of which are found in the Russell 2000 value index, and, in addition, it states in its prospectus that the universe of buy candidates come from this index, then you can be sure its benchmark is the Russell 2000 value index and needn't run any regressions. This would be true regardless of whether its regression of returns is higher against some other index. A holdings-based analysis can offer a different perspective on the objectives of a fund than the returns-based analysis, and vice versa.

Now that we have identified what the market and benchmark are under the guise of CAPM, what is alpha?

## THE BEGINNINGS OF THE MODERN ALPHA ERA

So what is alpha and what isn't it? The initial definition as we know it today comes from Sharpe's Capital Asset Pricing Model (though some attribute Jack Treynor as inventor or, at a minimum, a co-inventor). To begin, every investment carries two separate risks. One is the risk of being in the market, which Sharpe called systematic risk. This risk, later dubbed beta, cannot be diversified away. Unsystematic risk (idiosyncratic) is another kind of risk, best described as company-specific yet diversifiable. The CAPM implies that a portfolio's expected return hinges solely on its beta, which is its relationship to the market. The CAPM describes a method for measuring the return that an investor can expect for taking a given level of risk. This was an extension of Markowitz's thoughts in many ways, because he was Sharpe's advisor at Rand Corporation and he had a large influence on Sharpe.

Sharpe's CAPM uses regressed portfolio return (less risk-free return) against the market's return (also less risk-free return) to calculate a slope and an intercept, which are called beta and alpha. Beta is the risk term that specifies how much of the market's risk is accounted for in the portfolio's return. Alpha, on the other hand, is the intercept, and this implies how much return the portfolio is obtaining in and above the market, separate from any other factors.

However, risk is more complicated than just beta, because risk is divided into idiosyncratic or individual company specific risk and risk due to correlations of and within companies. To understand the latter risk, consider a company that creates hardware that is used in some other company's products, so for example consider an aircraft engine manufacturer. The correlation between an aircraft manufacturer and its suppliers is easily conceived. This can be observed by watching two companies' stock prices through time. Because their businesses are connected through their products, if the sales of aircraft fall, so do the sales of engines. Their business prospects and earnings are correlated, and this can be observed by visually plotting their stock prices. Statisticians often call this "chi by eye."

Correlations make risk a complicated feature, and one that people have trouble processing. So having estimates of risk and return, you can input these into a computer and find efficient portfolios. In this way, you can get more return for a given risk and less risk for a given return, and that is beautiful efficiency à la Markowitz. Prior to Markowitz, the investment mantra was simply do not put all your eggs in one basket or put them in a basket and watch them very closely, following the Ben Graham philosophy of weighing the assets in and of the company. There was little quantification. Markowitz and Sharpe brought quantification and mathematical elegance to investing, albeit much to Graham's chagrin.

The point of the CAPM was to compute a required rate of return of an asset given its level of risk relative to some risk-free rate. In practice, however, it has been reduced to a much simpler interpretation, even though it is wrong. The CAPM offers us an alpha and a beta, which represent the amount of return a portfolio (not an asset) offers above an index or market portfolio. That's the alpha, while beta represents a twofold interpretation in which neither is really appropriate but it's widely accepted to mean both whether a stock (or portfolio) is more volatile than the index (or market) and its correlation to the index (or market). Though these definitions come from portfolio managers and analysts and they are both widely accepted and used, neither one fully explains beta. Not to insult Mr. Beta, but he is nothing more than a regression coefficient. Either way, in practice, a stock with beta greater than 1 is expected to have greater volatility than its index, and if it is less than 1, it is expected to have lower volatility than its index. This is usually true but not necessarily so, as subsequent chapters will show. The alpha is what we are after, however. If one has alpha, then this implies that the portfolio-generating process, the underlying investment process, really does have an anomalous return feature associated with it, and it isn't some risk factor masquerading as alpha.

Although alpha is usually reserved for speaking about portfolios rather than stocks, it can be used for stocks, too. How it is interpreted, however, is important for the majority of financial and institutional consultants reference it all the time, as does Morningstar, Lipper, and other fund-rating agencies. In simple terms, if a portfolio has demonstrated positive alpha, it means that, relative to some index or benchmark, the portfolio has demonstrated outperformance for the same average level of risk (given beta equal to 1) as its index. Portfolios with negative alpha underperform relative to their index or benchmark. It is a relative world here we are talking about, by which we mean performance relative to a benchmark, not cash. It is not absolute return we're talking about, and this distinction is paramount when it comes to differentiating between long-only institutional asset management, mutual funds and hedge funds. Hedge funds live in an absolute return world, whereas long-only institutional asset management lives in a relative world.

Though academics of finance highly criticize this practitioner's view of alpha, 95 percent of the people in the asset-management business believe it. And you know what? This interpretation works! For instance, suppose you have three years of monthly returns of a large-cap core (or blend) portfolio and three years of monthly returns to the S&P 500. Now, subtract the benchmark's returns from the portfolio's return, and graph this excess return vs. the benchmark's return. The slope is beta and the intercept is alpha (approximately; strictly speaking, you need to subtract out the risk-free return beforehand). If the alpha is positive, you have a good portfolio that outperforms its index, and if, simultaneously, the slope (beta) is less than 1, you obtained that return for less risk than its index, too—or so it is interpreted.

## IMPORTANT HISTORY OF INVESTMENT MANAGEMENT

Why is alpha so earnestly sought after in modern quantitative investment management? Alpha is the legacy of focus by most analysts and portfolio managers as ordered by chief investment officers (CIOs) because of the history of the field of investment management. In the early days, analysts performed portfolio management, and management meant reading, digesting, and regurgitating balance-sheet information. Prior to 1929, the assets of a firm were the most important consideration, and stock selection was predominately based on how good the book value was. Later, after the 1929 crash, earnings became more important, and Graham, in an article in *Forbes*, said value has come to be exclusively associated with earnings power, and the investor no longer was paying attention to a company's assets, even its money in the bank.[4] In addition, these early analysts believed (some still do today) that they were ascertaining, by their fundamental analysis, a company's alpha simultaneously with its risk, and to a certain extent that was true. However, those early analysts never ascertained the co-varying risk this way, only the company-specific risk. This is because the typical fundamental analyst thought of individual companies as independent entities. There was a natural tendency to view investments in isolation, and not to think of the portfolio as a whole or of risks due to co-ownership of several correlated stocks.

A really cool analogy of correlation comes from watching how a flock of starlings or pigeons fly or how a large school of small fish behaves. Ever notice how the whole group of them flies in one continuous group—a portfolio of birds, weaving and diving—and, although it is clear that their flight paths are correlated, it is hard to pinpoint the leader of such a flock. You would have to be a scuba diver or watch Discovery channel to see identical behavior in a school of fish, but they also swarm and change directions, seemingly without any leader. Interestingly, if you get 50 people grouped together in a parking lot and tell everybody to keep an arm's length away from all your neighbors and try to stay near the same three or four people who are around you at all times, you get the same behavior as the fish and birds. Unfortunately for people, nobody will move unless you yourself are in the group, stand on the edge and start walking. The three to four people around you will follow you to keep you close, and their nearest neighbors will do the same, and then the whole group will start moving. The crowd will demonstrate the same behavior as the flock of birds and school of fish. In like fashion, stocks are similar. Correlation is palpable, but it is unobserved by watching a single bird, fish, person, or stock.

Alpha considerations alone also tend to create portfolios of higher risk and volatility, resulting in portfolios of lower information ratio (excess return over a benchmark divided by the tracking error of the portfolio, to be defined later) and you would have no idea what the tracking error is (or an estimate of it). In addition, the exposure of the portfolio to risk will be confused with the active bet or weight of various positions in the portfolio when thinking of alpha alone. For instance, you might have a portfolio that has 3 percent overweight relative to its benchmark in banks, say, when, in reality, there is a 4 percent exposure to banks simply because the portfolio also owns a couple of stocks that are highly correlated to banks that have not been accounted for consciously. Lastly, considering the alpha alone when constructing a portfolio usually leads position sizes to be directly proportional to the expected alpha or return for each stock. Thus, the highest proportion of money will be tied up in stocks that the analyst who runs the investment process believes has the highest return potential, regardless of its risk. This last point may result in unaccounted losses and larger-than-expected drawdowns.

In current quantitative efforts in modeling for alpha, the goal is primarily to define the factors that influence stocks or drive returns the most, and construct portfolios strongly leaning on those factors. Generally, this is done by regressing future returns against historical financial-statement data. The type of variables chosen, however, differs depending on the investor's time horizon. For shorter holding period models and strategies, trading data (bid, ask, daily volume, daily prices) may be used as the independent variables in these regressions. For a holding period of a quarter to several years, the independent variables are typically financial-statement data (balance-sheet, income-statement, and cash-flow data). For even longer holding periods of three years or more, the independent variables are macroeconomic in nature (GDP, unemployment rates, CPI, spread between long and short Treasury yields, yield curve slope). The reason the underlying factors change depending upon the holding period has much to do with the correlations of these variables with assets on these time scales. At least for the shortest and middle range holding periods, the factors are security or company specific. It is only for very long term holding periods—longer than three years—that economic variables are the stronger influencers of return, and these variables are not company specific. When investing in these time scales, thematic investing is usually the strategy employed, and it is less a quantitative practice than for the other two time horizons of investing. Players in this realm involve themselves in country-specific issues, currency plays, economic news, and a whole assembly of macro top-down perspectives. Quant's role in this endeavor is mostly fleeting.

In the majority of quant firms that manage assets today, the typical operations and day-to-day activities of quantitative analysts and portfolio managers is testing and modifying alpha models. That said, there are umpteen possibilities for constructing alpha models, and this keeps the quantitative analyst plenty busy!

## METHODS OF ALPHA SEARCHING

The search for alpha continues unabated since before the time of Graham. Curiously, the halls of academia have pretty well mapped out many features and subtleties of investing, certainly in the qualitative venue. Google knows where articles on alpha generation exist and with some thousands of dollars, one can shop Amazon, Borders, and Barnes & Noble and come away with hundreds of titles, subtitles, and chapters written about, discussed in depth, and opined on alpha. Many of these titles go back before Graham and Dodd's brilliant expose on *Security Analysis* in 1934.

Over the course of time, the number and frequency of published books on investing, which, by the way, are all about alpha, has a cyclical pattern peaking at market tops. As one might expect, books about risk analysis also peak right *after* the market tops. So alpha and risk publications, the yin and yang of investing, run countercyclical to each other. In addition, though much has been written from the fundamental side, taking 1934 as an anchor, fundamental investing has been under the microscope for 76 years or thereabouts. On the other side of the investment curriculum lies the relatively new field of quantitative investing, in the modern sense of the word, with computers doing much of the research. With the PC revolution came the ability to search for empirical patterns of return, influenced by economic and financial-statement data (i.e., factors), much faster than the human mind can do and, in addition, often with higher credibility. A lot has been published on the empirical side in the academic literature; however, much more work has not been published from the work of the practicing investor. What has been published is often of dubious practicality in the hands of the investment manager.

It is also the situation that the mapping of factors based on empirical observation has no standardization in which to offer overwhelmingly convincing evidence that a given factor is definitively a cause of stock return. There is no agreed upon method or statistical test that proves the validity of any empirical data set being responsible for the stock return time series. Much of this has to do with the unreasonable behavior of the stock market, and we will get into much of its nonlinear dynamic and chaotic behavior in future chapters. The stock market is not a repeatable event. Every day is an out-of-sample environment. The search for alpha will continue in quantitative terms simply because of this precarious and semi-random nature of the stock markets. In addition, the future is wide open for alpha searching in similar context for fixed income as quantitative approaches are in their infancy for these securities.

Lastly, much of the current research on alpha is beginning to offer explanations for the effect of certain factors on return. Many of these researchers, such as Jeremy C. Stein of Harvard, are attempting to offer fundamental explanations for factors that have been discovered (via the preponderance of the empirical evidence) to offer anomalous return, in the guise of the efficient market hypothesis. Still others, like Sheridan Titman from the University of Texas at Austin and Werner De Bondt of DePaul University, attempt to explain momentum strategies using behavioral finance theories.

In the simplest description of alpha, factors matter only to the extent that one can make economic sense of them. That is, you need to know that the anomalous outperformance of return from some factor is not due to Voodoo but has explanatory power related to some economically sensitive variable. Zip codes and weather forecasts should not have predictive power or consistent behavior in forecasting stock returns. For the practitioner, this is paramount for acceptance and for realization in an investment strategy. An alpha signal generated by some factor must have certain characteristics, including the following simple rules of thumb:

1. It must come from real economic variables.
2. The signal must be strong enough to overcome trading costs.
3. It must not be dominated by a single industry or security.
4. The time series of return obtained from the alpha source should offer little correlation with other sources of alpha.
5. It should not be misconstrued as a risk factor.
6. Return to this factor should have low variance.

7. The cross-sectional beta (or factor return) for the factor should also have low variance over time and maintain the same sign the majority of the time (this is coined *factor stationarity*).
8. The required turnover to implement the factor in a real strategy cannot be too high.

We'll now review these alpha characteristics one at a time. The first characteristic assures that the investment process under construction is not subject to spurious correlation sources, that is, that it comes from real economic variables. This is mostly a reality check. For instance, if you form a portfolio of inverted price, you can observe some empirical evidence that there are anomalous returns. However, 1/Price cannot be a source of real economic value, hence you could not use this factor, so it's rejected simply by this rule.

The second characteristic concerns the impact of trading costs on portfolio return. When sifting data empirically, it is often easier than you can imagine to observe some excess return with some factors. However, if the return is not sufficient to overcome trading costs, it can never be implemented. For instance, the reversal strategy (buying stocks that have gone down over the last week and selling stocks that have gone up in the last week) is arguably a nonworking strategy. There is alpha in reversal strategies, but the high-frequency trading required to implement it makes it a tenuous methodology for the average prudent investor because of the trading costs involved. In the current market, high-frequency trading firms and the proprietary trading desks of many large banks do utilize reversal strategies, but they have methods to overcome the cost of trading and, in fact, utilize sophistication in some ways so that the more they trade, the less the cost to the portfolio. This is unlike what is available to the average investor, however.

With respect to the third characteristic, generally, most quant strategies and applications of quant involve portfolio construction for the type-2 quant. In this vein, a particular factor that seems to work in only one sector or industry can, therefore, only be employed in a portfolio setting, if all the other sectors or industry also have their own model. It is uncommon to find single factors that work in only one industry and hard enough to find a single factor to work in each industry. One application of this does exist, and that is if you are building a model consisting of several factors for a given industry with the goal of building a portfolio specific to this industry. However, for the average investor, this is more risky than building a portfolio covering many sectors simply because of the lack of diversification and high cross-correlation (covariance) between the stocks in one industry. Many funds in the public domain that have high industry concentration could benefit from industry-specific models. (If managers of any of them are reading this book, they should omit this rule.)

For the fourth characteristic, that the time series of returns from differing alpha sources should be noncorrelating, first you should know that you derive a time series of returns from every alpha source. Because ultimately you will be building a model from several factors, you would like the return time series from each factor to be as independent from one another as possible. Just as diversification of stocks offers lower risk in the portfolio, choosing stocks from differing alpha sources also diversifies risks and, in fact, the two diversification methods are related. Though complete disconnect is impossible using economic or financial-statement variables to model security returns, it is wise to choose one's variables from diverse categories like valuation, profitability, cash flow, momentum, fundamentals, growth, and capital allocation. Though the alpha searching process usually examines several factors from each of these groups, typically factors within a group have more correlation than factors across groups. Graham knew this and it is the reason he considered independent financial-statement data for his investment methodology. Thus, choosing only valuation factors, say B/P, E/P, cash-flow/P, and S/P for your investment process is inherently risky because the final portfolio would mainly be constructed from a single alpha source, since these factors are typically highly correlated. This does not mean there will not be a period of time when you would have great gain. From March of 2009 to the end of the year, stocks bought simply by selection of low valuation alone would have outsized returns, but in 2008, your portfolio would have been destroyed by pure valuation alone.

With regard to the fifth characteristic, there are risk factors and there are alpha factors. It is safe to say that if a factor is not a risk factor, and it explains the return or the variance of return to some extent, it must be an alpha factor. A way to tell is if, in a regression equation with other factors known to be risk factors (like market returns [CAPM] or large-minus-small size from Fama-French equation), there is found a zero alpha, even though the factor increases the $R^2$ of the regression, then it's probably a risk factor. This would mean though it's helpful in explaining returns, it doesn't offer outperformance.

In other words, if the presence of the factor in the regression simultaneously raises the $R^2$ while decreasing the intercept coefficient, it is a risk factor rather than an alpha factor. A great example is a 12-month past-earnings growth. Though returns are colinear with this earnings growth, they are poor predictors of future returns. This is because many investors will have bid up the pricing of stocks that have shown historically good earnings growth concurrently with earnings announcements. However, 12-month past-earnings growth fails miserably at being a forecaster of future return. We will see that Graham liked to see earnings growth, but he examined it over years, not over simple 12-month measures. In this case, 12-month past-earnings growth is probably a risk factor because it regresses well with future return statistically, but offers little in the way of alpha. Generally any alpha factor that has been working for a long period of time becomes discovered by the market and ultimately arbitraged away and reduced in status to being a risk factor.

The next characteristic of alpha sources involves the volatility of the factor's return time series. The variance of these return time series should be low. It is not helpful if the factor's return time series is wildly oscillating over time. If so, it is difficult to harness the alpha in a portfolio. Unstable regression coefficients or, in simpler terms, unstable relationships of the factor with return usually follow this scenario. In other words, the factor's correlation with future return is nonstationary and it would be difficult to count on it consistently in an investment process simply because it would not be persistent.

We now have to spend a bit of time discussing beta. In a typical factor search for alpha, you regress a list of stocks' return against factors one date at a time or in a panel regression. In this way, the method obtains a beta for each and every time period, for each and every factor. So if there are 60 one-month periods, you obtain 60 betas for each factor in a time series. A requirement for usefulness is that the beta does not move around. So, if at the first time period the beta is 0.34, over the 60 months of calculation, beta cannot move from 0.34 to −.46 to 0.75 and finally settle at 0.22 and suggest usefulness. That would be unacceptable for a risk model and certainly for an alpha model, too. Hence, the variance of the time series of the beta cannot be too large. You should aim for small beta variance. Ultimately, these beta variances are chosen to build up a covariance matrix in risk forecasting; also, so you do not want them too large because one doesn't want a highly volatile portfolio. In addition, there is a relationship between stock volatility and beta volatility; the Stochastic Portfolio Theory (SPT) discussed in Chapter 9 explains how volatility takes away from long-term return. Generally, you want to own stocks of low volatility, unless you have very sophisticated optimization methods you can run under Stochastic Portfolio Theory, which is outside the scope of this book.

Lastly, the whole objective here is to build portfolios. Graham liked three-year holding periods generally or 50 percent returns, whichever came first. For the strategies Graham employed, purchasing low-valued stocks that are mispriced is the favorite of his process; however, you cannot know how long it will take the market to realize the mispricing. Hence, the typical stock has an unknown holding period, though it is usually fairly long by today's standards. In general, Graham's method has low portfolio turnover, as do most value investors' strategies. In addition, increasing turnover comes with increasing trading costs. Thus a factor that has a short-lived alpha—such as one that offers higher one-month returns relative to a benchmark that decays rapidly so that each month one must rebalance the portfolio at a high rate to sustain the investment advantage—is undesirable. In fact, for most institutional investors, wealth managers, and the typical Fidelity, Schwab, ETrade, or Ameritrade investor (not day traders), the trading costs of a high-turnover strategy cannot be overcome by the usual alpha obtained from financial-statement factors or pricing functions (i.e., price momentum). This, of course, does not include high-frequency trading methodologies, but their technology is very sophisticated and not for the average investor.

The next chapter introduces risk to the reader and covers it quite extensively. Risk modeling and alpha modeling are similar, but in alpha modeling one is not as concerned about the covariance structure as much as one is concerned about stable alpha. This will become clearer as we move forward to dissect risk.

# CHAPTER 2

# Risky Business

*There can be no doubt that the interplanetary and instellar spaces are not empty but are occupied by a material substance of body, which is certainly the largest, and probably the most uniform body of which we have any knowledge.*
—J. C. Maxwell in the *Encyclopedia Britannica* entry for "Ether"[1]

Ether, or aether, as it's been called, is defined as a medium in a state of absolute rest relative to the fixed stars, in which light is propagated and through which the earth moves as if it were transparent to it. On April 2, 1921, Albert Einstein delivered lectures at Princeton in relativity theory. While there, he was told of an experiment recently carried out that had found a nonzero aether drift. Einstein was overheard replying in German, "Raffiniert is der Herr Gott, aber boshaft ist er nicht!" which translated means "Subtle is the Lord, but malicious He is not!" When pressed, later he said, "I have not for a moment taken those (experimental) results seriously." Much later, science validated Einstein's summation because relativity theory couldn't accept aether's existence. But imagine facing Einstein, and risking ego and reputation by disagreeing with his theory.

Risks are real, though, and like aether, they are often undetectable. The exposure to failure, the existence of risk is mostly apparent after the fact. Part of this is due to risk being such a vague topic: no matter what you say, you are right, as long as you are talking about the "down" side of investing. It is the wicked stepsister to alpha really. Younger baby-boomers and older generation-X'ers picture the robot on "Lost in Space," waving his arms and frantically yelling, "Danger, danger, Will Robinson." This image conveys what risk is: very alarming and scary, but worthy of study. Calamity may never occur, but it *could* occur, and that is what scares the "bejeebers" out of most of us.

To start the conversation about risk, it is important to understand that after the emergence of Markowitz's method for specifying the optimal portfolio (mean-variance optimization), risk became synonymous with price fluctuation or volatility.[2] Prior to this interpretation by Markowitz, who showed cleverly that the overall normal variance of a portfolio could be less than the sum of its constituents for a given expected return, people didn't think about portfolios as some kind of entity. The stock to a portfolio is much like the person to a corporation; individually they seem very much independent, but in reality, in the aggregate, they are correlated. In the early days, a portfolio was considered as a collection of independent entities, narrowly defined, and risk was really just loss due to a company tanking. The ramifications of the collected sum of securities wasn't thought about much, and it is not thought about today by some dumb portfolio managers. We once worked with a portfolio manager (PM) who continually misunderstood the collective concept of a portfolio and what covariance is, so much so that his management style was strictly betting on price-momentum stocks as if they were lottery tickets. He was constantly overweighted on the momentum style, and with highly correlated stocks, too, I might add. Where there's hubris, there's surely a lack of talent, and he exposed his lack of talent through his portfolios. His returns vindicated this observation.

However, what began with Markowitz in 1952 was the beginnings of the concept of portfolio risk due to co-varying of stocks or, mathematically, the covariance of a portfolio. Thus began a 50-plus year history during which stock or portfolio variance was, by definition, risk. This is by no means the only or the best possible definition, but it lends itself to a great deal of analysis and it is intuitively comfortable, because when a stock's return fluctuates largely over time, it generally means its earnings are less consistent. Therefore, it may be thought of as less predictable and more risky. While conversely, a stock whose price remains fairly stationary is more predictable (as are its earnings), and hence is less risky. In this regard, it's suggested to think of the volatility of a stock price more as the symptom of risk, rather than as risk itself, because we shall demonstrate that risk is not variance and that variance is not even a good enough measure of volatility, let alone of risk going forward.

## EXPERIENCED VERSUS EXPOSED RISK

Consider this analogy: One dark, rainy evening you're driving down a rural road in New England and come across an old covered bridge hanging 20 feet over a rain swollen creek. You are not familiar with this bridge, but assume it is the fastest way to continue on your journey, because turning around is not acceptable. You proceed to drive across it slowly, and you cross it and continue on your way to reach Ben and Jerry's without incident. A few minutes later, another car approaches the same bridge from the same side. It, too, carefully crosses the bridge, but the bridge starts to creak and shake. The chronic neglect of bridge maintenance finally takes its toll. The bridge collapses under the weight of the car, and both the car and its occupants fall 20 feet into the rushing creek! What is the lesson we learn from this incident? You, as the first driver, experienced small risk, but your exposed risk was enormous!

Experience often looks to the past and considers the probability of future outcomes based on their occurrences in the past. In statistics, this is known as the frequentist approach, and it is derived empirically from easily collected past data and, frankly, is the major criticism of Nassim Taleb.[3] Taleb correctly reminds us that the past is never reproduced exactly as its historical record, and by forming histograms of past returns to obtain distributions of future returns expectation is quite inexact. Exposure considers the likelihood and potential risk of events that history (especially recent history) has not revealed. The difference between these two may be extreme. Traditionally, experienced risk in a portfolio has been measured by calculating standard deviation and portfolio betas. These measures grew up from approximations that were to make experienced performance and volatility easy to digest and interpret for the investor. Besides the fact that people put confidence in these dubious statistics, it's our belief that people also misunderstand experienced risk and expect that the previous year's portfolio volatility is also what their risk actually was over this same time period.

What your portfolios experienced may not be what you were exposed to. We often think that what we've experienced is what we've been exposed to in the markets, which is not always true. Exposures to risk are that: exposures. Experience is a risk coming true. One uses life insurance to cover one's exposure to death, but while you're living you have the exposure and you don't experience it until you die. A portfolio may be exposed to potential losses but not actually experience it. What we're trying to avoid in risk management is experiencing a risk that was not exposed in the first place, so that if your portfolio suffers a loss, you would at least have known you could lose money due to that effect.

This all assumes, of course, that volatility is risk, which it isn't. Unfortunately, these Modern Portfolio Theory (MPT) measures often lead to erroneous conclusions (statistically), particularly when they are coupled with their misinterpretation, as exposed risk measures compound inaccuracy.

Such was the life of growth-stock technology investors in the mid to late 1990s. In 1996 investors looked at the recent historical performance and volatility of technology stocks and decided there wasn't much risk. They poured dollars into technology and growth-style mutual funds while P/E's

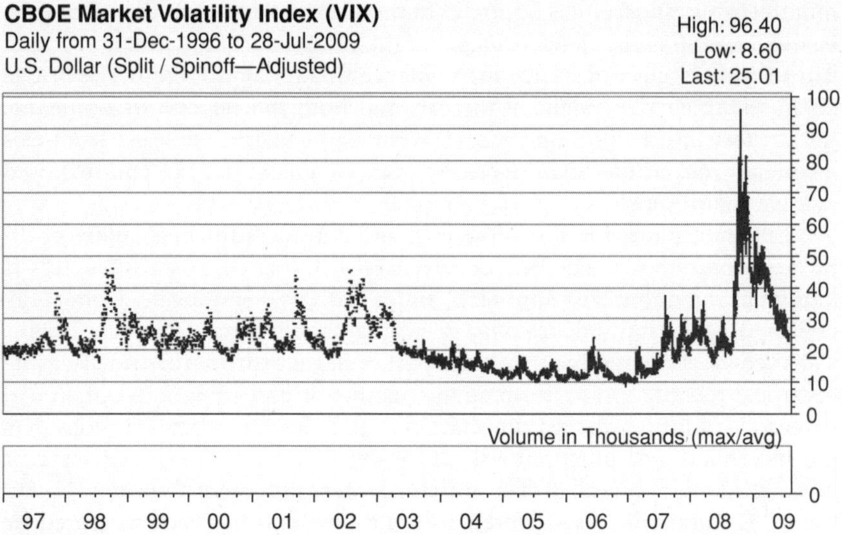


**FIGURE 2.1** The CBOE Market Volatility Index VIX
*Data source:* IDC/Exshare.

continued to climb. They did their risk analysis by continuously checking the rearview mirror, monitoring portfolio standard deviation and beta, all the while believing the risk wasn't too high as ascertained from experience. However, in the 1999 tech bubble, the bridge collapsed under the weight of all that heavy P/E and the real risk was exposed.

A more recent example was 2008. In that year the Volatility Index (VIX) climbed inordinately high compared to the last 15 years (daily data) as shown in Figure 2.1.[4] The VIX is highly correlated with the actual realized 30-day standard deviation of return of the S&P 500. Its value is a compendium of a chain of S&P index option implied volatilities, so it is a trader's view of what the future expected volatility will be for the S&P 500 over the next 30 days. A value of the VIX of 20 means that it's expected that the S&P 500 could swing within a range of 20 percent from its current value over the next 30 days, up or down.

In the chart shown in Figure 2.1, notice where the VIX went in early 2007, from the higher values of the tech bubble. During that process, investors mistakenly assumed this volatility reduction in these intervening years corresponded to a decreasing risk exposure, akin to the analogy of the car on the New England bridge referenced earlier. Simultaneously, in 2005 Alan Greenspan testified before Congress that, contrary to all of his past experience, increasing short-term rates results in an increase in long-term rates (after a 150 bps reduction in the Federal Funds rate occurred), whereas the inverted U.S. yield curve meant that long-term rates were south of short-term rates. In addition, we saw for the first time, in 2007, that the accumulated holdings of emerging market economies of U.S. Treasuries rose to absolute historical levels while U.S. equity markets were also recording record highs. This all portended to increasing risk exposure even while the VIX was signaling decreasing risk experience.

Likewise, from the low of 10 on the VIX in 2006 to a high of over 90 in late 2008, pandemonium struck in the markets. Low-quality and highly leveraged stocks were being priced for bankruptcy and were falling precipitously. Other stocks just kept falling, though not as much. When the VIX rises to such heights, this usually means that the market is increasing correlation, and all stocks fall simultaneously. Stocks hardly ever increase their correlation on the upside when the market rises. This is because they are more like individual entities whose future more strongly depends on their individual company financials and fortunes in a rising market. Not so on the downside.

To better understand the VIX and what it means in risk analysis, go to www.ivolatility.com, a site that uses interpretive graphics to demonstrate the role volatility plays in equity options.

When markets fall, three things happen: (1) stock returns correlate up, (2) the VIX rises significantly as traders' future views of volatility rise, and (3) stocks disconnect from their fundamentals. That is, the financial and economic factors that explain stock returns in normal environments suddenly become less useful, less predictive, and less correlated with return. All good quants know this, and it is observed in the correlation time series of fundamental factors with stock returns, so that, in up markets, fundamental factors and stock picking works (so to speak), and in down markets, it works less because fear and herd-like behavior are the dominant drivers of return.

In late 2008, the VIX was telling investors to run for the hills, get out of the market, sell, sell, sell! Investors did. Then in March of 2009, everything was priced so low, especially the low-quality highly leveraged companies, that investors stayed out of the market, predicated on the rearview mirror mentality. Then, when markets took off, beginning in March 2009, most investors sat out the gains. This crisis resulted in the S&P losing 55 percent in a one-and-a-half-year period. Those who got out of the market due to fear and hindsight didn't avail themselves of the gains of 2009, although they wouldn't have broken even entirely, even if they had participated in the rally; but it sure would have added balm to an open wound. Getting in the market in March of 2009 took courage that few investors could muster and the only indicating signal to use to get in the market would have been Ben

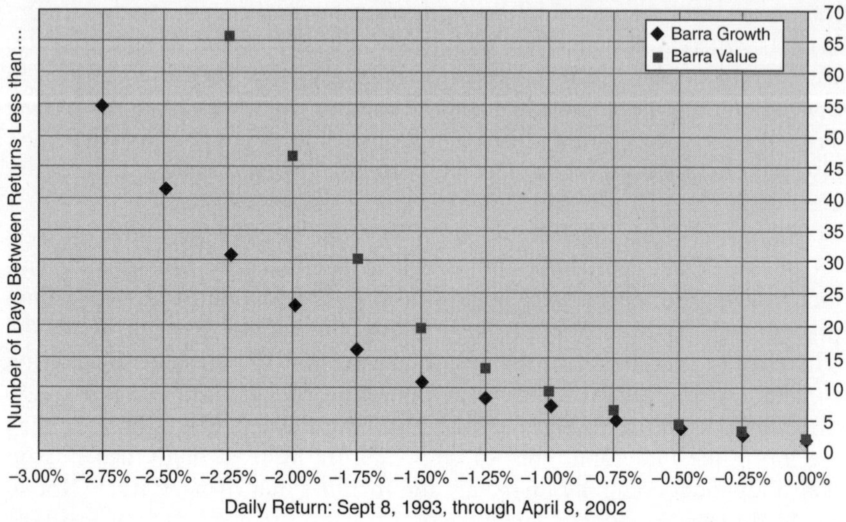


**FIGURE 2.2** Daily Return Lifetimes of Growth versus Value (S&P 500)*
*A daily return lower than –1.75 percent occurs for Value every 30 days, but every 16 days for Growth.

Graham's valuation strategy. Though he is no longer with us, I'm certain Ben would have told us there were bargains galore at that time.

We must acknowledge there is a difference between experienced versus exposed risk. How do we measure exposed risk? It's difficult. To get one's arms around exposure, one must look at the frequency of occurrence of the extreme events, not their sequence. This allows us to see what could occur. For instance, if you examined the number of times a large negative return movement occurred for the S&P 500 BarraValue and BarraGrowth indexes, and then calculated the average number of days between these extreme movements, you could create the exceedance lifetime graph shown in Figure 2.2.

The data for Figure 2.2 downloaded from FactSet is from index returns from September 8, 1993, through April 8, 2002, and it does not include the 1987 market drop. This chart depicts the possible exposure risk that is inherent in growth versus value styles.[5] The Y or ordinate axis lists the average number of days between daily returns of magnitude X or less plotted on the abscissa, where the abscissa are daily return values. For instance, a daily return of –1.75 percent or lower occurs roughly every 15 days for the S&P 500 BarraGrowth portfolio, whereas for a BarraValue portfolio it only occurs once in 30 days, as can be read from the graph in

Figure 2.2. This indicates that Growth portfolios by their very nature have had larger magnitude negative returns more frequently than did their Value counterparts.

The data to produce this chart was "experiential" (empirical) in nature; that is, it was created from historical return. In order for this chart to have relevance as a proxy for exposed risk, it is necessary for the data to be complete and representative of all the possible outcomes. Obviously, we can never have *all* possible outcomes, but if the frequency of data is high enough, we can have confidence that we are close to a complete distribution, which is why this chart utilizes daily returns over a long time period for daily data. To capture the same resolution and, hence, confidence in exposure, measurements using monthly data would require obtaining 2,239 months of data (186 years), which isn't possible in one person's lifetime.

By now you might be thinking, wait a minute, the –20.47 percent daily return that occurred on October 19, 1987 is not in the data for the exposure measure for BarraValue and BarraGrowth comparison, nor is the 2008 meltdown. Well, although it is not present in the daily data presented here, it is just as rare an event for Growth and Value. Typical of nonlinear (and chaotic) processes, the extreme-extreme events are often very similar among equity markets. This is, again, due to markets and stocks increasing their correlation when extinction-level events (ELE) occur, which are represented with the increasing VIX and which always seem to be to the downside (in the stock market, we can't say there's ever been a ELE event triggering huge upside). The Daily-Return-Lifetimes or Exceedance-Lifetime graphs for returns that occur less than once in 500 days are the same for value or growth, so the curves would overlap at these low-incidence events. Therefore, this data is not shown because there is no difference to be observed. This agrees with common sense, because major cataclysmic ELE events impact all markets similarly and are not usually predictable. Therefore, their impact is holistic and all-encompassing, regardless of style.

Importantly, events that occur less than once in 500 days are so extreme that their cause is from a different mechanism than that due to normal losses in normal markets. This point is the crux of an ongoing argument we have against those who criticize quantitative risk management. Unless we have God's risk model, we'll never predict ELE events like those in the movies *Armageddon* and *Deep Impact*.

In the example given, value (or the Ben Graham methodology) has shown itself to offer less exposure to risk than growth under average or normal circumstances. The heavier P/E growth portfolio's offer means there is a much smaller margin of safety than that required by Ben Graham's method of investing, so when valuations fall toward some underlying equilibrium value, it is a far larger fall for growth than value. The risk exposure of growth implies higher experienced volatility. Moreover, this volatility is asymmetrical, leaning toward negative returns rather frequently relative to value portfolios. We will continue this discussion at length, but we must segue to take a closer look at some rarer kinds of risks to a portfolio, namely, ELE events, or the more recent renaming of ELE events as if the concept is brand new, that is, infamous Black Swan events.

## THE BLACK SWAN: A MINOR ELE EVENT—ARE QUANTS TO BLAME?

In his remarkable book *The Black Swan*, Nassim Taleb re-introduces the topic of rare events, events so rare that they appear random and unpredictable.[6] The term *black swan* was chosen to represent unforeseen and previously unobserved phenomena and events that surprise us all. (The name was chosen because of the similarity with the discovery of the black swan in Europe, before which it was presumed all swans were white.) In the scheme of things, however, market dislocations are usually minor global events. Few people die when the S&P 500 moves downward 50 percent compared to real ELE events. Taleb's story in the book is mostly to make us aware of how random events influence us and how, in the stock market (or any market), we cannot account for their rise. Taleb goes on to criticize quants and risk managers for their feeble quantitative models based on the normal curve for statistics, and he appears to blame them for market meltdowns and for their model's failure to predict these random black-swan events, or, as we would rather call them, ELE events, which historically are not so rare.

Taleb asks the question: How relevant and useful is past experience as applied to current situations? Graham, on the other hand, said:

> *It is true that one of the elements that distinguishes economics, finance and security analysis from other practical disciplines is the uncertain validity of past phenomena as a guide to the present and future. Yet we have no right to reflect on lessons of the past until we have at least studied and understood them.*[7]

In addition, Graham said that if experience cannot help today's investor, then we must be logical and conclude that there is no such thing as investment in common stocks and that everyone interested in them should confess themselves speculators. The reason we like exploring the past has to do with the comfort we draw from our ability to use existing constructs and memorable ideas to explain historical developments, make current decisions, and estimate our future directions. That, of course, is why we may be late in recognizing significant shifts in the market in accordance with Taleb's accusations and ELE findings.

To that end, optimism and overconfidence have always accompanied bull markets, and pessimism always accompanied bear markets. In practice, most of us find three-day weather forecasts useful. We buy flood insurance in areas where floods have historically occurred, and, in fact, we make decisions every day based on past experience. So the logic of taking the outcomes of the past and counting them up to form a distribution with which to make future decisions does have some precedent. The normal distribution (Gaussian) is not representative of a future distribution, but it is representative for picking members out of a population and has no future values in it. Because the future has not happened yet, there isn't a full set of outcomes in a normal distribution created from past experience. When we use statistics like this to predict the future, we are making an assumption that the future will look like today or similar to today, all things being equal, and also assuming extreme events do not happen, altering the normal occurrences. This is what quants do. They are clearly aware that extreme events do happen, but useful models don't get discarded just because some random event can happen. We wear seat belts because they will offer protection in the majority of car accidents, but if an extreme event happens, like a 40-ton tractor-trailer hitting us head on at 60 mph, the seat belts won't offer much safety. Do we not wear seat belts because of the odd chance of the tractor-trailer collision? Obviously we wear them.

To add color, however, and to offer an apologetic for quants, consider that there is more than one cause and effect for almost all observable phenomena in the universe! Scientists usually attempt to understand the strongest influencers of an outcome or event, not necessarily all of the influencers of an outcome. So, in reality, there are multiple possible causes for every event, even those that are extreme, or black swan. Extreme events have different mechanisms (one or more) that trigger cascades and feedbacks, whereas everyday normal events, those that are not extreme, have a separate mechanism. The conundrum of explanation arises only when you try to link all observations, both from the world of extreme random events and from normal events, when, in reality, these are usually from separate causes. In the behavioral finance literature, this falls under the subject of multiple-equilibria, and it has been demonstrated in markets where there is deviation from no-arbitrage opportunities for a considerable amount of time and is of course noticed where structural mispricings occur for longer periods than a single equilibria mechanism would allow. In this context, highly nonlinear and chaotic market behavior occurs in which small triggers induce cascades and contagion, similar to the way very small changes in initial conditions bring out turbulence in fluid flow. The simple analogy is the game of Pick-Up Sticks, where the players have to remove a single stick from a randomly connected pile, without moving all the other sticks. Eventually, the interconnectedness of the associations among sticks results in an avalanche. Likewise, so behaves the market.

Quants generally are very aware of the unpredictable nature of random unforeseen events, and they do not waste their time trying to predict them. They spend their time building models to predict normal events with known causes that are predictable. Therefore, quants are *not* responsible for market meltdowns for two reasons. First, they do not claim they can predict random events, nor do they spend their time trying to predict them. Second, even if they could predict random events, that does not mean they are the cause of the event any more than the television weather forecaster is the cause of a tornado that they are predicting.

Take for example the principal teacher of ELEs, the financial markets. Thirsty bubbles, credit crunches, LTCM, currency crisis, October 1987, and August 2007 occurred, and they were not explained by the Gaussian model. Well, for ease of explanation, say there were two underlying distributions with two completely different mechanisms involved. One cause of market movements, say, results in a distribution of returns modeled like a Gaussian, whereas the other cause is best explained by some distribution that has extreme tails, infinite variance, and allows for discontinuous jumps. I have yet to meet a physicist or mathematician who would not agree with this categorization, and it satisfies Taleb's points exactly. Multiple causes are in effect simultaneously in most problems we encounter, each resulting in its own distribution of outcomes. However, when over 95 percent of the observations are due to the predictable cause, why wouldn't one avail oneself of the opportunity to model it? In particular, when one cannot separate the causes well enough, then we have havoc in an explanation, and in that case, error-free modeling is inhibited.

Being a student of history, I would like to offer two quotations, one from the supreme empiricist Isaac Newton and the second from the best theorist I know, Albert Einstein. First, Newton:

> *Thus far I have explained the phenomena of the heavens and of our sea by the force of gravity, but I have not yet assigned a cause to gravity. I have not as yet, been able to deduce from phenomena the reason for these properties of gravity. For whatever is not deduced from the phenomena must be called a hypothesis; and hypotheses whether metaphysical or physical, or based on occult qualities or mechanical, have no place in experimental philosophy.*[8]

Now from Einstein:

> *Newton forgive me; you found the only way which in your age was just about possible for a person with the highest powers of thought and creativity. The concepts which you created are guiding our thinking in physics even today, although we now know that they will have to be replaced by others farther removed from the sphere of immediate experience, for we know that science cannot grow out of empiricism alone.*[9]

These forefathers of empiricism (using past data to guide future predictions) and theory (observing past data and forming theories about cause) surely would disagree with denying the usefulness of past events to model the future. However, both would agree that extreme events do happen. To use the excuse of *karma* and avoid the science of observation is suicide and is not within the realm of the thinking person, in my mind, and it is a bitter path to walk along. I clearly concede the idea that we are too focused on the average value of things and don't look out for the tails that can bite hard. To live and let live is not enough; to live and help live is perhaps a little bit better, for a disease half known is half cured, hence we model what we know.

There are, indeed, random extreme events that occur that are not predictable. However, it is not a failure of those who make models that they cannot create models to predict these events. It is just sensible to tackle simpler problems first. We didn't throw Newton out when his laws failed to account for relativistic velocity; we shouldn't throw out Markowitz, Merton, Sharpe, Black, and Scholes either for their early contributions. In time they will be overtaken by Rachev and the Lévy-Stable distribution function, but in 1968, who could compute a numerical basis function on a piece of paper when computers were not around.[10] One reason the normal (Gaussian) distribution was used was simply because you could compute it; it had a closed-form analytical equation. However, I have also been a student of Newton, Kelvin, and Einstein, all of whom would and did make room for the Gaussian curve and normal statistics in their way of thinking, so as to not outlaw their use when feasible. The proper question to be proposed in determining whether to accept a normal distribution is whether the actual distribution of the data is sufficiently close to the model distribution so that the actual distribution can be replaced by an ideal one to facilitate the statistical inference. If this is so, the normal is fine. End of story. However, we will give examples later of when not to use the normal curve, because, indeed, not using it is also right at least half the time.

Now what's vexing but true is the following quote from Graham:

*The applicability of history almost always appears after the event. When it is all over, we can quote chapter and verse to demonstrate why what happened was bound to happen because it happened before. This is not really very helpful. The Danish philosopher, Kirkegaard made the statement that life can only be judged in reverse but it must be lived forwards. That certainly is true with respect to our experience in the stock market.*[11]

The reason we review this statement is because it should not be thought of as a coffin nail to those who would criticize the use of a normal curve to examine past data or as criticism for modeling regularly observed events. Understanding the statistical interpretation of a time series of past data is not related to the philosophical underpinnings of such a statement. Graham also purported and even had in his lecture notes the example of a stock reaching new highs; after a while it goes down to levels below previous highs, and you can take this example as a warrant for purchasing securities based on past or historical histories, at lower prices than the current high. Hence, Graham himself did not dismiss the lessons of history but used models, like this example. He even admonished the use of empirically determined methodologies when the data was of a regular variety, that is, of events that happen frequently enough to obviate their inclusion as extreme events or ELEs. So, indeed, Graham was an empiricist to some extent. However, it is also clear that anomalous investing strategies, uncovered from analyzing the past market through empirical analysis, do not constitute a proof of enhanced return availability through these methods. Graham was equally unsupportive of using price momentum as an applicable investment strategy, as his empirical work suggested, which is, however, contrary to many modern findings.[12]

## ACTIVE VERSUS PASSIVE RISK

Okay, back to standard risk management. In particular, we will discuss the major issues surrounding the fog of confusion about these passive versus active risk measures, the construction of a covariance risk matrix, and industry issues. To the typical portfolio manager or investor, passive risk involves setting constraints that will not be exceeded under any circumstance. For instance, the largest position size in the portfolio will be 5 percent of assets, or not to purchase less than 30 securities or not to have a larger percentage of banks in a portfolio than one has in one's benchmark. Passive risk control simply involves setting appropriate constraints and then living within these constraints, similar to a budget. Sometimes risk controls are even said to be a risk budget, something we will discuss in greater detail later.

Active risk control, on the other hand, is entirely different. Active risk control involves more vague definition sometimes while also allowing for more flexibility. Active risk control also pops up more often when you are involved in optimizing a portfolio; that is, when you have alpha estimates for the stocks you are interested in, when you have risk estimates (both kinds: stock specific, which is diversifiable, and market related, which is not) for these same stocks and you want to create a portfolio from these stocks maximizing alpha while minimizing risk.

There is a strong need to consider alpha and risk simultaneously. This assures that the bets you are taking when you construct the investment portfolio are, indeed, the bets you desire. By considering alpha and risk together, you can offer a consistent, more robust and reproducible methodology for weighting thc securities in the portfolio in the first place (the alternative to this is usually ad-hoc security weighting). Joint consideration also gives a tighter quality control against your benchmark and a more stable tracking error through time while assuring that the risk and reward of a security are properly matched, along with usually offering a higher risk adjusted return (a higher information ratio) in the final measure. Thus, when it comes to active risk management, you must specify a covariance matrix. This is a mathematical expression used to enunciate the associations between securities in a portfolio that is designed to manage the overall portfolio risk. This covariance matrix defines a risk that is usually driven by four basic types of factors: fundamental or endogenous (financial-statement data), exogenous models (macroeconomic factors), historical returns, and statistical or blind factor models for risk that arises from using methods like principal component analysis (PCA). Unfortunately, attention to risk models tends to be somewhat neglected within quant firms and the majority of attention to detail is given to the alpha model. Oftentimes quant firms outsource the risk model (wrongly), considering it secondary to obtaining returns.

The drawback of outsourcing the risk modeling, however, is it can end up being used just as a generic tool by portfolio managers. These risk models may not work in accordance with the underlying alpha model and may be shared with competitors, since multiple managers might end up using the same risk model. Risk models should not be dismissed easily, nor should an off-the-shelf model be implemented without serious consideration. Quantitative investors or asset managers who do so are missing important ways to add value to their or client returns. Using a canned risk model entails several portfolio-specific problems. If a manager's alpha model is out of sync with the markets (meaning fundamental factors are losing correlation with return, usually accompanying down markets), it is difficult to analyze how the risk model is performing. In cases where both alpha and risk models are out of sync with markets, it becomes nearly impossible to determine how far from the Markowitz optimal or efficient portfolio that the optimal portfolio lies.

Additionally, if the factors in the alpha model are not the same as the risk model, then the factor biases cannot be optimized. For example, if you have a growth-biased alpha model with no valuation factors, but you have no growth factors in your risk model but only value factors, then the optimization is like maximizing growth/value ratio rather than return/risk. This may result in unintended exposures. Another example would be if the momentum factor in the alpha model is 12-month return defined as the return measured from 13 months ago to 1 month ago, whereas the risk model momentum factor is the 12-month return measured from 12 months ago to the current period. In this case, the portfolio will have a large negative exposure to 1-month returns, a clearly unintended bet. This impact worsens the farther the difference between factors in the alpha and risk model are. Finally, as noted earlier, risk models purchased from a vendor are available to competitors, which may increase correlation between those managers, as we observed in the quant meltdown of August of 2007.

The prudent quant investor should break the old paradigm and begin spending equal time on risk and alpha models, because we believe there is significant value added in creating a risk model that pairs well with the alpha model. In this way, we hope to avoid obvious deficiencies of outsourced risk models and to capture the additional value that proprietary risk models can add to portfolio returns. With this in mind, frequently quants begin their research on the alpha model and then just stop their work when they have an alpha model they like, though, in reality, the construction of a risk model inherently models the returns first, on the way to modeling the variance of returns. In fact, the process of risk modeling begins with modeling returns. Therefore, it only makes sense for most quants to just continue their research when they decide on an alpha model, and to turn that model into the risk model (i.e., construct the covariance matrix from their own alpha model factors). Why chief investment officers do not insist on this, we just don't know. Or, for that matter, why don't investment consultants penalize an investment manager for using third-party risk models when they have their own alpha model? In our experience the reason is that many type-2 quants are not experienced enough with mathematical methods to construct their own covariance matrix.

For the average prudent investor, the creation of a covariance-based risk model is confusing. A covariance matrix is a wonderful thing, but how do you go about making one? If, for example, your investable universe is

1,000 stocks, taken from the Russell 1000 index, then the covariance matrix would be 1,000 × 1,000 if using historical returns to calculate this beast. In addition, to take each stock's corresponding historical returns and calculate each stock's variance and covariance by hand or with some statistical package is unseemly and time consuming. Besides, just using empirical data is the hindsight method we discussed earlier, and using historical data can easily reveal spurious correlations between unrelated stocks that cannot possibly be expected to continue going forward. In addition, if a stock has just done an initial public offering, there is no data. You also need a sample period of at least as many data as there are stocks, so in this example, a 1,000-stock universe would require, minimally, 1,000 returns per stock, or almost four years of daily trading data. So calculating a covariance matrix from historical returns is not the best way to go.

However, the key to building a useful risk model covariance matrix lies in the simple models of the CAPM, Fama-French, or Ben Graham recipe. The key is in the alpha model factors, because in their use to model returns, the data requirements are far less. Therefore, these models with 1, 3, or 6 factors would greatly reduce the dependency of the calculation from millions (1,000 × 1,000) to a much smaller matrix on the order of the number of factors. In addition, we can divide the factors into categories of common, industry, and exogenous factors, like commodity prices or economic variables that are not tied specifically to individual stocks like B/P, accruals, or free cash flow. The models then constitute the common factors associated with systematic (market) risk in the first instance. Then, you can build up industry or sector-level factors by combining the residuals of the regressions of the model common factors with returns in various creative ways to obtain the ultimate full covariance matrix. This is the simple explanation, but the risk model vendors all have their own little recipes and subtleties, making each risk model slightly different. The steps can be summarized as follows:

1. Define your investable universe: that universe of stocks that you'll always be choosing from to invest in.
2. Define your alpha model (whose factors become your risk model common factors); this could be the CAPM, the Fama-French, the Ben Graham method, or some construct of your own.
3. Calculate your factor values for your universe. These become your exposures to the factor. If you have B/P as a factor in your model, calculate the B/P for all stocks in your universe. Do the same for all other factors. The numerical value of B/P for a stock is then termed exposure. Quite often these are *z*-scored, too.
4. Regress your returns against your exposures (just as in CAPM, you regress future returns against the market to obtain a beta or the

Fama-French equation to get 3 betas). These regression coefficients or betas to your factors become your factor returns.

5. Do this cross-sectionally across all the stocks in the universe for a given date. This will produce a single beta for each factor for that date.
6. Move the date one time step or period and do it all over. Eventually, after, say, 60 months, there would be five years of cross-sectional regressions that yield betas that will also have a time series of 60 months.
7. Take each beta's time series and compute its variance. Then, compute the covariance between each factor's beta. The variance and covariance of the beta time series act as proxies for the variance of the stocks. These are the components of the covariance matrix. On-diagonal components are the variance of the factor returns, the variance of the betas, and off-diagonal elements are the covariance between factor returns.
8. Going forward, to calculate expected returns, multiply the stock weight vector by the exposure matrix times the beta vector for a given date. The exposure matrix is $N \times M$, where $N$ is the number of stocks and $M$ is the number of factors. The covariance matrix is $M \times M$, and the exposed risks, predicted through the model, are derived from it.

We leave out higher-order complexities of risk models having to do with the residuals, which are beyond the scope of this book. Then you're done. If you had 1,000 stocks in the universe, you would have gone from having to compute a $1{,}000 \times 1{,}000$ covariance matrix to computing one of size $M \times M$ where $M$ is the number of factors, typically on the order of 10 to 15 common factors, followed by a number of industry factors. If you follow these steps, you will have a risk model covariance matrix.

However, it is entirely possible for several securities to have their returns uncorrelated or lowly correlated, whereas their prices are strongly correlated. This is one of the reasons for the emergence of using a copula (I didn't say copulate!) to describe associations among stocks. It rightly considers nonlinear associations that a covariance matrix will completely miss. However, it is way beyond the scope of this book to discuss copulas because they are extremely wild mathematical animals and we are not lion tamers.

We cannot tell you why regression coefficients have been renamed factor returns and actual financial statement variables (B/P, E/P, FCF/P) have been renamed exposures, but that clearly is the convention in risk management. You must watch out, though, when you add exogenous factors or industry factors to the risk model because, often, the created industry factors are returns from stocks within an industry averaged or aggregated up. They are called factor returns, whereas the betas from the regression on these industry or exogenous factors are termed exposures. Confusing, we know, and silly, but that is the practice. When engineers from other fields move into finance, half their time is spent learning the nomenclature, although the math is not too hard. Going forward in this book, all regression coefficients will be called betas and anything else will be called exposure.

So, you ask, what is the covariance? It is very easy to see from the following simple equation but we caution you that these definitions are explicit and represent how you would calculate them from historical returns data. However, this is also how you would calculate the betas from the time series of the factor returns. Assume we have 60 monthly returns for some stock $x$, then, sum the difference of each return for some month from its mean.

$$\text{Variance}\,(x) = \left(\Sigma(x_i - u_x)^2\right)/60$$

In this equation, $x_i$ is a return for month $i$, and $u_x$ is the average return over the whole period for stock $x$. The covariance then between two stocks $x$ and $y$ is similar as seen below:

$$\text{Covariance}\,(x, y) = \left(\Sigma(x_i - u_x) * (y_i - u_y)\right)/60$$

Covariance can be thought of as the degree to which returns $x$ and $y$ move in tandem linearly. So if we now have a covariance matrix, we have the expected correlations of all the stocks within our investable universe, assuming we used an alpha model in the preceding recipe to create the covariance matrix rather than using empirical historical returns. This is because the alpha models represent predictive or forecasting of returns, so likewise would a risk matrix built from them. Using historical data offers the hindsight view we have been criticizing.

In summary, the process utilized in building a covariance matrix offers the investor a measurement (through regression) of what the betas to the factor exposures are in the risk model and betas to industries as well. In addition, the forecasted volatility and tracking error (to be defined in further chapters) elucidate that the risks of the portfolio are obtained from the full covariance matrix. Think of the covariance matrix as offering transparency to the risks the portfolio is exposed to. The total risk calculation is the stock weights, times the exposure matrix, times the covariance matrix, times the transpose of the exposure matrix, but all these calculations are done with matrix algebra. Hence, we have a recipe to calculate risks for any set of stock weights. To find the most appropriate stock weights, we take this risk matrix as one input to a mean-variance optimizer. Given the alpha forecast together with the risk forecast, you can solve for the appropriate weights of the portfolio. Additionally there are inputs specifying exactly how much risk the investor is willing to take and other constraints, like position size limits, industry limits, and so forth. We will discuss portfolio optimization in Chapter 9, however, because in the first instance of constructing the Graham quantitative model, we will not be using portfolio optimization.

Another issue of importance in active versus passive risk measures and their subsequent analysis involves industry exposure. Traditionally, S&P, one of the McGraw Hill companies, developed the Global Industry Classification Standard[13] (GICS) for the express purpose of offering to their clients a systemized methodology for categorizing companies into 10 sectors, 24 industry groups, 67 industries, and 147 subindustries. (In practice it is more like 66 industries and 139 subindustries, unless you are really a global investor.) These GICS classification schemes have become very useful to portfolio managers and others for measuring active weights versus benchmarks or even on an absolute return portfolio run by hedge funds, to give the manager a feel for what industry weights are in the portfolio. However, GICS classifications have their drawbacks for use in risk or alpha modeling. In addition, many other data providers besides S&P have their own classification schemes. For instance, FactSet offers 104 sectors and 128 industries. Another data provider that also offers risk models is Northfield Information Systems, as does Barra, and they use their own classification schemes in their risk models. In all of these methods, however, the drawback is that each and every company is put into a single industry. That begs the question, what about GE, Coca-Cola, conglomerates, or other multinational companies that have business in many industries? This is one of several issues that may confuse the investor, besides the fact that many of these categorization methods, though each is fine in its own right, mandates that whatever method you choose, you must stick with it over time and use the same one for the benchmark, the alpha model, and the risk model for consistency of process. This is not often insisted upon in practice.

The most egregious error is the one company, one industry mandate. Typically, an investment manager may have a model for determining whether to overweight some industry or sector, predicated on some industry-group classification by aggregating security-level returns or factors up into their assigned industries and creating industry-level momentum measures, for example, or aggregating up from the sum of stocks in an assigned industry their valuations or other fundamental variables. This is also how industry-group exposures are created in a risk model. For risk models we speak of exposures rather than weights, as when speaking about an alpha model. However, we mean betas, because these betas come directly out of the process used to compute the risk forecasting covariance matrix calculation. Significantly, this method utilizing the older types of specified factor risk models simply assumes that a stock will have a beta of 1 on its own assigned industry group and a beta of 0 on all other groups. Instead, a better method is to recognize that not all stocks in an industry necessarily have the same exposure to the industry and that some stocks may have significant exposure to other industries as well. This would mean that, rather than assigning a stock to a single sector or industry group, it could be assigned fractionally across all industries that it has a part in. This might mean that some company that does 60 percent of its business in one industry and 40 percent in another would result ultimately in a predicted beta from the risk model that is also, say, 0.76 one industry and 0.31 another. Although this is novel, and fully known and appreciated, few investment managers do it because of the amount of work required to separate out the stock's contribution to all industries. However, FactSet's MAC model does include this operation.

Just as there is multiple industry membership by some companies, there can also be multiple country membership. For instance, Baidu (BIDU), an Internet search provider in China, does business in China, but it is incorporated in the Cayman Islands in the Caribbean. It lists its American Depository Shares (ADR's) on the NASDAQ. However, there can be legal and/or regulatory obligations across countries for major multinationals. So, assigning some stocks to a single country might produce some misgivings, especially if the company obtains significant revenue across the globe. This is not addressed in most conventional vendor risk models either, even if they are designed for international or global portfolio mandates, but again is, in FactSet's MAC model.

The bar chart in Figure 2.3, however, will serve to demonstrate the results of just such an analysis. In this example we show the active weights of a portfolio in gray, and the active exposures in black for the identical industry group classification scheme used in an alpha model and risk model.

Active weight is simply the sum of the individual security portfolio weights in an industry from the portfolio, minus the same industry weighting of the benchmark. This is a very simple definition and very easy to calculate. It again assumes that the data provider (such as GICS, FactSet, Northfield, or Reuters) assigns stocks to their industry. The active exposure uses the same classification scheme; however, it comes from the risk model's (covariance matrix's) betas to these same industries. Nevertheless, in this case, a stock can have multiple betas to one industry, as opposed to 1 and 0 by most risk models, and they can be fractional values that need not sum to 1, either. The ramification of this is shown in Figure 2.3 because active weights may not equal active exposures. In almost every industry group, there is a mismatch in the heights of the bars for the two measures. In particular, consumer services, consumer durables, energy minerals, and health technology, for instance, all have opposing weights versus their exposures. Thus, although investment managers think they are positively exposed to health technology (i.e., overweight health tech) in reality, there is a negative exposure there. Why is this? Where does this negative exposure come from?

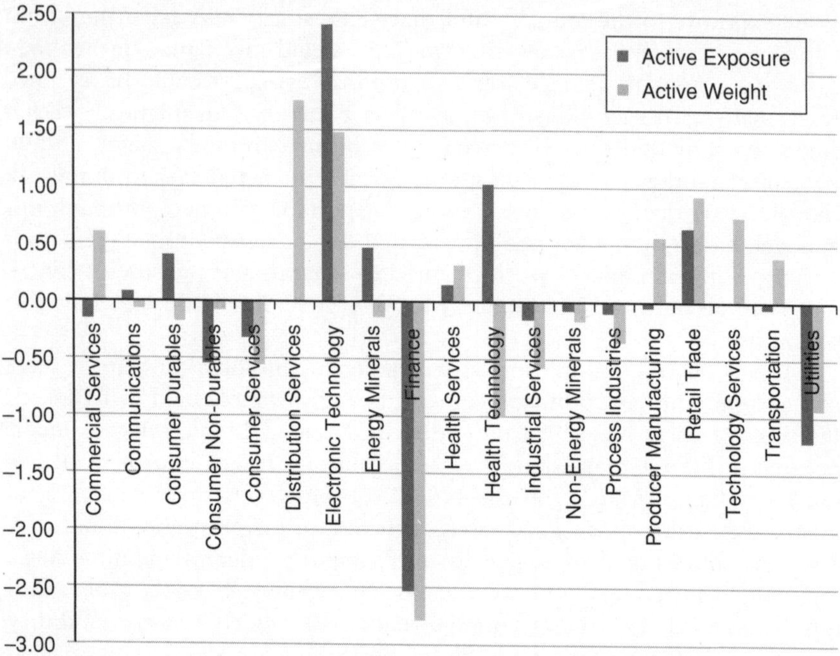


**FIGURE 2.3** Active Risk Exposures versus Active Portfolio Weights

It comes from the correlations (covariances) among stocks. This occurs specifically in this example because there are other stocks in the portfolio, assigned to other industry groups by the vendor, that have business interests, products, and processes associated with health technology, even though they are classified somewhere else, probably because the majority of their business is in some other industry. To give you an example, the next two figures, Figure 2.4 and Figure 2.5, illustrate the stock prices of two stocks shown in a completely different industry. The first involves Whirlpool Corporation. We downloaded from FactSet the daily price trace of Whirlpool (ticke: WHR) along with the Financial Select SPDR from State Street Global Advisors ETF (ticker: XLF) from November 2008 to November 2009. If you just glance at these two price histories, it will become immediately apparent through chi by eye that there is correlation between these two signals. The correlation over this time period measures 75 percent. Thus, in a properly defined risk model, Whirlpool would have some beta to the financial sector. We do not share with the reader why this would occur; that is another story for correlation does not imply causality. The question raised would be: Is this a spurious correlation in this example? It could be, but good statistical testing would

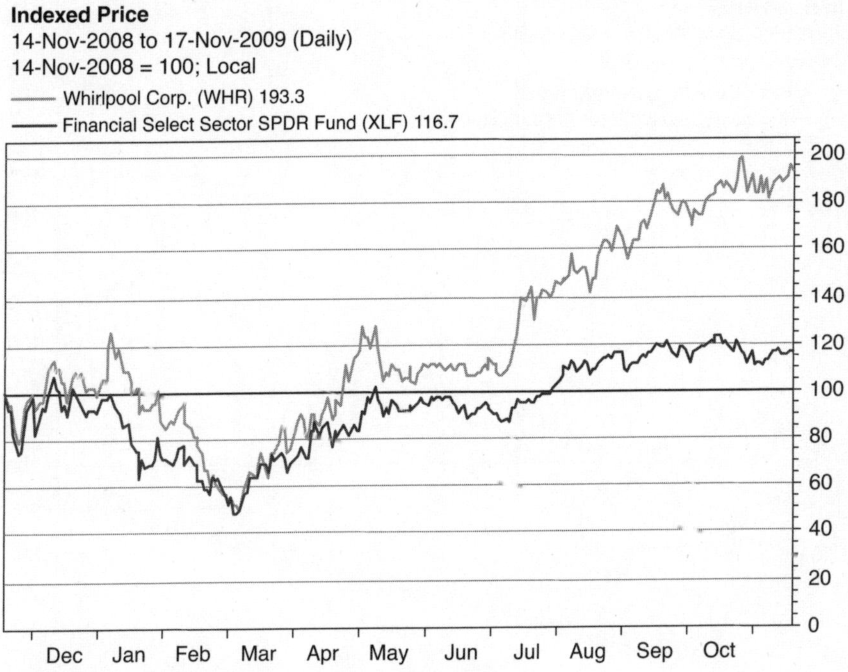


**FIGURE 2.4** Whirlpool and Financial Select SPDR
*Source:* © FactSet Research Systems 2009.
*Data Source:* Prices/Exshare.

minimize the possibility of including it in the risk model should that be the situation, and it would only calculate a worthwhile beta to the financial sector if it passes good testing.

Moreover, there are many, many stocks in this situation. Consider News Corporation (ticker: NWSA). News Corporation's price history for the same time period is plotted with the technology SPDR XLK in Figure 2.5. Again, the astute reader can visually see the correlation, which is measured at over 80 percent for this time period. The correlation exists and might be explained by the fact that News Corporation has a significant technology platform in its news distribution. Another example would be the old AT&T company after the breakup in January of 1984 but before the spin-out of Lucent Technologies (i.e., Bell Labs) in September 1996. Was AT&T a utility or a technology company? It had traces of both and, hence, exposures to both industries most probably. So, if a portfolio contains stocks that are assigned to a single industry by some vendor, and it owns stocks that, in reality, have products in multiple industries, it is very easy to see why the

**FIGURE 2.5** News Corporation and Technology Select SPDR
*Source:* © FactSet Research Systems 2009.
*Data Source:* Prices/Exshare.

actual industry exposure of the portfolio can be quite different than what is measured utilizing the weights of stocks in an assigned classification scheme. This industry exposure conundrum becomes more important when there are fewer stocks in the portfolio.

When you have a risk model built from common risk factors and subsequently properly conditioned on industries and countries, you can examine the possible risk of a portfolio by observing how the portfolio has performed in various market environments using stress-testing simulations. For instance, this would involve looking back in time to find a stressful period for stocks, like the Internet bubble, the Iraq invasion, LTCM debacle, and so forth. Then, having built a covariance matrix from that time, use the factor returns it was built on, together with the current exposures to see how a portfolio might behave, should that kind of market situation happen again. In essence, use the established covariance structure in the market from past major extreme events and test them against current portfolios exposures to see how they might behave. This is a sophisticated method, implemented in

FactSet, for instance, but it shows the versatility a risk model offers, should you have one.

## OTHER RISK MEASURES: VAR, C-VAR, AND ETL

There are other measures of risk that should be reviewed, and these are the up and comers. Though Nassim Taleb holds them in low esteem, these methods are gaining much credibility in risk analysis and forecast. The first consideration involves a risk metric called value at risk (VAR). The VAR of a portfolio is that amount of loss in a specified period that could occur at some confidence interval. For instance, say we have a million-dollar portfolio in an IRA at Fidelity. Then the daily VAR might be $35,000 at 95 percent confidence interval, or, in percentage terms, the VAR would comprise 3.5 percent of the portfolio's value, for example. Or another way to say it is that there is a 5 percent chance that the portfolio will fall by 3.5 percent of its value in the next day. Thus VAR is a growing measure of loss, and in this vein it is a more preferable risk measure in line with Ben Graham's view of risk. Value at risk is more intuitive, too, because variance as a risk measure is symmetric, meaning that a stock can be penalized for moving up as well as down, whereas VAR only looks at downside stock price movements.

The calculation of VAR can be done using historical measures of return, which is the "frequentist's" approach, such as taking the past year's daily returns, plotting the histogram of these returns, and looking at the left tail where 5 percent of the data lies. This would be a very easy method that anybody with a little Excel experience could perform. Unfortunately, this method plays exactly into the hands of those who criticize risk methodologies as being too hindsight oriented. The preferred methodology utilizes the risk model created for the portfolio.

In this latter method, pretend you have the covariance matrix created from calculating the variance and covariance of the time series of the factor betas, each set obtained from a single cross-sectional regression of the investor's universe for a given date. This was done recursively for say, 60 time periods, so that there is a set of 60 betas for each factor exposure for each date, and their variance and covariance measured through time is the source of the data in the covariance matrix. Now, pretend there exists a method for generating a new set of betas that has the exact same covariance matrix, so that the individual factor variances are the same, as are the factor covariances, but the actual values of the betas in time are different than the original set. An example is shown in Table 2.1. Here we show the original hypothetical betas obtained for some factor exposure A in the risk model. The rows are data points in time and would represent betas calculated from

**TABLE 2.1** Examples of Covariances and Monte Carlo Runs

| Factor A | | |
|---|---|---|
| | Ann. Stdev 2.09 | Ann. Stdev 2.09 |
| Num. | Org. Betas | New Betas |
| 1 | 0.56 | 0.43 |
| 2 | 0.46 | 0.48 |
| 3 | 0.55 | 0.40 |
| 4 | 0.54 | 0.28 |
| 5 | 0.43 | 0.55 |
| 6 | 0.23 | 0.27 |
| 7 | 0.24 | 0.59 |
| 8 | 0.28 | 0.40 |
| " | 0.52 | 0.66 |
| " | 0.35 | 0.24 |
| " | 0.30 | 0.40 |

a cross-sectional regression of returns versus factor exposures like B/P, P/E, dividends, or EPS growth, for instance, at that time. This is depicted in the middle column of the chart, which shows the beta time series. The standard deviation (square root of the variance) of the column's data is shown annualized at the top of the chart and has a value of 2.09 here.

The column on the far right is an alternative set of betas through time with the identical variance and standard deviation as the original set. Likewise, this new set of betas would also retain the same covariance with some other Factor B (not shown) as the original set of betas.

In this fashion, we could generate 5,000 other sets of betas for each factor while retaining the original variance and covariance structure of the original risk model. However, if we use these betas to forecast return, by multiplying them times the current factor exposures, we would generate a different return for each stock than we would have if we used the original betas. In fact, we could generate a distribution of returns—5,000 of them for each stock. A plot of this return distribution could be used to determine the VAR and it would be a more accurate VAR than using the historical time series of returns because it would be based on the covariance structure of the underlying assets modeled through time. In addition, because these 5,000 sets of betas would have been generated randomly, a completely different set of returns would end up being used to calculate the VAR than those obtained just by using a histogram distribution of the actual past returns. In fact, greater outliers could occur in this method, also, making the VAR from this method larger than it probably would be using historical returns, thus offering a margin of safety that Graham would approve of. This is the method implemented in FactSet's MC VAR calculation, where MC here stands for Monte Carlo, which is a method for generating random distributions. Google knows there is a lot more to VAR than this simple explanation, but in general this is how it works and what it is.

In practice, VAR will be breached minimally 5 percent of the time, assuming we are using the 95 percent VAR (obviously the investor is free to choose the confidence interval and 99 percent could also be chosen), so that means that 1 day in 20, there will be a loss greater than the VAR amount. Thus, the VAR can be most appropriately used for risk management in the following fashion. Consider an investment portfolio that has a VAR of 3.5 percent of assets at the 95 percent confidence interval. Now, consider a software program that says that if the VAR is greater than 3.5 percent of assets, "automagically" readjust the portfolio accordingly to reduce the VAR below the 3.5 percent of assets level. In essence, the intelligent investor could do these "what-ifs" manually by making portfolio changes and changing the asset allocation in such a way as to lower the calculated VAR. This would be done in an iterative fashion until the desired VAR level is obtained.

Foreseeable events are most appropriate for VAR measures, too, as is risk modeling in general. This again points to the confusion many have for risk modeling overall, insofar as their expectations are that risk modeling should catch extreme events. Such is just not the case. Unforeseen events cannot be modeled, and VAR is neither an omniscient predictor of extreme events nor a portfolio savior of losses; it is just another tool in one's belt for making predictions in normal markets. However, it is highly illustrative for exposing potential losses due to regular market movements (not ELE), and that's what it should be used for. Consider a portfolio positioned to have a daily VAR of 10 percent of assets, for instance. How would you feel if you had a portfolio of stocks and a couple of options that have a 1 in 20 possibility of losing 10 percent or more of the portfolio's value in a single day? Now, what if you didn't know it? Knowing the VAR can illustrate the risk exposures before they become experienced losses.

A technical drawback of VAR involves the size of losses that could occur. In the preceding example on the million-dollar portfolio, we mentioned that the portfolio might have a daily VAR of $35,000 or 3.5 percent of the portfolio. Of course, that is a completely made-up number, and we said that there's a 5 percent probability that losses could exceed this VAR. However, how great could the loss be? Could it be $45,000, $95,000, half the portfolio? VAR only gives us the probability that losses could exceed the VAR amount, and it says nothing about the amount that could be lost.

Hence, conditional VAR was invented, and it is a probability measure of the tail loss on average or the amount that could be lost in probability terms. It is essentially the average of all losses beyond the VAR. It is more difficult to calculate accurately, too, allowing for the quant critics to continue their onslaught demonizing quantitative methods.

The C-VAR or expected tail loss (ETL) is a very sophisticated tool, much of which is beyond the scope of this book. It allows for a fitting of a sophisticated mathematical function to the fat tails of the return distribution, much of which is an odd mixture of art and science. Remember that the tail comprises the rarer events of the return distribution, of which there are not many values, and averaging the losses to produce the C-VAR number means that you are averaging just a few numbers, making the C-VAR inaccurate, simply because there are too few data. Hence, the rise of very sophisticated measures for doing the tail calculation and fitting. Given the sophistication of calculating the ETL, there has actually been a patent that has been issued for mean-ETL optimization, in which a portfolio is optimized with respect to returns and tail losses.[14] They use a skewed *t*-distribution for the form of the return distribution tail fitting and *t*-copula to capture nonlinear associations (something that a covariance matrix misses) in their ETL calculation. Also, it is asymmetric, so unlike a covariance- or variance-based risk methodology, it does not treat upside returns like downside returns. This methodology is still cutting edge and state-of-the-art, but, as usual, increases in computer speed and technology will eventually bring this to the retail investor. For now, it is limited mostly to institutional investors.

## SUMMARY

Risk is easy to talk about, but not so readily defined, mostly because we cannot see risk, but we can see an individual stock move up and down. Therefore, the invisibility of risk exposure generally puts it behind our backs and out of our minds. However, volatility and covariance are a proxy for risk because risk, in reality, concerns losses only. When trying to lower portfolio volatility as an objective for a given level of expected return, risk exposure is important when there is a need to liquidate assets in a hurry. Even if you have a Graham portfolio of lowly valued underpriced stocks, the daily volatility of prices could mean you have to liquidate the portfolio in the midst of a market that has not yet recognized the real value in the Graham portfolio, even with the application of Graham's margin of safety.

A drawback to these conventional measures of risk involves the symmetry associated with the variance measure. Using variance as a risk measure implies that a trending stock price moving upward is also risky just because it, too, will increase the variance calculation. Therefore, in a rising market like the Internet bubble, as stocks rose, a variance estimate of risk would imply that the market is getting risky for all the wrong reasons. Indeed it was getting riskier, however the risk occurred due to valuations obtaining lofty levels, not due to stocks trending upward. Therefore, the alternative measures of risk involve using just the negative side of the return distribution like value-at-risk. In addition, the ETL, or C-VAR, variables are mitigating of the false symmetric risk idiosyncrasies. These measures involve making assessments of losses in probability terms. For instance, the statement that the maximum cumulative loss at a 95 percent confidence level is 8.9 percent of the portfolio over 10 days is a very useful statement to an investor.

These are more sophisticated concepts and involve providing a much better estimate of the underlying stock return distributions rather than just a normal distribution. However, if the tracking error of the portfolio is relatively low, this approximation for risk using variance is acceptable, because the portfolio's overall risks are not too different from the portfolio's benchmark, and the mean variance methodology and its associated factor-derived linear covariance risk matrix methodology is sufficient for risk monitoring.

An aspiring quant should not worry much about the criticisms directed at quants and modeling from the likes of Nassim Taleb and Scott Patterson. Much of the criticism is for publicity and is much to-do about nothing. Consider their understanding to be unrefined, though they are well read. They just have not been reading the right material to give their criticisms credibility. That rebuttal hangs on the experience of many contacts, friends, and graduates of most PhD programs in physics, mathematics, statistical, and financial engineering departments.

Finally, the correlations among stocks can be seen and experienced almost every day in investment portfolios, as seen by the likes of the co-occurrence of stocks like Whirlpool and News Corporation with sector specialty indexes. This resultant effect has impact in the risks of collections of stocks, and, unfortunately, certain measures of risk that have grown up under the guise of efficient market theory and modern portfolio theory are flawed as measures of volatility, as we will see in the next chapter.

# CHAPTER 3

# Beta Is Not "Sharpe" Enough

*We now know that science cannot grow out of empiricism alone, that in the constructions of science we need to use free invention which only a posteriori can be confronted with experience as to its usefulness.*

—Albert Einstein[1]

To my knowledge, Ben Graham never liked the term *beta*. Like Einstein, a student of what he studied, Graham allowed imagination to guide him, and he used the empirical evidence after the fact to be his judge. In a *Barron's* article, he said that what bothered him was that authorities equate beta with the concept of risk.[2] Price variability, yes; risk, no. Real risk, he wrote, is measured not by price fluctuations but by a loss of quality and earnings power through economic or management changes.

Due to Markowitz, the concept of risk has been extended to the possibility of decline in the market price of a security, even though it may be simply a cyclical or temporary effect. This possibility, of course, is feasible for any instrument traded on exchanges and for many not on the exchange (housing prices, for example). Graham argues that a certain level of price fluctuation (i.e., volatility) is normal, to be expected, and does not signify real risk. Real risk, in stocks, is solely due to the underlying business losing money and does not have to do with the stock price paid should the owner be forced to sell. In this definition, risk is one sided and only involves the left-hand side of the return distribution. Further, he would argue that an investor (but not a speculator) does not lose money simply because the price of a stock declines, assuming that the business itself has had no changes, it has cash flow, and its business prospects look good. Graham contends that if one selects a group of candidate stocks with his margin of safety, then there is still a good chance that even though this portfolio's market value may drop below cost occasionally over some period of time, this fact does not make the portfolio risky. In his definition, then, risk is there only if there is a reason to liquidate the portfolio in a fire sale or if the underlying securities suffer a serious degradation in their earnings power. Lastly, he believes there is risk in buying a security by paying too much for its underlying intrinsic value.

As for variance or standard deviation of return being a useful risk measure, in the same *Barron's* article Graham says that the idea of measuring investment risks by price fluctuations is repugnant to him, because it confuses what the stock market says with what actually happens to the owner's stake in the business.

On this subject, we have much to say. First, you need to understand that to Graham, a portfolio is a collection of pieces of companies. Often, his perspective is more like that of a private equities investor rather than a person who purchases stocks on the open market. This is similar to Warren Buffett's approach in that they can take control of a company and often force management's hand or influence policy and business within the company, whereas the typical investor with $250,000 spread across 30 or more companies cannot possibly do so. This kind of perspective more correctly defines Markowitz and Sharpe; their outlook is portfolio wide, and it is concerned with how to interpret risk of the portfolio as a whole. This distinction, between the company definition and the portfolio definition, is important to keep in mind when following a conversation on risk.

To begin, we need to review some definitions in greater detail. We will segue occasionally to relevant modern topics, but we will always come back to address volatility and beta. We start by explaining what mean and variance (the square root of variance is the standard deviation) originally meant. Simply, a distribution of data (heights of women, weight of men, speeds of cars on an expressway) has an associated population distribution, commonly called the density, and it is often displayed via a histogram. In a graph of this histogram distribution, the abscissa (the point [4,5] has 4 as the abscissa or $x$ axis and 5 as the ordinate or $y$ axis) is in units of the distribution, and the ordinate represents frequency of occurrence. Interpret the density as a probability, where the larger the value on the ordinate axis for some value on the abscissa means the greater the probability of finding that value. For instance, if the ordinate is number of cars and the abscissa is speed of cars, then where the peak is (in the curve of number of cars at a given speed), we have the highest probability of finding a car at that speed. Usually (and certainly for a normal distribution) the curve's peak marks the average value, that is, the average speed of the cars on the expressway. If one computes the standard deviation of the data, then, for a normal curve, 68.27 percent of the time, all the data will be found to be within +/−1 standard deviation from this mean. Among most of us humans, this results in the perception that, over long periods of time, the net result experienced is the average and 68.27 percent of the time fluctuations of the data will be between the average − standard deviation and the average + standard deviation.

When this supposition is true, we usually find the normal (Gaussian) or bell distribution. Although it is the cornerstone of modern statistics, it was investigated first in the eighteenth century when scientists observed an astonishing degree of regularity in errors of measurement. They found that the patterns they observed could be closely approximated by continuous curves, which they referred to as normal curves of errors, and they attributed these distributions to the laws of chance. These properties of errors were first studied by Abraham de Moivre (1667–1745), Pierre Laplace (1749–1827), and Carl Gauss (1777–1855), whose later portrait is well known and graced the face of the Deutsche Mark before the advent of the Euro. The graph of the normal curve has the familiar bell shape given by the Gaussian function named after, guess who, Herr Dr. Gauss whose name is also used as a unit to measure the magnitude of magnetic field, another area to which he contributed considerably.

The normal distribution arises when the errors of a measurement are given by chance; hence they are fully random and nonserially correlated, independent, and identically distributed. For instance, if 1,000 people were given a meter stick and asked to measure the height of a desk, the distribution of measured heights would display a normal distribution. This is so because the errors in measurement are random variables, not because the height of the desk is random. Thus, most phenomena that have a value distributed around some error that is random displays a normal curve for its density. The value about which the errors are distributed is the mean value, average, or expected value. In the case of investment return, this value is not constant, and neither are the causes of errors. To understand this, imagine another 1,000 people asked to measure the height of a desk, but now springs have been attached to the legs of the desk, which is also in a truck being driven down a bumpy road. Each of the participants has a turn in the back of the truck with the same meter stick and desk and has to measure the desk's height from the floor of the truck to the top of the desk. The height of the desk appears to be varying with time because the legs are flexing on the springs and the errors are a combination of the original random measurement error plus some function of the road surface and spring force constant. The resulting distribution of measurements will not be normal; they will be something else. Herein lies the difficulty in interpreting investment return measurements, because all anyone really knows is that the investment return mean varies with time and the errors are not random.[3]

When the previous supposition is not true, that is, when the mean is not at the maximum in the distribution or when the data is confined to greater or lesser than 68.27 percent of the mean +/−1 standard deviation, you are usually looking at data arising from some cause that results in some other distribution. Of course there are many, many types of distributions. For instance there are the binomial, Bernoulli, Poisson, Cauchy or Lorentzian, Pareto, Gumbel, Student's-t, Frechet, Weibull, and Lévy Stable distributions, just to name a few, all of which can be continuous or discrete. Some of these are symmetric about the mean (first moment) and some are not. Some have fat tails and some do not. You can even have distributions with infinite second moments (infinite variance). There are many distributions that need three or four parameters to define them rather than just the two consisting of mean and variance. Each of these named distributions has come about because some phenomena had been found whose errors or outcomes were not random, were not given merely by chance, or were explained by some other cause. Investment return is an example of data that produces some other distribution than normal and requires more than just the mean and variance to describe its characteristics properly.

This concept is significant and has profound implications in measuring performance and risk in investment portfolios. Since the early 1900s, market prices have been known to have non-normal distributions and maintain statistical dependence, meaning that the generating process (i.e., the market participants trading securities) for the underlying pricing is not constant with time, and the higher moments indicate large deviation from normal behavior. Even though this is well known, it appears that this information has been downplayed and excused away over the years in favor of the crucial assumptions that market returns follow a random walk resulting in random errors, which allow the implementation of well-known and easy-to-use statistical tools developed to examine normal data. Unfortunately, a random walk is an extremely poor approximation to financial reality as reviewed by many authors.[4] Risk Metrics Group, a publically traded company (ticker: RISK), until recently acquired by MSCI, published definitive data examining equity, money market, and foreign exchange return distributions and confirmed this result unequivocally back when they were part of J. P. Morgan.[5] Even Nassim Taleb, who criticizes the normal curve strongly in his later books, used it in his earlier work, a sophisticated text on dynamic hedging.[6]

R. Douglas Martin with others has also documented numerous times the occurrence of overly fat tails of both daily and monthly return time series of various stocks and demonstrated that fat-tailed skewed distributions are a better fit to the data than is a normal curve.[7] Many other authors can be found with a simple cursory examination of the academic literature (the most famous being Benoit Mandlebrot) documenting this very fact. In addition, Figure 3.1 demonstrates monthly return time series of some randomly

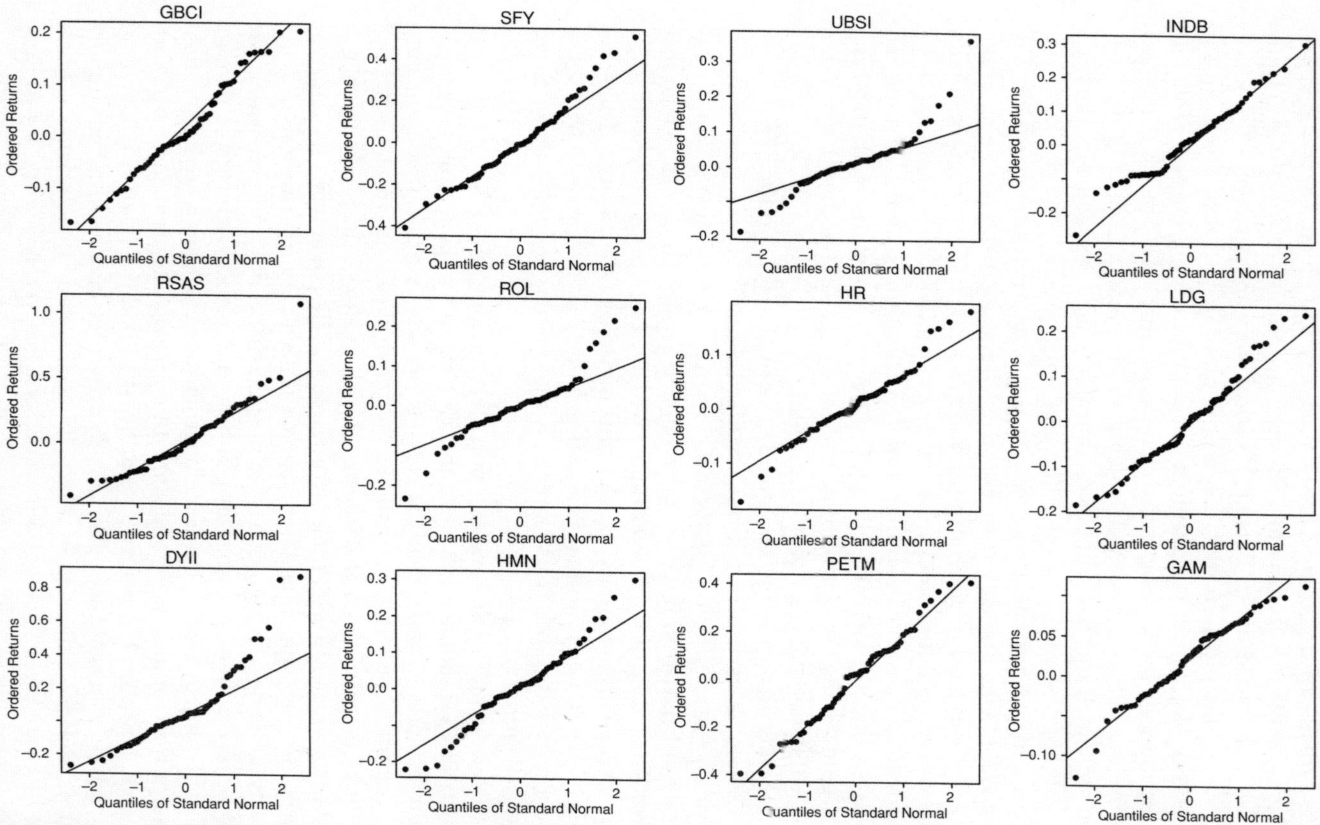


**FIGURE 3.1** Q-Q Pairs Plots of Selected Small-Cap Stocks

selected small-cap stocks in what is known as a Q-Q plot. Their tickers are displayed on the top of each plot. The price histories were downloaded from FactSet and loaded into S-Plus, a statistical software package, to produce these Q-Q pairs plots. In statistics, a Q-Q plot (Q stands for quantile) is a probability plot, which is a graphical method for comparing two probability distributions by plotting their quantiles against each other.[8] If the two distributions being compared are identical, the points in the Q-Q plot will lie on the line. If the distributions are linearly related, the points in the Q-Q plot will approximately lie on a line, but not necessarily on the line. Any deviation from a normal curve is shown as a deviation from the straight line in the graph. One can see clearly the strong deviation from normality in the data. This is typical of small-cap stocks in general, and it is also commonly found in most illiquid stocks (i.e., international, emerging markets, etc.). In particular, often the central part of a distribution is similar to a normal curve, but the tails are very different for the two distributions. In this case, you would see the linear central part of the Q-Q plot, but divergence in the lower left and upper right parts of the plot.

Treating financial time-series data as normal is a very difficult paradigm to break for a variety of reasons, only some of which are good reasons. However, our ability to identify structural changes in our thinking is extremely difficult, even if we are open minded enough to accept change that contradicts public or written testimony we have given previously. In the case of the academic community, much of the underlying theory is predicated so much on the standard normal as a starting point that to redo it all with more contemporary methods from statistics is too onerous and self-flagellating to right the wrong.

Later examples will show non-normal behavior to give a better sense of it all and why we should correct our thinking about its application in finance. In the meantime, know that the standard equity return distribution (and index return time series) typically has negative skewness (third moment of the distribution) and is *leptokurtotic* ("highly peaked," the fourth moment), neither of which are symptomatic of random walk phenomena or a normal distribution description and imply an asymmetric return distribution.

From the data in Figure 3.1, we see that stocks offer no pretension that they behave simply as normal distributions of returns. Therefore, to express their volatility by way of a normal distribution is a clear error. The original concept that variance is a good substitute for volatility remains a stubborn concept, however. Further, that volatility is a good proxy for risk in general is a concept that is old enough to legally drink! We concur with Ben Graham on this, that price fluctuation is not risk, and we add that variance is not a good enough price fluctuation measurement to even be a good measure of price fluctuation, let alone a good risk measure, as we will now show.

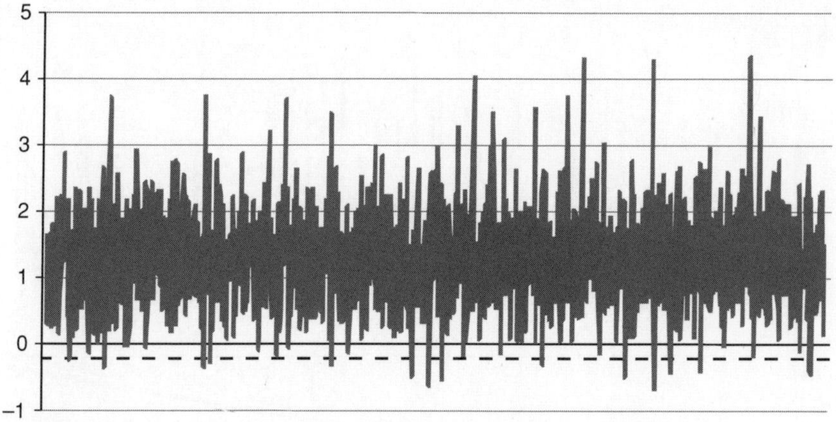


**FIGURE 3.2** Gaussian (Normal) Time-Series Plot

Continuing our discussion revisiting the idea that 68.27 percent of the time, returns fall between the mean −1 standard deviation and the mean +1 standard deviation, which any introductory statistics book makes clear. It is widely assumed that, if two portfolios have the same return time-series mean and standard deviation, then their performance and volatility should be identical. To show this inaccuracy, consider two portfolios that have just such properties: their mean and standard deviations are identical. Further, let one portfolio's return be described by a near normal distribution (Gaussian) and the other by a Frechet distribution. (Hint: I took a Frechet for this example simply because I like its cool analytical equation, no other reason other than F follows G in the alphabet. Okay, I am a math-head, to use the gear-head analogy. Anyway, this would work with any asymmetric distribution of which the Frechet is just one of several generalized extreme value distributions.)

Now, in Figures 3.2 and 3.3, I plot the two return time series. The graphs show daily return time series, but they are purely hypothetical, totally fabricated data created to dramatize the effect of volatility. Their means are 1.31 and standard deviations are 0.66 roughly. Statistical data are tabulated in Table 3.1 for these two time series.

The data include mean (first moment), standard deviation (second moment), partial standard deviations, skewness (third moment), kurtosis (fourth moment), and the minimum and maximum returns. We tabulate the data in Table 3.1.

Focus on the top row to see where the percentage of data found between the respective mean +/−1 standard deviation is very, very different for the

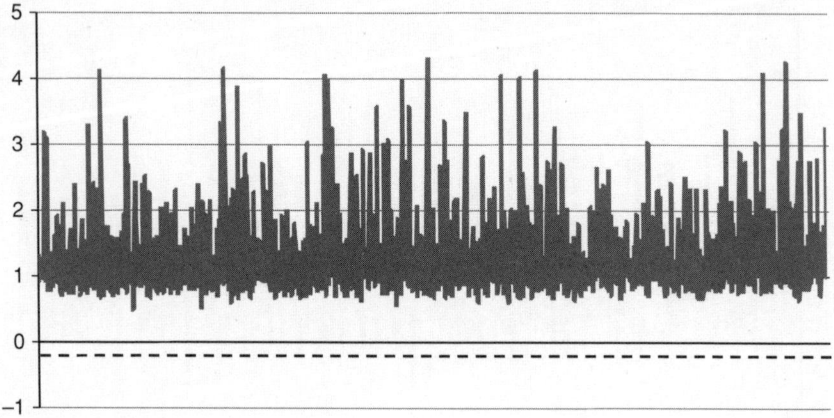


**FIGURE 3.3** Frechet Time-Series Plot

two distributions. This means that for the normal curve, 68.9 percent of the data, close to the theoretical value of 68.27 percent, is found bounded by the mean +/−1 standard deviation. However, the Frechet returns are found almost 85 percent of the time within one standard deviation of the mean. The plots also show how highly skewed to the positive the Frechet is relative to the normal, noted by the much larger upper partial moment (0.598) than its lower partial (0.169) documented in Table 3.1. One can see from the time series this effect, too. The plot also shows where we have spikes in the data upward but not downward, whereas the normal curve seems to the casual eye to appear more symmetric in the time series about its average value. Some of these qualities can even be visualized easily by studying the plot of the actual distributions from which these time series were created,

**TABLE 3.1** Comparative Statistics for Gaussian versus Frechet

| Parameter | Gaussian (Normal) | Frechet | Difference |
|---|---|---|---|
| Percent within +/−1 Std Dev | 68.9 | 84.6 | 15.7 |
| Mean | 1.317 | 1.319 | 0.002 |
| Standard Deviation | 0.678 | 0.652 | −0.026 |
| Lower Partial Moment | 0.382 | 0.169 | −0.213 |
| Upper Partial Moment | 0.455 | 0.598 | 0.143 |
| Skewness | 0.348 | 2.664 | 2.316 |
| Kurtosis | 0.888 | 8.437 | 7.549 |
| Min Return | −0.67 | 0.51 | 1.18 |
| Max Return | 4.32 | 4.36 | 0.04 |

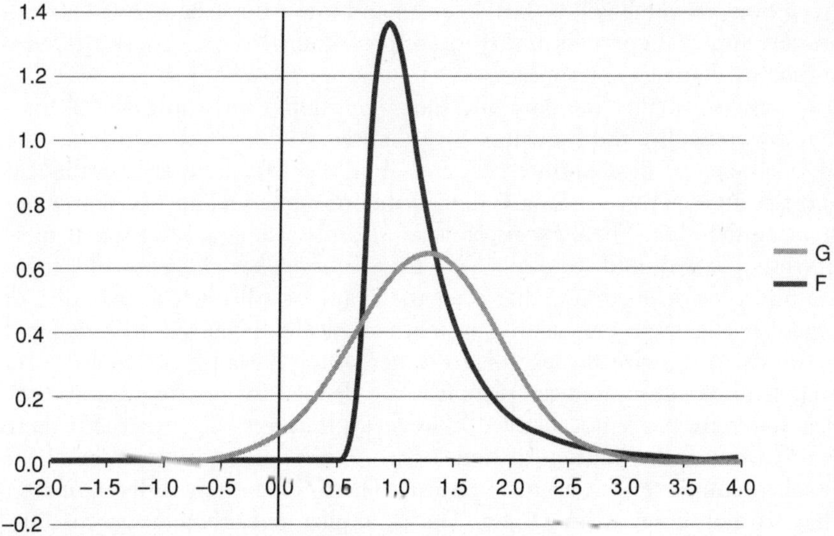


**FIGURE 3.4** Gaussian and Frechet Return Distributions

displayed in Figure 3.4 (F: Frechet; G: Gaussian). The plot that appears taller is the Frechet and it's obvious that it has more area under the curve in a narrower space than the Gaussian.

Note that the time series were created from the distributions, not the other way around in this numerical example, using the rejection method.[9] A reference function was needed to compute an accurate (and equal) mean and standard deviation for the Gaussian and Frechet distributions, and it was easier to do this in reverse. The statistics in Table 3.1 came from the time series, however, and slight discrepancies in their values are simply due to numerical round-off errors.

These curves show that not only is the Frechet narrower than the Gaussian (normal) curve, though they have identical standard deviations, but that the high peakedness (kurtosis = 8.437) relative to the normal curve's (kurtosis = 0.888), means that the data is more confined over time, nearer to the mean. It is this quality and precisely this quality that determines a portfolio's volatility. The fact that a given portfolio spends less time away from its mean return through time demonstrates a less volatile portfolio and lower risk when it comes time to liquidate, especially when liquidation needs to be done in a hurry, and that the portfolio will be less than its equilibrium value. However, a portfolio whose return distribution is something like the Gaussian's has higher volatility than a portfolio whose return distribution looks like the Frechet's, because there is a higher probability that, at any given time, its value will be farther from and lower than the mean. This extremely important point is mostly lost to professional investment consultants and many managers, it appears.

Now, to qualify the data and the conclusion a bit, I might add, first, that theoretically, the skewness of a Gaussian is zero (all odd moments of a symmetric distribution are zero), but the data here is hypothetical and not an exact match to a Gaussian due to numerical imprecision when creating the data. The kurtosis of a Gaussian is also equal to three (excess kurtosis is zero), and we don't have that value, either. Additionally, there are not a lot of portfolios that offer the shape of a Frechet distribution in practice. The engineer, scientist, or mathematically inclined reader also will be quick to criticize the use of a Frechet simply because the closed-form analytical equation used to create it is not defined for negative values (i.e., negative returns are not allowed). However, that does not mean that there is not a return distribution of some security that has the same shape of the Frechet, complete with negative returns. That is an entirely different matter that we will show a little later. The examples here, though, go to show the significance of the shape of the return distribution on the risk of the portfolio. More importantly, risk is not the volatility but the probability that the portfolio will be far away from its average value when it is liquidated. Thus, risk in this context is more like Ben Graham's definition, associated with losing money, not price fluctuation. Now that's a risk definition that makes intuitive sense that we can live with!

## BACK TO BETA

Now we return to the discussion of beta and why it is essentially a misapplied statistical parameter. First, beta is clearly defined in the CAPM and in the Fama-French models. It is given mathematically as the covariance of a portfolio with its benchmark, divided by the variance of the benchmark. Thus, it is easy to calculate without resorting to regression and is easily calculated using a standard spreadsheet given returns (not that regression is difficult, but one doesn't have to resort to finding risk-free rates and subtracting them from returns to obtain a beta). The interpretation of the standard beta, however, is hazardous because it relies on covariances between returns that are usually and mostly non-normal. Herein lies the rub: bivariate distributions can have zero covariance and yet still maintain linear dependency.[10] I will digress to explain the importance of this, but understand that beta is an attempt to calculate in a single parameter both the volatility of a portfolio relative to a benchmark and, simultaneously, the portfolio's correlation or association more generally with its benchmark.

Now, why the interpretation of beta is hazardous has to do with the covariance being in the numerator of its definition, because if two variables are linearly independent, then their covariance is always zero, which means they would have a zero beta. This is always true; however, the converse is not true. To say that a portfolio has a zero covariance or very low beta does not tell you whether the portfolio is truly independent of the benchmark. To understand linear dependence in simple investment returns, we are interested in whether a portfolio is a simple multiplier of the benchmark return. That is, if the benchmark moves X, will the portfolio move 0.92*X? Has it done so consistently? If so, they are linearly dependent. Or are the two unrelated, in which case they are linearly independent. Mathematically, this means we can express the return of the portfolio as a simple multiple of the benchmark if they are dependent, giving beta some validity. We determine this by calculating beta, but what if their covariance is zero (or very low), resulting in a zero or near zero beta? This would mean we cannot discern if they are dependent, rendering beta essentially meaningless.

When markets are turbulent, exhibiting high volatility, as in the tech bubble or credit crises of late 2008 and early 2009, asset returns went negative. As we've said, when asset returns turn south "en masse," they tend to increase correlation, and they tend to exhibit greater-than-average dependency. However, the computed covariance may not signal this to an investor and even though there's strong dependency between stocks and the market, the resulting beta could be off by a lot. Using beta as a signal for market association would be a very poor idea, as suggested by Ben Graham, though I don't know if he necessarily knew the mathematics behind why.

## BETA AND VOLATILITY

Now, fortunately, because of mathematics, we can do an interesting experiment to show another separate criticism of beta that has to do with the fact that beta can be entirely wrong about volatility. Assume there are two portfolios of equal beta but differing variance of return with the S&P 500. The data below depicts what the result of mandating two portfolios' betas to the S&P 500 to be equal and solving for a time series. In this example, we took five consecutive weekly returns of the S&P 500 and, after some math, ended up with an equation that looked like this[11]:

$$V(Y) - V(Z) - V(\text{S\&P} + Y) + V(\text{S\&P} + Z) = 0$$

This is a very easy equation to write and it basically says that the variance of a portfolio *Y* minus the variance of a portfolio *Z* minus the variance of

| Variance | | 1 | 2 | 3 | 4 | 5 | Beta |
|---|---|---|---|---|---|---|---|
| 6.01 | Y | 5.204 | 0.597 | −2.375 | 0.128 | 1.251 | −0.240 |
| 10.82 | Z | −2.375 | −0.617 | 4.455 | −2.104 | 5.305 | −0.240 |
| 9.85 | S&P | −2.576 | −2.934 | −0.925 | 5.724 | −0.973 | |

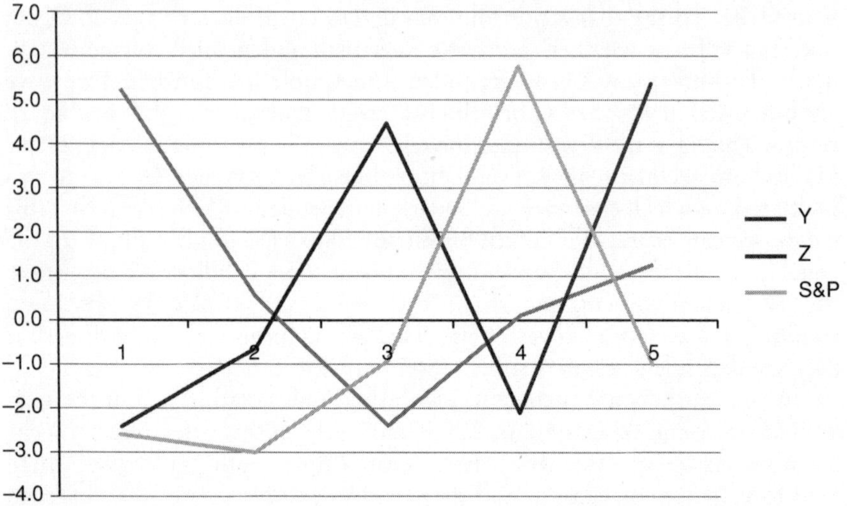


**FIGURE 3.5** Variance Example

a portfolio consisting of the S&P plus *Y*, plus the variance of a portfolio of the S&P plus *Z* equals zero. Thus, given five data points of the S&P's return in a simple spreadsheet, you can use random number generation to solve for *Y* and *Z* portfolios that make the equation true. One solution is shown in Figure 3.5 (there are other solutions, too).

We show the variance of *Y*, *Z*, and the S&P on the left column above the chart, the five returns for each, and the calculated but equal betas for this solution. Notice that portfolio *Z* has a higher variance of return than does the S&P, even though its beta is much smaller than 1 and negative, and the portfolio *Y* has a lower variance for the same beta. Thus, beta is not "Sharpe" enough, as we started this chapter expressing. It is unable to offer true insight into volatility.

Ultimately, this can result in the diversification process of asset allocation to offer less risk reduction or control than originally intended if using portfolio beta and/or covariance to assess asset relationships and volatility. The trend analysis characteristics determined from correlation and covariance measurements have been made too broad and are used as a panacea for all problems, and few people have bothered to question the significance of the results.

One alternative to beta is to separate out the problem so that volatility and association are measured independently. To demonstrate the effectiveness of this strategy, we looked at 5- and 10-year popular mutual fund performance, downloaded weekly return data from FactSet, and calculated various statistics on them. There were thirteen portfolios and three indexes, and the data is compiled in Table 3.2. The data collected and calculated includes the weekly mean return (first moment), standard deviation (the square root of the variance that is the second moment), minimum and maximum return skewness (third moment), kurtosis (fourth moment), the percentage of time the returns spent between the mean – standard deviation and the mean + standard deviation (named A-Vol in the table) and the betas to the three indexes (S&P 500, Dow Jones Industrials [DJI], and the Russell 3000 [R3K]). In addition, the row of numbers to the right of the table, on top of the named categories, represent that individual column's correlation with the standard deviation. The last two columns involve a more complicated but accurate determination of volatility. These include the percentage of time the portfolio's returns are bounded between the mean return and +/– the S&P 500's standard deviation (labeled +/– S&P's std A-Vol) and finally the g-factor.

## THE WAY TO A BETTER BETA: INTRODUCING THE G-FACTOR

Okay, so we play on words. In accordance with our idea of separating out the volatility measure from the association measure, let us first discuss volatility. The latter calculation of percentage of time spent bounded in a region around the mean return, using the index's standard deviation, demonstrates the volatility of a portfolio relative to that of the S&P 500 (or any other benchmark, for that matter). Using this percentage of time allows more perfect judgment of relative volatility between portfolios, because we can form a very illustrative ratio called the g-Factor.

Usually, when one speaks of return volatility, the obvious default measure is the standard deviation of return. However, we have already shown its limitation for describing volatility, such that portfolios with identical variance may spend more or less time within a region of the mean, bounded by the standard deviation (à la the Gaussian and Frechet comparison shown earlier), and, in fact, the data that follows, the correlation between standard deviation and A-Vol, is nearly zero. In addition, beta cannot be used because of its inability to conclusively determine linear dependency (through the covariance) and because it is not "Sharpe" enough to rank standard deviation correctly.

**TABLE 3.2** Statisties Captured for 13 Popular Mutual Funds

| Past 5 Years Weekly Return Time Series (2/11/2005–2/11/2010) | | | | | Correlations to Stdev- | | −0.3% | 89.8% | 88.4% | 90.9% | −96.4% | 93.6% |
|---|---|---|---|---|---|---|---|---|---|---|---|---|
| | Mean | Stdev | Min | Max | Skew | Kurt | A-Vol | S&P 500 Beta | DJI Beta | R3K Beta | +/− S&P Std A-Vol | g-Factor |
| Fidelity Magellan | 0.037 | 3.408 | −18.249 | 14.260 | −0.361 | 6.174 | 81.3% | 1.122 | 1.139 | 1.099 | 74.8% | 1.082 |
| Fidelity Value Fund | 0.083 | 3.812 | −19.063 | 18.291 | −0.253 | 5.897 | 83.2% | 1.261 | 1.275 | 1.236 | 72.9% | 1.110 |
| American Funds EuroPacific Growth A | 0.162 | 2.980 | −16.497 | 12.547 | −0.747 | 5.319 | 79.0% | 0.898 | 0.920 | 0.879 | 78.2% | 1.034 |
| American Funds Fundamental Invs A | 0.111 | 2.907 | −17.111 | 12.069 | −0.690 | 6.539 | 79.0% | 0.961 | 0.981 | 0.939 | 79.0% | 1.024 |
| American Funds Washington Mutual Invs A | 0.039 | 2.770 | −17.575 | 11.840 | −0.681 | 8.119 | 80.5% | 0.942 | 0.983 | 0.910 | 81.7% | 0.991 |
| Vanguard Windsor Fund | 0.040 | 3.329 | −20.203 | 15.879 | −0.277 | 8.665 | 81.3% | 1.122 | 1.156 | 1.090 | 77.1% | 1.050 |
| Vanguard Wellington Income Fund | 0.104 | 1.860 | −13.016 | 7.891 | −1.140 | 10.991 | 81.3% | 0.621 | 0.639 | 0.602 | 92.4% | 0.876 |
| Putnam Growth & Income Fund Class A | 0.009 | 3.174 | −19.756 | 13.746 | −0.459 | 7.735 | 80.2% | 1.072 | 1.111 | 1.037 | 77.1% | 1.050 |

| | | | | | | | | | | | | |
|---|---|---|---|---|---|---|---|---|---|---|---|---|
| Acadian Emerging Market Portfolio Instl Cl | 0.303 | 4.160 | −21.297 | 19.143 | −0.796 | 6.129 | 78.6% | 1.129 | 1.146 | 1.108 | 62.2% | 1.301 |
| Manning & Napier Fd, Inc. World Opp Srs Cl A | 0.167 | 2.950 | −19.129 | 9.709 | −1.319 | 7.723 | 78.2% | 0.881 | 0.899 | 0.862 | 77.5% | 1.044 |
| Templeton World Fund Class A | 0.083 | 2.748 | −17.738 | 11.919 | −0.864 | 8.267 | 80.5% | 0.879 | 0.909 | 0.855 | 82.8% | 0.977 |
| PNC International Equity Fd Class I | 0.123 | 3.179 | −18.571 | 12.019 | −1.025 | 5.539 | 77.9% | 0.928 | 0.950 | 0.911 | 75.2% | 1.076 |
| PNC Large Cap Value Fund Class I | 0.051 | 3.145 | −19.620 | 14.454 | −0.398 | 8.561 | 80.5% | 1.058 | 1.096 | 1.024 | 78.6% | 1.029 |
| S&P 500 | 0.047 | 2.910 | −18.140 | 12.092 | −0.616 | 7.705 | 80.9% | 0.996 | 1.032 | 0.965 | 80.9% | 1.000 |
| DJ Industrial Average | 0.072 | 2.744 | −18.092 | 11.307 | −0.707 | 8.456 | 77.9% | 0.918 | 0.996 | 0.884 | 79.0% | 1.024 |
| Russell 3000 | 0.062 | 2.993 | −17.961 | 12.862 | −0.538 | 7.149 | 80.9% | 1.024 | 1.055 | 0.996 | 80.5% | 1.005 |

*(Continued)*

**TABLE 3.2** *(Continued)*

| Past 10 Years Weekly Return Time Series (2/11/2000–2/11/2010) | | | | | | Correlations to Stdev- | 61.4% | 78.7% | 73.2% | 82.1% | −97.9% | 97.0% |
|---|---|---|---|---|---|---|---|---|---|---|---|---|
| | Mean | Stdev | Min | Max | Skew | Kurt | A-Vol | S&P 500 Beta | DJI Beta | R3K Beta | +/− S&P Std A-Vol | g-Factor |
| Fidelity Magellan | −0.003 | 3.056 | −18.249 | 14.260 | −0.340 | 5.788 | 78.9% | 1.080 | 1.042 | 1.059 | 75.7% | 1.033 |
| Fidelity Value Fund | 0.178 | 3.157 | −19.063 | 18.291 | −0.418 | 7.311 | 82.2% | 1.034 | 1.039 | 1.013 | 76.1% | 1.028 |
| American Funds EuroPacific Growth A | 0.082 | 2.584 | −16.497 | 12.547 | −0.628 | 5.496 | 76.6% | 0.791 | 0.772 | 0.782 | 79.3% | 0.986 |
| American Funds Fundamental Invs A | 0.090 | 2.590 | −17.111 | 12.069 | −0.691 | 6.138 | 77.4% | 0.905 | 0.888 | 0.886 | 79.5% | 0.983 |
| American Funds Washington Mutual Invs A | 0.086 | 2.481 | −17.575 | 11.840 | −0.602 | 7.148 | 78.0% | 0.856 | 0.881 | 0.824 | 81.8% | 0.956 |
| Vanguard Windsor Fund | 0.117 | 2.966 | −20.203 | 15.879 | −0.341 | 7.745 | 78.2% | 1.024 | 1.037 | 0.992 | 75.7% | 1.033 |
| Vanguard Wellington Income Fund | 0.131 | 1.674 | −13.016 | 7.891 | −1.028 | 9.683 | 77.0% | 0.566 | 0.584 | 0.545 | 93.5% | 0.836 |

| | | | | | | | | | | | | |
|---|---|---|---|---|---|---|---|---|---|---|---|---|
| Putnam Growth & Income Fund Class A | 0.048 | 2.776 | −19.756 | 13.746 | −0.459 | 7.467 | 78.4% | 0.965 | 0.986 | 0.930 | 78.0% | 1.002 |
| Acadian Emerging Market Portfolio Instl Cl | 0.274 | 3.513 | −21.297 | 19.143 | −0.827 | 6.838 | 79.1% | 0.897 | 0.868 | 0.894 | 67.4% | 1.159 |
| Manning & Napier Fd, Inc.World Opp Srs Cl A | 0.185 | 2.545 | −19.129 | 9.709 | −1.348 | 8.587 | 77.8% | 0.726 | 0.728 | 0.717 | 80.5% | 0.971 |
| Templeton World Fund Class A | 0.083 | 2.440 | −17.738 | 11.919 | −0.845 | 8.001 | 78.0% | 0.793 | 0.788 | 0.778 | 83.1% | 0.940 |
| PNC International Equity Fd Class I | 0.021 | 2.801 | −18.571 | 12.019 | −0.998 | 6.112 | 78.0% | 0.834 | 0.814 | 0.827 | 77.0% | 1.015 |
| PNC Large Cap Value Fund Class I | 0.089 | 2.724 | −19.620 | 14.454 | −0.427 | 8.470 | 79.3% | 0.924 | 0.951 | 0.891 | 79.5% | 0.983 |
| S&P 500 | 0.017 | 2.743 | −18.140 | 12.092 | −0.526 | 5.896 | 78.2% | 0.998 | 0.983 | 0.969 | 78.2% | 1.000 |
| DJ Industrial Average | 0.062 | 2.657 | −18.092 | 11.307 | −0.670 | 6.520 | 76.8% | 0.922 | 0.998 | 0.884 | 78.4% | 0.998 |
| Russell 3000 | 0.037 | 2.813 | −17.961 | 12.862 | −0.505 | 5.675 | 78.4% | 1.020 | 0.997 | 0.998 | 76.6% | 1.020 |

In fact, in Table 3.2, the correlation of standard deviation with beta for the 5 years' worth of data for 13 popular mutual funds is 89.8 percent, but over 10 years it has a lower value of 37 percent. Thus, there is a need for a better mousetrap here, and the g-Factor is just that. In simple terms, the g-Factor is the ratio of percentage of time the benchmark's return stays within +/−1 standard deviation of its return to the percentage of time the portfolio's return stays within +/−1 standard deviation, using the benchmark's standard deviation measure in both the numerator and denominator. So if the S&P has a standard deviation of magnitude SD, then the formula for the g-Factor is simply:

$$\text{g-Factor} = (\%\text{ of time S\&P is within } +/- \text{ SD})/ (\%\text{ of time portfolio is within } +/- \text{ SD})$$

Remember that in this equation, the denominator uses the S&P's standard deviation, not the portfolio's. The g-Factor in essence, then, is a ratio suggesting whether the portfolio spends more or less time in the vicinity of its mean than the benchmark. Thus, a portfolio with a g-Factor greater than 1 means that portfolio is more volatile than the index. Literally, it would imply the portfolio spends less time within a constant distance (a distance determined by the standard deviation of its benchmark) from its mean return than does the index. The opposite would be true for a g-Factor less than 1. In that case, the portfolio spends more time in the vicinity of its mean than does its benchmark. The g-Factor is our own invention so you will not find it anywhere else.

From these popular mutual funds, we can see many interesting details. We outline in dark gray in Table 3.2 those funds that had a beta greater than 1 and with light gray those with a beta less than 1. Moreover, we calculated betas to all three indexes, not wanting to make a mistake of assigning a benchmark to a fund since we do not rightly know which index the portfolio manager has benchmarked to. However, surely the income fund and the international fund would most probably be benchmarked to the Lehman Aggregate and the EAFE Growth index, whose data we have no access to.

There is a large discrepancy between the data collected from the last 5- and 10-year periods generally. It is clear that the years of 2008–2009 had a huge impact on the portfolios' characteristics overall because the 10-year numbers include a longer period of more restive behavior in the markets in their time series, dampening the impact of the credit crisis of 2008. We call attention to the 5-year period and want the reader to focus on the beta to the S&P and the g-Factor columns to the right of the table. American

EuroPacific Growth, American Fundamental Investors, Manning & Napier, PNC International, and the Dow Jones Index all show g-Factors greater than 1, whereas their betas are less than 1. This implies that, although they are classified as funds of lower risk (i.e., lower volatility) than the S&P 500, if accounting for it by beta, they actually are more risky as categorized by the g-Factor, the more robust measure. Note, however, that the g-Factor says absolutely nothing about association or correlation with the benchmark or index. It is strictly a volatility measure. Notice also that the g-Factor correlates to the fund's return standard deviation (cross-sectionally) at 93.6 versus 89.8 percent for beta. Given the previous beta discussions, the g-Factor is the more robust volatility measure, even more robust than the standard deviation alone, due to the fact that these funds are all highly skewed, asymmetric, and leptokurtotic, as seen in Table 3.2.

Every one of these popular mutual funds has a kurtosis of the same magnitude as the Frechet (around 8, give or take) and has negative skew. Not one fund is represented well by a normal curve. Thus, the percentage of time the returns spend within a constant distance from the mean, as represented by the g-Factor ratio, is a far better indication of their volatility.

American Washington Mutual, Vanguard Wellington Income (a bond fund), and Templeton World Fund are the only three funds that were less volatile than the S&P 500 over the last five years, according to the g-Factor calculation.

For the 10 years' worth of return time series, there are three funds that have higher volatility than the S&P 500, though their betas to the S&P are below 1. These are Putnam Growth & Income, Acadian Emerging Markets fund, and PNC International Fund. Again, over 10 years, the skewness of all mutual funds are negative and their kurtosis is well above that of Gaussian or normal distribution of returns, averaging 7.2 for the 13 funds, which is well above the kurtosis value of 3 for a normal distribution. Clearly, managed portfolios' returns are something other than a normal distribution, rendering the standard deviation and beta poor measures of volatility and association.

For a good comparison of the return distribution of these actual mutual funds, Figure 3.6 shows a histogram of 10 years' worth of daily data for Fidelity Magellan obtained from FactSet, plotted with a normal distribution using the same mean and standard deviation. Also shown is a Frechet distribution, plotted essentially backward, and aligned with the other two distributions, using a suitably chosen mean and standard deviation to visually match Magellan's values.

The dotted line represents the Magellan Fund's return distribution, while the lighter solid line is the normal distribution and the darkest line is the Frechet. This picture offers a good guide as to the non-normality of equity returns in a portfolio, and it also demonstrates the highly negative skew,

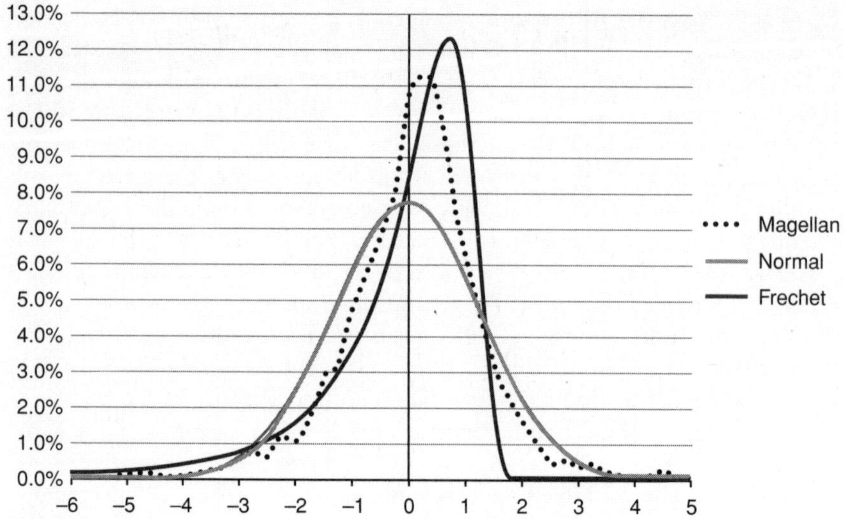


**FIGURE 3.6** Magellan, a Normal (Gaussian), and a Frechet Distribution

which more closely follows the Frechet's tail decay more than the Gaussian. Obviously, the Frechet misses on the upside but again captures the leptokurtic peak quite well. In general, this visual and the previous data serve the reader well to make clear the mistake of suggesting that returns follow a normal distribution, that beta can describe funds' behavior well, and that the standard deviation is a good volatility measure, let alone a good proxy for risk.

Figure 3.6 also shows that, although a mathematician and even a finance professor would shudder over the use of a Frechet to describe returns (because it is technically not defined for values less than zero mathematically), it is very clear from the image that portfolio returns may occasionally take on nearly the shape of a Frechet.[12] Portfolio returns are not constrained by our ideal image of them, nor by the notion that years of the finance literature using the normal curve to describe returns (or log returns, more accurately) forces their compliance. It is probably safe to say that 10 years of daily returns of Fidelity Magellan should be sufficient to remedy the closed mindset about how portfolio return distributions are supposed to look. However, it would be refreshing indeed if finance academics included a multidisciplinary approach to the analysis of return, as is done very simply here.

The lesson here is a philosophical one, to some extent, and you should remember that mathematics reside only in the human mind; nature is not constrained nor defined by mathematics. There is no such thing as a straight line, a flat surface, a triangle, and so forth. Those are constructs of the human mind, and nature (of which markets are a natural phenomena, being a symptom of human behavior) is not bound simply by mathematical formulas describing geometric shapes. For instance, at the atomic level, nothing is flat. The surface of the smoothest table is bumpy at the atomic level as observed through scanning electron microscopes. Hence, the shapes we can contrive and create smooth mathematical functions to describe do not necessitate the required conditions that natural phenomena (of which market reactants are) need to reproduce them. Mathematics only describes reality; reality does not need mathematics for it to exist. Most college graduates are left with a misunderstanding of mathematics as a natural phenomenon because of professional bias, self-importance, and the overwhelming worship that Western society gives to analytical prowess. In reality, mathematics only exists in the imagination of the human species. You should never let nature be defined by mathematics but understand that it is just another descriptive language, similar to words, mostly used to describe nature's behavior. However, under all circumstances, Mother Nature does not know mathematics exists and it is not confined by it.

## TRACKING ERROR: THE DEVIANT DIFFERENTIAL MEASURER

We have essentially come to the most misunderstood measure of portfolio analysis ever devised by humankind, that of tracking error (TE), which, in its simplest explanation, is the standard deviation of a portfolio's excess return over time. It is usually reported in the sacrosanct SEC mandated (for mutual funds) 1-, 3-, 5-, and 10-year values. What you should remember is that *TE does not require a portfolio's return to be bounded 67 percent of the time within plus or minus the tracking error of the benchmark to define it*. No, it does not. It does not mean that if a portfolio has a TE of 4 percent and the benchmark's return is 8 percent that a portfolio's return 67 percent of the time is between 4 and 12 percent absolutely. First of all, it is not so predictable that past measures will mean certainty about the future value either. Secondly, suppose the average excess return is 16 percent with the 4 percent tracking error? Then how could the portfolio be bounded between 4 percent and 12 percent most of the time? It is entirely possible for a portfolio to have excess return that is greater or lesser than the reported tracking error, and the standard misused definition prohibits this.

Tracking error is the standard deviation about the excess return, not the benchmark's return. Thus, it is centered about the return given by the

**TABLE 3.3** Tracking Error Numbers

| | | | | Port Abs Ret Bnds | | Port Bnd about Bench | |
|---|---|---|---|---|---|---|---|
| Port | Bench | XS | TE | Lwr Bnd | Upr Bnd | Lwr Bnd | Upr Bnd |
| 3.50 | 5.00 | −1.50 | 4.00 | −0.50 | 7.50 | −5.50 | 2.50 |
| 5.00 | 6.00 | −1.00 | 6.00 | −1.00 | 11.00 | −7.00 | 5.00 |
| 7.50 | 7.00 | 0.50 | 8.00 | −0.50 | 15.50 | −7.50 | 8.50 |
| 9.00 | 8.00 | 1.00 | 4.00 | 5.00 | 13.00 | −3.00 | 5.00 |
| 11.00 | 9.00 | 2.00 | 6.00 | 5.00 | 17.00 | −4.00 | 8.00 |
| 13.00 | 10.00 | 3.00 | 8.00 | 5.00 | 21.00 | −5.00 | 11.00 |

difference between the portfolio and the benchmark, not the benchmark alone. Assuming normality (which of course we have already shown is few and far between or meager and distant amid found in finance), you could say that if the TE is 4 percent and the excess return is 16 percent (assuming we have a really, really good investment manager!) and the benchmark's return is 8 percent, then the portfolio is bound between an excess return of 12 and 20 percent, implying the portfolio is bound between 20 percent and 28 percent absolutely. This is easier to see with a chart.

Table 3.3 serves to illustrate this using more realistic numbers. Here we show portfolio returns, benchmark returns, excess, and tracking error of hypothetical portfolios and benchmarks.

In Table 3.3, we show what the lower (and upper) bounds could be 67 percent of the time for the absolute returns of the portfolio, given the tracking error and average portfolio return. These are the columns labeled portfolio absolute return bands (Port Abs Ret Bnds). These columns are the absolute expected returns to expect 67 percent of the time for the values of excess return and TE charted given the portfolio's average return. Then, we show how much lower (and higher) from the bench return the portfolio can be found 67 percent of the time, assuming normality. These are labeled portfolio bands about benchmark (Port Bnd about Bench). Thus, a portfolio with a 2 percent excess return, exhibiting a 6 percent tracking error, could have a return −4 percent below the benchmark and up to 8 percent above the benchmark (second row from the bottom).

This result is independent of what the actual bench and portfolio returns actually are as long as the difference of Portfolio return minus Bench return equals 2 and the TE is 6. Notice, now, that that is not the same as saying the returns are found 67 percent of the time within +/−6 percent of the bench, which, in this example (second-to-last row), would provide values of −6 and +6, not −4 and +8 that are indicated in the chart. For this example, the portfolio is not found 67 percent of the time between the bench−6 percent (at 3 percent) and the bench+6 percent (at 15 percent) but rather between bench−4 percent (at 5 percent) and the bench+8 percent (at 17 percent). It is surprising that so many professional institutional consultants make this error when interpreting the tracking error. This should serve to clarify what TE is, however. You can easily verify these conclusions doing your own computational experiment in Excel.[13]

## SUMMARY

We have covered a variety of topics in this book so far but have left much uncovered. The levels of detail cannot go too deep because we would leave the major theme of applying Graham's methods to the investment process behind in the endeavor. So far we have begun discussing alpha, what it is, why people look for it, and what it is responsible for. Also we listed the considerations one must have in examining factors for use in a model. We covered risk in great detail, from a philosophical perspective to practical applications and discussed the importance of what quantitative risk models can and cannot do and how expectations will always be let down for expecting too much. Models cannot and I believe never will be able to predict extreme events. Losses due to market failures are generally not within the purview of modeling. Quantitative models can only contain the foreknowledge their authors have, no more. However, risk models can put a number on a risk measure, making relative comparisons between portfolios easier and allowing for portfolio asset allocations to be performed more reproducibly. In addition, modern risk models do more than quantify risk. If correctly applied and used in normal market environments, their steady application will mitigate portfolio losses. The best preparation for ELE events, those Black Swan events that happen so unexpectedly, is to employ the use of the Motorcycle Safety Foundations SIPDE acronym. Search, interpret, predict, decide, and execute. Finally, the newer methods of stress-testing a portfolio by using covariance matrices of past events combined with current exposures to measure the impact of ELE events may also lead us to newer methods of ELE avoidance. In addition, future applications of CVAR and ETL methodologies will serve to allow for further testing of portfolios beyond their "normal" environments, allowing risk remedies to be applied consistently across portfolios.

In this chapter, we discussed the failure of the classic beta statistic in performing its charter, that of offering information about correlation to and volatility relative to the market. We introduced a nonparametric measure of volatility, the g-Factor, rendering beta to what it is, a regression coefficient, nothing more. We turned to expressing the largest mutual funds, certainly many well known in terms of their return distributions rather than their stock holdings. This characterization shed light on just how wrong and erroneous application of normality is to even everyday investments, even for the ubiquitous mutual fund. Moreover, because we have fixed ideas on the shape of investment returns, we fool ourselves to believe we can confine the shape and hence the mathematical form of an investment distribution. In other words, it is showing a lack of knowledge to insinuate that a return distribution in the shape of a Frechet cannot happen. For the Fidelity Magellan fund, it almost did!

We also demonstrate that many investors misunderstand even a concept as simple as the tracking error. It is no wonder portfolio returns vary so widely across the universe of investors, because most investors do not even understand what they think they know. In the next chapter, we begin to describe the Graham methodology, having been educated on alpha, risk, beta, volatility, and returns. Let's see what Graham has to say about stocks now.

# CHAPTER 4

# Mr. Graham, I Give You Intelligence

*It follows at once that each planet must exert a perturbing force on every other planet in the solar system. The consequence must be, that the displacement of the sun from its center of gravity may have the effect that the centripetal force does not always tend toward an immobile center and that the planets neither revolve exactly in ellipses nor revolve twice in the same orbit. Each time a planet revolves around the sun it traces a fresh orbit, as happens also with the motion of the moon, and each orbit is dependent upon the combined motions of all the planets, not to mention their actions upon each other. Unless I am much mistaken, it would exceed the force of human wit to consider so many causes of motion at the same time and to define the motions by exact laws which would allow of any easy calculation.*

—Isaac Newton, *The Principia*[1]

The three-body problem arising from this characterization by Newton is mathematically very intractable. It came about from considering just two planets interacting with the sun and each other—three bodies in total. From the time that Euler first devised the equations that would generate the trajectory of the planets in 1760 for the theory Newton hypothesized before 1687, it took over 40 years to get a solution by Laplace. The fact that Newton saw the evidence strictly from empirical measurements, from recordings of astronomers of his day, never ceases to amaze me. Isaac Newton exudes superintelligence. In the same way, Ben Graham's studies of the markets, businesses, and the economy exude a deep understanding of the relevant issues and, much like Newton, he wasn't always able to cast his foresight into mathematical expressions. That, too, came later. As Laplace was to Euler, and Euler was to Newton, so was Fama-French to Markowitz, and

Markowitz to Graham. Also, as you will see in Chapter 9, the chaotic trajectories of planets are exactly analogous to the price trending of stocks, insofar as they move in predictable patterns but never in exactly the same way.

This chapter will retell the story of Ben Graham's successful investment insight leading to strategy. Snippets of Graham's voice have been written at various points of the book so far with the idea in mind to show the man's color, character, and resolve to educate the investor and investing public about what not to do, as much as what to do. In addition, the previous chapters laid the groundwork for the reader to get up to speed, get on the learning curve, and gain an appreciation for what quants are, how they think, what the issues are, and what their critics say. We told the story of the rise of modeling in the search for return, starting with the CAPM, Fama-French, the stories of alpha and beta, and we answered the questions about normality and introduced the g-Factor. We also covered risk management, risk modeling, and forecasting through the covariance matrix and also stock industry assignment and lack thereof. The order of the pedagogy was intentional, though it may seem peculiar; it was done this way to make easier reading as one subject flows into another.

Of course, I am a quant and "the best investment is in the tools of one's own trade."[2] There is enough background material (albeit with little to no mathematics) in the previous chapters in quantitative methods and processes for two reasons: (1) to write an apologetic, and (2) to allow easier interpretation (now that the reader is quant-armed) of the subsequent chapters. The apologetic was required because of the various books and articles criticizing quantitative methodologies in general since the credit crisis arose beginning in late 2007.[3] Most of these writings are by non-quants or quant wannabees, and there is a need to tell the quant side of the story. In addition, to apply Graham's methods in a truly modern quantitative fashion, you need relevant background to understand the quant principles involved and enough experience to trust the credible make-up of properly applied statistical methods. So far, that has been the attempt to offer the reader, including a serious but simple expose of quantitative history.

Now this chapter will be like a summary of *The Intelligent Investor*. The reader who is familiar with Graham's book should not forgo the telling of it here, however, because the modern version (notwithstanding Jason Zweig's excellent explanations throughout the 2003 revised version, except to my knowledge, Jason Zweig has never managed other people's money) hasn't been revealed through the quant's eyes as of yet. Before we begin, though, we need to discuss CAPM, and Fama-French once again, but this time we will traverse previously undisturbed ground. We will speak of these models as if they are just mathematical expressions for a moment, to set a stage for the creation of the Graham equivalent expression.

From a mathematical standpoint, the CAPM equation is neither novel nor new. It is a ninth-grade algebra equation; in fact, it is probably the first one we all learned. It has one equation and one unknown. The intercept is simply a result of the outcome of plotting $X$ versus $Y$ for any data and fitting a straight line to it. So then, why did Sharpe receive the 1990 Nobel Prize in economics? This has everything to do with the concept behind it and nothing to do with the very simple mathematics. Likewise, the Fama-French equation, the inheritor of the homage originally paid to the CAPM, is also a very simple equation. Eugene Fama and Ken French found that whether alone or in concert with other fundamental factors, beta, the slope in the regression of a stock's return on a market return, has little information about average returns. Hence, the strong criticism and mathematical uncertainty argued, displayed, and leveled in previous chapters about beta in this book. However, Fama-French[4] found that market capitalization, earnings to price, leverage, and book to price have explanatory power in explaining returns individually. Used in concert (i.e., combined), market capitalization and book to price did a very good job of explaining the cross-section of returns on the NYSE, AMEX, and NASDAQ stock markets from 1963 to 1990, so much so that the reported alpha in their regressions was zero (intercept is 0), which implies they have explained everything! Now they go on to show that the market factor, beta, is a necessary addition in their equation to explain the large difference in returns between stocks and 1-month T-Bills, so they include beta in their final incarnate formula. Hence, alpha in this sense is the extra return of stocks over short-term bonds through time.

## FAMA-FRENCH EQUATION

When Fama-French (or any quant for that matter) uses the term *cross-section of returns*, they are referring to a method described in the following recipe. First, gather returns for a given period of time for some stock $i$, and form a column of return data for $N$ stocks. Then form columns made from factors like book to price ($B/P$) and market cap ($MCap$) for each stock, such that we have the following equation setup for regression:

$$(R_i - R_f) = \beta_m * (R_m - R_f) + \beta_v * B/P_i + \beta_s * MCap_i + \alpha_i$$

In this equation, $R_m$ is the 6-month market return; $R_f$ is the return of a risk-free asset like 1-month T-Bill; the betas are the output coefficients of the regression for market, valuation, and size; and alpha is the intercept of the regression. If there are $N$ stocks, then there are $N$ equations of this type, each with a single $B/P$ and $MCap$ for each stock $i$, while the market beta term multiplier ($R_m - R_f$) remains constant for that set of $N$ equations for the given time period of the regression. If we combine $M$ periods as in a panel regression, than there are $N \times M$ equations to solve simultaneously and determine the best fit, given the model. The final result gives the three betas and the alpha. Then, if this equation fits the data well, we say we have explained the cross-section of stock returns with it, as opposed to explaining the time series of an individual stock's returns. Now again, mathematically, this is simply $y = m_1x_1 + m_2x_2 + m_3x_3 + b$, a very simple ninth-grade algebra equation. Similarly, we can construct an equation using Ben Graham's factors, assuming he has defined them thoroughly enough for us. Here is a listing of the factors of his methodology directly from *The Intelligent Investor*:

Adequate size of the enterprise
A sufficiently strong financial condition
Earnings stability
Dividend record
Earnings growth
Moderate price/earnings ratio
Moderate ratio of price to assets

To gain a qualitative appreciation of the seriousness of these factors, let's review them somewhat. To begin, the size of a company can be measured by total sales or revenue, market capitalization, net income, or asset size, or it can be in the top third among its industry peers by any of these measures. The criterion for size is not necessarily really given by some formula, but when used by Graham it is meant to convey a firm that has some history, has a positive position in terms of market share of its products, and has a definition of large that does no harm to the overall investment strategy. The generally accepted method would be to utilize market cap (number of outstanding shares times stock price), and indeed, this is the closest measure of most indexes' (though not actually) constitution, or how they weight the stocks in their index.

A strong financial condition can be measured by current ratio, which is the sum of cash (and equivalent) and other securities, accounts receivable, inventory, and any short-term asset that could be converted to cash in a rush to liquidation, divided by current liabilities. Typically Graham wanted current assets to be a minimum of twice current liabilities. Given that working capital is defined as current assets minus current liabilities, the minimum requirement, therefore, is that working capital is at least half the current assets. This would exclude highly leveraged companies. So during the 2008 credit crisis, highly leveraged stocks that did so poorly in 2008 but rebounded abundantly in 2009 wouldn't have been in the Graham-styled portfolio and the prudent investor wouldn't have had their portfolio whipsawed so violently if investing using the Graham methodologies.

Additionally, Graham is clear in stating that working capital must have debt and preferred stock liabilities deducted from the number to be a valid measure. Whether using the current ratio (current assets/current liabilities) or working capital (current assets – current liabilities), either is an acceptable measure for balance-sheet health, but just examining current ratio looking for values greater than 2.0 is the easier measure.

Earnings stability was a picky point for Graham, because he liked to see earnings in each year of a 10-year period. Since earnings, which are defined explicitly as revenues minus the sum of sales expenses, operating expenses, and taxes, are thought of as the single most important determinant of stock prices, Graham felt the past was a good measure here, too (which philosophically supports reasons for back-testing quant models). He seldom paid attention to forecasted earnings. Moreover, in a 1932 article in *Forbes*, Graham criticized the preponderance, at the time, of analysts overlooking current assets and book value in favor of a new trend, at the time, of favoring earnings outlook. He went on to say that the then-current situation in which stock prices were below company liquidating values would never have occurred if analysts were not preoccupied with looking for future earnings and paid some attention to assets. He blamed this on the cult of performance sought by pension-fund managers. Moreover, he adds that if the shares sell persistently below liquidating value, then perhaps that would be the best thing for the shareholders, but he scolds business managers for resisting that, for fear of their own job loss because they are often willing to sacrifice their shareholders' last dollar to keep the company going. Hence, in Graham's mind, the importance of the balance sheet should never be overlooked (i.e., "a strong financial condition") in favor of paying too much attention to future earnings. In particular, Graham paid little attention to earnings estimates in general, and he felt that the only earnings worth measuring were historical earnings. Score one for the quant discipline.

Dividends to Graham were very important, and his look-back period for dividend payments was 20 years. It has even been said in current circles that only Warren Buffett can invest shareholders' money better than shareholders and that perhaps there is too much cash in technology stocks and that companies owe it to shareholders to start distributing earnings.[5] Since dividends have made up more than 40 percent of the return to the S&P 500 since 1926, there is certainly no harm in wanting some cash back from your investments. In addition, there has been academic evidence that when current dividends are low, so goes the stock, and when they are high, so goes future earnings.[6]

**TABLE 4.1** Average 12-Month Rolling Total Return and Standard Deviation of Dividend Sorts (December 1985 to June 2003)

| | Avg Compound Annual Return | Excess Return over Non-Div Universe | Std Deviation of Return |
|---|---|---|---|
| Div Yld Range% | | | |
| No-Dividend | 5.85% | | 22.31% |
| 0–1 | 7.88% | 2.03% | 15.08% |
| 1–2 | 9.16% | 3.31% | 15.8% |
| 2–3 | 9.27% | 3.41% | 14.80% |
| 3–4 | 9.96% | 4.11% | 14.96% |
| 4–5 | 8.74% | 2.89% | 15.52% |
| 5–6 | 6.21% | 035% | 14.51% |
| 6–7 | 5.96% | 0.11% | 13.63% |
| 7–8 | 5.94% | 0.08% | 12.74% |
| 8–9 | 5.41% | −0.44% | 13.76% |
| 9–10 | 3.08% | −2.78% | 17.93% |
| Wilshire 5000 | 9.15% | | 16.28% |

The CEO of Federated Clover Investment Advisors, Michael Jones, and I have compiled total return of the varying subsets of dividend-yielding stocks and measured them against a nondividend-paying universe over time, using a universe of the Wilshire 5000. Table 4.1 shows the performance of the portfolios by listing the 12-month rolling compound annual return for the dividend-yielding portfolios, the nondividend-paying universe, and the Wilshire 5000, along with their standard deviation over the time period of the study. Nondividend-paying stocks posted poor results, gaining 5.85 percent versus a return of 9.15 percent for the Wilshire 5000 Index. Stocks in the groups with dividend yields between 1 and 4 percent outperformed the Wilshire during this time period and showed lower volatility, as measured by standard deviation of return.

The dividend yield range of 3–4 percent was the best performing cohort, beating the nondividend-paying universe by a hefty 4.11 percent per year. Returns worsen significantly for portfolios with dividend yields above 5 percent. We believe this is because these portfolios contain a few companies in distress that are often about to eliminate their dividends. These stocks often suffer severe price erosion when their dividends are reduced or eliminated. The effect of this minority group drags down the Wilshire's total portfolio return, too.

There has always been good theory in reinvesting dividends rather than paying them out for a firm. The idea was that if a company has shown good growth in its recent history, it was tempting to believe these profits could be counted on to contribute substantially to future growth, so that these stocks could be primarily valued in terms of the expected growth rate over the next decade, and dividends not paid could be justified. It is very difficult to argue in favor of owning stocks that do not pay dividends, given the performance data, however, albeit the dividend payor's stocks are typically thought of as income issuers and are not usually associated with the glitz and glamour of the Googles, eBays, and Ciscos of the world. Nowadays, even Microsoft and Oracle pay a small dividend, and, of course, tax policies can certainly effect dividend payouts.

Earnings growth was equally important to Graham, but not more important than balance sheet assets. He liked to see earnings growth of about 33 percent over 10 years. However, he added that he would like to see this number in a rolling 3-year period, over the last 10 years. It is an easy formula to obtain, but why? First, this amounts to 2.89 percent annual earnings growth applied over 10 years, which is pretty lame by today's standards. However, it was the earnings growth with stability that was important to him. A steady grower offers a margin of safety. Moreover, he looked at historical earnings growth, not at estimates of future growth, because he believed earnings estimates were pie in the sky and that anything could happen in the future. There really is no such thing as forward looking, a statement prominently offered time and time again by fundamental analysts. Nobody has future information.

Finally, to Graham, a moderate price to earnings (P/E) and price to book (P/B) were requirements and should be somewhat related to corporate bond yields. In particular, the acceptable P/E should be related to the reciprocal of twice the current average high-quality AAA bond yield. Therefore, if the current AAA average yield is 6 percent, then the greatest P/E acceptable would be 1/(2*.06) or 8.3. If the current AAA average yield is 8 percent, the highest P/E acceptable would be 1/(2*.08) or 6.25. This being the case, however, he also stipulated to never buy a stock with a P/E greater than 10, no matter how low high-quality corporate bonds go. This makes Graham a real value investor. For book value, Graham did not like paying more than 1.5 times book. However, he would accept a higher book if the P/E were lower. He gave a formula of P/B*P/E, which should always be less than 22.5, which comes about from multiplying a P/E of 15 times a P/B of 1.5; this then would give a margin of acceptable safety. It was his decision, too, that keeping this multiplier of P/E and P/B less than 22.5 will keep one from over-emphasizing earnings in lieu of assets, a predominant philosophy of Graham's taught to him from overly depressed assets in the Great Depression and the assertion of overly forward looking earnings emphasis right after the Depression.

In discussing book value, however, we must review several subtleties of book-value issues. These include the impact of good will and the occurrence of value traps. Ben Graham's prize student, Warren Buffett, recently stated in his 2009 annual report that "In aggregate, our businesses are worth considerably more than the values at which they are carried on our books." He goes on to demonstrate how book value growth is paramount to how he measures success. Graham defined book value as the value of assets on the balance sheet eliminating good will, trade names, patents, franchises, leasing agreements, and so forth, so that the book is clearly only tangible assets.[7] For common stocks, book is the shareholder's equity.

A common definition of a value trap is a stock that has depreciated significantly in price from recent highs, only to be purchased and then continue to fall. However, this is only half right. A real value trap is a stock whose valuation measures (P/E, P/B, P/S, P/CF) remain depressed so that the stock always remains a low valued stock, because there is no price appreciation over time. In this stronger definition, the stock once purchased may not decline anymore, but stays at a level price for eternity (or so it seems) so that no gain is made, either. However, because the valuation never changes, it is a value trap. The Graham methodology, in general, is to find underappreciated stocks in the marketplace and construct a portfolio of them, but only if the market indeed underappreciates their value so that sooner or later, the market will eventually catch up and properly value them, so that the investor realizes the appreciation of price. A value trap is a stock that looks underappreciated by the market as measured by valuation, but in reality is low priced for good reasons and is a value illusion. In that case, the stock is rightfully low valued, and it will stay depressed for much longer than a typical investment period (three years for Graham). In addition, Graham expected an investor to hold onto a stock until a return objective of 50 percent was reached for such securities. Thus, even if after three years a positive return but less than 10 percent is realized, one might attribute such a stock to be a value trap, because the return over three years is so low that opportunity costs prevailed over the investment return. Thus the Graham factors together serve to counter the possibility of purchasing just such stock and helps identify those stocks that offer upside as well. This explains why investing based on low valuation alone is not a great idea in and of itself.

Separately, Jeremy Grantham at GMO, who launched one of the first quant funds in 1982, said during an interview with Steve Forbes recently,[8] "Prices used to mean revert in under 10 years, but our research today shows more like 7 years." Thus we may think about shortening the look-back period a bit for dividends, earnings stability, and growth, for Graham's method, but we must be cognizant of doing so.

That summarizes the technical side of *The Intelligent Investor*. However, the softer underbelly of this featured work of Graham's conveys much less about analyzing securities and much more about investment principles and investor behavior. That said, his opening chapters are about the history of the stock market, again showing the great use of available historical data Mr. Graham utilized as a teaching moment, but also to underpin his investment strategy, which was exactly identical to that of modern quantaphilias. He goes on to separate out the investor from the speculator, concluding that his thoughts are for the investor and not for the speculator.

Now, in demonstrating the taxonomy of trading into these regimes of investing and speculating, each of which has many subclasses, attention is given to technical approaches that fall under speculative investing by his notion. The most common of which is momentum investing, which, in its simplest form, urges an investor to buy a stock because it has gone up recently and to sell it because it has gone down recently. He then goes on to chastise this method because, after over 50 years of investing, he has never seen long-term and lasting wealth occur from this strategy. We point out this very example, because it is the only example where Mr. Graham diverges from the modern quant, and that is in the area of momentum investing. This particular topic will be examined in much greater detail later on.

The qualitative descriptions continue, separating out the investor again into two subcategories of defensive and enterprising. In his world, they are still both value investors, and his definition is that the underlying principles are the same but the level of security interrogation differentiates the two. The defensive investor seriously emphasizes the avoidance of losses, whereas the enterprising investor spends more time and skill if they have it, identifying special candidate stocks that might have more upside potential than average. He points out situations or fads of investing herding that the investor needs to be aware of and avoid. For instance, a common practice is to identify a hot-growth industry like the Internet or, in his day, the airlines, and later, the computer industry, and invest in companies in these industries, hoping for return. The problem is, he says, the obvious prospects for growth in an industry do not translate into obvious returns for investors simply because there is no way to identify the most promising companies within those industries, and the return only comes from those top-surviving companies. You can verify this with easy empirical comparatives from the past and present. How many auto companies were there in the early days and how many Internet companies were there in 1999? More have gone out of business and lost more investors' money than have stayed in business. Betting you can pick the survivors of an emerging industry is very difficult.

Graham's focus is often about best practices and saving us from ourselves. That certainly is what *The Intelligent Investor* is about—being patient, disciplined, and teachable, and that those qualities will allow for gains in the market even greater than those with extensive knowledge or experience in finance, accounting, and stock market anecdotes who do not practice those virtues. For instance, a portfolio manager I worked with, who, at the height of the sell-off in February of 2009, before the correction took place, stated the obvious: stocks are being priced for bankruptcy, though many of them have earnings and no debt! "Certainly even those with some debt have fallen far enough to be worth something!" he said. He bought many of these stocks. Ruby Tuesday, for instance, was trading between $6 to $7 a share prior to September of 2008 for a while. Then, from October 2008 to March 6, 2009, it fell to $0.95 cents a share. At this point, it was priced to go out of business, but subsequently by April 9, it was trading for $6.61 a share again. Graham said that "99 out of 100 issues at some price are cheap enough to buy and at some other price they would be so dear that they should be sold," and he wanted to embed in the reader a tendency to measure and quantify (which is exactly what any quant would argue for). So in the ensuing example of Ruby Tuesday (ticker: RT), the advice we garner from Graham is that the investor should stick with purchasing stocks selling for low multiples of their net tangible assets.[9]

In the data in Figure 4.1, for instance, we show the calculation of the current ratio for Ruby Tuesday during the melee of its share price falling to

**Ruby Tuesday Inc. (Ticker: RT)** FactSet Fundamentals
**Balance Sheet—Quarterly**

| | 31-May-09 | 28-Feb-09 | 30-Nov-08 | 31-Aug-08 | 31-May-08 |
|---|---|---|---|---|---|
| Total Assets | 1,124.2 | 1,149.0 | 1,173.5 | 1,239.8 | 1,271.9 |
| Total Assets per Share | 17.38 | 17.82 | 18.20 | 18.64 | 18.98 |
| Total Liabilities | 707.8 | 745.1 | 775.5 | 805.4 | 840.4 |
| Total Liabilities per Share | 10.98 | 11.56 | 12.03 | 12.49 | 13.04 |
| Total Shareholders' Equity | 416.4 | 403.9 | 398.0 | 434.3 | 431.5 |
| Equity per Share | 6.46 | 6.26 | 6.17 | 6.74 | 6.69 |
| Current Ratio | 1.58 | 1.54 | 1.51 | 1.49 | 1.46 |

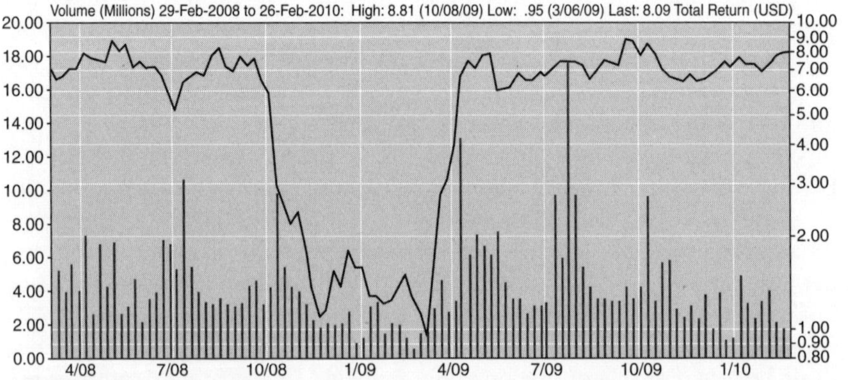


**FIGURE 4.1** Ruby Tuesday

\$0.95 per share. The data were downloaded from FactSet. The data shows that total assets per share stayed pretty even from May 2008 right through to May of 2009 and that the net tangible assets (equity per share) were about one times the share price (right scale of price graph, trading volume is left scale). The current ratio is below Graham's ratio of 2, so it would not have passed a Graham screen. However, when the stock traded below net assets, essentially anytime below \$6 share, the stock was a buy, and when it dropped to \$0.95, tangible book to price would have gone roughly from 1 to 6 (P/B going from 1 to 0.2) and the stock was a steal! What an opportunity!

The ultimate result of this kind of investment strategy is one of conservation of principle, but, indeed, it has better outcomes over the long term than chasing glamorous stocks in the growth style, where forecasting future earnings is distant and vacuous as compared to measuring something as simple as net asset values. Thus, Graham's odyssey is really about true value discovery, about separating what the current market price says about a stock versus its real underlying intrinsic value, and that is the story of *The Intelligent Investor*.

## THE GRAHAM FORMULA

Putting the Graham method into the prototypical quant formula yields something that has the following form:

$$(R_i - R_f) = \beta_m * WC_i + \beta_{es} * ES_i + \beta_{dy} * DivYld_i + \beta_{eg} * EGr_i + \beta_{v1} * \mathrm{E/P}_i + \beta_{v2} * \mathrm{B/P}_i + \beta_s * MCap_i + \alpha_i$$

In this equation *WC* is working capital, *ES* is earnings strength, *DivYld* is dividend yield, *EGr* is earnings growth, *P/E* is price to earnings, *P/B* is book to price, and *MCap* is market capitalization. This is the Graham formula in the modern context of quantitative investing. We shall leave it here for a moment and begin to visit the elements required for any quantitative model, using standard econometric "like" methodologies. We add that it is important to order the variables such that if you calculated the correlation of the variable factor with the left side of the equation, it is positive. For instance, you would not use *P/B* as one variable and *E/P* for another. You would use B/P and E/P so that they have the same sign of their correlation with return. This is very important in a model, especially if it is a model predicated fully on sorting by factors as opposed to regression. For if one variable generates high returns for low values, as a valuation factor would, and some other variable generates high returns for high values of that variable, in the model the two variables fight each other.

This particular format is what will be used in all the variations of Graham type models in the rest of the book. We will show individual factor returns from sorts on these factors and investigate their properties, returns, and statistics. Also, the reader should not confuse the wording of *factor returns* in this setting, with the wide use of the term meaning regression coefficients or betas when discussing risk. In alpha modeling, the term *factor returns* means the returns due to sorting a universe of stocks by the factor, buying them, and then holding them for a pre-selected period of time.

## FACTORS FOR USE IN QUANT MODELS

Now, when it comes to building models, the starting point is always about individual factors. Some of them are the ones already discussed as in CAPM, Fama-French, or Graham's formula, discussed earlier. However, there are many more factors available to the average investor, specifically when discussing holding periods of common stocks from as short as three months to as long as three years. This is the traditional holding period for most retail mutual funds and even for the majority of equity or fixed income investing for pensions, endowments, and other institutions. These factors are derived mostly from financial statement data, when using a bottoms-up approach (which by definition implies a method for building a portfolio starting from individual stock selection or ranking methodologies) consisting of factors taken from balance sheet, income, or cash-flow statements. From these financial statements, the factors get classified into fundamental or valuation categories. Generally, a factor is called a valuation factor if it contains price in the numerator (as in price to book, price to sales, or price to cash flow, for example) or denominator, as in earnings yield, which is the inverse of price to earnings. The factors can easily be ascertained or even invented by—well—anybody. However, the academic literature and sell-side shops publish numerous quantities of these factors, their performance through time (which we will discuss), and other essential statistics measured from them.

The next set of factors includes those from the world of technical analysis (historically called chartists). These kinds of factors all really fall under the label of momentum; however, some are short term and some longer term and they are used differently. In many momentum measures, trading volume also is included in some formulation. Among the professional investment community, it is funny to hear people differentiate technical indicators (which is what they call factors such as MACD and stochastics) from price momentum indicators. For the electrical engineers and physicists who have been doing signal processing, they are all in the same class because there is only one medium of information, namely, the price. Sometimes the finance community really lives in its own world when it comes to using conventional nomenclature of mathematics.

The factors representing price momentum can take on many different mathematical formulas. Generally, momentum factors are created from the price trajectory and/or the return profile. The most common momentum factors are the 6-month return factor and the 12-month return factor, studied vociferously in the academic literature. The relation between returns and price is naturally evident but the direct formula is:

$$R = 1/P * dp/dt$$

so that return is exactly the first derivative of price times 1/price. However, it can be daily returns, weekly, monthly, semi-annually, and so forth, and the formula is typically given as $(P_i/P_{i-1}) - 1$ when computing returns in a spreadsheet.

Examples of differing momentum measures include the following:

- $P_0/P_{-n}-1$ where $n$ takes the value of 3, 6, 9, 12, or 18 months. This is the most common definition.
- Correlation of price trace with a line that has a 45-degree slope measured over 9 months.
- Regress a line ($y = mx + b$) to the price trace over 3, 6, 9, and 12 months and obtain the slope coefficient. The $m$ is a momentum measure for the stock.
- The 50-day and 200-day moving average of price.
- Measure the 52-week high, then measure the current price, and take the ratio, price/52week.
- Measure the average trading volume over 50 days (DTV50) and the trading volume over 200 days (DTV200); form the ratio DTV50/DTV200 and multiply it by 6-month price return.
- Stochastic oscillator, MACD, Up/Dn ratios, etc.
- Regress the raw monthly return against a linear equation composed of past 1 to 12 including past 24- and 36-month returns, and then use this equation to predict next month's return and rank the output.
- Defined as a sum of quarterly weight of security in the portfolio times the portfolio's return for that quarter going back 10 years (or until purchase date of the security) normalized by dividing by the number of quarters.
- Straight 6 monthly cumulative return (i.e., the sum of 6 one-month returns).
- Stock-specific momentum defined as the intercept coefficient (the alpha) of a regression model using CAPM and Fama-French three-factor model.

- A factor-related beta-type momentum that is the coefficient for the slope in CAPM or the three factors in Fama-French.
- Relative-strength indicator (100 – 100 / (1 + avg(up)/avg(dn)), where average up (down) is the average return measured when the stock is up (down) for a specified period of time.

You can make up many more of these momentum indicators quite easily using your imagination. Some momentum indicators can be complicated. For instance, a description of MACD from FactSet is:

> *Moving Average Convergence/Divergence (MACD) measures the relationship between exponential moving averages of prices. An exponential moving average (or EMA) is calculated by applying a percentage of today's closing price to yesterday's moving average value. It tends to place more weight on recent prices than a simple moving average. Generally, MACD is a trend-following momentum indicator of buy/sell signals. It uses three EMAs: a short EMA, a long EMA, and an EMA of the difference between the two, used as a signal or trigger line. The MACD line represents the difference between the long and short EMA. When the MACD line falls below its signal line, divergence goes from positive to negative and this represents a sell signal. Similarly, when MACD rises above its signal line, divergence swings from negative to positive and this is considered a buy signal. The farther Divergence is above (below) zero, the more overbought (oversold) the security. Default values of 12 (Shorter EMA), 26 (Longer EMA), and 9 (Signal) are typically used for sell signals. Values of 8, 17, and 9 are commonly used to track buy signals.*

Generally, anything that decomposes price trending into some functional and mathematical form can be utilized as a momentum factor. They all work to a lesser or greater extent. The point to remember about momentum factors is that they are all based on gaining some indicator of the trend of price in the past, and they are used in alpha modeling to forecast the future direction of price. Now, there is very good evidence that there have been returns to momentum factors in the stock market.[10] Many portfolio managers and stock analysts subscribe to this view, that momentum strategies yield significant profits over time. Many different kinds of momentum strategies are documented that indicate the basic premise that buying stocks with high returns over the previous 3, 6, 12, or up to 24 months and selling stocks with poor returns over the same time period earn consistent profits.

Although these results have been well accepted by many professional investors in the long-only institutional world and hedge funds, the source of the profits and the interpretation of the evidence are the only issues still widely debated. Nonetheless, Google knows there are a ton of academic papers on this subject going back to the early 1990s, which can be found easily.[11] A comprehensive review of the momentum literature[12] exists, which documents the empirical observation of momentum offering anomalous returns to investors. It also offers support for the fundamental interpretation of why momentum offers anomalous returns, which Jeremy Stein of Harvard has so well postulated. His explanation has much to do with the speed of news flow about a company and lists it as a diffusion process, citing bad news traveling more slowly than good news as the responsible investor behavior for the anomalous return.

The reader should understand that the literature references in support of momentum are from empirical measurements in which an index worth of stocks (~1,000 to 3,000) are sorted by past momentum measures, then, typically, the top decile (10 percent of the stocks ranked by momentum) are purchased, and the bottom decile (10 percent of the stocks) by rank are shorted (on paper). Then, the returns over differing holding periods are recorded and statistics acquired. Typically, any factor's responsiveness to equity return is measured in just such a format, not just momentum. In summary, however, momentum is a portfolio selection method rather than a stock selection process if used simply as a one-factor model. The reason for this has to do with the success of the strategy being slightly better than a coin toss in so many circumstances, so you want the law of large numbers in your favor when employing it. In addition, you will also choose differing stocks resulting in differing portfolios depending on the exact form of momentum chosen, but the portfolios will have much overlap. In addition, profits can come from the shorts or longs as both have been reported in the literature (and from my own experience), depending, again, on what formulas were chosen to define momentum. The common themes to momentum investing from the literature include the following:

- Google knows there is a momentum anomaly and that it is statistically and economically significant even after considering transaction costs.
- There is a January effect that is impacted by firm size.
- There is a time scale in which momentum investing is optimal both in terms of the look-back period for portfolio formation and for the holding period.
- Time scales longer than two years and shorter than one month are more reversal oriented and are probably where contrarian (value) investing and reversal trading strategies work best. The implications are that

momentum strategies have higher turnover than contrarian strategies, and this is demonstrated in mutual funds that use momentum heavily.[10]

- There is reason to offer a lag from the time the portfolio is formed from historical return information until you actually create the portfolio, somewhere between one week to one month, because of short-term return reversals.
- In all cases, momentum strategies pick portfolios, not stocks, and have periods of time when their strategy is not in favor.

The evidence and pro-examples of momentum offering returns among the cross-section of stocks are just too many to refute intelligently. We have to confess, however, that Graham's intelligent investor, unlike the (unintelligent) speculator, would never utilize momentum strategies. In particular, Graham said that most speculators were guided by these mechanical indicators in his day, and that momentum investing was an unsound business practice. In addition, he said that after 50 years of investing experience, there was no lasting wealth created using these methods on Wall Street, but that con-examples of momentum failing were not enough to offer proof of his convictions in this regard either. For this reason we shall adhere to use only the factors Graham suggests for stock selection in his model, but later we will show results from a model of Graham's including additional momentum factors.

One thing to keep in mind when using any factor is that there are periods of time when a factor may lose efficacy. For example, momentum investing was a complete disaster in 2009, and for many quants, it led to large losses. If one bought the top 100 past winning stocks while shorting the past 100 losers, rebalancing monthly, using the universe of the Russell 1000™, one would have produced a return under negative 100 percent, a record loss! Joe Mezrich, a quant's quant, working for the sell-side research firm of Nomura Securities, has stated this is the largest loss going back to the 1970s in his database using momentum as a factor.[13] Also, there has been a considerable decrease in the efficacy of using momentum as a factor since October 2000 when Regulation FD was introduced in the United States.[14] A solution may involve utilizing either short-term momentum or momentum on stocks where there is far less analyst coverage anyway (usually stocks with lower trading volume, as in small caps or emerging markets, which have lower analyst coverage if any). Stocks with high analyst estimate dispersion, when the disagreement in earnings estimates between analysts is high, also have been offered for future momentum returns, but this is unlikely.

An empirical study to test momentum and earnings dispersion to draw some conclusions about their current and future efficacy involved downloading data to form six factors using the Russell 1000™ (R1K) universe and the Russell 1000 Growth™ (R1KG) index constituents from December 31, 1993, until December 31, 2007, using FactSet. The results are presented here. The attempt was to measure the effectiveness of earnings dispersion and earnings diffusion in the large-cap space using a control of four price momentum factors. The six factors were:

| | |
|---|---|
| Earnings dispersion: | total number of estimates / stdev(estimates) |
| Earnings diffusion: | (up estimates – down estimates) / total number of estimates |
| Ratio52: | closing price / 52 week high |
| t-Stat: | the t-Stat of a correlation calculation of a stock's price with a 45-degree line measured over 9 months |
| RelVol: | (50-day trading volume / 200-day trading volume) * past 6-month return |
| C200DMA: | closing price / 200-day moving average |
| 6-month return: | $P_{-6}/P_0 - 1$ |

We then measured the forward 6-month returns (with 1-month lag) for *octiles*, which are formed for each month of the study, consisting of roughly 125 stocks for the R1K (RUI) universe and 86 stocks for the R1KG (RLG) universe for each cohort. We tracked the returns of the octiles through time and had the following conclusions. First, what we observe is that the effectiveness of each of these factors has fallen considerably after the tech bubble. The years between June of 2002 and December of 2006 were especially ineffective for these factors in the large-cap space, as measured by the spread between the top octile and bottom octile cohorts of stocks, because the top minus bottom octile spread has been observed to decrease from then until now. Additionally, 2007 was a year of good stock selection for momentum. This was observed across the board for all six factors and, in particular, a large-cap growth product that I managed did very well that year, having strong momentum in its underlying model.

The highest volatility observed from the data was for the ratio52 factor for both R1K and R1KG universes and, in addition, ratio52 has a negative average spread over the last five years. Clearly, ratio52 is not a good factor for the large-cap stocks, and it demonstrates how a basic difference in momentum formulation can have dramatic differences on returns. Earnings dispersion and diffusion showed lower volatility in their top-bottom spread, with returns lower than any of the price momentum factors. However, they have not been greatly effective in the latest five years either, and purchasing stocks from the R1K and R1KG using these factors independently would not have given outsized returns against the benchmarks.

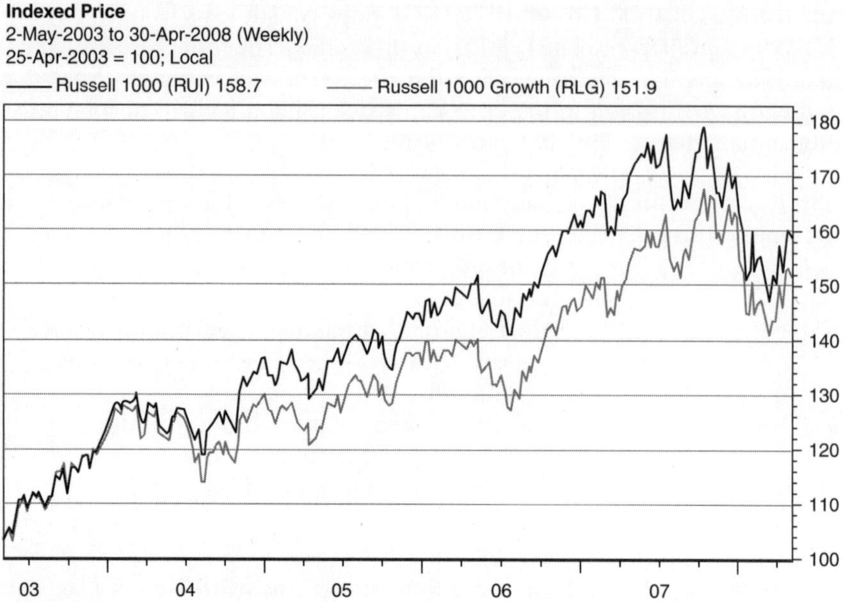


**FIGURE 4.2** Russell 1000 and Russell 1000 Growth Indexes
*Source:* © FactSet Research Systems 2009.
*Data Source:* Prices/Exshare.

Earnings diffusion, RelVol, and past 6-month price return have been the most effective in the last five years of the six factors, for a universe of the Russell 1000. The effectiveness of these factors wanes, however, when you measure them against the R1KG universe, because it is the momentum of stocks, not in the R1KG, but in the R1K that have been winning. This is why the R1K has beaten the R1KG for the majority of the last five years, as illustrated in Figure 4.2. Let's now turn to how to run such an experiment.

## MOMENTUM: INCREASING INVESTOR INTEREST

In teaching bottom-up modeling to interns and younger researchers in finance, it has always been helpful to do an actual study using some factor(s) to review the methodology and functional forms of the factors used and tests performed, and then have them run a similar model trying to reproduce results (not the same decimal-point accuracy, but to ascertain the trends). Thus, we will proceed with an example to give you a mark to model, too.

The next example also involves momentum again, but here, it is measured against a Russell 2000™ index constituent universe. This work was done some time ago, but it will serve to document the methodology utilized in factor testing, in particular the efficacy of momentum on small-cap stocks.

In this study, we took the time-period of December 31, 1991 to May 31, 2007, and downloaded from FactSet the R2K index and constituent's return for 6-month and 12-month periods and read this data into S-Plus™.[15] Then, for these differing time periods, we formed regression models run against market (R2K Cap Weighted Index), sector (Standard & Poors Global Industry Classification Standard, i.e., GICS), industry (GICS), and individual stock return. In this fashion, we sought to remove from an individual stock's return the contribution from the market (benchmark), sector, and industry, leaving the residuals of the regression as the true idiosyncratic effect. To remind you, residuals here are the difference between the model's predicted value of returns and the actual values of returns.

Three models are depicted mathematically in the next section. The first equation describes a fit of *future* stock return ($R_{i,t}$) to *past* market ($R_{\text{mkt}}$), sector ($R_{\text{sec}}$) and industry ($R_{\text{ind}}$) returns, and individual stock returns ($R_i$), where all were evaluated over a 6-month *previous* time period. The second model added past 3-month stock returns to the equation, in an attempt to affect shorter interval momentum to the return forecast. The third equation is similar but evaluated returns over 12 months, where the final two terms add the latest past-6-month and past-3-month returns to the equation. The market definition here means the full R2K index. Equally weighting all stocks in a given sector and averaging their returns over the time period in question created the sector return. The industry return is identically created, which is an equally weighted return from all stocks in a given industry. Thus, the final term(s) represents historical monthly returns of a given stock in Equation 4.1 (6-month past returns), as does the final two terms of Equation 4.2, (past 6 and past 3 months), and final three terms of Equation 4.3 (past 12, 6, and 3 months), which allows for autoregressive behavior.

$$6R_{i,t} = w_m * 6R_{\text{mkt},t-1} + w_{\text{sec}} * 6R_{\text{sec},t-1} + w_{\text{ind}} * 6R_{ind,t-1} + w_i * 6R_{i,t-1} \tag{4.1}$$

$$6R_{i,t} = w_m * 6R_{\text{mkt},t-1} + w_{\text{sec}} * 6R_{\text{sec},t-1} + w_{\text{ind}} * 6R_{\text{ind},t-1} + w_i * 6R_{i,t-1} + w_i * 3R_{i,t-1} \tag{4.2}$$

$$12R_{i,t} = w_m * 12R_{\text{mkt},t-1} + w_{\text{sec}} * 12R_{\text{sec},t-1} + w_{\text{ind}} * 12R_{\text{ind},t-1} + w_i * 12R_{i,t-1} + w_i * 6R_{i,t-1} + w_i * 3R_{i,t} \tag{4.3}$$

The experiment proceeds as follows: First, for a given month ending date, say December 31, 1991, ascertain the past-6-month return for each individual stock in the R2K index. This would be returns from June 30, 1990 to December 31, 1991. Save the data. Collect all stocks in a given sector using the GICS classification and assignment from S&P (any vendor's assignment could work). Average the returns from all stocks in a sector. This gives the 6-month return over the same time period for the sector. Do the same for the industries. Also archive the R2K equally weighted return over this same time period. At this juncture, we have all the data for the right side of Equation (4.1).

The left side of the equation would be individual stock returns for the time period January 31, 1992 to July 31, 1992. We forgo using the month of January, because one generally uses a lag from the time the portfolio is formed from historical return information until you actually create the portfolio, somewhere between one week to one month later due to short-term return reversals, which you are trying to avoid. From these data, regress the future returns (dependent variable, left side of the equation) against the other independent variables found on the right side of the equation. From the regression, the coefficients $w_m$, $w_{\text{sec}}$, $w_{\text{ind}}$, and $w_i$ found in the equations are determined, as are other statistics. We also have a model then, in which to rank stocks going forward. Even today, we could take the R2K index constituents, determine the values of the factors on the right side of the equation, multiply them by their corresponding coefficients, and predict or forecast each stock in the index's next 6-month return using this kind of model. That is exactly what we did in this example. For brevity, however, out-of-sample testing is forgone and omitted for the benefit of the teaching moment in this example. Also, we ignore the impact of look-ahead bias and survivorship bias for the same reasons, but wish to assure you that all these topics will be discussed later and were accounted for in this study.

When you use the model to do a forecast, the goal is to rank the stocks by the forecast, best to worse (highest predicted 6-month return to lowest predicted 6-month return), for a given month-ending date. Doing this recursively one month at a time from December 31, 1991 to May 31, 2007, creates a time series of forecasts, each done in a similar but separate fashion for every stock in the index. This is done for each of the three models. Once this is done and you have the forecasts (ranks) for the stocks, the next step involves gathering the realized returns of the stocks for those identical time periods. That is, given each stock's 6-month return forecast rank (good to bad for 2,000 stocks) starting on a given date, obtain the real 6-month return for each stock for that same time period. Then, the top-ranked decile (octile, quintile, or quartile) of stocks' actual realized returns are averaged as well as the bottom-ranked decile (octile, quintile, or quartile) realized returns, and the spread between the two is measured, as well as many other statistics gathered. Generally, one needs enough stocks in a cohort to offer decent statistics, so if one has 2,000 stocks, 200 is enough, cross-sectionally, and deciles are used. If you have an industry of stocks and there are only 40 stocks in it, say, then even a quartile may not be enough. So from these three models, quintiles for sectors and deciles cross-sectionally were formed and performance was measured via the aforementioned techniques.

In all, therefore, we examined three sets of predicted excess returns cross-sectionally and created associated statistics and portfolio time-series plots. The data show significant improvement over ordinary 6-month momentum as a predictor of stock return. We also applied the first equation to quintiled sectors alone to compute their excess returns over the R2K index and show graphs of performance. That is, we did the same across sectors, so we could ascertain the impact of the models, using just the stocks in individual sectors, rather than the whole index constituents.

We focus the discussion here to the three equations used in forming portfolios from the R2K universe. First we show universe aggregate population data in Figure 4.3, where we filtered the R2K universe by allowing only those stocks over \$2/share and that have a monthly average daily liquidity of over \$200,000 per day. Obviously, from Figure 4.3, this cutoff criteria

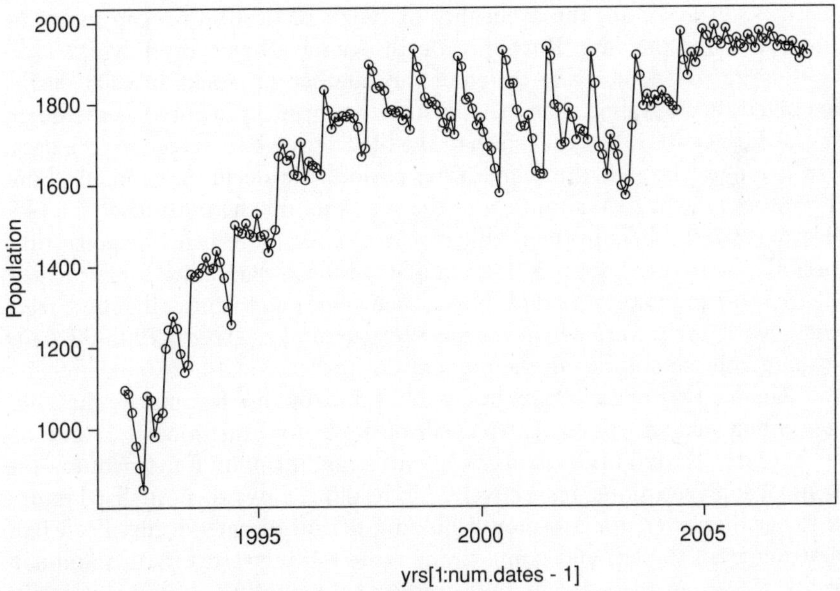


**FIGURE 4.3** Population of Stocks in Universe

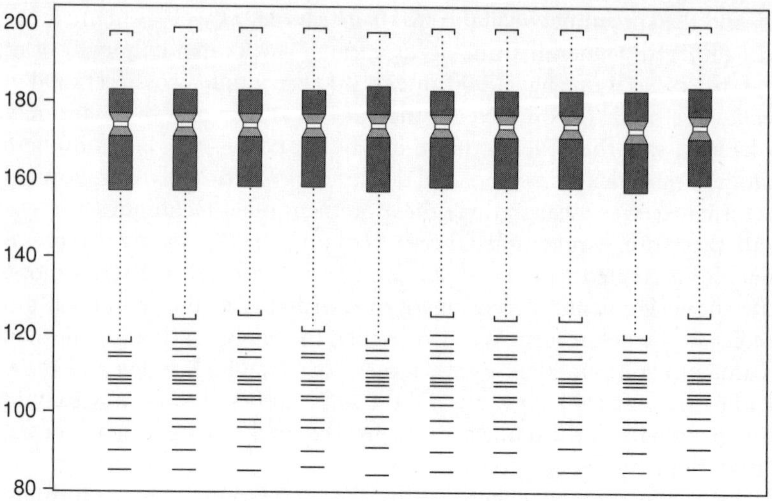


**FIGURE 4.4** Cross-Section of Stock's Decile Count

was more strongly in effect earlier in the time period of the study than more recently. In addition, the cyclicality of index reconstitution can easily be observed from the data (Russell reconstitutes the index every July 1).

Figure 4.4 depicts the count of the number of stocks in each decile, averaged through time. The median stock count is represented as the notch in the dark centers, and the width of the block covers 50 percent of the data. On average, through the whole time period, the deciles contained about 170 stocks each, thereabouts, and the whiskers on the bottom of the plot demonstrate outliers in the number of stocks for months in the given time period. So, there are not 2,000 stocks all the time in the Russell 2000 because of attrition and takeovers throughout each year, and historically, there were times with far fewer, which meant $2/share and average $200,000 daily trading volume criteria cut the population further.

The next set of bar charts in Figures 4.5 through 4.8 comprise the average annualized returns of a given decile of stocks for Equations (4.1) (data6), (4.2) (data63), and (4.3) (data1263), and straight 6-month momentum, the control analyzed alone, respectively. All the data shows an annualized return number, however, for a 6-month holding period of each decile. Each bar, starting from the left and going to the right, is the average return (annualized), measured through the time frame of the analysis, to a given decile, starting from the worst-ranked stocks and moving to the best. You would

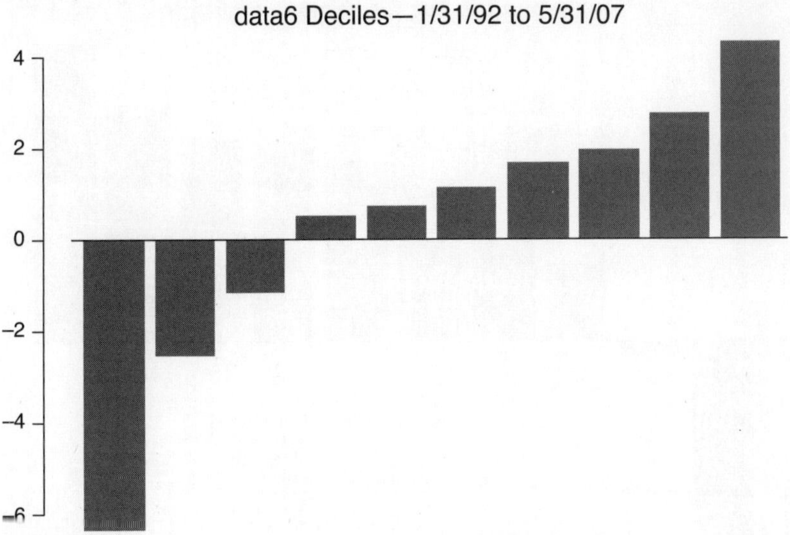


**FIGURE 4.5** Data6 of Equation (4.1) over a 15-Year Period

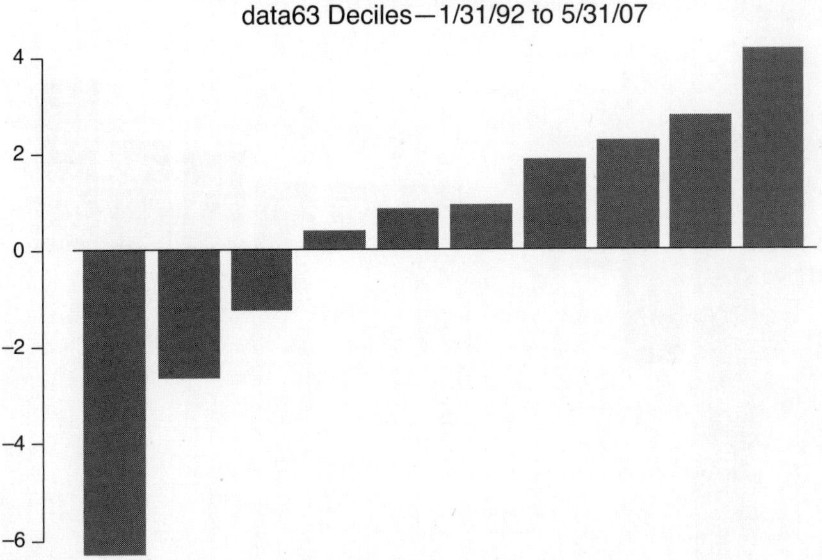


**FIGURE 4.6** Data63 of Equation (4.2) over a 15-Year Period

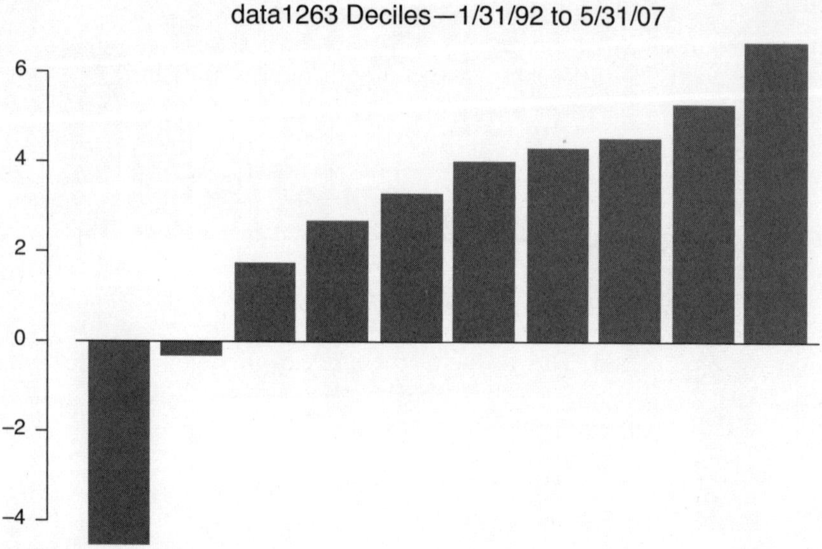


**FIGURE 4.7** Data1263 of Equation (4.3) over a 15-Year Period

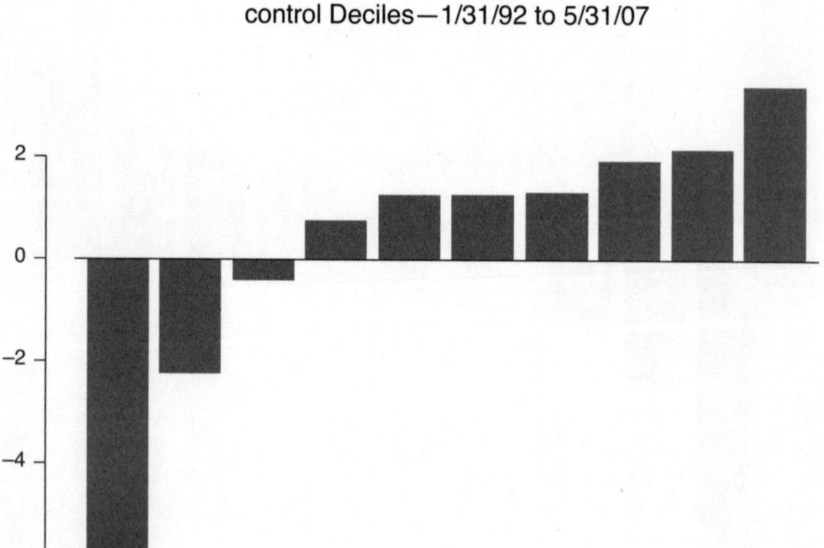


**FIGURE 4.8** Control Sample of a Pure 6-Month Price Momentum

expect to see a bar chart with this characteristic and trend if the model (and underlying factors) are any good at all.

The addition of the latest past-3-month returns adds little in efficacy here, as can be seen in the charts for (data6) compared to (data63). Therefore, the model of Equation (4.2) offers no advantage over the model in Equation (4.1). That is, the average returns for the model of Equation (4.2)'s top deciles are not improved (observably) by adding the shorter momentum factors to each model's successively longer dominant time frame. However, the inclusion of the past-6-month and 3-month momentum measures in the Equation (4.3) model (data1263) offers no substantial improvement even though the top decile reports an average 6 percent versus 4 percent return over the time period. This is due to the model in Equation (4.3) showing 12-month return results whereas models in Equations (4.1) and (4.2) report 6-month holding-period returns. The spread between the top and bottom deciles remains roughly constant for Equations (4.1) and (4.2). In all cases however, the three models offer improvement over using a single 6-month return momentum factor.

Figure 4.8 uses a 6-month return as a single momentum factor, in a one-factor model. Examining the top decile average return of about 2.5 percent shows it does not come close to the 4 percent return of Equations 4.1 and 4.2 and is even further from the 6 percent of Equation 4.3. Its bottom decile, the potential shorts though, is closer to –6 percent of Equations 4.1 and 4.2, whereas the shorts of Equation 4.3 are only –4 percent, but that is a figure for a 12-month holding period. In general, if these were the only model results you had, you would conclude that Equations (4.1), (4.2), and (4.3) all are an improvement over a single 6-month momentum factor in stock selection. Be mindful that in practice, you are purchasing 170 stocks on average for each decile or bucket and then holding them for 6 months, except for the results shown for Equation (4.3), which is a 12-month holding period. Later, we will show annualized figures for all models. Also, the portfolio turnover is not reported here, but it is high, as are momentum models generally.

Figure 4.9 offers a picture of the time-series performance of Equation (4.1) where we plot the excess return over the R2K in rolling 6-month return profiles for the top decile and the bottom decile of each model. The expectation is that the top decile should mostly show positive return versus the benchmark, and the bottom decile should underperform versus the bench the majority of time. In Figure 4.9, the top decile's average excess rolling 6-month return is shown as the cross-hatched lines, whereas the bottom decile's excess return is drawn as the black-circled dotted line. This is the standard format for all time-series plots we will show.

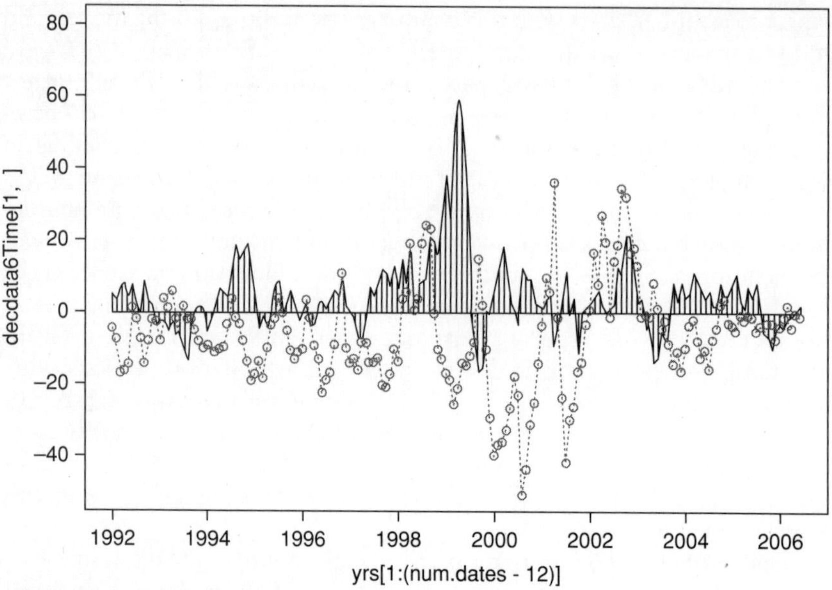


**FIGURE 4.9** Top and Bottom Quintile 6-Month Rolling Return Time Series of Equation (4.1)

From this chart of the first model (Eq. 4.1, data6), we see that the top decile (hashed curve) has mostly outperformed, especially during the stock market technology bubble of 1999. Momentum has worked "hugely successfully" in the past, but notice that it peters out as we move to the later half of the first decade of the millennia. It is also interesting that even when the tech bubble crashed, using the form of momentum given by the first equation would have obviated losses relative to the R2K benchmark. Remember, this is a plot of excess return, however, so that there were still negative absolute returns after the technology meltdown using this momentum model but higher returns than the index itself. The observations are similar for the second model (data63, whole63) as they are for the first model as depicted in Figure 4.10. There is very little performance differential between models (1) and (2) as visualized in the time-series plots and as measured in the earlier bar-chart plots.

Figure 4.11 shows similar behavior for Equation (4.3) that includes 3-month past momentum measures along with 6-month past returns to what is essentially a 12-month momentum model. This model offers significant average return improvement over the other two as measured and shown by the bar chart, but a major drawback is that all the extra return that gives

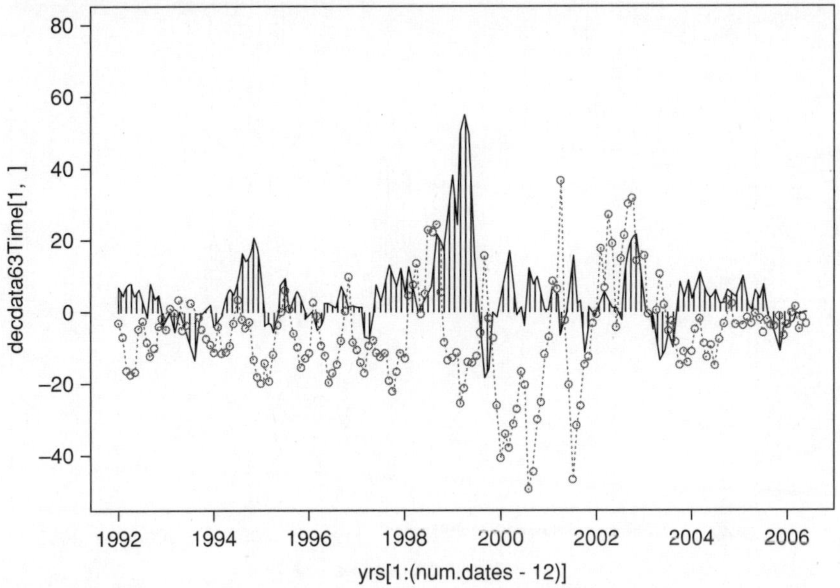


**FIGURE 4.10** Top and Bottom Quintile 6-Month Rolling Return Time Series of Equation (4.2)

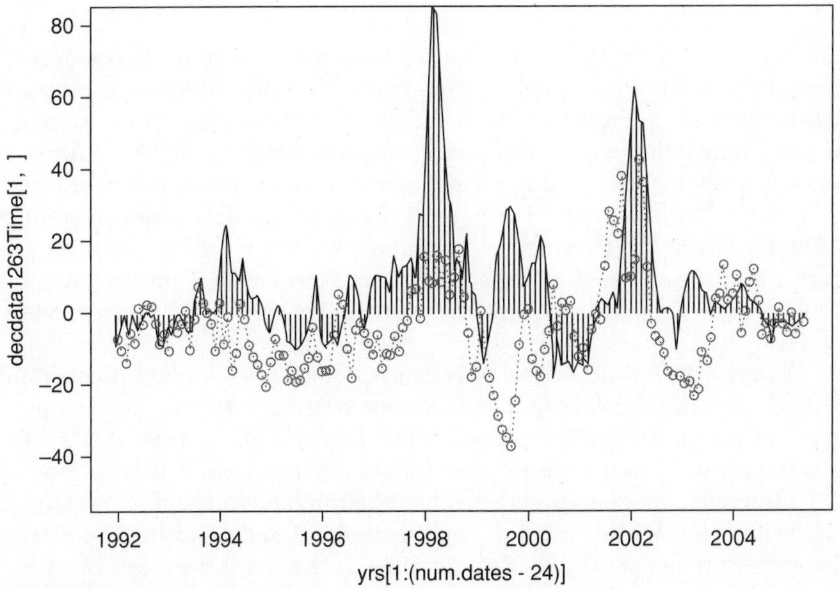


**FIGURE 4.11** Top and Bottom Quintile 6-Month Rolling Return Time Series of Equation (4.3)

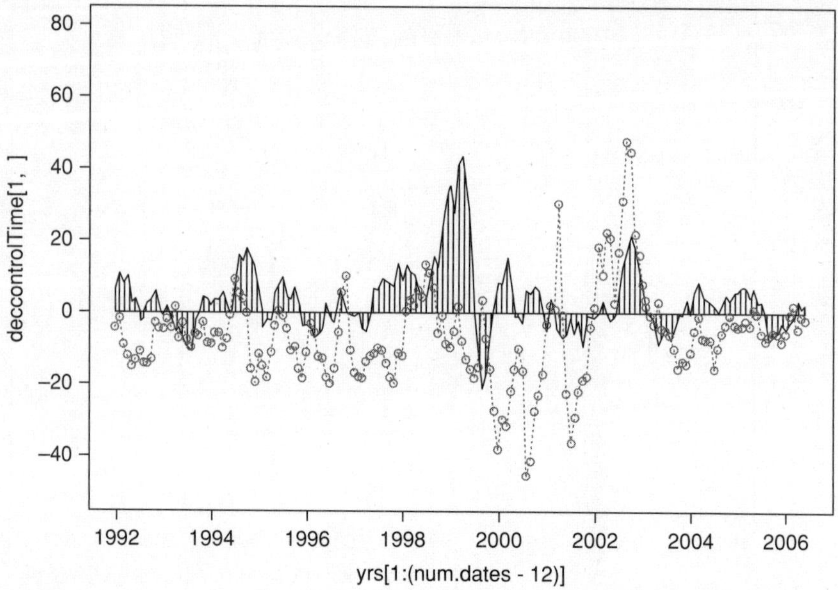


**FIGURE 4.12** Top and Bottom Quintile 6-Month Rolling Return Time Series of Momentum (Control)

this model's top decile a decent spread from top to bottom deciles occurs during the technology bubble and in 2003. This model does not offer as consistent returns through time as the other models either. Thus, by plotting the time series of outperformance or excess return versus the returns of the universe of stocks used to create the model, there are apparent reasons to reject a particular model. Figure 4.12 shows the time series of rolling 6-month return for the single-momentum factor of 6-month historical return (the control), used to rank stocks and forecast their future 6-month return (with 1-month lag). You can see similar patterns, but with lower returns.

Figure 4.12 for the control of ordinary 6-month stock price momentum has an obvious difference in its return time series as compared to the other momentum models. In particular, notice that, for the bottom decile, the return pattern is more negative than for the other models.

Generally, we comment that these idiosyncratic momentum measures worked quite strongly during the Internet bubble, and they offer significant hit rates in the upper deciles through time as charted in Figure 4.13. A hit rate is the percentage of time a given decile's return outperformed the R2K index, averaged through all time. We forgo showing each model's data but

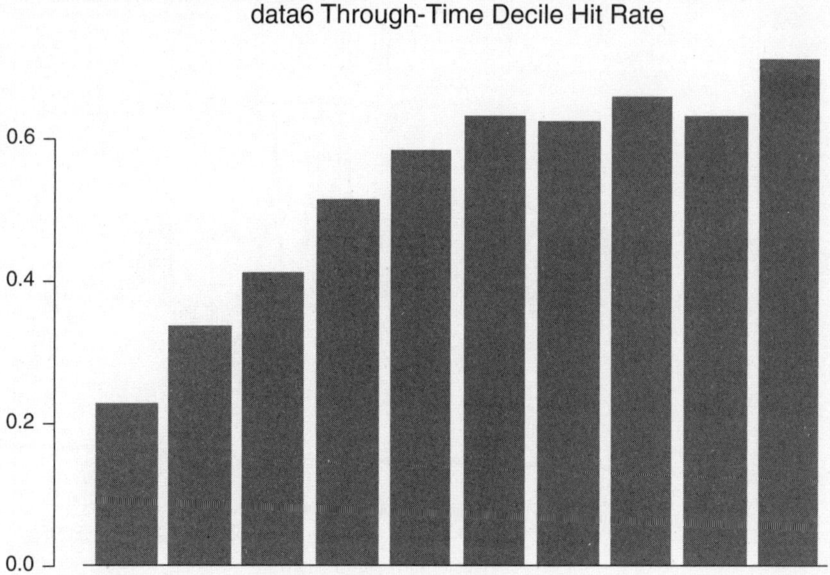


**FIGURE 4.13** Through-Time Hit Rate of Equation (4.1)

demonstrate the data using a bar chart for the first model only. This is just one of the many measures utilized in selecting models and factors. Figure 4.13 shows that only 20 percent of the time did the bottom decile (far left bar) outperform the R2K throughout the time period of this study, but we see that deciles 1 through 6 (middle to far right bars) had outperformed their index over 50 percent of the time, and, for decile 1, it beat the index well over 60 percent of the time.

Finally, we plot the spreads, that is, the top decile's return minus the bottom decile's rolling 6-month return for the three momentum models, as well as the control (standard 6-month momentum model) in Figure 4.14, all on the same vertical (ordinate) scale. These graphs are very useful to garner in one quick glance how well the model ranks good stocks from bad stocks, because the visual representation of the spread in performance allows you to quickly ascertain whether the underlying models are any good or not. Think of them as a portfolio that is simultaneously long the top decile and short the bottom decile. This is very important and actually reveals more than a chart of numbers. This is because, by reporting average return numbers, often in this step there is implicitly a misinterpretation or misreliance on the standard deviation of the average return number. This brings us back to the concept of focusing on averages and missing the deviation.

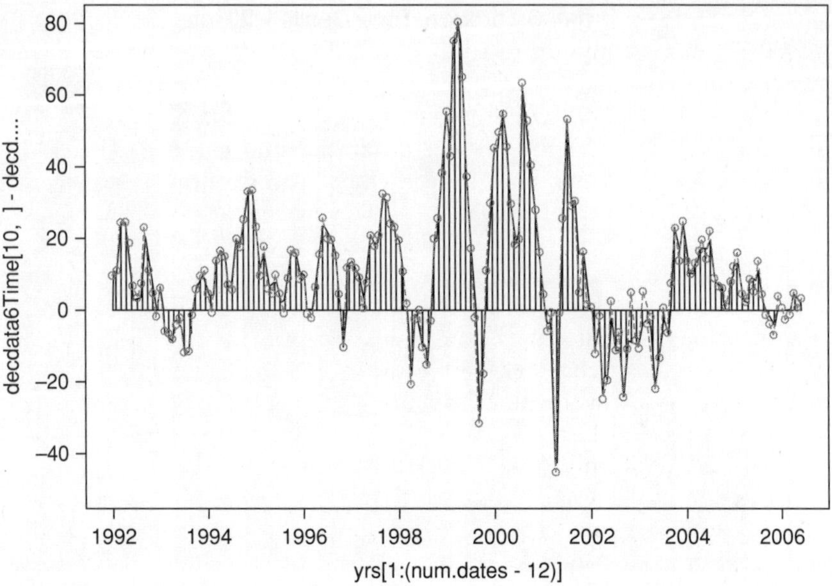


**FIGURE 4.14** Top Decile minus Bottom Decile for Equation (4.1)

For instance, if we report the top decile's average return as 6 percent and the bottom decile return as –4 percent over a 15-year back test, we entirely overestimate the goodness of the model if we are not also forced to cogitate the impact of the return variation. In other words, if you are told that the top decile has an average 6 percent return over the benchmark, with a standard deviation of 35 percent, versus –4 percent return of the bottom decile with a concomitant standard deviation of 43 percent, then you realize the quality (or lack thereof) of the models. I contend that the spread of top minus bottom decile returns, plotted in a time series, captures the essence of the numbers in a quick glance. Figure 4.14 does this for Equation (4.1).

From the plot in Figure 4.14, we see the spread between the rolling 6-month return of the top decile of the first model, minus the bottom decile's return. This indicates that the model is essentially sound because the top decile consistently outperforms the bottom decile. If this does not occur, then the soundness of the underlying model has to be questioned. This is a solid fundamental principle of modeling stock returns, and it has nothing to do with comparing this particular model with any other, because it is a paramount condition with any model that top decile must outperform the bottom decile, consistently.

Also, from this chart, we can see that from 2002 almost to 2004, the bottom decile outperforms the top decile. Now, this is a sufficiently long enough time to put a portfolio manager in a mutual fund out of business, should the manager's sole method for purchasing stock be momentum. Hence the peril of a single-factor model. In addition, the fact that momentum has not worked in 2008 and 2009 shows there is precedent in history for two years of underperformance. You must be aware of history in a factor to set expectations of performance going forward, which is why we agree with Graham's statement that if experience cannot help today's investor, then we must be logical and conclude that there is no such thing as investment in common stocks and that those interested in them should confess themselves speculators.

We see similar behavior from Equation (4.2) in the losing years of 2002 to 2004 as shown in the plot in Figure 4.15. Let the momentum investor beware. In the third model, the period between 2002 and 2004 has the problem mitigated only to have 2000–2002 have negative spreads between top decile performance and bottom decile performance. This is troublesome for the momentum models, and you can see the single-factor model of just 6-month momentum alone only has a single year 2003 as the problem child.

Though similar throughout, there is greater spread in the three models than in the control model, the single 6-month momentum factor. Also,

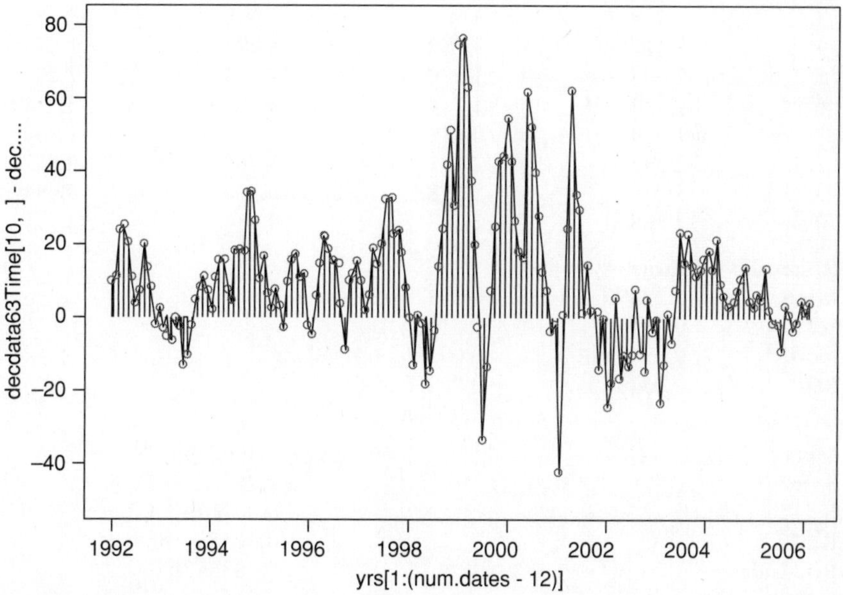


**FIGURE 4.15** Top Decile minus Bottom Decile for Equation (4.2)

unfortunately in all cases, the momentum trails off toward the end of the study, especially in the most recent time period, because, again, momentum as a recent factor has been losing efficacy.

We chart the *annualized* excess return over the R2K using these idiosyncratic momentum models along with the associated regression coefficients and *t*-stats of the regression below, ordered from left to right, Equation (4.1) (data6) to Equation (4.3) (data1263).

The first column of Table 4.2 is for the model constructed from Equation (4.1) where future 6-month return is regressed against past 6-month market, sector, industry, and stock return. What is interesting is how strongly the individual stock returns are impacted by the benchmark (the market) and negatively correlated, too, as shown by the negative regression coefficient

**TABLE 4.2** Decile Performance and Regression Statistics of Idiosyncratic Momentum Models

| | Decile Excess Returns over R2K | | | |
|---|---|---|---|---|
| | **data6** | **data63** | **data1263** | **control** |
| 1 | 8.859 | 8.494 | 6.655 | 6.946 |
| 2 | 5.637 | 5.657 | 5.287 | 4.370 |
| 3 | 3.999 | 4.561 | 4.549 | 3.918 |
| 4 | 3.417 | 3.770 | 4.295 | 2.672 |
| 5 | 2.305 | 1.890 | 4.015 | 2.572 |
| 6 | 1.522 | 1.714 | 3.295 | 2.565 |
| 7 | 1.044 | 0.814 | 2.684 | 1.553 |
| 8 | −2.292 | −2.431 | 1.767 | −0.837 |
| 9 | −5.046 | −5.178 | −0.330 | −4.441 |
| 10 | −12.368 | −12.203 | −4.556 | −12.511 |
| **Regression Coefficients (*t*-stats)** | | | | |
| Mkt6 | −0.2939/(−37.6) | −0.2942/(−37.6) | | |
| Sec6 | 0.0156/(1.91) | 0.0153/(1.9) | | |
| Ind6 | 0.0947/(14.3) | 0.0951/(14.4) | | |
| Ret6 | 0.0516/(25.4) | 0.0627/(24.6) | | |
| Ret6m3 | | −0.0238/(−7.2) | | |
| Mkt12 | | | −0.4062/(49.7) | |
| Sec12 | | | −0.0677/(−8.4) | |
| Ind12 | | | −0.0071/(−1.1) | |
| Ret12 | | | −0.0285/(−10.8) | |
| Ret12m6 | | | 0.0886/(20.0) | |
| Ret12m3 | | | 0.0152/(2.9) | |

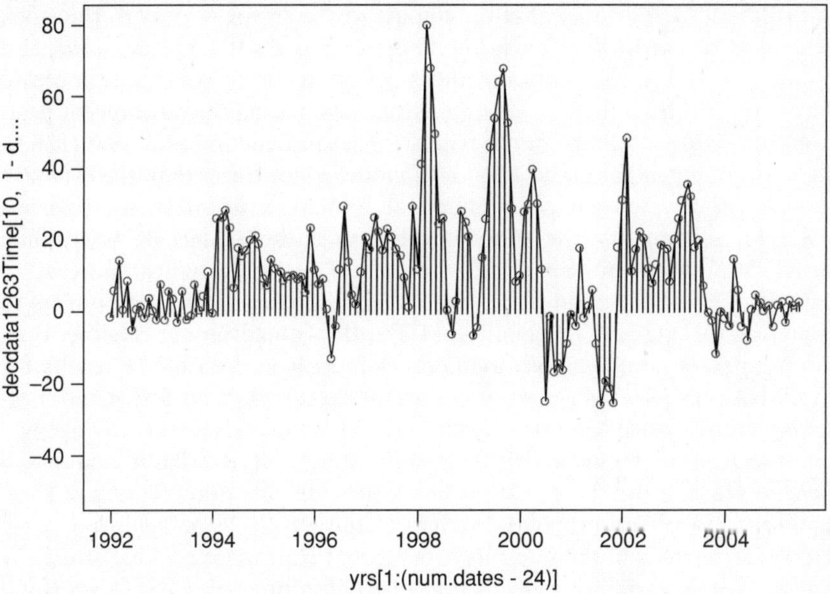


**FIGURE 4.16** Top Decile minus Bottom Decile for Equation (4.3)

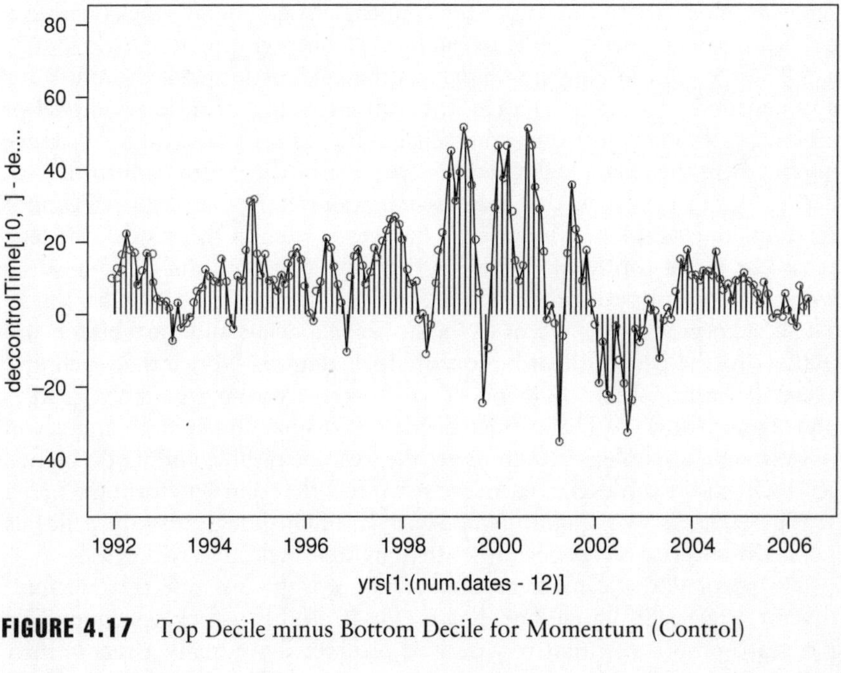


**FIGURE 4.17** Top Decile minus Bottom Decile for Momentum (Control)

of −0.2939. Also, notice that the impact of the sector returns to the stock returns is the smallest effect in the first two models (0.015 coefficient and *t*-stat of 1.9) and that industry and stock momentum contribute more to future returns than does sector momentum. By adding the most recent past-3-month returns to the 6-month regression, as in Equation (4.3) (data1263), there is not much gain. The 12-month model is not better than the 6-month models either when you see numbers all annualized to make comparisons possible. In summary, the idiosyncratic momentum models are better than ordinary 6-month momentum as a predictor of future return and easy to calculate; however, adding the shorter-term autoregressive components to Equation (4.1), giving us Equation (4.2), offers no advantage. Neither does adding past-3- and 6-month momentum models as seen in the results for Equation (4.3). We also state an important caveat when modeling and measuring performance against a benchmark. These models are created using a cross-section of stocks arising from some source. In this latest example, a benchmark like the Russell 2000 index provides the universe of stocks to build the model and provides a stable reference to measure against as well. However, there is nothing in this process that states that ranking stocks by any economic variable(s) means that one will ultimately create a portfolio of stocks that will beat the index. Each decile has a significant breadth of stocks, such that some stocks outperform the index and some underperform the index. Figure 4.18 typifies what occurs when model building, and it serves to elucidate to the reader the challenge of getting all stocks within a cohort (decile, octile, quintile, or quartile) to outperform an index.

The box plot in Figure 4.18 depicts the median decile excess return for another model (so named model_5, because it was a proprietary model of a quant asset manager) versus its benchmark, as represented by the center notch where the dark block covers 50 percent of the return data from each decile. We can tell you that this model, proprietary to a firm we cannot reveal, is one of the best models we have ever seen. In this model, the left-most bar is the top decile, whereas the right-most column of data is the worst or bottom performers. These are the results of a 20-year back test. The brackets cover 95 percent of the stocks in a decile and the whiskers are outliers to the general distribution of stock returns. Notice that each and every decile has stocks both under- and overperforming its index (values above and below 0). The average decile returns may be favorable, but you have to own a whole portfolio to get the average results, and if you owned all stocks in the top decile, there are still a few that underperform the index at times. This is why quant methods are so often thought of in practice as portfolio selection strategies rather than as stock selection strategies.

In particular, the more granular one goes, the less effective are multifactor, regression-based modeling methods used for stock selection. This is a reason most quantitatively derived products have many assets in their

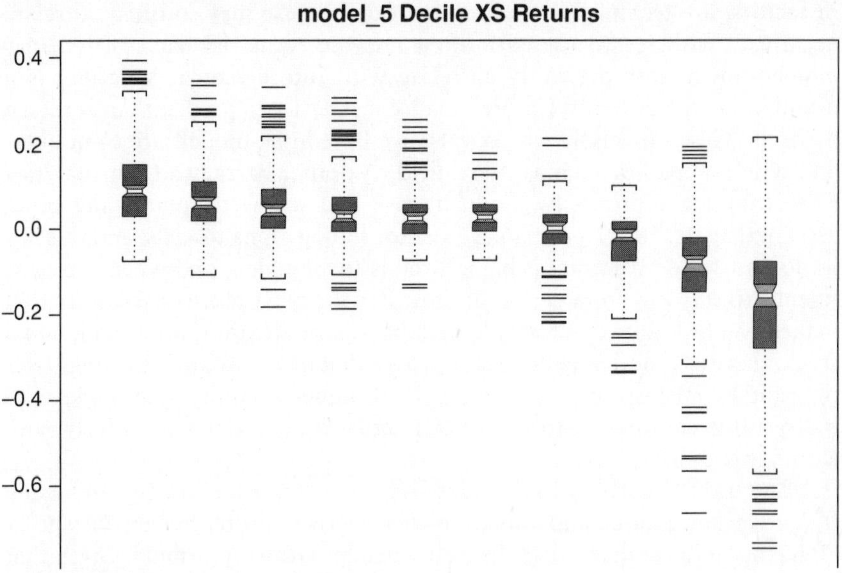


**FIGURE 4.18** Box Plot of Median Excess Return over Benchmark for Quant Manager's Model

portfolio, counting on the law of large numbers to obtain the average results. It is also why these kinds of models are used as screens for fundamentally managed portfolios where they will perform further research to whittle down the selections to smaller portfolios. These kinds of models are generally not so good at picking individual stocks, but they are great at deciphering broader trends among groups of stocks. Even in the bottom decile (far right), shown here, there are some stocks that outperformed the index as one can see. Also remember that these empirical results involve equally weighted portfolios within each decile. Since most investors weight their stocks unequally, results can be considerably different under differing weighting schemes. We will cover this topic when we ultimately get to discuss portfolio construction and optimization later.

## VOLATILITY AS A FACTOR IN ALPHA MODELS

We now have valuation, fundamental, and momentum factors utilized in building factor models. We have to segue to review the indicators that utilize volatility now, either from standard deviation measures (which we have shown are inaccurate descriptors of return distributions) or from tail functions, designed to look at the downside return only. These vol functions, or factors, are technical in nature, too, but because they so often correlate negatively with return they are often referred to as risk factors, whereas momentum factors positively correlate with future return. Volatility is a useful indicator of return simply because it is easier to predict than is return by itself. This is precisely why covariance-based risk models are so popular and why companies such as Northfield, Axioma, Barra, and FinAnalytica exist; they make profits by modeling risk and selling to quants and other asset managers. Fewer companies exist for selling alpha models, and this has to do with when volatility is high, it tends to stay high, and when it is low, it tends to stay low for a period of time. It is the persistence of volatility that makes you feel quite comfortable with its use. In addition, for an individual stock, there is a fundamental reason stocks that have disparate earnings over time and express earnings uncertainty have higher volatility than stocks with more stable earnings histories. Price fluctuation correlates negatively with earnings stability.

The use of volatility in the next section is not related to risk modeling (i.e., covariance modeling) but is applied directly in the regression with other alpha factors as in the CAPM, Fama-French, or Graham formula. Given that stock volatility is a proxy for earnings stability, it makes sense to include it in an alpha model. For example, stocks with high volatility have been shown to have low average returns.[16] In particular, stocks with high idiosyncratic (high individual) volatility relative to the market have lower returns, generally, than stocks with low average volatility, and this phenomenon is not explained by exposures to size, book-to-market, momentum, and liquidity effects. Volatility is a very powerful predictive factor. Portfolio managers who, in the technology bubble of 2000 and in the credit crisis of 2008, essentially stayed away from stocks that had high past volatility did much better than the indexes and their peers in those years.

In this study, we took the time period of January 31, 1992 to May 31, 2007, and downloaded from FactSet the Russell 2000 (R2K) index and constituents' return and volatility as measured as the standard deviation of daily return over 3-month, 6-month, and 12-month periods. We read this data into our favorite statistical package, S+Plus (but one could use "R" as well). Then, for these differing time periods, we formed regression models against market (R2K Cap Weighted Index), sector (GICS), industry (GICS), and stock volatility, defined as the standard deviation of daily returns. In this fashion, we sought to remove from an individual stock's volatility the contribution from the market (benchmark), sector, and industry, leaving the residuals of the regression as the true idiosyncratic volatility effect.

We did not use the g-Factor as our definition of volatility in this example, because of the ease of computation to obtain the standard deviation of return, and it served the point very well as a teaching moment.

Two models were constructed and are depicted mathematically in Equations (4.4) and (4.5). Though they look like Equations (4.1), (4.2), and (4.3), they are not the same. Those equations had stock price momentum in them for factors, whereas these have stock price volatility (i.e., standard deviation of daily price return over 6 months). Equation (4.4) describes a fit of future stock 6-month excess return ($XS_i$) of the R2K index constituents, to past market ($V_{\text{mkt}}$), sector ($V_{\text{sec}}$) and industry ($V_{\text{ind}}$) volatility where each measure is the aggregated volatility from the stocks in the market, sector, and industry respectively. The second model, Equation (4.5), adds a further past stock volatility to Equation (4.5) in an attempt to add an autoregressive component to the model. Thus, the last term in Equation (4.5) goes back a period further than the other independent variables as indicated by the $(t{-}2)$ subscript. From regression results of these models, deciles are easily formed from the predicted excess returns and realized values, exactly as demonstrated in the momentum example previously discussed at length.

$$6XS_{i,t} = w_m * 6V_{\text{mkt},t-1} + w_{\text{sec}} * 6V_{\text{sec},t-1} + w_{\text{ind}} * 6V_{\text{ind},t-1} + w_i * 6V_{i,t-1} \tag{4.4}$$

$$6XS_{i,t} = w_m * 6V_{mkt,t-1} + w_{\text{sec}} * 6V_{\text{sec},t-1} + w_{\text{ind}} * 6V_{\text{ind},t-1} + w_i * 6V_{i,t-1} + w_i * 6V_{i,t-2} \tag{4.5}$$

Equation (4.5), where we add an autoregressive term to Equation (4.4), yields no improvement in decile performance so its results are omitted, but we show the equation because we wanted to confirm the ease with which you can append a new factor to an existing model. This is commonly done within the quant industry.

We concentrate on the 6-month returns for the results presented because the trends identified are similar for all holding periods, though the actual reported average returns may be different. Lastly, for a control, individual stock volatility (labeled Vol6Mon in the charts) was used as a lone factor with deciles formed from it, allowing comparison with the other model similar to the control of 6-month momentum we gave in the momentum example earlier.

The empirical analysis proceeded as follows. First, returns for a given 6-month period of time were collected for all stocks in the Russell 2000 index and the index returns were subtracted from the individual stock returns. Then, the standard deviation of daily returns for all stocks was measured for the preceding 6-month time period. This gave the term on the left of the equal sign for model in Equation (4.4) and the last term on the right of the model in Equation (4.4). Next, stocks were placed into buckets of their assigned industry (again, any vendor's assignment is acceptable as long as it is consistently used for the whole of the study), and the standard deviations of daily returns were averaged. Then, this was done identically for assigned sectors. Finally, the standard deviation of the R2K index daily return was measured. Thus, all factors for the model in Equation (4.4) would be known, and regressing the excess future 6-month returns against past data could be performed and coefficients $w_{\mathrm{mkt}}$, $w_{\mathrm{sec}}$, $w_{\mathrm{ind}}$, and $w_i$ solved for. The model is then used to predict, forecast, and rank all stocks by the model's scores for a given period and results sorted from best to worst prediction. We then obtain the actual realized 6-month excess returns for all stocks in the sample for each and every time period and align them with forecasted performance. Since we have almost 2,000 stocks for every time period, we can form deciles sorted by the stocks, model ranks and tabulate realized return for each bucket.

Figure 4.19 for model (4.4) shows the top to bottom spreads of excess return over the R2K. The top decile's time-series performance minus the bottom decile's performance measured using a 6-month holding period is shown in the dark hatched plot. What is most consistent is the reverse behavior of the models during the technology bubble period as compared to the momentum models we showed earlier. The model is not differentiated in

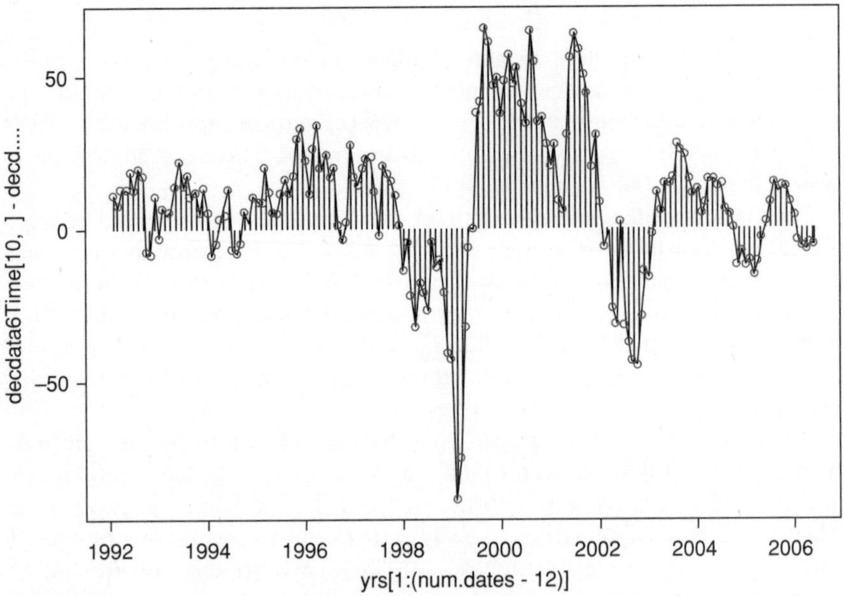


**FIGURE 4.19** Model (4.4) Top-Bottom Decile Spread

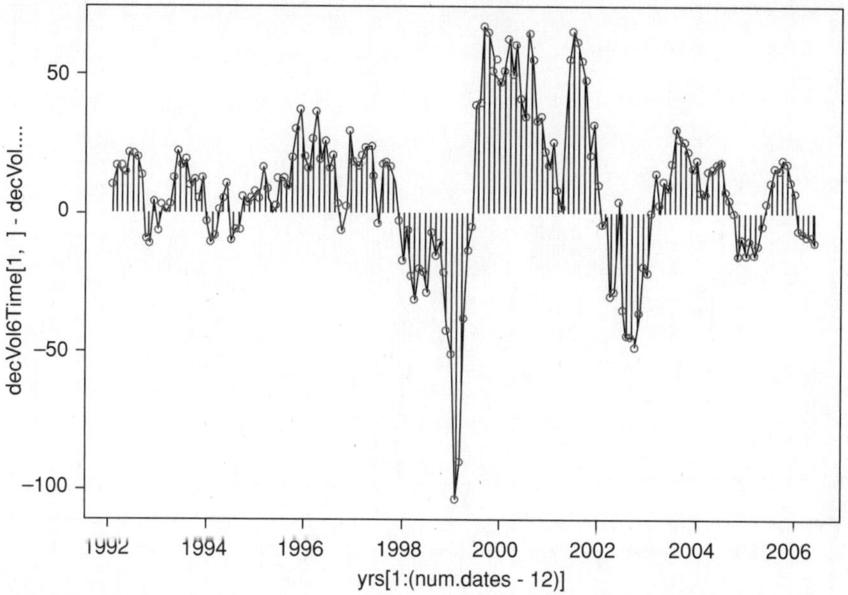


**FIGURE 4.20** Top-Bottom Decile Spread for 6-Month Volatility (Control)

these plots from individual stock volatility (the control) shown in Figure 4.20 and offers little performance advantage as compared to it either.

The top and bottom deciles of excess return over the R2K are shown in Figure 4.21 for the model in Equation (4.4), and ordinary stock volatility is shown in Figure 4.22. There are very few reportable differences between these two models. Considering the higher level of difficulty in incorporating what was thought to be market, sector, and industry contributions to the excess return of stocks, it appears it is not worth the effort extended. In practice, often many tests are run by adding more complicated formulas to a model, to determine whether a factor or combination of factors is relevant in building the model that will become the cornerstone of your investment process. In this case, the differences seen in a time series of excess performance over a benchmark are so subtle from the more complex model as to be worth neglecting, taking the more parsimonious result as more workable and God's truth. This expresses a total agreement with Einstein who stated, "Reduce every problem to its most simplest form and no simpler."[17] In general, always take the simple model when more advanced models offer no advantage. In addition, you may also be subject to overfitting when the advanced model is only a slightly better performer.

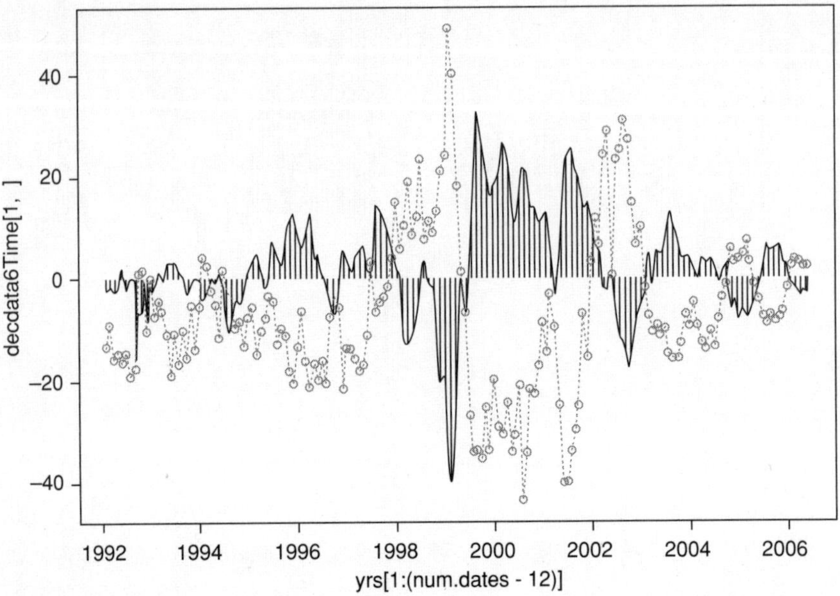


**FIGURE 4.21** Model of Equation (4.4) Top (Hashed) and Bottom (Dots) Decile XS Return

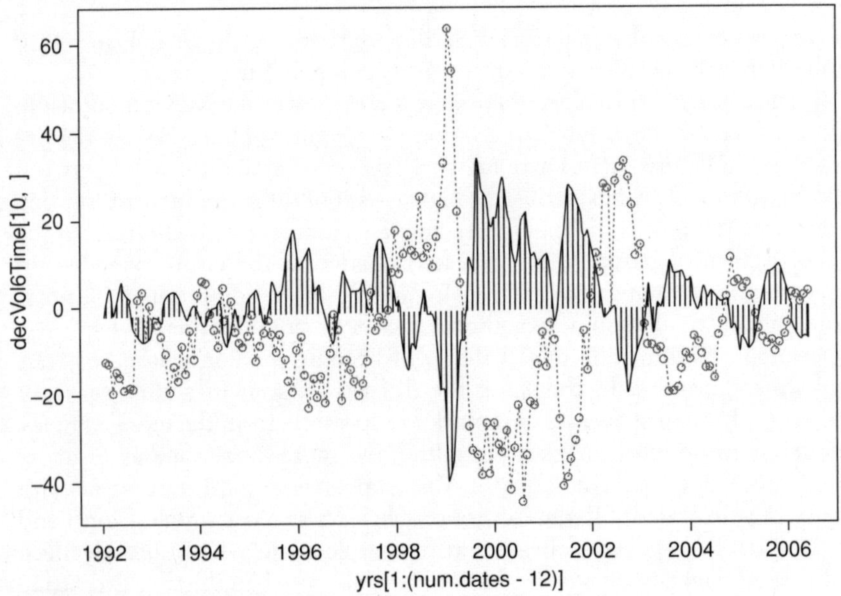


**FIGURE 4.22** Top (Hashed) and Bottom (Dots) Decile Returns for 6-month Volatility (Control)

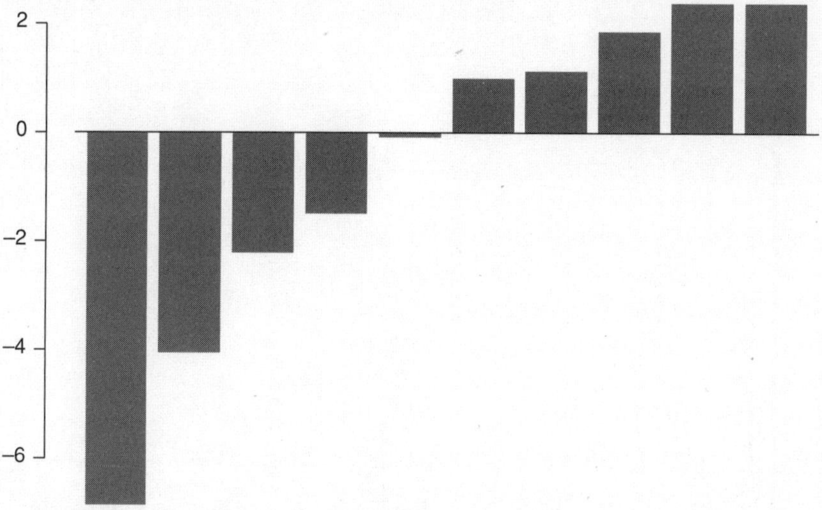


**FIGURE 4.23** Model (4.4) Decile XS Return—1/31/1992 to 5/31/2007

The decile excess return bar plots, showing the average decile performance for the whole period of the study, are displayed in Figure 4.23. The leftmost bar plots negative return for the model of Equation (4.4) and represents low model score and high volatility. Since stock volatility is generally negatively correlated to return, the plot is reversed for the individual stock volatility control factor as shown in Figure 4.24. This is due to this

**FIGURE 4.24** Control Decile XS Return—1/31/1992 to 5/31/2007

**TABLE 4.3** Acceptable Suite of Factors for Use in Quant Modeling

| | MOST COMMON FACTORS UTILIZED IN QUANT MODELS | |
|---|---|---|
| VALUATION | | |
| | P/B | |
| | P/SALES | |
| | P/CASHFLOW | |
| | P/E | Forward and Backward |
| | Dividend Yield | |
| | Total Yield | |
| | Operating CF/P | |
| | Free CF/P | |
| | EBITDA/P | |
| GROWTH | | |
| | % Change in FF1 Earnings Estimates vs. Actual LTM Earnings | |
| | % Change in FF2 Earnings Estimates vs. FF1 Earn. Est. | |
| | Last 3 Years Sales Growth | |
| | EPS Growth | |
| FUNDAMENTAL | | |
| | Change in Net Margin | |
| | Accruals | |
| | Change in Working Capital | |
| | Book Value Growth | |
| | Return on Assets | |
| | Return on Equity | |
| | Unexpected Earnings | |
| | Earnings Diffusion | |
| | Earnings Dispersions | |

| | | |
|---|---|---|
| EXOGENOUS | | |
| | Market Cap | |
| | Firm Value | |
| | Enterprise Value | |
| | Change in Share Count | |
| **MOMENTUM** | **MATHEMATICAL FORMULA** | **LOOKBACK PERIOD** |
| tStat | (Correlation*(N-2)^(0.5))/(1.0-(Correlation ^(2))^(0.5) | N Trading Days |
| EStat | Error Estimate of tStat | N Trading Days |
| c-Stat | (Covariance*(N-2)^(0.5))/(1.0-(Covariance)^(2))^(0.5) | N Trading Days |
| Ratio52 | Current Price/last 52 week high | 12 months |
| Slope-N | Coefficient of Regressed Price with Line of Slope 1 | N Trading Days |
| Moving Average 50 | Sum(Price,50)/50 | 50 Trade days |
| Moving Average 200 | Sum(Price,200)/200 | 200 trade days |
| Ema50 | ExpMovAvg(Price,50) | 50 Trade days |
| Ema200 | ExpMovAvg(Price,200) | 200 trade days |
| RelStren | 100 - 100 /(1 + average(up days)/average(down days)) | 190 Trading Days |
| Move3 | (P-4/P-1) - 1 | 4 months |
| Move6 | (P-7/P-1) - 1 | 7 months |
| Move9 | (P-10/P-1) - 1 | 10 months |
| Move12 | (P-13/P-1) - 1 | 13 months |
| Move15 | (P-16/P-1) - 1 | 16 months |
| C200DMA | Price Now / 200 Day Moving Average | 200 day trade |
| RelVol | (Sum50DayTradeVolume / Sum200DayTradeVolume) * Move6 | 200 day trade |

single-factor model having low volatility offering higher return in its first decile, in exact accordance with the model in Equation (4.4), but because the scores of the model in Equation (4.4) in the first decile correlate with higher volatility and lower return, they are reversed.

We present this confusing plot to show that you typically want to sort the data before comparing factors and models such that they are all correlated positively with future return. This is a subtle but important point, and we mention it because more than a few quants have had some factors within a model reversed from other factors in the same model, offsetting the gains that they could have made otherwise, had they sorted their factors correctly. When managing other peoples' money, this can be a terrible error.

Usually, you examine a model with respect to some reference for which you have good data and when expectations are known, thus the reason for inserting a 6-month momentum factor and a 6-month volatility factor as controls. Here, we created a model to educate the reader in model construction, analysis, and testing. In practice, however, you would hope there would be a greater separation in terms of performance from these differing models, but sometimes there is not. Both the time-series graphs of top and bottom deciles, along with their spreads, indicate that ordinary daily stock volatility (as measured by standard deviation) would do the job as well as or better than a model incorporating sector- and industry-level volatility. As it stands, a simple measure of calculating the daily standard deviation of stock returns is simple and requires no further data reduction. It remains to be seen if a model constructed using g-Factor methodology may indeed offer higher discrimination and better returns.

Naturally, you collect hit ratios and other numbers in determining the effectiveness of a factor. In later chapters we will offer the laundry list of factors tests that need to be done and review what measurements are likely to indicate the best methods to determine factor and model efficacy.

The factors useful to begin formal studies are categorized as valuation, fundamental, growth, exogenous, momentum, and risk. There are many possibilities in these categories. Table 4.3 will serve Graham's enterprising investor to explore possibilities in constructing quant models, less the volatility factor substituting for risk. The table just lists available factors and their definitions and offers an example of possibilities. Do not necessarily take these as mandated formulas.

CHAPTER 5

# Modeling Pitfalls and Perils

*"I have recently had a question which was difficult for me to understand. So I came here to today to bring with me a battle on the question." Trying a lot of discussion with him, I could suddenly comprehend the matter. Next day I visited him again and said to him, "Thank you. I've completely solved the problem." My solution was really for the very concept of time, that is, that time is not absolutely defined but there is an inseparable connection between time and the signal velocity. With this conception, the foregoing extraordinary difficulty could be thoroughly solved. Five weeks after my recognition of this, the present theory of special relativity was completed.*

—Albert Einstein in his Kyoto address, December 14, 1922[1]

There are times when wrestling with modeling results, it is important to consider what goes into the process. In particular, episodes arise where the results do not make sense based on some preconceived notion, and that notion has to be revisited. In such cases, reviewing where most modeling pitfalls arise often shines light on the problem, rendering a unique solution. Using a sounding board can often help to explore your thinking processes We visit that subject in this chapter and, like Einstein needed, offer views to the enterprising quant investor to function as the acoustic mirror sounding board, so to speak. To begin, we chatter a bit.

The starting point in any stock selection model has to do with investment philosophy and the universe of stocks chosen in which to obtain data. For Graham, in his day, there was a strong home bias because global diversification was not yet part of the vernacular. Even today, among retail investors in the United States, there is a strong bias to invest in U.S. markets before seeking exposure in the international arena. This is changing and there is a growing impetus to avail oneself of stocks headquartered in other countries these days. Moreover, the rise of Brazil, China, and India in this modern era is calling for more attention, as is the impact that sovereign wealth funds are having as they find investing opportunities for the huge accumulation of growing foreign reserves that many of the emerging market and middle eastern oil states have. For instance, China continues to buy U.S. Treasuries with its rapidly increasing current account surplus. The developed world continues to call for China to allow market forces to push their currency (Renminbi or Yuan) down. These secular forces are provoking discussions about China diversifying their reserves into other currencies and assets, which would ultimately create more demand for stocks.

It is increasingly obvious that allocating a larger percentage of assets in global markets will reward the shrewd enterprising investor going forward, especially as the developed world's GDP slows relative to its recent past and the size of the contribution to global GDP from emerging markets increases, because developed countries are suffering from middle-aged spread.

## DATA AVAILABILITY, LOOK-AHEAD, AND SURVIVORSHIP BIASES

The first step in building a quantitative model and process is to specify the universe of stocks in which investments will be made. It is important to consider the data availability, because some markets are just so illiquid that data collection is scare (e.g., micro-cap stocks or the pink sheets, vs. the S&P 100 for comparison). In addition, investors must consider the impact of several complications in data collection, namely, survivorship bias. Survivorship bias arises when only surviving companies remain in the database. This is common when examining mutual fund historical data, for many funds that were unsuccessful because of poor performance or were unable to raise sufficient assets went out of business. Moreover, when funds or firms go out of business, there is a bias toward remaining firms (funds) that were successful, resulting in an overestimation of performance when analyzing the historical database. A point-in-time data provider, Charter Oak Investment Systems, has this to offer:

> *The Point in Time concept, originally developed by Marcus C. Bogue III, Ph.D. at Charter Oak Investment Systems, Inc. properly restores the alignment of companies' historical market-related and fundamental elements, thereby removing random biases and data distortions which result from historical back-testing of restated company data using lag assumptions.*

A similar concern is look-ahead bias in data. Not too long ago, many databases containing fundamental data would actually replace data when, for instance, earnings were restated. Say, for example, that IBM released an earnings announcement on January 28 for the previous quarter ending December 31. The database vendors would then put that data in the database for December 31, but in actuality, the marketplace did not know what those earnings were until January 28. Likewise, even if the company restated their earnings 10 months later, the vendor would replace the December 31 earnings number with the restated data, when, in fact, the marketplace never knew that number until October of the following year. This is why the trend nowadays, for all quants who know their business, is for point-in-time data. Point-in-time data contains only information that the market knew on the date the market knew it; that is, a database that has only the information in it that was concurrent with what the market actually knew on that date. Therefore, nobody can come and edit the data after the fact to update any information. This allows reliable and consistent back-testing, not worrying about whether data is restated or not. It provides information to quants exactly as the market knew that information on the same day the investing public knew that information, on a day-to-day basis.

Look-ahead bias reveals itself in another way. It occurs in a model when there is overlap between forecasted periods of future return (the response or dependent variable) and predictor variables (independent variables). For instance, when downloading data, it is possible to unknowingly obtain some fundamental data from a database that is not point-in-time on some monthly ending date that the market did not know until, say, 28 days later. Hence, the data would show a P/E, say, for September 30 ending, when the market did not know it until October 24, but now there is, as the dependent variable, a return beginning on October 1. This means there is overlap in time between the independent and dependent variables. Another example would be a momentum function measuring returns from, say, August 31, 1998 to February 28, 1999, a 6-month momentum signal and the investor inadvertently uses a future return of, say, January 31 until June 30, 1999. In this case, the past momentum overlaps one month with the future return.

Now, there are some applicable steps the quantitative investor can take to mitigate some of the issues with look-ahead and survivorship bias. The first step is to always lag the data. That is, when gathering data to create a model, use a time lag between the data used to rank the stocks and the beginning of the time period in which to begin measuring return.

So, for example, if we create a model using data from December 31, 1990 to December 31, 2009, and this model is based on 12-month returns, then the first time period of data is December 31, 1989 to December 31,

1990, which is the time period of data collection for the predictor or independent variables (the right side of the model equations) consisting of valuation, fundamental, momentum, exogenous, and risk factors. Then, normally we would start to measure the performance of the model, by holding stocks ranked by the model as of January 31, 1991, creating a one-month lag to build the portfolio. Two months would even be better because many stocks do not announce their earnings from the last quarter of the prior year until February. Thus, if we started portfolio formation dates, say, on February 28, 1991, we would be sure that the majority of the companies would have reported and the market would have known their actual earnings by the portfolio formation date of February 28. The restated data of course would have put that earnings number back in the data on December 31, 1990, but by the time the holding period for portfolio formation got started, the market prices would have already reacted to the announcement.

This is one remedy often utilized; however, it does have drawbacks as just mentioned and obviously is not as good as original point-in-time data. To explain this drawback more clearly, consider postearnings announcement drift. For stocks that announce earnings before the lag begins, with either a strongly negative or positive earnings surprise, by the time the portfolio is formed and returns begin to be monitored using the lag method, the price may have moved down or up considerably by expiration of the lag, and the measured return would not be as accurate.

The survivorship bias issue is not as easily remedied, however, and really is problematic in modeling mutual funds. Academic researchers quite often go back and include the funds that actually merge or liquidate[2] in the data. However, that is tougher to do for the retail investor, and it is very time consuming. For databases of companies, it is not as large a problem. To see why, consider a typical index like the Russell 2000 or the S&P 500. When these indexes reconstitute every year, it is only at reconstitution time that they actually have 2000 and 500 stocks each, respectively. As the year progresses, companies are acquired, go bankrupt, get delisted, and so forth, and the number of stocks in the index falls. Sometimes this effect can be substantial and is particularly evident in small-cap indexes like the R2K. However, this also means that the performance bias that occurs because of survivorship exists in the reference index used against which to measure performance. In addition, if an investor is using these indexes to constitute the universe of stocks in which to create a model, the survivorship is exactly accounted for when measuring relative performance against an index; it is, however, not mitigated when constructing an absolute return model (i.e., as in a hedge fund). Thus, there is some natural selection working to mitigate the impact of survivorship bias when working with stocks as compared to mutual funds in this fashion. In addition, we must always remember that, typically, there are more mutual funds than actual stocks available for purchase, and the mutual fund birthing and demise rate is far higher for funds than stocks in the United States, which again serves to force the survivorship bias into a larger issue for modeling mutual funds than when working on stock-selection models. This mitigates but does not eradicate survivorship bias in company databases, however.

Thus, be mindful of the available data when selecting an investable universe. Pricing data is the easiest to acquire, unfortunately and since the Graham methodology makes use only of financial-statement data, access to this kind of data is more important. There are no momentum or volatility factors in the Graham methodology, so pricing is only important to compute valuation factors of P/B and P/E. Also, U.S. data and large-cap global companies are also the easiest (and cheapest) data to acquire.

Now there are some people so cheap that when they pull a dollar bill out of their wallet, George Washington is wearing sunglasses because he never sees the light of day. Alexander Hamilton, in these people's wallets, has gone blind. These investors will probably want to obtain free data over the Internet because, assuredly, Google knows where to get some. Nonetheless, there are serious concerns when using this free data. First, it is not clean. That is, there is no guarantee that the closing-price data is, indeed, what the last trade of the day was. Second, the price given is not guaranteed even to be for the security quoted. Third, there is no way of knowing if the data came from any of the actual exchanges or who scrubbed it, whether it is split adjusted in history or if it will continue to be made available going forward in time. Generally, using free stock market data from the Internet is not akin to creating a robust, stable consistent process for investing. My hunch is that Ben Graham would not have used free data from the Internet, had it been available in his day. Lastly, the data may not be timely. How many days from when a company reports earnings and other information to when it is posted on the Internet for downloading? Latency can be important, as can be stale pricing. Nevertheless, it is my belief that a great many people use this data regardless, but whenever you can obtain data from a reputable vendor and/or exchange, the lower the possibility for error in quantitative modeling.

## BUILDING MODELS YOU CAN TRUST

Another topic you must digest when it comes to quantitative modeling has to do with whether you can trust the model or not. This is a very large topic covering many disciplines in statistics and finance, and it even has bearing on your investment philosophy. Some of the trust comes from confidence in the art and some from the reported statistics ascertained by the quantitative process. Trust is also based on whether the major factors supporting the model come from your confidence in their stock-selection efficacy (i.e., people trust Ben Graham's investment methodology and philosophy, hence they will tend to trust a quantitative process built on the crucible of Ben's experience). In addition, investors accustomed to fundamental analysis or a traditional investment process point out that the major criticism of quantitative investing is that of its hindsight bias. We will deal with these issues one at a time in reverse order.

First, hindsight bias obviously exists. In earlier chapters, we noted that we all utilize past experience to make decisions about our future every day. In addition, Ben Graham did not utilize earnings estimate forecasts because he felt they were too inaccurate and had human bias (overly optimistic projections, for one) built in. However, many fundamental analysts purport to utilize earnings estimates all the time, even while they criticize the predictions of quants. This is hypocritical, and what exacerbates the criticism is that critics are generally unaware of the hypocritical nature of their accusations. Also, we have never known of a fundamental analyst who used "future" data in their analysis. (If you know of any who do, please invest with them, for they are way, way above average). Analysis is all backward looking and there can be no such thing as forward-looking insight. That is not even a reasonable statement to make.

Fundamental managers often depict quants as analogous to driving a car on a highway while looking in the rearview mirror to anticipate the future direction of the road from what they have already driven over, and a sharp right bend can easily overtake the quants' suppositions of the future direction of the road. Conversely, they position themselves as looking through the front windshield where they can actually see the future of the road they will be traveling over. The problem with this picture is that the future of a company's fortunes more closely follows its past than a highway does, and it has everything to do with the serial correlation of a stock price. In addition, a company's future is not seen clearly like the surface of a road. It is vague, unclear, and even the management of the company does not have a great view of its own future, let alone an analyst looking in from outside. It is deceptive to believe that because you are thinking about future business sales and future margins of a company, that mere thinking about it can predict the company's future with any accuracy, or that your thinking is a more accurate art than is the science of forming relationships with past trends and forecasting the future through quantitative techniques. This kind of talk adds no value but is popular; it falls within the camp of good marketing. It offers no higher returns than quantitative methodologies. In fact, Josef Lakonishok of LSV Asset Management presented a talk at the Nomura conference in May of 2010 that studied returns from quant vs. fundamentally managed assets in the large-cap space and found several things:

1. The variation among quants in alpha is as wide as among fundamentally managed portfolios.
2. The returns to quant have been as consistent as fundamentally managed firms except for the 2008–2009 time frame and that failure can be traced to the use of price momentum as a factor, which has seen an unprecedented failure in its stock selection efficacy recently.

Consider that long before quantitative strategies were widely in practice, mutual funds, on average, still underperformed their indexes, and the great majority of their returns led to Vanguard's beginnings and to John Bogle's criticisms, reported earlier in this book, which argued that investment managers cannot beat the market in the long run. Those comments were aimed at traditional asset management, not at the modern quants, because there were not any in business at the time (though I am sure he would say the same about quants today).

The second issue involving trust has to do with the investment philosophy of the quant, because you must remember that, to the quant, the black box (so to speak) is not black but it is quite clearly encased and entirely transparent. The model is the embodiment of the quant's investing philosophy, and the factors in the underlying model were chosen for a reason. The perma-bear, Jeremy Grantham, at GMO lost 60 percent of GMO's asset base in the tech bubble. Clients fired GMO because their investments underperformed the bench, but the company's principles made them get out of growth stocks when valuations got way out of hand. What the company was doing was entirely transparent at the time. Therefore, the investment philosophy utilized in a quant process can express conviction, avoid human behavioral biases, and maintain robustness by offering reproducibility and higher quality control than can a purely traditional asset management process. This is all part of the three elements of trust: reliability, competence, and sincerity. A quant process demonstrates reliability by good testing, periodic in-depth analysis, and good performance in the back-testing process. Competence comes about from the selection of financial and economic data utilized in constructing the model, certainly using Graham's factors one can lean on. Lastly, sincerity is a human element, and as long as quant investors have focused their attention on the first principle of money management, which is to avoid losing money and taking undue risk, sincerity becomes automatically embodied in the quantitative process.

Furthermore, sincerity implies complete transparency, which mandates honesty with the quantitative process constructed. By asking yourself, "Have

I made assumptions based on good financial and economic sense?" or "Am I really being objective in using this factor?" clarity of purpose and objective will be illuminated. To give an example of this, consider that Graham used a look-back period of dividends consisting of payment over the last 20 years. Quant investors should ask themselves, "Is this still relevant today?" because of the rapidity of the economic environment these days. If the investment objective is more small-cap related, dividends in general are hardly paid in that asset size cohort. So the answer chosen will ultimately be incorporated in the quantitative model, and the investor's trust in that model will be partially dependent upon how the investor answers those questions. The more thought, sincerity, and attention given to answering those questions, the more trustworthy will be the model.

The last element involved in gaining trust of the model comes about directly from the quantitative approaches, methods, and measures calculated through the algorithms of model construction. These are technical in nature and are borrowed from the fields of statistics and physics both in terms of formulation and practice. The good news here is that these methods can be taught and are required to gain model confidence and avoid model risk, whereas investment philosophy is more nebulous and only comes about from experience, taught to us by great investors like Ben Graham, Warren Buffett, Jeremy Grantham, Peter Lynch, Bill Gross, and Robert Rodriguez.

To begin the systematic measures, you must employ standard measures of return, as in 6- and 12-month return from portfolios constructed from ranked stocks from the model, as well as the standard deviation of return, the skewness, and kurtosis of the return distribution from the model's top, middle, and bottom decile return time series must be calculated regularly from a portfolio's return distributions. The tracking error, Sharpe ratio, information ratio, information coefficient (correlation of model's rank with ranked stock's return), and hit rates (of which there are two kinds) are components needed in decision making about whether to accept or reject a model. The two hit rates are the percentage of times the decile (or octile, quintile, or quartile) outperforms its index (or outperforms cash if it is an absolute return model) and the average percentage of stocks within a decile that outperforms its index over time. Also, drawdowns, up and down capture ratios, and examining the model in different environments should also be performed. There are additional tests that can be done that we will reveal when we review actual examples. These tests are for the more sophisticated enterprising investor and involve sample bootstraps, for instance. All these tests serve to create confidence and reliability in the model in addition to mitigating the chance of constructing a model based on spurious relationships and associations of factors with returns. These measures are the performance characteristics calculated from the return time series of model results, but they suggest nothing about the statistics calculated from the model's output before you run the model to rank stocks and produce returns.

In the model itself, the output of the regression involves coefficients mainly and the statistics associated with confidence in these coefficients are *t*-stats and what we like more, *p*-values. Other features of the model and various incarnations of the model that investors like to see are stable coefficients across time series and from model to model. For instance, if you have a model with B/P as a factor, and you run regressions of future return over differing subtime-periods, you can create a time series of regression coefficients to this factor. So say you have a one-factor model of 15 years of monthly data on B/P and the concomitant return for stocks constituting the Russell 1000 index. Then, if you regress lagged future 6-month stock return against B/P in 3-year rolling time segments and you see that the regression coefficient varies wildly from 0.34 to −0.26 and back to 0.27 multiple times over the course of 15 years, then this would suggest this factor is not stable and probably should be avoided for use in a stock-selection model. This is not to say that B/P behaves that way; it is just an example. Thus a major theme is model stability over time and in differing environments, and by monitoring the time-series behavior of the betas to factors you willingly remove structural inconsistencies in model construction. This will become clearer as you work through some examples.

## SCENARIO, OUT-OF-SAMPLE, AND SHOCK TESTING

Lastly and importantly are testing through different market environments or, to use military jargon, scenario testing. There are many ways to slice and dice the market and the most common methods are simply to examine how a factor or model behaves in up and down markets, growth and value markets, and high-volatility and low-volatility markets. Recently, because of the junk rally in 2009, we have been called to closely examine models in both high-quality and low-quality markets. Likewise, State Street Global Research has defined five different market environments in a regime map determined by examining the cross-border flows from 45 countries covered by MSCI, which consist of two positive environments for securities, called leverage and liquidity abounds, and two negative for equities called riot point and safety first.[3] They have a neutral signal, too. We cannot show the map because it must be color coded. However, Figure 5.1 depicts what regimes the market is in at various times historically. From this timeline, one would collect model performance in one regime, examine its behavior and

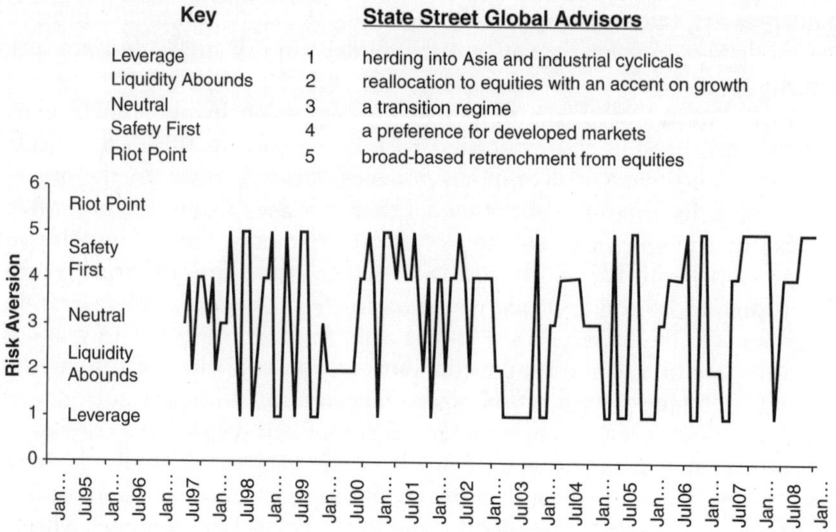


**FIGURE 5.1** State Street Global Advisors Regime Map

performance only within that regime, and compare it to its performance in other regimes. Again, model stability is what you are looking for.

It is extremely difficult for one model, composed of a single investment philosophy, to perform adequately in all time periods. This was seen in earlier plots of factors, where we saw that, during the technology bubble, model failure usually occurred and efficacy waned as you moved from one time period to another. If, in fact, you have great performance in all time periods and all markets, then that is usually a signal that there is look-ahead bias or a large amount of data mining going on, or some weird calculation error. Only God's model is that good! You must be very careful to avoid hubris with a model, and if it performs too well, that should be interpreted as a negative signal.

Due to technological change, market psychology, and business cycles, the economy is in a constant state of flux and is, in fact, dynamic. Certain sectors of the economy will outperform others. By testing the models in differing environments, the impact that any one cycle has on the model is tested, allowing careful selection of the final model and avoiding selecting a model that works best strictly in one scenario.

You are somewhat free to create market time periods in which to test a factor suite or model through, but you should be aware of two things: (1) there must be an amount of time in a single market to produce enough data to offer statistical significance, and (2) it should be determined by some quantitative or reproducible measure. For instance, you can create volatility regimes by using the VIX as a signal. Periods of time when the VIX is above the median VIX measured over the last 20 years is one regime; periods when it is below the 20-year median VIX is another. Also you could compare the long-term versus short-term VIX, the one-year vs. thirty-day VIX. In general, the difference between the two is zero over long time frames, so monitoring whether the short-term VIX is greater than the long- term VIX can easily be used as a flag for the kind of market environment you are in.

Another measure to test through is when markets are dominated by growth stocks versus value stocks; you could use this measure when the Russell 1000 Growth index is outperforming the Russell 1000 Value index, for instance. It is not necessarily a condition that these periods of time defining differing markets have a time scale appropriate to invest in. For instance, you don't need to have a continuous environment in existence greater than the expected holding period for the investment process you are building to test through, for in fact, you would concatenate the small periods together to make a longer continuous stretch of time to test through. This is because, in production, you cannot predict the future market environment, and the ying and yang of market forces create any market scenario it wants. Therefore, testing across market environments is not akin to investing in particular prolonged markets. In other words, suppose you have defined a market environment of a high-frequency nature, say, of the order of three weeks in a single down state that switches to the up state about every three or four weeks and later down again and so on. But if you have 16 years of weekly return data of the switching environment, then the continuous sum of a single state is 8 years of data, which is enough time in which to test a model through, though the longest consecutive period of a state may have only been, say, for 6 weeks. For testing purposes, it is not a requirement that the market environments be continuously sequential, just that the sum of time over all periods be long enough to offer statistical significance in testing.

Other examples include removing periods of time thought to be extraordinary for model building. For instance, some quants we know remove the technology bubble from the time period used when creating the model, but they put it back in again when running the back-test performance measure. They do this because they tend to think of the technology bubble of 2000 as an anomaly that they believe will not occur for a generation. They also can show that the technology bubble was a period of time when valuation measures completely broke down and that if they include this time period when constructing a valuation model, indeed they obtain regression coefficients to value factors that are unstable. However, they say, if you remove just 1.5 years of bubble from a 20-year history of the data, the valuation factor coefficients stabilize completely. Are they justified in doing this? Well, do you have more trust in a model created with or without the bubble period included? It is a very personal question. Graham's investment philosophy did not change much through the crash of 1929, which leads me to believe your investment philosophy embodied in your quantitative model should not, either (except on the margins). You can interpret this to mean that you should choose to ignore or include the technology bubble in your testing process but do so consistently.

At this juncture it is important to discuss out-of-sample testing and its ramifications in model results. Out-of-sample testing is a methodology that was invented to reduce the possibility of data mining and for obtaining model validation. For instance, assume you have 20 years' worth of returns (the dependent or response variable) and fundamental data (the independent, explanatory, or predictor variables) with which to construct a model. The idea behind out-of-sample testing is to fit a model to some major period of time, like 15 years, and to hold out the last 5 years' worth of data with which to test your model through later, with the hope of validating the model by testing to see if it is effective in a period of time that was not used to build the model. It is akin to putting the model through a real investment period, except you don't have to wait 5 years of real time to see if the model's working. For example, if the forecaster withholds all data about events occurring after the end of the fit period, the evaluation is identical to the real world in which we stand in the present and forecast the future. If we utilize any data from the out-of-sample period, we risk infecting the whole experiment.

This is a good idea, but it is mostly misapplied, and there are serious drawbacks to out-of-sample testing. First, it is a widely held belief that models created from a data set (in-sample) do not guarantee significant out-of-sample predictability. This is usually interpreted that the in-sample model construction process may be subject to data mining and is more likely to be contaminated by spurious correlations and, therefore, should be discounted. Similarly, in-sample tests tend to reject the null hypothesis of *no predictability* more often than do their out-of-sample counterparts. It is with this conventional wisdom that researchers are encouraged to pursue out-of-sample testing on their models.

However, to create an out-of-sample population, sample splitting must occur, which results in a loss of information and lower predictive power due to smaller sample sizes. Therefore, it may fail to detect predictability that the in-sample test would have found in some future real out-of-sample period. Also, to claim that out-of-sample testing is without data mining is incorrect because out-of-sample testing is mostly used in a cross-validation construct. That is, the researcher keeps iterating over different models with the in-sample data, until they obtain a preferred out-of-sample result. Read that last sentence again aloud. Thus, out-of-sample inference is subject to exactly the same potential of data snooping as is in-sample testing. In addition, the literature citations encouraging the use of out-of-sample testing come almost entirely from comparing models created from overlapping time periods (nesting). It can be highly misleading to compare in-sample nested models with out-of-sample tests. Hence, bootstrapping the model in-sample returns to get more random samples on which to build the model can offer higher confidence in model construction than can the iterative out-of-sample testing technique.

Bootstrapping with replacement is such a powerful statistical method that it is absolutely uncanny, but it is not a miracle-working machine either, though when we reveal it here, you may think it is! It is the Hannibal of the statistics world nonetheless. It began to appear rigorously in the statistical literature after 1979 and is used to offer confidence about any statistic measured from a subset of a larger population, offering insight about the statistic's value of the larger population. The most common application of the bootstrap is to estimate confidence intervals about the mean of a large population, based on drawing a small sample out of the much larger population. However, it can also be used to replicate the large population from the smaller sample and allow confidence limits that will apply to the larger sample. Statistical packages like SAS, S-Plus, and R all have precanned functions available for bootstrapping.

For instance, suppose you lack a huge population, a long time period, or a large universe of stocks in a dataset. Say, for example that you have only 5 years' worth of data and wish you had 20. Any mean, median, or standard deviation computed from the 5 years' worth of weekly data ($5 \times 52$ or 260 data points) would not represent accurately what the mean of the 20 years' worth of data might be, if you had it. In this situation, all you need to do is draw another sample from the original sample, with replacement. Thus, each drawn data point has the probability of being drawn 1/260, just as if you were drawing from the original larger population with no replacement. This is the bootstrap. Statistics calculated from these new samples, created from the original sample, offer a distribution of the statistic. From this distribution, we can ascertain confidence intervals.

To see this method at work, suppose you have 5 years' worth of weekly returns data, but wish to have 20 years of data or more. If you draw sets of data from the five years of returns, 100 times, you will create 100 sets of replicated datasets, each as long as the original 5 years' worth of data. Each dataset might have drawn multiple times the same value, of course (that is what replacement does), and each dataset will have its own mean, standard deviation, or any statistic you want to calculate. Thus, you will have 100 means, 100 standard deviations, and so forth, one from each replicated dataset. These 100 values will create a distribution of means, from which you can calculate confidence intervals. Therefore, you record these means, and you can read the 95 percent confidence interval about the mean from this distribution. You can be highly confident (but not absolutely sure) that the real mean from the much larger dataset you do not have will fall within this confidence interval. It must be added that this is what is known as a non-parametric approach and that no assumption about normality or about the larger distribution actually is necessary; it computes accurately the variability of the measure desired. Not only is it powerful, but it is loads of fun to calculate if you have any geeky genes in you at all!

The programming languages R and S+Plus both have built in bootstrap functions. Every budding quant should immediately download the Comprehensive R Archive Network from http://cran.r-project.org/ and install R on your laptop. First, for those with the blind Alexander Hamilton $10 bills in their wallets, they will especially love R because it has most of the same functionality as MATLAB or Octave, S+Plus, and has a complete statistical package available along with many other specialty libraries all freely available in the R network.

Rather than do out-of-sample testing and hold back 5 years' worth of data out of 20, use the whole 20 years' worth of data to create the model and test the model through. Then run bootstraps on the returns to create confidence limits about average return, Sharpe ratio, variance of return, and so forth. This is the preferred method and it can even easily be done in Excel using its "rand()," random number generator function.

Another great type of model building, in my opinion, involves any of the dynamic methods of model construction. These are examples of a great use of out-of-sample testing with hold-out periods, provided they are forecasting forward in time by just one period. So, for example, assume you have 20 years' worth of data again, the idea is to use the first 5 years of data to build a model and forecast 6 months ahead. Then, move forward in time 6 months, incorporating those 6 months ahead of data, while omitting from the back end the first 6 months' worth of data. In this fashion, you have a rolling model in which the coefficients from the regression are changed ever so slightly, so that the model evolves slowly and incorporates the new view one period at a time. Assuming monthly data, each forecast has 59 data points in this example, identical to the previous forecast with only the one new data point added in each iteration, replacing the one data point falling off. Hint: 48 months or longer are needed, though, for general model stability, using financial statement data ascertained from experience.

In general for out-of-sample testing, the expert literature on the subject would contend there is no evidence that model distortions due to data mining are more prevalent for in-sample tests than out-of-sample tests,[4] too, and concludes that results of in-sample tests of predictability will typically be more credible than results of out-of-sample tests. Another published work undertook an extensive analysis of both in-sample and out-of-sample tests of stock return predictability.[5] They conclude that there is not a great deal of difference or discrepancy between results for in-sample or out-of-sample testing in predictive models for a number of commonly used financial variables and claim that the literature appears to overstate the degree of disparity between in-sample and out-of-sample test results. A third paper concludes that firm-specific regressions perform more poorly than pooled regressions and that out-of-sample predictions from firm-specific regressions are no more accurate then pooled in-sample regressions.[6] Basically, our views would suggest that if the model outperforms above expectation during the out-of-sample test period, we would overestimate its capability, and if it underperforms, we might reject the model. Or at the very least, we might change it to get better performance in the out-of-sample time period (i.e., data mining).

A real world example occurred once when we showed results of a model back test, of 167 six-month holding period returns from the top ranked stocks of a model. As we debated about putting a model into production based on these results, a fundamental analyst suggested we run a paper portfolio for six months to see how the model would work out-of-sample. We then explained that if we did that, it would mean we would now have 168 data points in which to make an analysis, and that if this last six-month return was really good, we would be completely overconfident in the model. If it underperformed, we would throw away the model. In essence, therefore, we would be using the last data point and it alone in which to make a decision. Moreover, if that was so, we need not create a model to run over the previous 167 six-month holding periods. We could have just sat down and bought stocks using these factors, held them for six months on paper, and our decision would have been just as good. The occurrence of this event informs me that most people do not really understand quantitative and statistical methods applied to finance. It is seemingly unreasonable to someone trained in the hard sciences that anyone would think like this. Thus, the motivation to write this book came from this experience expressly.

However, there are many ways of performing out-of-sample testing properly. Google knows many methods. To be truthful, out-of-sample testing is extremely useful when one has noisy data. Now, financial data is not really noisy, not in the true sense of the word; the data is real and somewhat accurate. For instance, P/B is a number, profits and earnings are actually accurate numbers, the noise in financial data is not white noise, the cause of its noise is estimation error. When you have data that is hidden among true white noise, like a 50 micro-amp signal among a 500 micro-amp noisy background collected from some radio-astronomy or optically detected magnetic resonance signal, this is white noise and then holding out a sample from the data used in model construction is useful. Then, the signal found in sample with a noisy background is given a theory and fit to a model of this theory. The model is then used to predict the out-of-sample data and one can test the model's predictions versus the out-of-sample data. In this usage, rightfully so, one doesn't adjust the model to get a good fit to the out-of-sample data. To adjust the model predicated on the out-of-sample results in this vein is clearly data mining.

We favor building multifactor models and testing through differing market environments for a stock selection model, but using the whole time period in which to build a model. However, you can create subperiods of the whole market (growth, value, up, down, high volatility, low volatility, junk, quality) and build models just from each period. Afterward, they can be tested through the whole time period to see which one is most stable. Then, of course, if you have a regime-switching model, to advise about what state of the market you are in, you could use whichever model works best in the regime you are in for production. This would be the best of all worlds, I suppose.

Another great idea is to shock the model. Suppose we use the whole time period of data to create a model. Next, copy the in-sample data so as not to corrupt the original data set and prepare the copied data set to run the model through for testing, but first, manually infuse some hypothetical and outlandish values for the fundamental, valuation, or momentum factors (the exposures) in the copied model. Doing this shocks the independent predictor variables of the data while keeping the factor returns (the betas) constant, after you have already created the model on their real values. Then, when the model is used to rank the stocks using the shocked data, one can measure its effectiveness and stock selection capabilities on this corrupted data set.

Finally, another form of stress testing can be performed using the backtested results from your alpha or risk model, whereby you go back in time to some stressful period, oil price spike, LTCM debacle, Iraq invasion, 9/11, or Internet bubble and obtain the factor returns, the betas from the risk model in that period. Then, using these old betas, multiply them by current exposures (factors) and calculate the returns. The difference between the returns calculated using old betas versus new betas suggests the possibilities that could occur. If it spells doom to your portfolio, then when Lady Luck is not on your side, she's departed and you'd better get on the boat with her by making adjustments to the model or portfolio and move on.

## DATA SNOOPING AND MINING

*Data snooping* or *data mining* generally refers to finding correlations between data and assuming relationships within data that do not actually exist (i.e., correlation does not prove causality). Data snooping is a real issue in finance where many analysts have time to pore over large amounts of data in the pursuit of an infallible predictor of excess returns. Although it is impossible to completely avoid, there are steps to reduce the possibility of data snooping and to minimize its effects. For instance, the dangers of data snooping are more severe when large bets are placed on a single factor. Thus, testing for robustness both individually and in the context of a combined factor model through scenario analysis and statistical confidence interval testing is recommended. In this regard, the role of probability theory needs to be utilized in model construction, not simply correlative structural assessments, which is why we seek time-stable correlations and regression-coefficient betas along with significant *t*-stats.

Factors need to be tested in a variety of market environments and in economic sectors. It is our philosophy to combine quantitative analysis with a traditional fundamental approach. This is precisely why we are using Ben Graham's method and building a quantitative model around it. Whenever historical information is used as a guide to forecast the future, there is a risk that there may be a schism with the past. The risk is always present that nuances of the past do not occur in the future, or that future nuances were not there in the past to model. By maintaining awareness of economic and fundamental changes while monitoring the performance of the models, the risk of being caught unprepared in an unexpected market environment is reduced (but not eliminated). The use of quantitative models does not require eliminating the role of human intelligence in the process. It just means removing human involvement where it does not add value, where it interferes with selecting optimal portfolios, or where it may introduce unwanted behavioral biases. It is within this context that the enterprising investors can devote their energy to controlling the quality of their process by advocating and using a quantitative model.

In Graham's method, all of his factors have a strong basis in economic theory and the financial literature. Perhaps the first and best defense against the criticism of data mining is that the factors must make economic sense. Using factors based on financial statement or publicly available data that offer a fundamental, bottom-up approach is not only wise, but applying them correctly offers a margin of safety both from model risk and investment risk. Each stock can be analyzed individually to understand why the model has chosen to add it to the portfolio by examining its underlying factors and fundamentally interpreting its foundations.

## STATISTICAL SIGNIFICANCE AND OTHER FASCINATIONS

It is unfortunate that we have to cover some esoteric, statistical material in this section, but it is necessary in order to explain why some people criticize the use of quantitative methods in finance. By no means, however, will these topics be covered in expert depth or will an attempt be made to convey expertise. The first topic involves heteroskedacity, which is measured from the outcome of a regression model's residuals.

So, to begin, what are residuals? When you have a model created forecasting stock returns, you measure the prediction versus the actual returns in the time series. The difference between the forecast and the actual returns are the residuals. Now, this is for in-sample data only; it is only measured for the data used to make the model. After the model is created, then you use the model to make in-sample forecasts and measure the difference between the model's forecast and the actual returns used to make the model.

To make this understandable, suppose you have 1,000 stocks' returns for a given time period and hence $N \times 1000$ valuation, fundamental, and momentum variables for use as the independent (predictor) variables. Let $N = 3$, just for fun, so we have B/P, earnings growth, and six-month price momentum as our three factors for each stock so that our model equation looks like this:

$$R_i = w_{v,i} * B/\mathrm{P}_i + w_{f,i} * \mathrm{EarnGro}_i + w_{m,i} * 6\mathrm{MonMom}_i + \mathrm{alpha}$$

where $R$ is future six-month return, the $w$'s are coefficients determined by regression for valuation, fundamental, and momentum, respectively, and the subscript $i$ represents stock $i$. Next, pretend we have 15 years' worth of monthly ending data, hence we have $12 \times 15$ time periods or 180 time periods. This constitutes the back-test period. Thus, combining all this data, we have a column of returns on the left side of the model equation that is 1000 stocks $\times$ 180 time periods long, or 180,000 rows of data. Likewise, on the right are three columns of data, each also 180,000 elements long. Since each of the time periods is composed of six-month returns for a given single month-ending date, we have overlaid time periods or nested data, and because all time periods are concatenated, we have pooled data. This would be one big nested-pooled regression calculation if the regression were done this way (and many times it is).

The left side of the model equation makes up actual future returns over the back-test period. Now, given that we have this model regressed, we have solved for the $w$'s and alpha term, which is the intercept of the regression in this simple format. Think of the intercept using the $Y = mX + b$ simple linear construct while plotting $X$ versus $Y$. This would represent a line given by the equation using slope ($m$) and intercept ($b$) coefficients determined through regression; slope $m$ and intercept $b$ would cross the $Y$ axis at height $b$. Alpha in this simple analogy is the intercept.

After we perform the regression, we have the coefficients and we can use the right side of the model now to make forecasts given the values for the stocks of B/P, earnings growth, and past momentum for a given time period. Thus, for each stock's actual future return $R_i$, we have a forecast $F_i$. Again, remembering the term *future return* here means only a return six months ahead of the period in which you measure B/P, earnings growth, and six-month momentum. It does not mean out-of-sample future return. So if we plot the left side of the equation, the $R_i$'s versus the right side's calculated $F_i$'s, in a scatter plot, we would get a picture as shown in Figure 5.2, using the first 100 data points of this hypothetical model.

The ordinate is the forecasted returns $F_i$ and the actual returns are $R_i$ on the abscissa. Now do not let the fact that all returns are positive in this example throw you; it is purely a hypothetical illustration. Obviously, if the model fit the data perfectly, all the data points would lie in a straight line. The difference, formed by $R_i - F_i$, constitutes the residuals of the regression, and a plot of this difference is shown in Figure 5.3 for the first 100 data points.

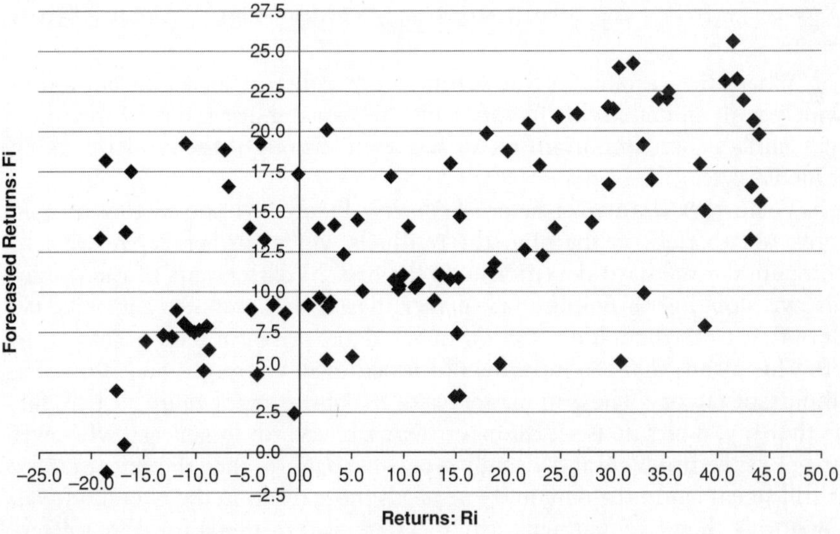


**FIGURE 5.2** Scatter Plot of Actual versus Forecasted Returns

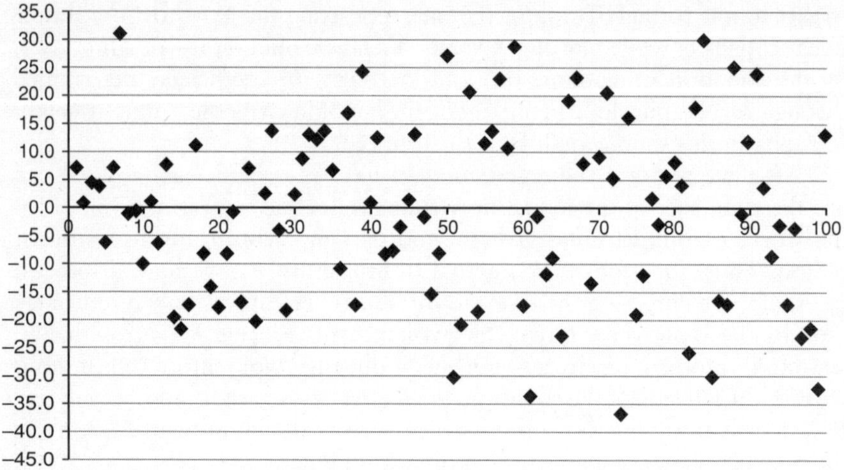


**FIGURE 5.3** Residuals of Actual versus Forecasted Returns

The interpretation of this particular plot serves to illustrate the impact of heteroskedacity. Notice as one observes the spread of the data, as one moves from left to right, that it widens or tends to increase with the $X$ axis. This means that the variance of the error terms from the regression is not constant. The model now becomes:

$$R_i = w_{v,i} * B/\mathrm{P}_i + w_{f,i} * \mathrm{EarnGro}_i + w_{m,i} * 6\mathrm{MonMom}_i + \mathrm{Alpha} + \mathrm{Errors}$$

Where the variance of the errors is not constant anymore but varies widely with an underlying factor. Thus the growing dispersion of the residuals implies some important factor has been left out of the model, making it incomplete.

To further dramatize heteroskedacity, Figure 5.4 shows that as you move left to right in the plot, the residuals widen further. If we were to compute the standard deviation over the first 20 data points of the residuals, we would get a number far smaller than if we computed the standard deviation from the middle section of the data, say from data points 50 to 70. This means that the model is ill-formed or ill-conceived and is missing important factors. The graphic serves to make this point more clearly, for, as they say, a picture is worth more than a kiloword. In general, whenever one plots the residuals and visually sees some pattern, then that means there is still signal left in the data and one needs more terms in the overall model. Obviously there are mathematical and statistical methods for signal detection in residuals but they're beyond the scope of this book.

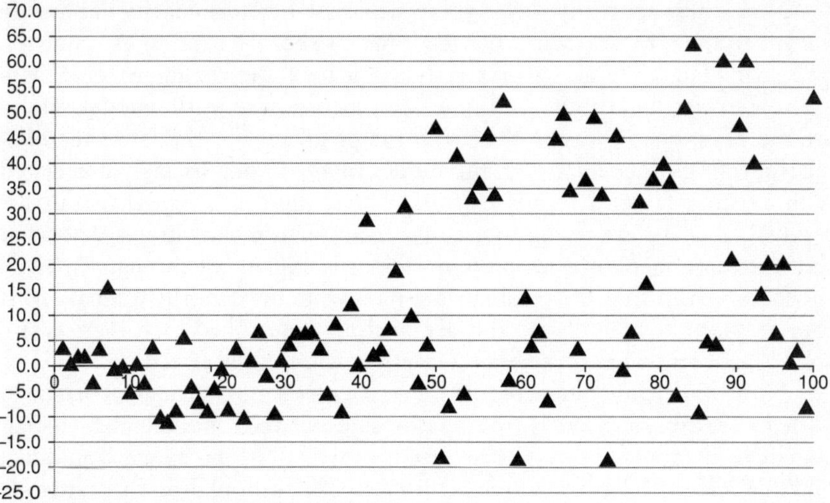


**FIGURE 5.4** Residuals Displaying Heteroskedacity

To offer a real-world example of heteroskedacity in motion, consider a drivers' course. Suppose we have 100 16-year-olds who have never driven before. In the beginning of the course, we force the students to negotiate a narrow swerving road course outlined with orange cones. At first, many of the students run over the cones, and there will be a wide dispersion of how many cones the students hit. However, as they progress through the course and gain experience, they hit the cones less and less. Finally, at end of the course, the dispersion has mostly gone away. Hence there is a nonconstant variance of performance of the students with time. Another example would be income as a function of education. The more years of education you have, the larger the probability of higher income and hence a wider dispersion. This matches intuition as, most likely, the income from among 100 PhD's varies much more widely than does the income from 100 high school dropouts. Consider the income disparity between a brain surgeon and a history professor of a 4-year college in central Idaho who have roughly the same number of years in university compared to the difference in income between a mason worker and garage mechanic. So if we formed a model of income as a function of years of education and age of worker, we would probably see a divergence of the residuals of the model if we plotted the residuals versus years of education—for, though income generally increases with years of experience (i.e., age of worker), it hardly varies as much as it does with education.

Now, there are many ways experts deal with heteroskedacity but mostly it's left to them to deal with. For us, it means that we need to examine the underlying factors to see which is responsible for the effect and to see if there are some other important factors we can incorporate in the model. Those are the practioner's way to deal with the problem. For the latter method, incorporating other factors in the model (that are not strongly correlated with existing factors) means essentially that there is a signal left in the residuals that we are trying to account for it. This demonstrates that what the regression method is trying to do for us is explain all the signals, given the factors such that the residuals are like white noise in their behavior. If they are not like white noise and demonstrate heteroskedacity, there is still some signal left. That is the easiest interpretation of the effect.

Now, financial-statement data in general is not strongly correlated with future return. That is, the relationship between individual financial-statement data and future returns is not nearly as strong as we would like and that most MBA's believe when they get out of school. It is difficult to get your mind around the weak relationship between financial-statement data with company performance after you spend two years analyzing case study after case study while deep in the bowels of accounting details investigating its impact on a company's earnings. So, you must be mindful that a correlation of even a powerful factor like price to book is only of the order of 5 percent or so. This is weak, even though it is a good factor. The three most powerful factors based on cross-sectional correlation alone with future six-month return are valuation, momentum, and individual (idiosyncratic) volatility. So if you correlate B/P, six-month momentum, and six-month daily stock volatility, you have about the largest correlations with future six-month return that you will find for individual stocks, meaning they have a long-term average correlation of around 5 percent each, give or take. At this point most of you would give up and buy an index fund. Well, it turns out that this little bit of correlation is all that is necessary to obtain outsized returns. It is also important to understand that, when you perform a regression of returns against the typical suite of economically important, financial-statement variables, the $R^2$ of the regression, which is a kind of measure of goodness of fit, is usually also small. It is not unusual to obtain an $R^2$ of less than 20 percent for explanatory variables in stock selection models, and it is nothing to be shy about if achieved.

Additionally, you must remember that in an ideal situation, all the factors that make up a model would be completely uncorrelated with each other, making what mathematicians would call an orthogonal set. Nonetheless, in finance that is not the case. We state that, again, it is just not the situation with financial-statement data that the predictor variables are independent of each other. Statisticians refer to this problem of correlated variables as co-linearity. Even the variables utilized in a model as good as Ben Graham's are going to have some correlation. Statistical independence of the explanatory, predictor, or independent variables—whatever one likes to call them—is a concern in modeling. The correlation between the independent variables constitutes a weakness in calculating regression coefficients. It turns out that the more correlation there is between the explanatory variables, the greater the standard errors and the less precisely the regression coefficients will be estimated from the data set. Thus, the choice of factors is important, almost as important that they be logically connected with return in a fundamental way (i.e., economic variables as opposed to weather conditions, zip codes, and dress sizes) as that they have weak correlation with each other. This means, generally, that if one chooses valuation factors like price to book and price to earnings for input in a model, that one might want to consider the ramifications of having both of these highly correlated variables in the regression equation—because they are correlated means that they each explain some identical portion of the return.

So given the fact that financial-statement data are more weakly correlated with future return than desired and have correlations among one another that are far from zero, what's a quant to do? The technical treatment involves employing a principal component analysis (PCA) where the underlying factors are in a sense rotated and added together to form orthogonal factors with which to run models. The purpose of PCA is to reduce a data set containing a large number of variables to a new data set containing far fewer new variables but that are represented by a fraction of the variability contained in the original data, so that following PCA provides a number of principal components, each of which constitutes a compact representation of the original data. This is commonly done in many fields of econometrics, some social sciences, and statistical weather forecasting especially. It is often used when modeling yield curves and interest rates in fixed-income-investment quant approaches.

However, there is a loss of explanatory power due to these newly created PCA factors being combinations of the previous factors mixing their interpretation. For instance, how does one interpret "$0.78*B/P + 0.24*ROE - 0.32*Momentum$" as a single factor? For this reason, fundamentally trained analysts and clients usually reject such a methodology, though factor analysis has been shown to be effective everywhere it has been applied. Surely proprietary trading desks and hedge funds that lack transparency frequently treat the data more often like this, but typical type-2 quants in an institutional long-only asset-management shop usually avoid PCA.

If you have to avoid factor analysis like PCA, the evidence that even heuristics (sorting) built from fundamental data can offer outsized returns implies that even with these constraints, constructing a model from correlated financial-statement data works because of the impact of cause and effect.[7] In essence, simple sorts on valuation combined with momentum factors can produce a portfolio that outperforms. Cliff Asness founded AQR Capital Management and has built a successful business around this application and its exploitation. To see why, we must return to physics and employ instances of observable cause-and- effect examples to illustrate how this can occur. Just because there is a problem with the mathematics in standard regression when co-linearity exists is no reason to believe nature is confined by this constraint, for this is just a mathematical difficulty. For "reality must take precedence over public relations, for nature cannot be fooled," said the late physicist Richard Feynman.[8] One example, therefore, involves something as natural as weather forecasting and another uses car pricing, offering a market phenomenon as proxy.

Components of weather-forecasting data such as precipitation; humidity; ground reflectivity; snowfall cover; wind velocity; cloud cover; and average, minimum, and maximum daily temperatures that are used in a deterministic (Navier-Stokes mathematical models of several linked differential equations) solution to weather prediction have inherent correlations to one with another. Relevant predictor variables are almost always mutually correlated in nature. The fact that these correlations between weather's fundamental variables exist does not inhibit their impact on what the future weather will be, for they are the influencers of weather. For instance, cloud cover and daily temperature have an inherent correlation, as does ground infrared reflectivity and snow cover, yet the cause and effect between these variables and future weather are inherent in the process, hence they offer clues to future weather, even though they are correlated.

Another example is very simple but involves the pricing of used cars. This is a Hannibal of an example. Suppose we wanted to create a model for pricing used cars, given three predicting variables: vintage, miles, and make. Google knows it does not take gifted brilliance to conclude that age of the vehicle and miles on the odometer are correlated, yet both are indeed necessary to determine a price for the car. Also the make of the vehicle has to have an association with year because there is always a beginning vintage for a given make, and we would certainly want to know the make of the vehicle to gauge the car's price. For instance, it cannot be that a 1995 BMW M3 with 32,000 miles will cost the same as 1995 Dodge Colt with 32,000 miles on the odometer. Oops, the Dodge Colt stopped production in 1994, see what we mean? Now, obviously, the "other" major contribution to the used car price includes the accessories. In addition, to a given buyer, color, and whether the car was driven in winter along with other qualitative features that are not in a three-factor model (consisting of vintage, miles, and make) offer small contributions to the predicted price. But probably those three are the major drivers (pun intended) of used car prices and, like our stock selection model, capture the majority of the variance of the response, though they are correlated. In this very simple market analogy, the predicting independent variables are indeed correlated and yet the used-car pricing model still works due to the cause of the effect implicit in this example.

The fact that one can find natural examples and market examples where correlated independent variables exist to collectively offer insight into the model's response doesn't negate the responsibility of the investor to choose predictor variables with as little correlation as one can find. Again, the reason we want to avoid the factor correlation is because, intrinsically, the mathematical methods involved in regression have a tough time assigning what part of the explanation to two variables that are correlated. For instance, take the extreme example of two variables that have correlation of 0.93, a very high correlation but not 1.0 in a model with three other variables not correlated with any other. The numerical method employed to solve the regression in a least-squares sense does not easily determine which variable to attribute explanation to. If the order of the variables is X1 and X2, it will assign most of the variance to X1. If the variable the algorithm gets to first is X2 before X1, then most of X2 will get assigned the majority of the explanatory power. With two variables this highly correlated, often the regression coefficients get assigned numbers like +0.87 and −0.92 so that they are effectively canceling out their contributions. If only one of these factors was in the model it, would get a coefficient of maybe −0.06. So the problem of handling the correlation comes down to poor mathematical algorithms, not necessarily to badly designed model specification. We say *necessarily*, because having two factors in a model correlated greater than 50 percent means the user is being lazy, because one variable is probably a proxy for the other, and if the user is making mistakes of that magnitude, the user is probably making other important errors, too.

In practice, since financial-statement data are correlated, the co-linearity is not that large a problem, especially if the model built from the data is utilized on data where the variables are not much different from the training set. That is, if the correlation between two variables is on the order of, say, 35 percent, for the period of time the regression is being run, then, as long as the out-of-sample data maintains a correlation between the factors of the same magnitude, the model's predictions should be acceptable. Most of the problems in co-linearity occur when it is found that the variable's correlation is very different outside the time period of where the regression was run, after extrapolating a model using variables that are correlated in regressions (i.e. out-of-sample testing).

This being said, there are many advanced ways to deal with the co-linearity condition, but, for the average investor, it is way too much trouble to assert these mechanisms, and the payback just is not worth the effort. My experience has been that, whether you have a bit of overconditioning in the model due to cross-factor correlations of the order of 30 percent level or less, ultimately it just doesn't matter for model performance when considering the weak statistics determined from multifactor models applied to stock selecting bottom-up models in general. Along similar lines, subtle accounting differences usually do not matter much, either. For example, when one is considering a free-cash-flow-to-price factor, whether free-cash flow is defined as operating income minus dividends paid minus capital expenditures, or leaving out the dividends paid term, returns to either factor are completely within the error of the result, so one cannot conclude there is any difference at the model level. Though they indeed imply something completely different at the explanatory level to an accountant, in modeling, it is no big deal, though fundamental analysts usually try to make it one.

## CHOOSING AN INVESTMENT PHILOSOPHY

Your choice of investment philosophy centers around what you are trying to accomplish. In particular, it involves belief about how markets operate, where returns come from, what inefficiencies can be exploited, and what risk exposures you will purposefully accept. Generally, this book takes the perspective of the long-term investor talking about saving for retirement, so this constitutes the focus we have adopted, which is well in line with Graham's attention. In addition, we concentrate on mid- to large-cap equities in the United States and, later, on global markets. This concentration allows for the universe of stocks chosen. As written previously, the very first step is to define the investment area you want to concentrate on, and from this, choose the universe of stocks in which the intelligent investor will concentrate. These days, even fundamentally run investment firms utilize quantitative screening to eliminate undesirable stocks, thereby reducing the size of the universe in which to focus. It is often as easy as restricting yourself to only stocks in the Russell 1000 Value index if you are a value investor. In so doing, you are outsourcing the definition of value to some vendor, however. For the professional money manager, this mitigates a kind of risk involving a client's (usually an institution such as a pension, endowment, or

Taft-Hartley [i.e., a union] plan) investment policy statement and/or asset allocation. It is easy to tell a client, "We only own stocks in a given style index," so that all that we can own are designated "value" by an independent third party. For an individual investor, however, whose objective is only return, this strategy may reduce the opportunity set available. In the situation of this book, we are restricting ourselves to stocks that Graham would focus on, and his methodology is both a screen and a stock ranking and/or forecasting algorithm combination, obviously the best of both worlds. The limitations and constraints we place on the universe should be decided based on data availability, country exposures, investment style, and liquidity.

Now, the prudent investor would say let's begin with a large universe of a global nature and let the Graham method reduce it down to a manageable portfolio. We can do this, especially today, because it is not nearly as difficult as it was even 10 years ago to buy foreign-exchange traded and headquartered companies, thanks to technology. If, however, U.S. readers are more comfortable applying home bias, they can restrict the universe to U.S. trading stocks only. What is most important is that there is historical data available to test the factors and model through and current data to prudently examine stocks for purchase based on the model. Graham mostly invested in the United States in his early days, widening his opportunity set as technology and the evolution of foreign GDP growth increased, offering more liquidity and information on foreign markets. Likewise, with growing GDP and maturing markets, liquidity has increased globally, too, so much so that style and quality represent the last bastion to overcome in planning your investment focus.

In the examples utilized here we will use a universe of the S&P 1500 (the large-cap, mid-cap, and small-cap S&P indexes, combined) for ease of use. If the universe is larger (i.e., global, for instance), the creation, testing, and running of factors and models methodology is identical, but it may take longer simply because of bigger calculations on your PC or server because the number of securities is larger.

## GROWTH, VALUE, QUALITY

Jeremy Grantham said that there are no quality funds, though there are growth and value funds. He said this in late 2009, referencing the phenomenal returns incurred by stocks that were of low quality in that year. Historically, GMO, his firm, is a high-quality value investor and has a remarkable reputation and return history. However, he was taking some criticism for poorer relative 2009 returns due to this "purposeful portfolio positioning"

(PPP). This is, of course, true in all ways, and though Mr. Grantham (Mr. Graham and Mr. Buffett, too) has competitors, he does not have many peers. Grantham, Graham, and Buffett's philosophy of examining balance-sheet health (high current ratios of current assets to current liabilities) and not paying too much for a company should not be ignored.

This being said, the prudent intelligent enterprising investor should, therefore, pay homage to these successful sages' wisdom. We will, however, make a distinction between being a pure value investor versus being a Ben Graham value investor. Let us define these two main strategies first, using pragmatic and easy-to-understand definitions. Value investors are people who have an anathema to price; that is, they are overly price conscious, and we do not mean that in a bad way. However, they continuously ask the question, "Is the multiple too high, relative to my other investment opportunities?" first in their decision making. Thus, they may buy a low-quality highly leveraged stock because there is a price at which the resulting debt load makes the company a good value to them, regardless of the debt. These types of value investors made lots of money beginning in March of 2009, because they bought stocks that were cheap on the valuation multiples but that may have had high debt and were of lower quality.

Growth investors, on the other hand, are not the opposite of a value investor, and this is where many investors miss it. Growth investors are not looking at high multiples as buy candidates, but it just so happens that those stocks that the market has deemed have higher growing earnings potential have often already priced those future earnings, hence their multiples are high. Nevertheless, there are some companies whose valuation multiples are high but that do not have good earnings prospects. An example may be a company rumored to be taken over, or a designated merger or acquisition candidate already announced. The valuation would have risen simply because the announced takeover price is a premium to the pre-announced market price.

A quality company is usually one with little debt or one that is lowly levered. In particular, ranking stocks by factors of total debt to EBITDA, cash over total debt, year over year cash (and cash equivalents) increases, and leverage[9] (net debt over enterprise value) all are useful in gauging the junk versus quality relationship. Junk is perhaps an acronym, but low quality has many poor characteristics for a company, and most value investors (but not "value only" investors as described in the last paragraph) avoid it. Even growth investors often stay away from low quality. Only in the case of exceptional future earnings potential and forecasts would an investor dare to own a low-quality company usually. You might conclude that the IPO's from the Internet heyday of 1999 was basically junk or low-quality stocks coming to market, because so many of them had no earnings. Nada, zippo, nein, nyet earnings, making any debt they had in an EBITDA to debt ratio zero! Of course, that makes a conundrum out of companies with no earnings and no debt. Forgetting what you call them, you have to have faith in their quest to obtain earnings in the future. These are stocks in which Graham would never invest.

Graham, the quintessential value investor, mandates that investors understand a company's business, not pay too high a price relative to the bond market yields, insist a company is backward looking in terms of earnings and payouts, ensure a company has a healthy balance sheet (low debt), and be confident the company is not too small (so that earnings are likely to be maintained) and offers a margin of safety. He also always commented that investors should be able to sleep at night while owning a company's stock even if the price would not be known the next day, trusting in the market to someday awaken to the true value of the strength of the company and price it accordingly. As long as the earnings stream and cash flows were at a sufficient level, profits would eventually ensue to the shareholders. This concept was the sleeping pill to investors because Graham's method tended to offer metrics for companies that were difficult to achieve, and failure to meet a Graham criterion rendered a no-interest verdict on its purchase. As a result, the Graham methodology will favor larger-cap stocks with longer track records. Modern investors who subscribe to Graham include such names as Marty Zweig, Ken Fisher, Matthew Kaufler, and David Dreman, who all employ derivations of the Graham and Buffett strategies.

This makes Ben Graham not only a value investor, but an absolute one at that. Unlike many quantitative value investors who look at candidate companies whose valuations are at the low end of a sorting of companies' valuations, Ben felt at times there were no stocks to buy because the valuations across the board were too high for a given time. His absolute perspective of value was exhibited by Warren Buffett who said, in February of 2009, that there were plenty of good candidate companies in the market at that time, due to such low prices occurring in the credit crisis. This implied that, at other times, nothing is of a good value and it is time to get out of the market, take your profits, and wait for opportunities. Since many mutual fund managers (both quant and fundamental) have benchmark risk (whereas Ben did not measure himself against a benchmark), they must be mostly fully invested in the market at all times. If they receive cash from investors, they cannot sit on it and wait for value opportunities to arise, as Ben could, so they usually invest right away. To do so means they must sort by value and choose from among the lowest group, even if, on average, prices are high, as too are valuations. This is especially true of institutional managers. These kinds of investors are termed relative-value investors.

## INVESTMENT CONSULTANT AS DUTCH UNCLE

We must segue to report on the difficulty of managing assets institutionally, because of the role investment consultants have taken on over the last years. Consultants, also known in the business as gatekeepers, are often hired by a pension, endowment, or firm because of the pressure exerted on their oversight committee by legal requirements to carry out fiduciary duty. They are called gatekeepers because they insert themselves between the actual client and the money manager hired. They usually control the client and keep manager and client at arm's length. Now, imagine yourself as a union representative or CFO of some firm on the investment committee. You have a full-time job requiring your real skill and expertise and also are on the board of the pension, so your demands are split. Which job gets shortchanged? So, to cover yourself you hire an investment consultant from a firm like Callan, Mercer, Lipper, Russell, or countless others. Your job is much easier now, because you have outsourced much of the work, but not the obligation of your duty as fiduciary. You can, however, act in good faith to any government authority investigating or reviewing your mandate by asserting that you hired expertise. Now, consider realistically that most of these people with the responsibility of serving on investment committees are there for resume padding and/or just do not have the necessary experience to manage or police the assets they are in charge of, hence outsourcing the fiduciary effort is prudent. Indeed, there is expertise with these consultants, but they are paid for their investment manager selection and ongoing monitoring and, in addition, help set investment policy, guidelines, and asset allocation. This last function, setting the asset allocation, is what often conflicts with the hired money manager's process and makes institutional asset management less efficient than it could be.

The investment consultant will work with the firm to set the asset allocation based on prudent guidelines and risk measures. Then, they perform a manager search for the allocation, interview, and help select the manager. In most instances, the firm will go with the consultant's choices. Now, suppose the asset allocation is composed of 30 percent large-cap core (like S&P 500), 10 percent small-cap value, 10 percent small-cap growth, 15 percent international, 5 percent emerging market, 20 percent investment grade corporate debt, 5 percent government (Treasuries and agencies), and 5 percent cash (short-term notes and money market). We are not stating that this is a correct allocation, but just by way of example, suppose you are the large-cap manager in this allocation, using the Ben Graham method to run your portfolio. Suppose also that it is the height of the Internet bubble and valuations, relative to corporate debt yields, are just too high. Remember that Graham said the acceptable P/E should be related to the reciprocal of twice the current average high-quality corporate AAA bond yield. So, in this market environment, as the money manager, you want to go to cash with 20 percent of your assets. However, the consultant who hired you says no because the consultant determined that he wants only 5 percent in cash in total. If you as the manager take your 20 percent of the 30 percent of allocation you manage and move to cash, then, suddenly, 20 percent of 30 percent is 6 percent and cash in total is now at 11 percent of the client's pension. Therefore, if the large-cap manager did that, that manager would get fired. The manager is forced to invest in a market she does not want to participate in because the consultant will tell the manager that she is not hired to be in cash but to be in stocks.

Now, in honesty, the consultant who hired the large-cap manager should be aware of the methodology and process the manager uses and should have prepared herself for situations like this example, where the asset allocation can be quite different from what is desired. However, we have experienced situations in which that was not the case, and the consultant required the manager to be fully invested even when she would not be with their own money, bypassing the specific risk-management overlay that the manager has, independent of the total risk management the consultant is specifying or preferring.

Another bad example of consultant micromanaging of client money we have experienced involved a well-known mutual fund advisory committee that sub-advised (outsourced) the money management for the fund. In this role, acting as fiduciaries, they devised a scheme in which they hired three separate managers to each use their process to manage a portfolio of only 20 stocks each, but by definition, a manager could not use their process to manage a portfolio like this. For instance, the total fund had supposedly 60 positions. Each manager was required to own 20 stocks and be fully invested at all times and each could not own 19 or 21 stocks, but 20. However, all three managers were small-cap-value style managers, so there could be co-ownership of stocks that, in reality, might result in only 50 stocks in the portfolio, or 40. Each manager could not clearly see the positions of the other two managers, and so risk overlays were either not applied or totally redundant. Asset allocation went out the window with common sense in this case, and risk exposures could drift anywhere with this idea for a product. Moreover, the position size limitations had high restrictions (boundaries), so each manager's hands were tied in reality to manage this portfolio's positions and risk. It would have been far better for the client to have a single manager run this product.

In addition, because consultants usually measure managers relative to a benchmark, the managers are also restricted in how they can manage. If Exxon is 5 percent of the benchmark, the risk of not owning it may be too high to avoid, even though their process may hate the stock. This outlines the peril of hiring consultants who seemingly know better, but as gatekeepers with the client their first inclination is to protect their fees. Therefore, they behave as if they know what's best for the client even though most of them have actually never managed money and they guard the relationship between manager and client vigorously to remain in control of the assets and concomitantly their own fees.

So relative value managers are alive and well and often have that style imposed on them as a result of the constraints set by the institutional consultants. This is why Ben Graham, Warren Buffett, and many other very good investment managers refrained from building businesses from consultant-involved money when they began. Later, after they had much success with their investment strategy, institutional money came to them and consultants, too, but they never let their investment process be held captive by a consultant's requirements. In the rush to build a business and gain assets under management, we're afraid too many asset managers laid down in front of consultants and compromised their strategies and risk management to garner stable fee income. Let the investor beware! This is why we recommend employing the methods outlined by Graham as detailed in this book, because then you need less to invest with professionally compromised mutual funds going forward.

## WHERE ARE THE RELATIVE GROWTH MANAGERS?

One can make the claim that there is an equivalent-relative-growth manager too, versus an absolute-growth manager, but we are not aware of any classification of absolute versus relative mandate in any growth funds to date as there are for value managers. Also, as stated before, there just are not any quality managers per se, or at least not any characterized by that acronym, though many managers do indeed end up owning high-quality companies as an outgrowth of their process.

This is indeed true for most quantitatively managed assets. If, in the model-building process you form factors from financial-statement data, then regress them against future returns to form a model, using that model going forward in time will select higher-quality portfolios. This is because over long time periods, higher-quality assets outperform lower-quality assets so much that the factor bets or leanings (i.e., literally the regression coefficients) inherent in the model-construction process will result in biases toward higher quality. The higher-ranked stocks will be of higher quality necessarily, and it cannot be any other way. This is because any stock-selection model predicated on back-testing, if done correctly, will result in higher-ranked stocks being the higher performers. Thus, stock characteristics associated with the higher-performing cohorts of stocks, whatever it is predicated on, will be found in those higher performers, in this case higher-quality versus lower-quality.

Likewise, you could sort stocks historically by performance—say, rolling 12-month returns separating the top from bottom performers—and just examine each cohort's fundamental characteristics for a 20-year period per se. In so doing, you would find that a trait among the top performers is quality. This is not to say that there are not periods of time when less consistent traits are not occasionally associated with outperformers, but what would be consistent is quality. Hence, the models and resultant processes obtained from quantitative techniques do have a quality bias to them. A real example came from some quants we know who outperformed their benchmark, the S&P 500 in 2008, by 700 basis points (7 percent), only to give up so much more in 2009 due to the low-quality rally that ensued. Their investment process would not select a low-quality stock, no matter how low the price went. Therefore, they stayed away from junk and underperformed their bench because they did not own the stocks within the S&P that were low-quality and rallying. However, their process in the past avoided such low-quality stocks, such as Enron and Worldcom (when they bubbled), and the large banks, GM, Chrysler, and so forth in the credit crisis when their debt levels so overwhelmed their balance sheets that falling returns resulted. This became a bragging attribution for the manager, though they trailed their benchmark.

Also, the majority of quant processes have a value bias in them, too, again due to a characteristic trait of top performers to be value stocks. This was one reason (but not the only one) of the systemic loss of quant firms in August of 2007. The amount of overlapping ownership of stocks due to the correlation among models predicated strongly on value resulted in a loss due to trading illiquidity when exogenous deleveraging occurred. The main driver of these losses was the fire-sale liquidation of portfolios that happened to be similarly quantitatively constructed.[10] Everybody was rushing to raise cash and trying to exit from the same stocks, which resulted in massive losses occurring in that month. To those investors who did not vacate the markets but held their stocks, the rebound just one month later recouped all losses. It would have been better if these quant managers had gone on vacation for the month rather than react to the market. This deleveraging of hedge funds was related to the beginning of much larger than expected subprime mortgage losses that began to occur in 2007 due to the start of the credit crisis of 2008.

And so we have value, growth, and quality. The Graham method will result primarily in value with quality overlaid. As for growth, Mr. Graham has much to say and it is worth expounding on that a bit. To give color, in 1930s when Graham was perfecting his investing magic, much of the stock market capitalization was based on raw IME, that is, industrial conglomerates, materials, energy, and utilities. These kinds of industries had substantial inventory of component parts, property, plant, and equipment. The U.S. economy was based heavily in manufacturing. In addition, because of World War I, there was a dominance of U.S. manufactured goods in the world economy, because, Europe and its factories were partially destroyed. Asia offered a very small component of total global GDP at this time, too. This continuance of U.S. dominance in manufacturing and heavy industry continued right on through most of Ben Graham's career, through World War II and its aftermath and into the 1960s so that, again, tangible assets on the balance sheet remained a pivotal focus of him and his methods. For example, consider the state of the globe right after World War II. The United States was the only country with surviving factories. Most of the developed world was bombed to smithereens. Therefore, in the early days of security analysis, the focus was strongly on balance-sheet assets because the U.S. economy was dominated by businesses in which balance-sheet assets were very large, catching the attention of analysts rather than earnings expectations. This was Graham's emphasis until the day he died.

In the economy of today, however, service firms dominate the economy. Microsoft, Oracle, Cisco, even Intel and the banks of today do not have enough tangible assets—let alone the whole consumer discretionary and staples sectors—to have their value captured by tangible assets alone. Software, acquired brands, customer lists, product portfolios, patents, royalty agreements, licensing, and so forth dominate these companies' net worth, but these things are not itemized so easily on the balance sheet. Moreover, in today's economy, the United States no longer has a monopoly on global GDP. In fact, it has increasingly become a smaller player since the 1960s when Japan began its ascendancy. Thus, the impetus for today's value analysts is to consider free cash flow rather than balance-sheet assets as the heftier contributor to valuation, and free cash flow to price has become a favorite factor these days.

As we said earlier, nonvalue stocks are not growth stocks, but the converse is true, nongrowth stocks are usually value stocks. If common stocks that are expected to increase their earnings at considerably better than the average rate are growth stocks, than those not meeting those requirements obviously are value stocks and are priced accordingly. However, they also might be low-quality stocks. Most growth companies have a tie to technological progress in some way, so by choosing these prospects, investors in some way are also tying themselves to science. However, investors are really fooling themselves, because there are not many measurable parameters with which to quantitatively validate a company's level of growth until after the fact. In this sense, growth investing is different from value investing because in growth investing, investors attempt to gauge a company's expectations, whereas in value investing, a value company in fact has many variables at hand to determine its value.

If either strategy is attempting to mimic science, value investing is closer for its quantification capabilities alone, let alone that growth investing is indeed prognostication by its very essence. One can surmise that there is safety in growth to some extent, but it is difficult to be quantitative about how much to pay for expected growth that may or may not materialize. Moreover, unusually rapid growth in a company cannot keep up in perpetuity. Thus, identifying a growth company from past experience often means that the high growth period is now ready to expire as its hefty increase in size (moving from a small-cap stock to a large-cap stock in 5 years, say) makes a repetition of this growth much more difficult. Moreover, its appreciation will have been priced into its valuation accordingly, making those stocks sell at high prices relative to current earnings and at higher multiples of their net profits over the past period. These ideas led Graham to write, "Wonders can be accomplished with the right growth stock selections, bought at the right levels and later sold for a huge rise and before their probable decline. But the average (growth) investor can no more expect to accomplish this than to find money growing on trees."[11]

In summary, we have discussed much of the concern around quants and any investor deciding to build an investment philosophy and process based on quantitative approaches. Also, many of the topics discussed in this chapter are thrown up as criticisms of the quant process, which is why we spent so much time and detail expounding the issues and hailing the remedies. These criticisms hardly stand on their merits when properly considered and mitigated through ordinary and prudent modeling decisions.

CHAPTER 6

# Testing the Graham Crackers . . . er, Factors

*I know indeed that some men, even of great reputation, unduly influenced by certain prejudices, have found it difficult to accept this new principle [of gravity] and have repeatedly preferred uncertainties to certainties. It is not my intention to carp at their reputation; rather, I wish to give you in brief, kind reader, the basis for making a fair judgment of the issue for yourself.*

—Roger Cotes, Editor's Preface to the Second Edition of *The Principia*[1]

We now turn to the testing of the Graham factors, which are paramount for the success of turning the Graham process into a quantitative model. Like Cotes, however, we let the data speak for itself, because there are many critics of quantitative methodologies, and with the simple results presented here you can see so for yourself. With factor testing come the beginnings of model construction for the prudent investor, but without some examples it will be difficult to turn the hearts of the critics toward Graham and his recipes.

The previous chapters have outlined what we consider necessary background (and urgent information in light of today's credit and global crises) before beginning the process of discovering a prudent investment methodology. To understand the prior history of modeling and finance theory as well as to appreciate the art of modeling, we have attempted to arm you with the knowledge required to offset the many criticisms that have ignored the rich application of modeling in so many fields. To that end, arguments have been made to educate you so you can avoid the temptation to place blame on the quant process. Most of the criticisms the media have portrayed and its popular put-downs of market participants are really ignorant of what quantitative processes are about, and the prior chapters lay the groundwork to restore the proper context of modeling and investing to the prudent and enterprising investor. Next, we push the ship off the dock and jump into the boat; that means we actually start discussing the technical know-how: the process this book aims to teach.

This chapter may be the meatiest chapter in the book, introducing actual tests that are required to get you to the point of accepting or rejecting a factor, that is, to arrive at a go/no-go point. If it takes nine months for a woman to have a baby, you cannot take nine women and make a baby in one month. Another analogy concerning vitamins is relevant to drive this point home. Taking one vitamin can be helpful, but you do not become nine times more healthy taking nine vitamins. This is also true in creating quantitative models for stock selection. Though we may have created a useful stock-selection model using Graham's formula, it does not mean that we can make it nine times better by looking for more variables to cut the universe of possible stock choices for investing. There are diminishing returns with effort in this vein. A portfolio of stocks weaned from the Graham method is like fine wine that must be left in the bottle in order to ferment properly. Remember, Beaujolais Nouveau is mostly a fad. Young wines are not aged properly. This can be the hardest lesson to learn, because it is extremely difficult for the educated, intelligent, and enterprising investor to not do something. The tendency to re-juggle the portfolio after putting dollars to work in the market, to rebalance holdings, is very strong. Continuing to research new methods for predicting returns can also be more useless than useful. Stocks picked according to Graham's margin-of-safety principles are undervalued and there is no telling when the market will recognize their intrinsic value and re-price the stock. Thus, the investor can only wait.

## THE FIRST TESTS: SORTING

The first test is to sort stocks by each factor. These factor sorts are called factor exposures or loadings when they graduate to inclusion in a multifactor model. They essentially constitute the actual value of the factor for a given stock. For instance, if some factors are P/B and accruals, then the stock's factor exposures are the value of its P/B and its accrual. Later, the subsequent regression coefficients obtained from regressing these factor exposures against return are termed factor returns. The name origin comes down to units. If you make a model from an equation that has returns on the left side of the equation and factors multiplied by regression coefficients on the right side, then the combination of a single factor times its regression coefficient means that the units must end up being return. So if P/B is the factor with units of dollars per share/dollars per book, the dollars term cancels and the regression coefficient must have units of return to make the math right. That is, all the units on the right side of the model equation must end up with the same units as the left side of the equation. Hence, regression coefficients are renamed factor returns. This naming process is used for all factors' regression coefficients, though intrinsically, the units of the coefficient are totally determined by the factor they are multiplied by. The product of the factor return times the exposure must be unit-less because it must equal return, which is defined as:

$$\text{Return} = 1/\text{Price} * dP/dt$$

So the rate of change of price, divided by price is unit-less.

This first step is simple sorting based on factors, which allows us to determine whether it is worth investing time to combine one factor with another to build a model. This test was used on the examples for control on the momentum and volatility research discussed earlier in Chapter 4. Sorting a single factor, forming portfolios from the top and bottom sorts, and holding them for a period of time while measuring performance is heuristic in nature and easy to do, and it is the first step in building a model for stock returns.

Results of sorts based on the Ben Graham factors are presented in the next section. All sorts were carefully designed to eliminate or minimize errors due to look-ahead bias and survivorship bias, while keeping a home bias in place, because the S&P 1500 (S&P 500 large-cap index, S&P 400 mid-cap index, and S&P 600 small-cap index) universe was used. The time period of the study was from December 31, 1989 to December 31, 2009, using monthly ending data. Note that the results, though convincing, do not prove anything, because empirical back tests cannot consist of enough data to contain all and every market situation that can occur. Therefore, the results are not a complete set, though other inexperienced authors contend differently.[2] The results can only suggest that the underlying investment theory works in that it offers outsized returns and connects the factors to return in an associated way, but it cannot prove it in any way, shape, or form. The data comes from the FactSet Fundamentals database and the sorts were run with their software, too, namely, their alpha Testing platform. These tests were run as quintile tests, meaning the universe was broken up into five categories for each factor, literally based on the magnitude of the factor. In addition, if the data was not existent for some factor, resulting in an "#N/A," that stock was excluded from the results. Also, for any given year, the starting universe would consist of 1,500 stocks, but as the months in the year progressed, mergers and company actions would reduce the number of stocks in the universe through time until the next index reconstitution.

**TABLE 6.1** FactSet Fundamentals Definition of Basic Graham Factors

| | Factors | Formula |
|---|---|---|
| 1 | Book Value to Price | 1 / (FG_PBK) |
| 2 | Earnings to Price | 1 / (FG_PE) |
| 3 | Div/MCap | (FG_DPS) / (FG_MKT_VALUE) |
| 4 | Current Ratio | FG_CUR_ASSETS / FG_CUR_LIABS |
| 5 | Size | FG_MKT_VALUE |
| 6 | Earn Growth | FG_EPS_1YGR |
| 7 | Earn Stability | STD16(FG_EPS_1YGR) |
| 8 | Earn Stability_2 | (FG_SALES – FG_COGS – FG_SGA – FG_INC_TAX / FG_MKT_VALUE) |
| 9 | Graham Formula | Factors 1 through 7, each with a weight of 1 |
| 10 | Graham Formula_2 | Factors 1 through 6 and factor 8, each with a weight of 1 |

One difficulty, not easily corrected in a back test, is a requirement by Ben Graham that the acceptable P/E should be related to the reciprocal of twice the current average high-quality AAA corporate-bond yield. In this particular back test, we do not have a database of historical bond yields to measure. Historically, this is a drawback of the method employed. However, for current investing, the yield is easily ascertained from any high-quality corporate bond fund. Fidelity, Pimco, Vanguard, and many other fund families all offer such funds. Also, they can easily be found in FactSet.

The data in Table 6.1 documents the FactSet Fundamentals definition of the Graham factors used in the sorts and offers the exact code used in the software.

Each factor was run separately in the back test for sorting, and the models (9) and (10) also, where each factor was given equal weight to a model, respectively. The first data we show is the average three-month return of the factor cohorts. Table 6.2 shows the absolute return for each quintile for each factor and for the two Graham models.

We offset the second earnings stability definition and the second Graham model that uses it for ease of reading the table. The difference in returns between the two models with differing earnings stability definition varies little, though the two definitions of earnings stability used alone clearly demonstrate unique and widely disparate results over the period of the study. Now, the average individual investor is most concerned with absolute returns, which is why the data is shown here in this format. Only institutional investors care about relative returns to a benchmark. However, in both cases,

**TABLE 6.2** Three-Month Returns (Dec. 31, 1989 to Dec. 31, 2009)

| Factor/Quintile | 1 | 2 | 3 | 4 | 5 |
|---|---|---|---|---|---|
| Book Value to Price | 4.16 | 3.22 | 3.00 | 2.69 | 2.78 |
| Earnings to Price | 4.71 | 3.23 | 2.84 | 2.56 | 2.27 |
| Div/MCap | 5.44 | 3.31 | 2.70 | 2.53 | 2.90 |
| Current Ratio | 2.80 | 3.18 | 3.24 | 3.20 | 2.89 |
| Size | 4.78 | 3.22 | 2.92 | 2.66 | 2.29 |
| Earn Growth | 3.84 | 3.55 | 2.91 | 2.43 | 2.52 |
| Earn Stability | 2.96 | 3.48 | 3.21 | 2.95 | 2.89 |
| EarnStab_2 | 3.76 | 3.41 | 3.03 | 2.44 | 2.67 |
| Graham Formula | 4.17 | 3.30 | 3.03 | 2.64 | 2.40 |
| Graham Formula_2 | 4.02 | 3.22 | 3.01 | 2.68 | 2.43 |

the desirable result is to see a model in which just the first fractile, in this case quintile, outperforms the last fractile.

In this data set, we hope to see that the numbers in column 1 are larger than the numbers in column 5. This is a prerequisite for any factor in any model and, of course, for entire models, too. Why this is so has to do with the economic theory underlying the modeling effort. There is no economic theory that says selecting stocks by any particular financial statement data will contrive a portfolio of stocks that will beat some benchmark. This is because the benchmark is itself a managed portfolio selected using S&P's, Russell's, or MSCI's formulas for index constitution (passive indeed, stated sarcastically!). Hence, we can only compare performance versus a benchmark for some factor, not necessitate a strategy for beating the managed portfolio benchmark. However, we are on good economic ground for specifying that, if a factor explains returns at all, it has to be that sorting by that factor must have the top sort be different from the bottom sort, on average. If we believe the market misprices securities for periods of time and moves away from the nonarbitrage condition, then sorting by valuation where we compare low valuation versus high valuation, it must be the case that the differential is in favor of low valuation. That said however, it must be made clear that there's no guarantee, nor is their supporting theory that the top quintile would outperform some index.

In Table 6.2, that is the situation for all but the beloved current ratio, the ratio of net current assets to net current liabilities and the first earnings stability measure. Obviously, though a necessary measure by Graham for picking healthy balance sheets, current ratio alone is not necessarily a good picker of stocks, at least not as measured from the empirical data.

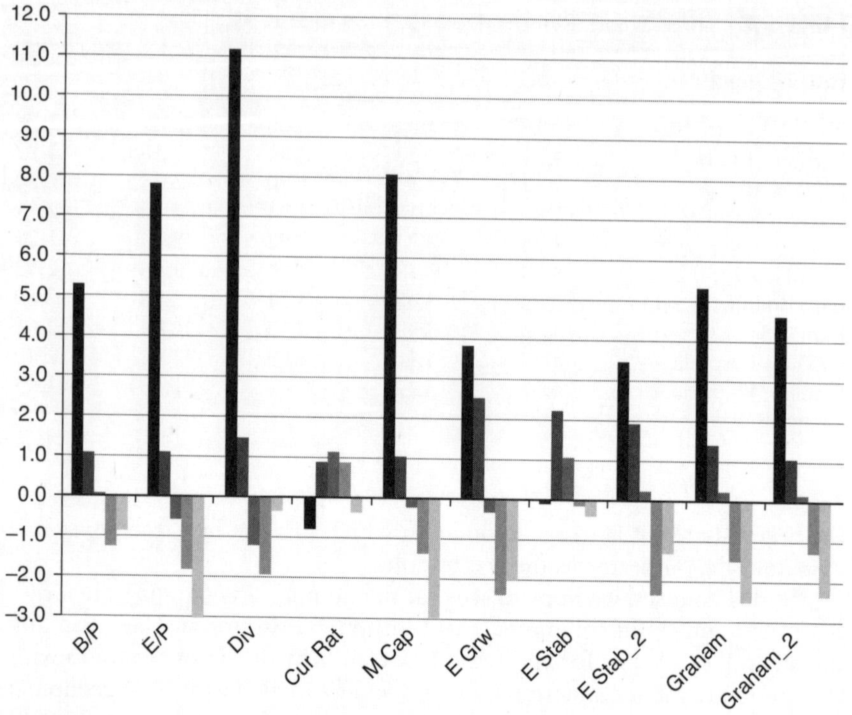


**FIGURE 6.1** Quintiled Excess Returns of Graham Factor Cohorts

Figure 6.1 illustrates a more comprehensive description of the utility of these factors and the two Graham models, created by equally weighting the individual factors. In Figure 6.1, we annualized the returns and then subtracted the annualized return of a hypothetical benchmark consisting of the S&P 500 index. For each factor group (of which there are ten), we show the five quintile excess returns on an annualized basis and what those results are for this study.

Figure 6.1 illustrates the way a typical quant looks at the empirical data set. Each factor's five quintiles of excess returns are shown. What is worth a kiloword is easily seen by the height of the first quintile and the depth of the fifth quintile, all except for the current ratio in the middle of the chart and the E Stab where there is hardly any differentiation between top, middle, and bottom quintiles for these two factors. The current ratio offers very little stock selectivity over time as represented here in the returns. The same can be said of the first definition of earnings stability, which is defined as the standard deviation over 16 quarters of reported earnings per share.

Notice, too, that the first definition of the Graham formula, which utilizes this earnings stability measure, seemingly outperforms the second definition of the Graham formula_2, which uses the better definition of earnings stability.

Now, in reviewing this data, it is easy to convince yourself of the efficacy of factors such as E/P, dividend yield, and size (as measured by market cap) in selecting stocks for purchase. First, remember that this is last-12-months E/P, not forecasted E/P, because Graham clearly felt that it is close to ridiculous to try to forecast earnings and did not use analysts' forecasted earnings values. Second, these results are returns averaged over 20 years, and inherent in averaging is a tendency to ignore the fluctuation of the data. So, if we report from the empirical evidence that the top quintile of stocks outperforms the index by almost 8 percent for E/P sorting on average, we fail to realize that it did so with some standard deviation. To realize the impact of this statement, take a look at the time series plot in Figure 6.2 of rolling 12-month return from sorting stocks based on last-12-months E/P over the time period of the study.

From September 27, 1997, until just beyond March 15, 2000, sorting and buying the highest E/P stocks resulted in underperforming the S&P 500 index. For two-and-a-half years, this method was under water. Though over the long term it made money, does the investor have the stomach for

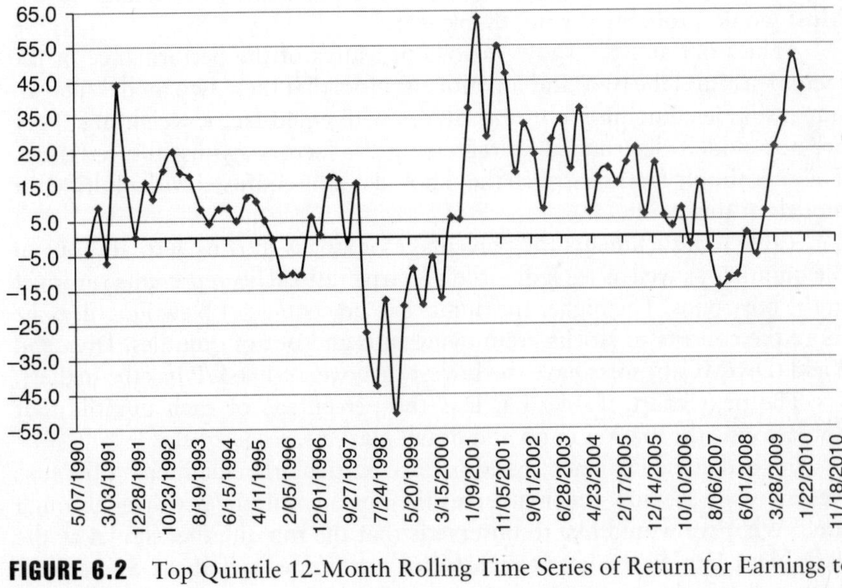


**FIGURE 6.2** Top Quintile 12-Month Rolling Time Series of Return for Earnings to Price (E/P)

**TABLE 6.3** Factor Statistics and Sharpe Ratio

| | % in New Fractiles | | | | | Sharpe Ratio | | | | |
|---|---|---|---|---|---|---|---|---|---|---|
| Factor | 1 | 2 | 3 | 4 | 5 | 1 | 2 | 3 | 4 | 5 |
| Book Value to Price | 21.2 | 36.7 | 36.4 | 28.4 | 12.4 | 0.36 | 0.28 | 0.25 | 0.23 | 0.23 |
| Earnings to Price | 29.3 | 47.1 | 46.1 | 38.8 | 22.1 | 0.42 | 0.28 | 0.25 | 0.22 | 0.16 |
| Div/MCap | 1.5 | 3.6 | 6.1 | 9.4 | 7.2 | 0.55 | 0.28 | 0.24 | 0.20 | 0.25 |
| Current Ratio | 10.7 | 19.8 | 22.0 | 19.0 | 10.4 | 0.21 | 0.26 | 0.29 | 0.30 | 0.29 |
| Size | 9.6 | 16.2 | 16.1 | 12.1 | 4.8 | 0.44 | 0.27 | 0.23 | 0.22 | 0.19 |
| Earn Growth | 20.3 | 21.1 | 21.5 | 23.8 | 25.0 | 0.35 | 0.33 | 0.26 | 0.19 | 0.18 |
| Earn Stability | 2.7 | 4.6 | 6.1 | 6.0 | 4.2 | 0.24 | 0.31 | 0.28 | 0.26 | 0.27 |
| EarnStab_2 | 19.7 | 37.3 | 40.9 | 34.4 | 25.9 | 0.34 | 0.30 | 0.27 | 0.19 | 0.19 |
| Graham Formula | 26.3 | 42.9 | 44.3 | 34.8 | 16.5 | 0.36 | 0.28 | 0.26 | 0.22 | 0.20 |
| Graham Formula_2 | 24.1 | 42.8 | 44.6 | 37.9 | 17.9 | 0.35 | 0.27 | 0.25 | 0.23 | 0.21 |

annualized returns −45 percent *below* the index if buying stocks based on E/P alone, which would mean buying only those stocks with the lowest price-to-earnings ratios and using that criterion alone in selecting stocks? Most would probably say no, thank you.

Tables 6.3 and 6.4 show various measures of the performance of the factor sorts and the two Graham models. Note that these two models constitute a simple combination of the factors with equal factor weighting. They are not models determined by regressing the factors against future return. They are simply factor sorts, so they should not be confused with multifactor models at this point.

Table 6.3 documents the percentage of stocks moving into and out of the quintiles as well as each quintile's Sharpe ratio. This represents turnover in the portfolios. The higher the number in percentage of New Fractiles, the more the cohorts of stocks are moving into and out of quintiles. Dividend Yield (Div/MCap) sorts have the lowest turnover, while E/P has the highest.

The next chart, Table 6.4, lists the percentage of each quintile that outperforms the market in up and down markets, respectively.

In particular, Figures 6.3 and 6.4 are particularly enlightening because we can easily see how the first versus the bottom quintile performs through time. What we would like to observe is that the top quintile, shown as the dark black bars to the left of each factor's group, is well above 50 percent, meaning that the majority of stocks in the highest quintile were beating

**TABLE 6.4** Factor Statistics and Hit Rates

| | % > Up Bench | | | | | % > Down Bench | | | | |
|---|---|---|---|---|---|---|---|---|---|---|
| **Factor** | **1** | **2** | **3** | **4** | **5** | **1** | **2** | **3** | **4** | **5** |
| Book Value to Price | 66.0 | 56.0 | 55.4 | 51.0 | 50.4 | 78.6 | 79.6 | 77.1 | 71.1 | 68.6 |
| Earnings to Price | 75.5 | 54.1 | 53.5 | 41.6 | 52.3 | 82.1 | 76.1 | 70.0 | 67.5 | 50.7 |
| Div/MCap | 64.5 | 63.5 | 49.7 | 45.3 | 46.6 | 77.1 | 76.1 | 73.6 | 63.9 | 61.4 |
| Current Ratio | 64.2 | 69.2 | 62.9 | 58.5 | 40.9 | 67.9 | 72.5 | 73.6 | 71.1 | 82.9 |
| Size | 73.6 | 59.8 | 57.3 | 60.4 | 40.9 | 78.6 | 76.1 | 66.4 | 67.5 | 65.0 |
| Earn Growth | 67.9 | 65.4 | 49.7 | 45.3 | 42.8 | 82.1 | 79.6 | 73.6 | 60.4 | 61.4 |
| Earn Stability | 66.0 | 69.2 | 62.9 | 47.2 | 48.5 | 75.0 | 79.6 | 80.7 | 63.9 | 65.0 |
| EarnStab_2 | 58.5 | 63.5 | 59.2 | 52.9 | 56.0 | 78.6 | 83.2 | 73.6 | 71.1 | 43.6 |
| Graham Formula | 71.7 | 61.7 | 61.0 | 52.9 | 46.6 | 78.6 | 72.5 | 73.6 | 74.6 | 75.7 |
| Graham Formula_2 | 67.9 | 59.8 | 64.8 | 51.0 | 40.9 | 82.1 | 79.6 | 70.0 | 71.1 | 75.7 |

the market over time. Likewise, we would like the bottom quintile to have smaller numbers, preferably below 50 percent, indicating that this quintile of stocks loses to the market in up and down periods.

The *Y* axes are the same for the two plots, and we can see that, in general, the winnings of the factors and models occur more in down markets than in up markets. This makes the Graham portfolios (models) and their

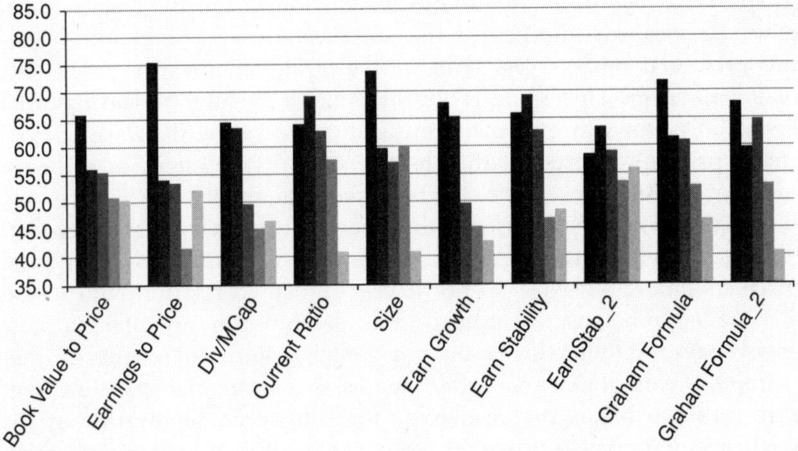


**FIGURE 6.3** Percent within Quintile Greater than Up Bench

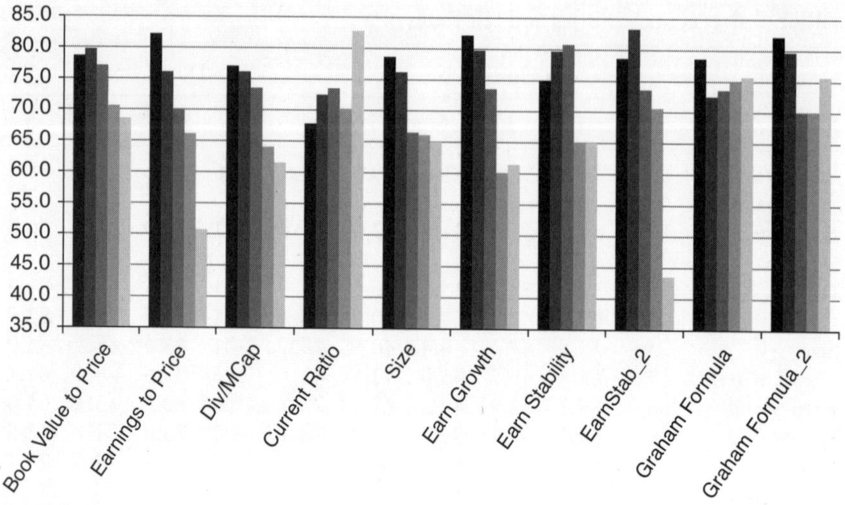


**FIGURE 6.4** Percent within Quintile Greater than Down Bench

subsequent factors more conservative or defensive, and this is how Graham positioned his portfolios in a general way.

The information ratio (IR) is the excess return over bench divided by the standard deviation of the excess return time series (also known as the tracking error). Table 6.5 documents the values for the factors and the two models. The information coefficient, or IC as it is called, is harder to define; it is the correlation of the stock's return in each quintile, with the stock's ranking by the factor or model. Obviously the IC T-stats, then, are the statistical significance of the correlation. We would like to see T-stats greater than 2 or less than –2 indicating significance; otherwise, it is not significant. This T-stat is not the same as the factor *t*-Stat reported earlier. That factor was a momentum signal representing the statistic from the fit of price momentum with a line at a 45 degree angle, a real price momentum measure. As can be seen from the data, the ICs are all very low, even though the factors themselves do generally offer relevance in separating winner from loser stocks. Again, to the chagrin of most MBAs, typical financial-statement data just do not have as much correlation with return as they are led to believe by the academic community. In my opinion, most B-schools have too much theory and not enough empiricism to back the theory's claim. We do not claim to offer theories that relate financial-statement data to returns; that is the academic's job. However, in my role as the practioner, empiricism suggests the main drivers of stock returns are often market trading forces more than underlying business financials, especially

**TABLE 6.5** Factor Stats; ICs and Significance

| Factor | Information Ratio | | | | | Information Coefficient | | | | | IC T-Stat | | | | |
|---|---|---|---|---|---|---|---|---|---|---|---|---|---|---|---|
| | 1 | 2 | 3 | 4 | 5 | 1 | 2 | 3 | 4 | 5 | 1 | 2 | 3 | 4 | 5 |
| Book Value to Price | 0.86 | 0.62 | 0.59 | 0.56 | 0.73 | 0.03 | 0.01 | 0.02 | 0.02 | 0.00 | 0.31 | 0.17 | 0.24 | 0.24 | −0.03 |
| Earnings to Price | 1.11 | 0.62 | 0.51 | 0.53 | 0.41 | 0.03 | 0.04 | 0.01 | 0.00 | 0.00 | 0.32 | 0.40 | 0.18 | −0.02 | −0.04 |
| Div/MCap | 1.14 | 0.88 | 0.62 | 0.37 | 0.42 | 0.02 | 0.03 | 0.01 | 0.01 | 0.00 | 0.17 | 0.32 | 0.07 | 0.19 | 0.03 |
| Current Ratio | 0.56 | 0.71 | 0.74 | 0.79 | 0.53 | −0.04 | 0.00 | 0.00 | 0.01 | −0.01 | −0.47 | −0.01 | 0.00 | 0.14 | −0.06 |
| Size | 1.07 | 0.61 | 0.58 | 0.54 | 0.56 | 0.04 | 0.02 | 0.01 | 0.00 | 0.00 | 0.51 | 0.21 | 0.13 | −0.04 | 0.00 |
| Earn Growth | 1.02 | 0.96 | 0.62 | 0.38 | 0.37 | 0.00 | 0.01 | 0.00 | 0.01 | −0.01 | −0.05 | 0.06 | 0.07 | 0.13 | −0.13 |
| Earn Stability | 0.61 | 0.90 | 0.75 | 0.62 | 0.61 | 0.01 | 0.01 | 0.01 | 0.00 | 0.00 | 0.15 | 0.09 | 0.13 | 0.00 | 0.00 |
| EarnStab_2 | 0.79 | 0.73 | 0.64 | 0.48 | 0.59 | 0.00 | 0.02 | 0.01 | 0.01 | 0.01 | 0.05 | 0.26 | 0.08 | 0.15 | 0.11 |
| Graham Formula | 0.94 | 0.65 | 0.64 | 0.53 | 0.62 | 0.02 | 0.01 | −0.01 | 0.03 | 0.00 | 0.21 | 0.08 | −0.09 | 0.31 | 0.04 |
| Graham Formula_2 | 0.87 | 0.65 | 0.65 | 0.54 | 0.66 | 0.02 | 0.02 | 0.00 | 0.00 | 0.01 | 0.13 | 0.18 | −0.01 | 0.01 | 0.08 |

in down markets when fear is leading the investment decisions rather than fundamentals. It is precisely why the Graham method works over time in that significant mispricing occurs because traders take the stock way out of line with fundamentals.

The IRs reported in Table 6.5 came directly out of FactSet and represent very good numbers for the top quintile of returns. IRs nearing 1 are indeed pretty fabulous. We will see in scenario testing that those numbers are not necessarily matched in differing market environments. Table 6.6 illustrates the CAPM beta, its T-stat, and $R^2$ from the regression of factor quintile returns with benchmark return time series. Remember, the $R^2$ represents the amount of variance that is explained by the model, so that an $R^2$ of 0.55 implies that 55 percent of the variance of return is explained by the factor. The higher the $R^2$, the higher the explanatory power of the factor in the return time series is implied. As can be seen from this data, the majority of the factors have betas less than 1.

Now as we documented in Chapter 3, beta is a poor measure of volatility and correlation with the index. However, it is a standard output of most modeling software, and when used comparatively, allows relative ranking between portfolios. In this case, relative ranking between the volatility and correlation between factors and the two Graham formulas can be ascertained. But no, beta is not nearly as informative as the g-Factor calculation. In the data in Table 6.6, most all factors demonstrate less volatility than the index (beta less than 1), with substantial enough T-stat (exceeding absolute values over 2) and $R^2$s to offer significance in a statistical sense to the beta values.

The statistical significance of the beta is not to be confused with what the criticism of beta has been throughout this book. It can clearly be a statistically significant measure, but its interpretation as *the* measure of portfolio volatility and correlation with the benchmark is what is in question. Rather, it is merely a regression coefficient and leaving its definition at that is absolutely fine with me. It is adding connotation to its meaning beyond that of a regression coefficient that is faulty in my view, and the g-Factor is a much better purposefully designed measure for portfolio volatility. Table 6.7 demonstrates real differences between beta and the g-Factor.

In this table, see how the betas, almost across the board, are less than 1, whereas the g-Factor, across the board, is almost always greater than 1. We already know that the g-Factor measures volatility more accurately, and in this case, the majority of the betas clearly have the wrong indication with respect to volatility. For confirmation of this result, all we have to do is look at the last five columns where we see the ratio of the standard deviation of return for each factor's quintiles divided by the standard deviation of return for the S&P 500. These ratios are clearly in the direction of the g-Factor's

**TABLE 6.6** Factor Stats; Beta and Significance

| | Beta | | | | | T-Stat Beta | | | | | $R^2$ for Beta | | | | |
|---|---|---|---|---|---|---|---|---|---|---|---|---|---|---|---|
| Factor | 1 | 2 | 3 | 4 | 5 | 1 | 2 | 3 | 4 | 5 | 1 | 2 | 3 | 4 | 5 |
| Book Value to Price | 0.81 | 0.79 | 0.83 | 0.83 | 0.92 | 9.8 | 11.4 | 13.0 | 16.2 | 19.7 | 0.55 | 0.62 | 0.68 | 0.77 | 0.83 |
| Earnings to Price | 0.84 | 0.80 | 0.77 | 0.83 | 0.94 | 10.5 | 11.5 | 12.6 | 17.7 | 18.7 | 0.58 | 0.62 | 0.67 | 0.80 | 0.82 |
| Div/MCap | 0.94 | 0.90 | 0.81 | 0.80 | 0.72 | 12.2 | 16.2 | 18.0 | 12.3 | 9.5 | 0.65 | 0.77 | 0.80 | 0.66 | 0.54 |
| Current Ratio | 0.93 | 0.90 | 0.84 | 0.80 | 0.69 | 14.8 | 14.1 | 13.9 | 15.3 | 12.8 | 0.73 | 0.72 | 0.71 | 0.75 | 0.67 |
| Size | 0.79 | 0.83 | 0.87 | 0.86 | 0.84 | 9.5 | 11.3 | 13.5 | 16.0 | 27.7 | 0.54 | 0.62 | 0.70 | 0.76 | 0.91 |
| Earn Growth | 0.87 | 0.85 | 0.79 | 0.83 | 0.87 | 14.0 | 15.2 | 14.9 | 14.3 | 12.4 | 0.71 | 0.75 | 0.74 | 0.72 | 0.66 |
| Earn Stability | 0.86 | 0.88 | 0.85 | 0.82 | 0.78 | 13.8 | 14.8 | 14.3 | 14.3 | 15.0 | 0.71 | 0.74 | 0.72 | 0.72 | 0.74 |
| EarnStab_2 | 0.79 | 0.81 | 0.80 | 0.86 | 1.00 | 10.8 | 12.1 | 13.6 | 18.0 | 17.5 | 0.59 | 0.65 | 0.70 | 0.80 | 0.80 |
| Graham Formula | 0.85 | 0.82 | 0.83 | 0.85 | 0.84 | 11.0 | 11.4 | 13.7 | 15.9 | 26.5 | 0.61 | 0.62 | 0.70 | 0.76 | 0.90 |
| Graham Formula_2 | 0.84 | 0.85 | 0.86 | 0.82 | 0.83 | 10.7 | 12.2 | 14.3 | 15.6 | 27.8 | 0.59 | 0.65 | 0.72 | 0.75 | 0.91 |

**TABLE 6.7** Factor Stats; Beta versus g-Factor

| | Beta | | | | | g-Factor | | | | | Stdev Ratio | | | | |
|---|---|---|---|---|---|---|---|---|---|---|---|---|---|---|---|
| Factor | 1 | 2 | 3 | 4 | 5 | 1 | 2 | 3 | 4 | 5 | 1 | 2 | 3 | 4 | 5 |
| Book Value to Price | 0.81 | 0.79 | 0.83 | 0.83 | 0.92 | 1.035 | 0.983 | 1.000 | 0.983 | 1.035 | 1.089 | 0.998 | 1.000 | 0.948 | 1.001 |
| Earnings to Price | 0.84 | 0.80 | 0.77 | 0.83 | 0.94 | 1.054 | 1.035 | 0.983 | 0.967 | 1.073 | 1.096 | 1.006 | 0.940 | 0.927 | 1.041 |
| Div/MCap | 0.94 | 0.90 | 0.81 | 0.80 | 0.72 | 1.030 | 1.017 | 0.967 | 0.983 | 1.035 | 1.007 | 1.025 | 0.901 | 0.979 | 0.978 |
| Current Ratio | 0.93 | 0.90 | 0.84 | 0.80 | 0.69 | 1.135 | 1.017 | 1.017 | 0.952 | 0.952 | 1.080 | 1.064 | 0.989 | 0.918 | 0.837 |
| Size | 0.79 | 0.83 | 0.87 | 0.86 | 0.84 | 1.073 | 1.054 | 1.113 | 0.983 | 0.983 | 1.075 | 1.046 | 1.041 | 0.984 | 0.883 |
| Earn Growth | 0.87 | 0.85 | 0.79 | 0.83 | 0.87 | 1.017 | 1.017 | 0.967 | 1.000 | 0.967 | 1.024 | 0.983 | 0.921 | 0.976 | 1.072 |
| Earn Stability | 0.86 | 0.88 | 0.85 | 0.82 | 0.78 | 1.054 | 1.000 | 0.983 | 0.983 | 0.967 | 1.024 | 1.018 | 0.999 | 0.966 | 0.903 |
| EarnStab_2 | 0.79 | 0.81 | 0.80 | 0.86 | 1.00 | 1.000 | 1.000 | 0.983 | 1.017 | 1.180 | 1.024 | 1.006 | 0.955 | 0.956 | 1.114 |
| Graham Formula | 0.85 | 0.82 | 0.83 | 0.85 | 0.84 | 1.035 | 1.000 | 1.000 | 1.035 | 0.983 | 1.094 | 1.030 | 0.991 | 0.971 | 0.886 |
| Graham Formula_2 | 0.84 | 0.85 | 0.86 | 0.82 | 0.83 | 1.054 | 1.017 | 1.017 | 1.054 | 0.983 | 1.086 | 1.044 | 1.007 | 0.944 | 0.868 |

leanings, implying they are more volatile than the index for most quintiles because there are only a few instances where the disagreement between g-Factor and the ratio of standard deviations varies.

## TIME-SERIES PLOTS

All data presented so far represents, for the most part, the average or cumulative values calculated from the back test, over the entire time period of the study. Next, we demonstrate an analysis that involves examining the time series of the data, specifically, the rolling 12-month absolute returns of the quintiles and the excess returns over the S&P 500. As said previously, most investors are interested in absolute returns. However, the alternative to every investor is purchasing the index, so we show excess returns, allowing prudent investors to examine for themselves whether they believe the Graham method, applied in a quantitative model, is worth the effort. Obviously, the evidence will demand a verdict.

Now, the number-one criterion with models is that the top quintile beat the bottom quintile. The first graphs are of the top minus the bottom quintile charts, through time. What the investor should look for in these area graphs is the preponderance of the time, the curves are mostly colored above zero. This would represent how performance would have been for the top versus the bottom quintile in the time period of the study. So if one was long the top quintile and short the bottom, the rolling 12-month return measures would follow this kind of signature, indicating out- or underperformance. The first graph is for book to price seen in Figure 6.5. Generally, low P/B is better, so in this case, the top quintile consists of those stocks in the S&P 1500 universe that have high B/P (i.e., low P/B).

One can see that during the time period of the study, B/P has been a good stock selection factor, as Graham believed and as is demonstrated empirically here. Take the time to integrate the percentage of time the chart is above zero to gather in your mind the efficacy of book to price. Next, the earnings to price time series is plotted in Figure 6.6.

Again, you can see that purchasing high E/P stocks based on the last 12-month measure has worked pretty well over time. We remind you that forward earnings is not nearly as extensive as historical earnings to price, and Graham never paid much attention to forward-earnings estimates. Next is the dividend yield plotted in Figure 6.7.

The data here are a little more aggregated than in Chapter 4, where we reviewed dividend yield more formally and studied a larger universe by breaking up the universe into yield buckets of 1-percent increments. This work here demonstrates that dividend yield still had efficacy in stock

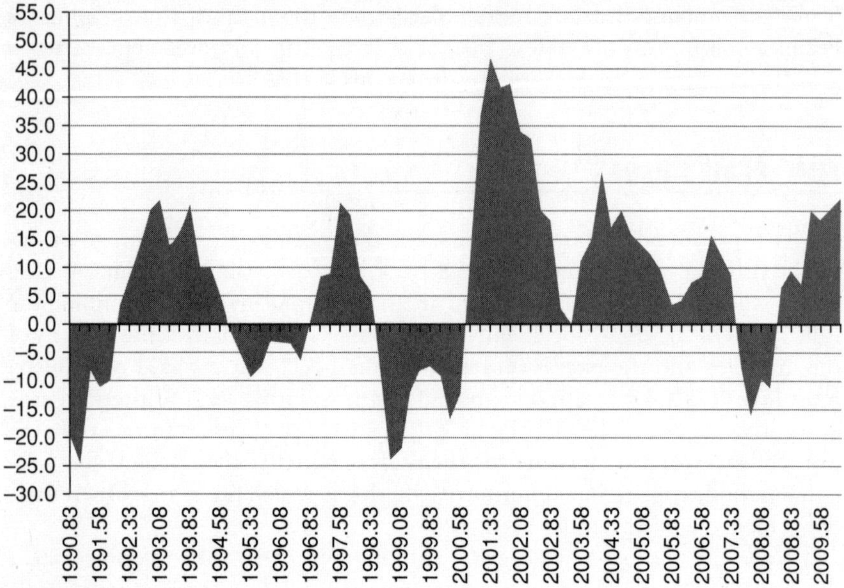


**FIGURE 6.5** Book to Price

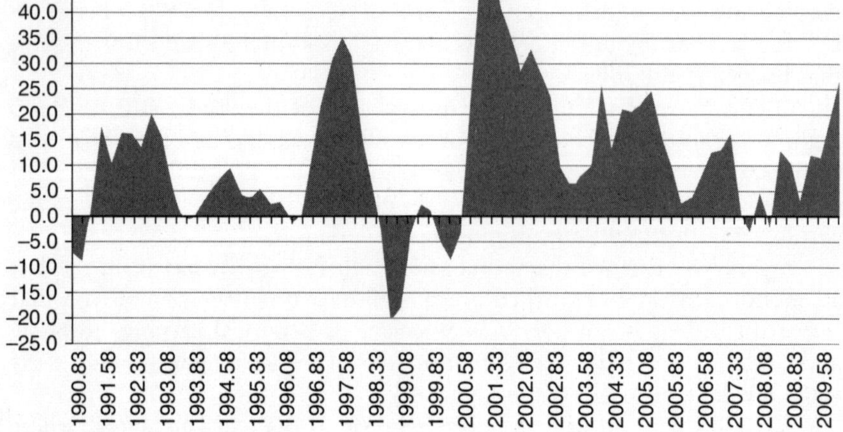


**FIGURE 6.6** Earnings to Price

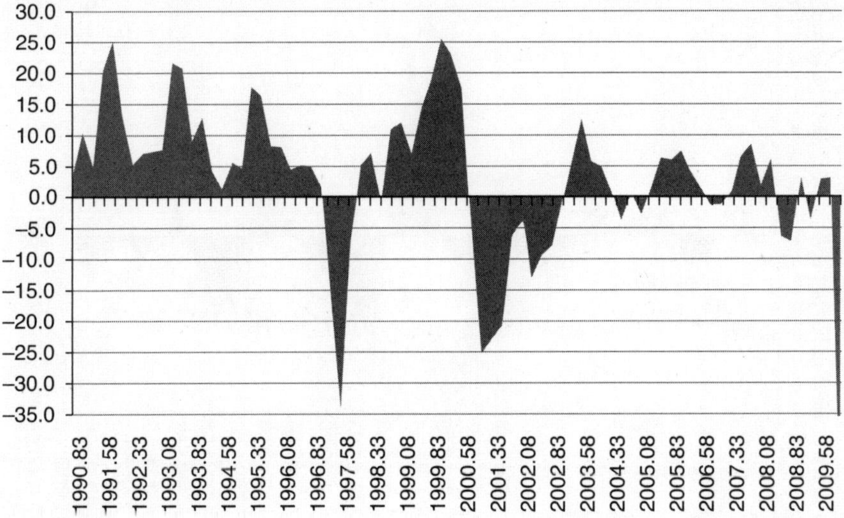


**FIGURE 6.7** Dividend Yield

selection in the past, but as we moved to more recent times, its effectiveness seems to have fallen off.

Next, we examine the current ratio, and the display of empirical evidence demonstrates that buying stocks based on current ratio alone offers very little help at all in stock selectivity, as discussed once already. This can be seen in Figure 6.8.

As can be seen in the current ratio time series, it is only during the pop of the Internet bubble that the ratio of current assets to liabilities was helpful. In times of duress, investors seek safety in balance-sheet health (i.e., quality). Surprisingly, in 2008, when there was a flight to quality, the current ratio did not help decide exactly what quality to run to, albeit it is the quintessential measurer of balance-sheet health.

Market capitalization, as a proxy for size, has demonstrated and still does demonstrate abundant return in the smallest quintile of stocks versus the largest as seen in the time series of size selection shown in Figure 6.9.

Generally, Morningstar-Ibbotson has demonstrated this phenomenon of large-caps and small-caps return differential in very long time-frame data series going back to the 1920s. In addition, size, of course, is one of the Fama-French factors, so buying stocks predicated on size should obviously be one criterion in a model. Just about every vendor's risk model has size, log of size, or square root of market capitalization in it. Thus it is a necessary component of returns that Graham foresaw.

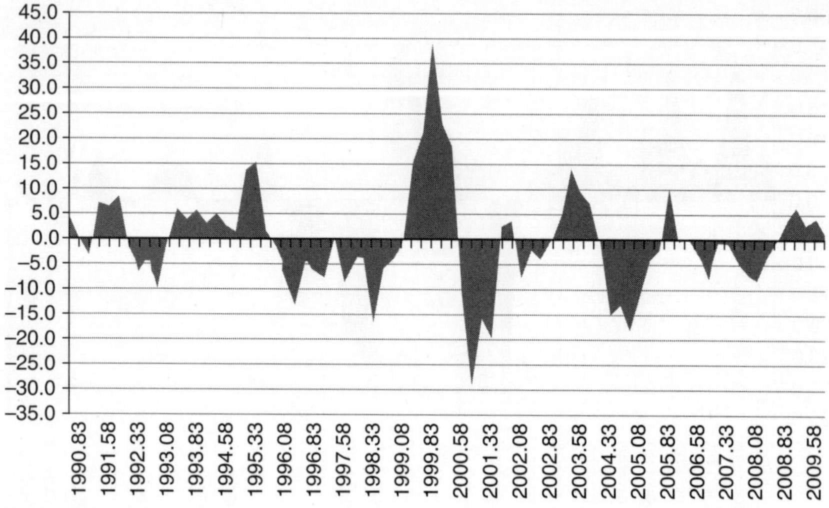


**FIGURE 6.8** Current Ratio

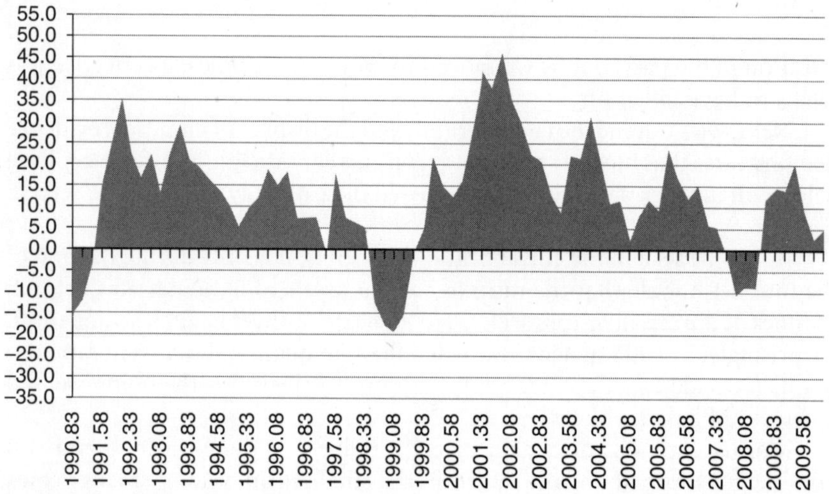


**FIGURE 6.9** Market Capitalization (Size)

Earnings growth as measured from the FactSet fundamental database using the growth of earnings per share over the last year (FG_EPS_1YGR) factor is also a decent factor as shown in the time series of Figure 6.10, though it has not been helpful more recently. However, I would bet on Mr. Graham and its inclusion in the Graham model as a highly significant contributor, because sometimes a factor that excludes stocks but does not

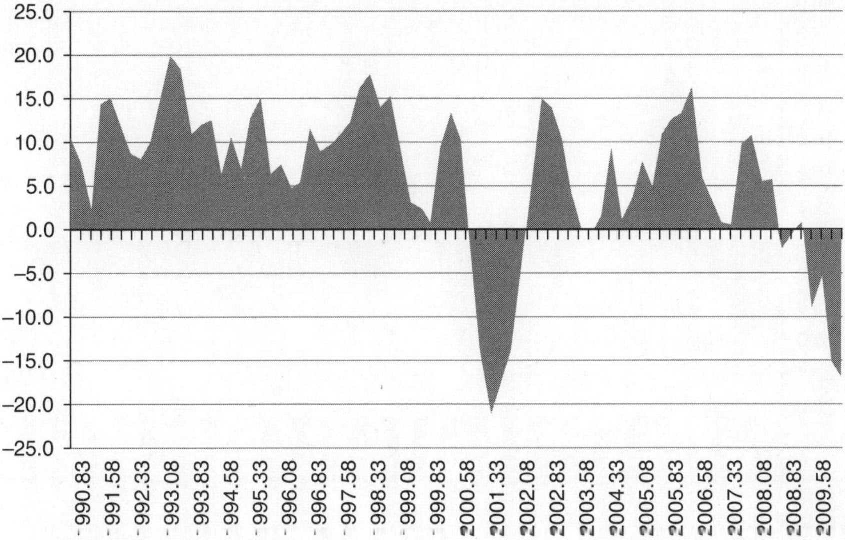


**FIGURE 6.10** Earnings Growth

necessarily add alpha is still useful in an investment strategy. EPS growth is one of those factors.

There are two definitions of earnings stability in this study. The first makes use of the standard deviation of "earnings per share growth," measured over 16 quarters and its time series of top minus bottom quintiles performance (shown in Figure 6.11).

The examination of this time series does not exactly instill confidence in its usage as a factor in the Graham model, and this is why we went to an earnings stability definition more consistent with Ben Graham's definition of sales minus cost of goods sold, minus selling general and administrative expense minus income taxes paid. All of this is normalized by market cap as foretold in the following equation using FactSet mnemonics:

$$\text{E Stab\_2} = (\text{FG\_SALES-FG\_COGS-FG\_SGA-FG\_INC\_TAX})/(\text{FG\_MKT\_VALUE})$$

This factor's 12-month rolling time series of top minus bottom quintile is plotted in Figure 6.12. It was especially efficacious right after the technology bubble collapsed.

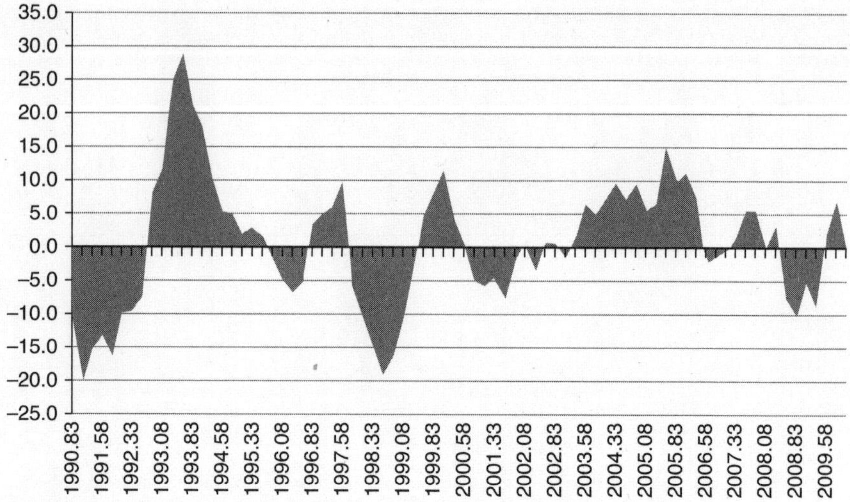


**FIGURE 6.11** Earnings Stability

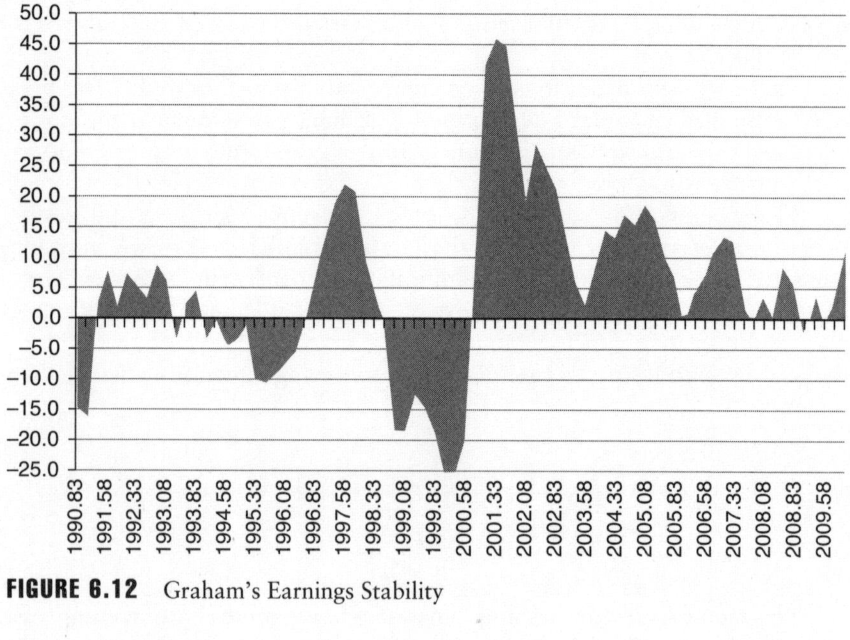


**FIGURE 6.12** Graham's Earnings Stability

This formula seems to have worked more recently, and the empirical evidence is that the majority of the area of the curve is found above zero and in the more recent time frame, too. It is interesting that it became a strong factor after the tech bubble, but wasn't much of a stock selector before that time period.

An example of a more sophisticated test on the second earnings stability factor involves bootstrapping to get a more accurate interpretation of the average value of return of the top and bottom quintiles as compared to the S&P 500 more generally. A numerical experiment was performed where we took the quarterly returns of the factor's top and bottom quintiles (1 and 5) along with the S&P 500 and bootstrapped, with replacement, the 20-year return time series. To review, we randomly selected a return from each of the top, bottom, and S&P 20-year quarterly time series and placed them consecutively in a spreadsheet column, until we obtained another hypothetical 20-year quarterly return time series, built from the original data set. Then, we calculated the average return of the new hypothetical time series for each of the three data sets. We did this more than 500 times, each time calculating the hypothetical time series average return. Then, we plotted the distribution of the average returns we acquired in this manner. The results are plotted in Figure 6.13.

The *X* axis is return, and the *Y* axis represents the number of times that average return was found among the 5,000+ sampled, 20-year quarterly

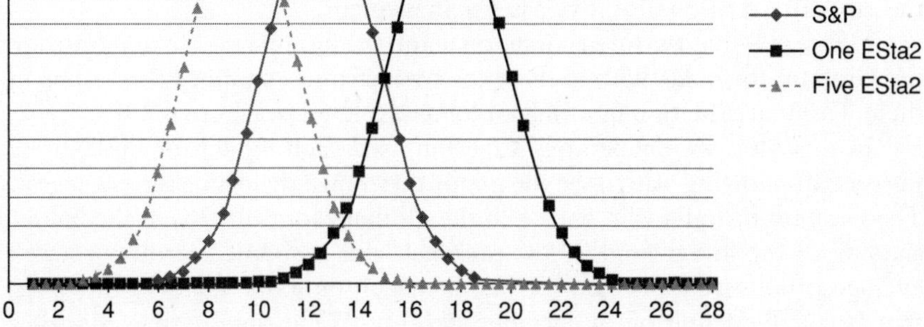


**FIGURE 6.13** Bootstrapping the Top and Bottom Quintile Mean Return of Graham's Earning Stability Factor along with the S&P 500

return time series we created from the original data sets. The bottom quintile average quarterly return is found on the left of the plot; the top quintile's return distribution is shown on the right; the S&P 500's return is in the middle. Now, each distribution shows what the real return's possible values are, so that it is a probability plot. The main likelihood is that the real return is at the center of each distribution, but there are probabilities that the return is either greater or lesser than this main value for each curve.

So, for instance, take the top quintile (One EStab2) and the S&P 500. Notice that, around the 15 percent return value, they overlap. This can be interpreted to mean that there is a possibility that the mean return of the top quintile could equal that of the S&P 500 at this point, both being 15 percent. In fact, there is a small probability that the mean quarterly return of the S&P 500 got as high as 17, and there is a small probability that the mean quarterly return of the top quintile actually got as low as 12 percent.

The results of the bootstrapped experiment then, are that there is no guarantee that the top quintile of quarterly returns from stocks bought predicated on the earnings stability factor did beat the S&P 500, but there is high probability that it did! Even if these two distributions were widely disparate, so that there is no overlap, that is still no guarantee that going forward in time this behavior would continue as strongly. In other words, the empirical evidence does not offer proof that past relationships will hold in the future. But it is better than random guessing! What these plots offer is the breadth of likelihood that the calculated means from the original time series has these values and the confidence in what the average values actually could be can be derived from it. Look for low overlap between the first quintile and the benchmark S&P 500 generally for any given factor in these types of bootstrapped plots. This is the kind of experiment that separates out the girly men from the manly girls, and it is highly recommended that you run them.

Showing these results—using just one small tool out of the vast selection in the statistician's toolbox—will hopefully allow you to begin to appreciate the modern art of quantitative asset management.

Figure 6.14 has two area curves on it and the figure serves to demonstrate the Graham formulas with each of the two earnings stability definitions in them. Compare the two in a single plot as depicted in Figure 6.14.

In this plot, we deliberately superimposed each model for the express purpose of allowing you to see the minor difference their time series suggest. The Graham formula is in back and the Graham formula_2 is in the lighter shading of the foreground. Now, each model is a simple equally weighted average of all seven Graham factors, in which only one factor is different, that being the definition of earnings stability. What the interpretation implies is that, although the second definition of earnings stability—that of Graham's specific formula—is better on a stand-alone basis, in concert with

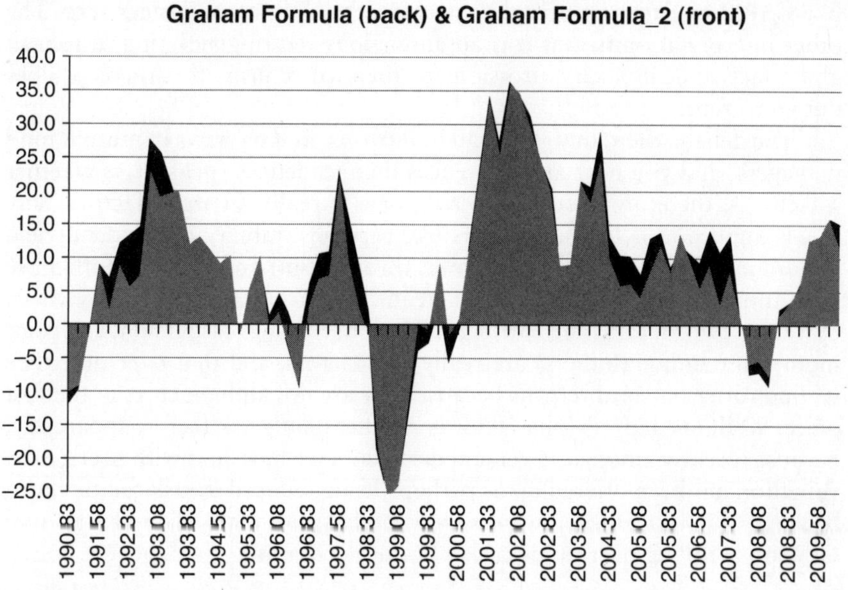


**FIGURE 6.14** Two Graham Models Time Series of Returns

other factors, it is a moot point. So, from a statistician's perspective, either is useful, whereas from a fundamental analyst's perspective, one would choose Graham's definition of earnings stability.

Now, the comfort to the intelligent investor is that the Graham equally weighted model return time series, reported here, looks pretty good. In general, one can be confident that the top quintile has most often outperformed the bottom quintile of stocks. This is what we are after, and this graph offers the kiloword viewpoint.

Now, the Graham factors studied to this point have been assumed to be alpha factors, and in our testing we do see anomalous return from sorting on these factors. But think back to the definitions of CAPM and the Fama-French model. Could these be risk factors rather than alpha factors? In these equations, the authors concluded that the factors in their models were risk factors and explained the variance of return well. In their data, the alpha term, the intercept of the regression when using these factors, was tiny (near zero if not so). Hence, they regarded market, large-small, and valuation all as risk factors. The emergence of definitions for CAPM and the Fama-French in modern times has allowed us to describe factors in these two different viewpoints: One is a risk factor and the other is a source of alpha, so coined as an alpha factor. It is a risk factor if, when used in a regression equation like CAPM or Fama-French, the intercept, the alpha term, is near zero. The other interpretation is that it is an anomalous return-generating factor, an alpha factor, if, in such regressions to forward returns, the intercept does not go to zero.

The debate, then, that you read in *Barrons*, in interviews of mutual fund managers, and you hear at conferences that academics speak at, is whether a factor is, therefore, a source of risk, or is it really an alpha factor? Why this is important is because factors like earnings stability or dividend-yield factor have shown wavering responses through time and more recently have been thought of as running out of steam. The accusations then have been that these two factors (and earnings diffusion, earnings dispersion, and price momentum, among others) are really risk factors, and that over time they will not offer outsized returns because they are not alpha factors in the first place. Well, one lady's alpha factor is another man's risk factor, apparently, because recently among the general discussion we have had with peers, even valuation has been offered up as perhaps being reduced to risk-factor status because of its nonefficaciousness over the last few years. You can be sure Graham is rolling over in his casket at this accusation.

## THE NEXT TESTS: SCENARIO ANALYSIS

The next series of tests for the factors involve what we call "scenario tests." Though there are many ways of creating scenarios, the method we chose is very simple and divided into six categories. These are: up and down markets, growth and value markets, and high- and low-volatility environments. The methods we chose to delineate these categories are as follows: Taking the time period of the study from December 31, 1989 to December 31, 2009, we download from FactSet, our data provider, the Russell 2000 stock index prices; the S&P 500 stock index prices; the Russell 2000 Growth and Value index prices; and the VIX, the options board volatility index. Then, we compute the three-month quarterly returns from these data to coincide in time with the returns from our factors. For the VIX we just utilize its level as discussed later.

For the up and down market delineator, we calculate the average three-month return over the entire time period. Then, starting at the beginning of time, we simply ask, is the current three-month return greater than the average value? If so, it is an up market, and if not, it is a down market. So the definition we use to determine up and down is not positive and negative returns, but whether the return beat the average 20-year three-month return. We could use the median and be sure that 50 percent of the time one has either an up or down value, but to use just positive or negative returns means, we may create a scenario that has 70 percent of the time in an up state, for instance, not allowing enough data for the down-state measure to offer statistical significance. In general, when bifurcating a market into two categories for testing, we want roughly equal populations for a given state.

For the growth and value delineator, we acquire the Russell 2000 value (R2KV) and growth (R2KG) indexes. We tabulate their three-month returns and simply ask the question: Did the R2KG beat the R2KV index in this period? If yes, it is a growth environment; otherwise, it is a value market.

For high versus low volatility, we utilize the VIX index and, with its levels tabulated over the identical time period, we simply ask: Is the current value of the VIX greater or lesser than its 20-year median value? Using this measure, we get 50 percent of the data in high-volatility and low-volatility market environments, respectively. Alternatively, one could use the one-month VIX and the one-year VIX and bifurcate the time periods into whether the one-month VIX is above or below the one-year VIX. This works because the long-term difference between the two "vixens" is zero. However, over the short run, their difference fluctuates but eventually moves toward the equilibrium value whenever it is mispriced.

The next set of figures graphs the up and down, growth versus value, and high-volatility versus low-volatility environments, as defined in the manner outlined in the previous paragraphs. We plot the S&P 500 (scaled to fit the plot) as the background for up/down, growth/value markets and the VIX (scaled) as the background for the high and low volatility delineator. Figure 6.15 is the first graph for up/down scenario.

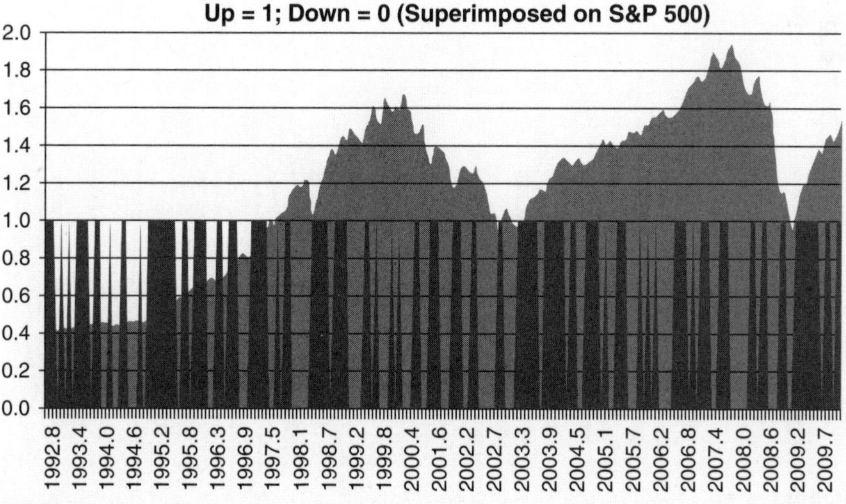


**FIGURE 6.15** Up and Down Market Scenarios

In Figure 6.15, it is not so clear that the up markets coincide with up markets in the S&P, namely because of the overarching secular trend of rising S&P 500 over these 20 years. In addition, we can see that the up market times, as defined in this way from the Russell 2000 index, may not ever persist for long periods of time and appear as transient signals. This is acceptable for testing purposes, but it is not necessarily acceptable for using a model in a production environment for Ben Graham style investing (though it can act as a trading signal perhaps for higher frequency day traders). In production, we seek model stability and usually low turnover of the portfolio. This would mean that we would want a model that does fairly well in up and down markets, and this is what scenario testing is about.

Therefore, we can separate out the time periods into these up and down markets, concatenating or conjoining the pieces of time that collectively exist in the same market environment, and examine the effectiveness of the model in that environment alone, computing averages and standard deviations of return absolutely or versus a benchmark. Then, those results quantify model behavior in a specific market, from whose results we either confirm model acceptance of or deny its use in production. The growth/value transition is plotted in Figure 6.16.

This last chart is the growth versus value market environment scheduler. Though its signifies different times than up and down market scheduler,

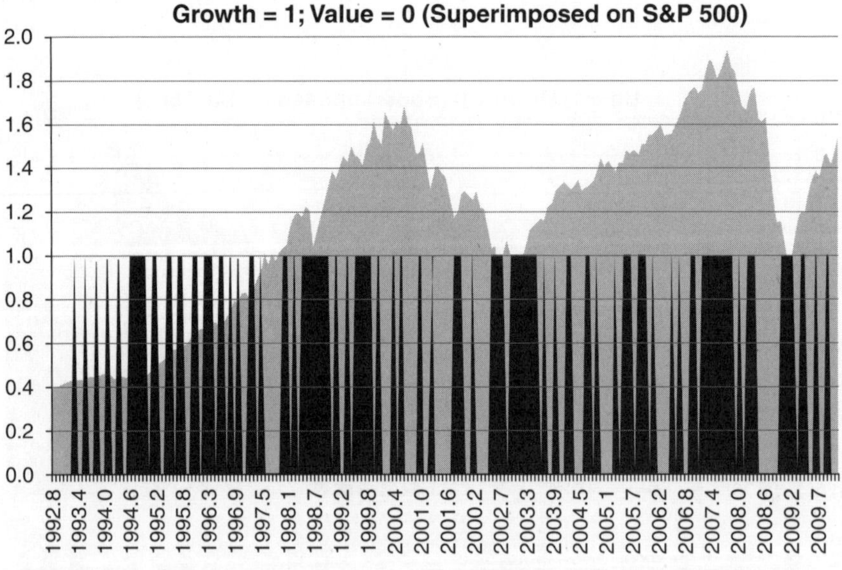


**FIGURE 6.16** Growth and Value Market Scenarios

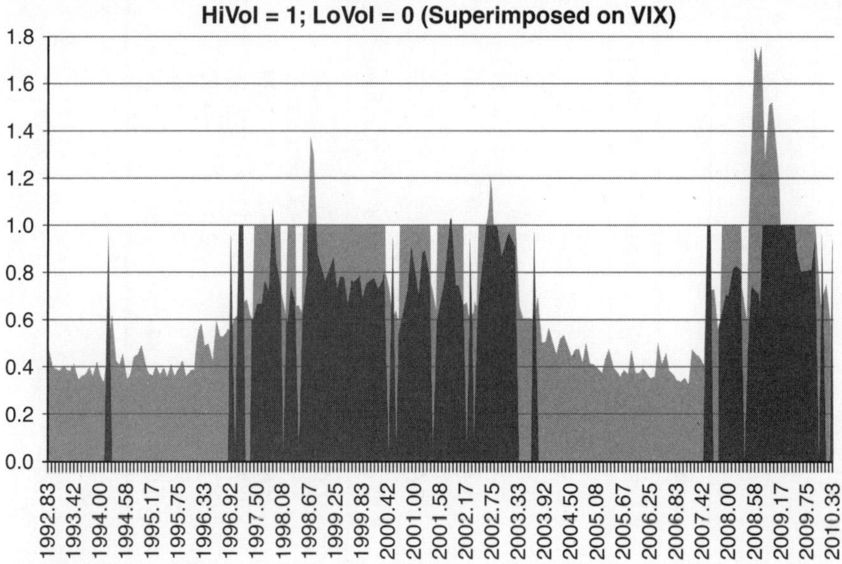


**FIGURE 6.17** High- and Low-Volatility Market Scenarios

it follows a similar higher frequency pattern, rendering it more useful in a literal sense for market trading rather than investing. Nevertheless, it offers a good distinction of markets for testing purposes with concatenation of like market environments to create a continuous time period to test through, though not contiguous in time. Figure 6.17 shows the high versus low volatility scheduler that is unlike the other two.

The volatility market indicator is widely accepted among most audiences we have found, as it is easy to demonstrate that volatility regimes do exist and they persist for longer periods of time. This makes market delineation by VIX values easy to process and understand. We add that these are not the only methods to create scenarios, as discussed earlier. The method by State Street Global Advisor mentioned earlier in this chapter is another great method, more sophisticated then these but one needs fund flow data to articulate them. The reader can brainstorm many other scenarios; however, it is believed that these three market bifurcations are just very easy to do for the average investor—even for the less than average investor!

Now that the time periods are put together, it is a simple spreadsheet activity to organize and collect returns for each market scenario's time periods and measure their statistics. Table 6.8 shows average excess returns over the S&P across the whole period, and each submarket scenario for the top and bottom quintiles. Again, we are looking for top quintile returns to

**TABLE 6.8** Average 12-Month Returns over S&P 500

| | Avg 12 Month XS Returns over S&P | | | | | | | | | |
|---|---|---|---|---|---|---|---|---|---|---|
| Top Quintile | B/P | E/P | DivYld | Cur Rat | MCap | E Grow | E Stab | E Stab_2 | Graham | Graham_2 |
| All Periods | 7.48 | 9.44 | 1.92 | 0.07 | 9.76 | 4.43 | 1.54 | 4.91 | 6.95 | 6.28 |
| Up | 13.42 | 14.03 | 4.09 | 5.11 | 14.55 | 9.39 | 6.95 | 10.27 | 12.31 | 11.67 |
| Down | 1.01 | 4.43 | −0.45 | −5.42 | 4.54 | −0.99 | −4.35 | −0.93 | 1.10 | 0.41 |
| Growth | 8.34 | 10.04 | 3.85 | 0.70 | 10.66 | 4.57 | 1.97 | 6.04 | 8.11 | 7.05 |
| Value | 6.49 | 8.75 | −0.31 | −0.66 | 8.72 | 4.26 | 1.05 | 3.60 | 5.60 | 5.39 |
| HiVol | 6.95 | 7.81 | −4.79 | −0.85 | 8.53 | 0.93 | −1.72 | 4.06 | 5.65 | 5.84 |
| LoVol | 7.97 | 10.93 | 8.07 | 0.91 | 10.90 | 7.63 | 4.54 | 5.69 | 8.13 | 6.68 |
| **Bottom Quintile** | **B/P** | **E/P** | **DivYld** | **Cur Rat** | **MCap** | **E Grow** | **E Stab** | **E Stab_2** | **Graham** | **Graham_2** |
| All Periods | −0.74 | −2.29 | 0.74 | 0.72 | −2.40 | −1.00 | −0.57 | −0.76 | −2.08 | −1.98 |
| Up | 3.23 | 2.74 | 5.89 | 4.82 | 1.74 | 5.43 | 3.66 | 4.43 | 1.73 | 1.69 |
| Down | −5.07 | −7.77 | −4.87 | −3.75 | −6.92 | −8.01 | −5.19 | −6.42 | −6.24 | −5.99 |
| Growth | 0.79 | −1.37 | 1.22 | 1.17 | 0.04 | 0.20 | 1.52 | 0.32 | −0.58 | −0.29 |
| Value | −2.52 | −3.36 | 0.19 | 0.21 | −5.23 | −2.39 | −2.99 | −2.02 | −3.82 | −3.93 |
| HiVol | −1.52 | −5.25 | 0.66 | −0.56 | −2.79 | −1.98 | 0.79 | −2.55 | −1.87 | −2.04 |
| LoVol | −0.02 | 0.42 | 0.82 | 1.90 | −2.05 | −0.09 | −1.82 | 0.87 | −2.27 | −1.93 |

exceed that of the bottom quintile. The reader should always consider the bottom quintiles as short candidate portfolios generally, though we have to qualify that there is no underlying economic theory that mandates that multifactor models in a general sense must have the top quintile outperform the market or the bottom quintile underperform the benchmark. However, there is economic theory underlying the quant process that says the top quintile should outperform the bottom quintile. So any factor or model used to rank stocks must have the top cohort outperform the bottom cohort if they are correlated with returns in any way, if the cause of stock returns is associated with that factor or model. But this is not the same thing as stating that the top and bottom fractiles must out- or underperform another portfolio formed some other way, as a benchmark is.

The user can only hope that their process would beat the bench, but there is no guarantee of this, and this includes Graham's process as well. Conditioning an investment methodology on the mispricing of securities, as does the Graham process, generally offers high probability that it will offer outsized returns relative to the S&P 500, but it does not offer guarantees that it will. The hope of outperformance of the Graham method over a capitalization weighted benchmark is predicated on the theory that the cap-weighted benchmark is, by its construction, inefficient. We will speak more about this in Chapter 9 when we discuss Stochastic Portfolio Theory. For now, the empirically determined average excess returns over the S&P 500 are listed for all scenarios in Table 6.8.

The kiloword viewpoint is in the accompanying bar charts of Figures 6.18 and 6.19. First we illustrate that, in down markets, there is clearly less performance than can be expected from factor models. This is mostly because, in down markets, fundamental factors disconnect from the stock market generally because of fear being the most prominent factor effecting stock returns. That is, correlations between factors and returns falls precipitously, whereas correlations between stocks rise so that the underlying financial-statement information that people make investment decisions on they ignore, and people sell, mostly out of panic, giving little to no thought to business factors in their ensuing decisions.

High-volatility markets also have a history of offering little alpha from financial-statement factors. However, as seen here, there is some efficacy with the Graham factors in high-volatility environments, due to his margin of safety principle. Notice, specifically, how the factors tend to perform in low-volatility environments better than in high-volatility markets. This again will be discussed in Chapter 9 when speaking about SPT, because high-volatility stocks are shown to be a drag on long-term performance, as corroborated by the empirical evidence. So the interpretation is that the factors and equally weighted Graham models work in five out of the six

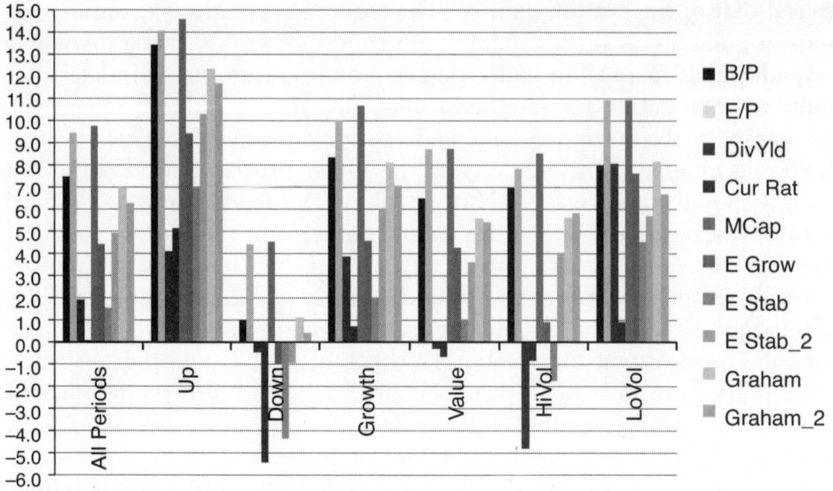


**FIGURE 6.18** Top Quintile Excess Return over the S&P 500

environments, but in down markets we might consider that we would trail the benchmark.

The bottom quintiles demonstrate underperformance across most factors in most environments, as seen in Figure 6.19. In up markets, the rising tide raises all ships and portfolio gets carried along for the ride. In up markets, most factors work not necessarily because of factor efficacy but because

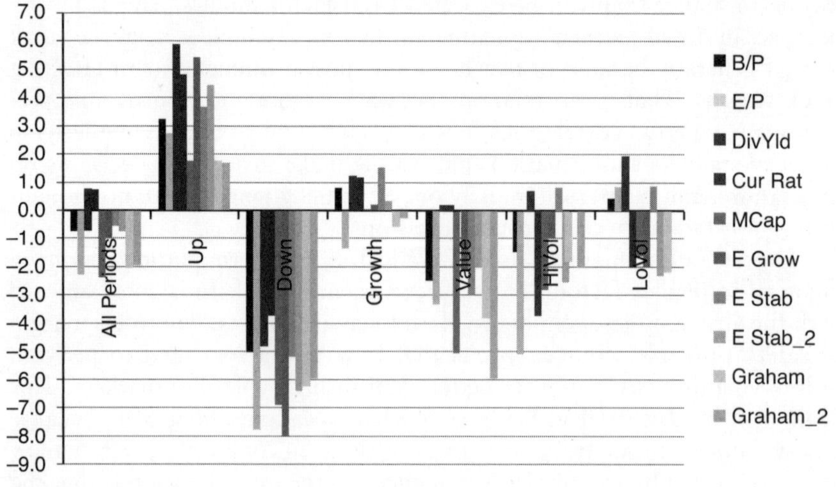


**FIGURE 6.19** Bottom Quintile Excess Return over the S&P 500

all stocks rise when the tide rises; even bottom quintiled stocks can have outperformance of the bench in up markets. However, Figure 6.19 shows that, on average, the bottom quintile stocks host a losing category, in general, and should be avoided. Also, consider that these are all equally weighted quintile portfolios so that beating a cap-weighted benchmark is easier in up markets, because, during up markets, unlike most, the entire breadth of stocks are rising rather than just those of the highest capitalization.

Now, to most individual investors, absolute returns are all that matter. However, these days, it is just too easy to go buy an index. A cap-weighted index is usually sought, and to the typical investing public the S&P 500 is the market and the index most widely known and favored. Hence, relative to an index, we would ask how performance is often. The next data set involves considering performance in addition to how widely disparate it is over time from the index. Hence, we show the information ratio of the quintile portfolios. The information ratio is simply the excess return over the benchmark, divided by the standard deviation of that excess return (also known as the tracking error) and can be thought of as a risk-adjusted performance measure. This figure is decidedly important to institutional investors, and we include it now simply because we can.

We boldly outline those IRs' values that are negative for ease of observation in Table 6.9. Remember, only the numerator in the IR ratio can be a negative number, so negative IRs are reflecting negative excess returns, though the absolute value determines how closely it mimics the index through the tracking error in the measure's denominator.

What is an important takeaway from Table 6.9 involves the extraordinary size of the IR in low-volatility markets relative to other markets for the top quintile, relative to other market environments. It can be easily seen in the kiloword view of Figure 6.20, where we bar chart the top quintile's IR in all scenarios. The reason that investors obtain larger returns in low-volatility environments is due to a factor-based method like Ben Graham's, which is associated with investor behavior in these markets. Generally, when volatility is low, there is little fear in the market, and it is a stock selector's paradise because cross-correlation between stocks is quite low. Investors are concerned about business basics and the fundamentals of financial-statement data, in addition to being wary about paying too much for a stock, so valuation-based metrics tend to work well. In the Graham factors there is strong emphasis on valuation and balance-sheet health, so in these low-volatility time frames, we tend to get decent returns and lower tracking error in general. When volatility in the market is lower overall, so is tracking error to a bench and, consequently, the denominator in the IR calculation is smaller and the IR ratio goes up. Therefore, in up markets investors gets higher returns on average, but in low-volatility

**TABLE 6.9** Information Ratio of Top and Bottom Quintiles

| | Information Ratio | | | | | | | | | |
|---|---|---|---|---|---|---|---|---|---|---|
| **Top Quintile** | **B/P** | **E/P** | **DivYld** | **Cur Rat** | **MCap** | **E Grow** | **E Stab** | **E Stab_2** | **Graham** | **Graham_2** |
| All Periods | 0.34 | 0.45 | 0.12 | 0.00 | 0.48 | 0.27 | 0.09 | 0.24 | 0.35 | 0.31 |
| Up | 0.58 | 0.62 | 0.27 | 0.29 | 0.67 | 0.59 | 0.41 | 0.49 | 0.58 | 0.55 |
| Down | 0.05 | 0.24 | −0.03 | −0.38 | 0.26 | −0.07 | −0.28 | −0.05 | 0.06 | 0.02 |
| Growth | 0.32 | 0.40 | 0.25 | 0.03 | 0.45 | 0.25 | 0.10 | 0.25 | 0.34 | 0.30 |
| Value | 0.37 | 0.57 | −0.02 | −0.05 | 0.58 | 0.32 | 0.08 | 0.23 | 0.36 | 0.35 |
| HiVol | 0.24 | 0.28 | −0.33 | −0.04 | 0.32 | 0.05 | −0.08 | 0.15 | 0.21 | 0.22 |
| LoVol | 0.59 | 0.84 | 0.56 | 0.07 | 0.98 | 0.66 | 0.43 | 0.43 | 0.68 | 0.56 |
| **Bottom Quintile** | **B/P** | **E/P** | **DivYld** | **Cur Rat** | **MCap** | **E Grow** | **E Stab** | **E Stab_2** | **Graham** | **Graham_2** |
| All Periods | −0.06 | −0.16 | 0.04 | 0.04 | −0.20 | −0.05 | −0.04 | −0.05 | −0.18 | −0.18 |
| Up | 0.26 | 0.18 | 0.29 | 0.31 | 0.14 | 0.26 | 0.23 | 0.29 | 0.15 | 0.15 |
| Down | −0.46 | −0.63 | −0.27 | −0.24 | −0.66 | −0.47 | −0.39 | −0.49 | −0.65 | −0.62 |
| Growth | 0.05 | −0.08 | 0.05 | 0.06 | 0.00 | 0.01 | 0.09 | 0.02 | −0.04 | −0.02 |
| Value | −0.28 | −0.29 | 0.01 | 0.02 | −0.61 | −0.18 | −0.26 | −0.17 | −0.50 | −0.52 |
| HiVol | −0.10 | −0.30 | 0.02 | −0.03 | −0.18 | −0.08 | 0.04 | −0.14 | −0.13 | −0.14 |
| LoVol | 0.00 | 0.04 | 0.08 | 0.20 | −0.26 | −0.01 | −0.22 | 0.07 | −0.31 | −0.28 |

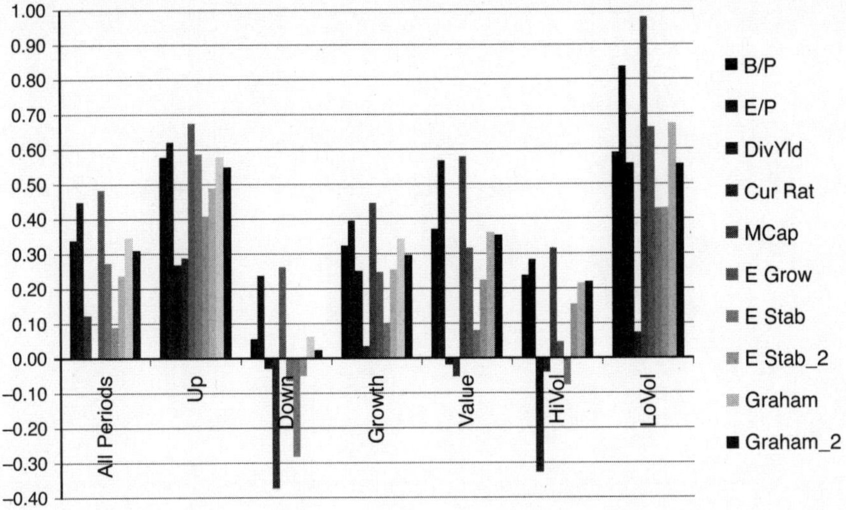


**FIGURE 6.20** Bar Charts of Information Ratio (XS Return/Tracking Error)

environments investors track the benchmark more closely and higher IRs persist.

In summary of these last chapters, we have demonstrated the pitfalls and perils of quant modeling, and in this chapter have taken the Graham factors, sorted stocks by them, and measured performance of these sorts. Then, we showed how to construct three very simple market environments and test models through them. Given the efficacy of these factors in stock selection as proposed by Graham, we now can move forward to examine various ways of combining these factors to form an investment process predicated on the Graham factors, manifested in a quant model.

CHAPTER 7

# Building Models from Factors

*Although he lived three hundred years before our time, the spiritual situation with which (Baruch) Spinoza had to cope peculiarly resembles our own. The reason for this is that he was utterly convinced of the causal dependence of all phenomena, at a time when the success accompanying the efforts to achieve a knowledge of the causal relationship of natural phenomena was still quite modest.*

—Albert Einstein, overheard at dinner by his secretary Helen Dukas, toward the end of his life

Baruch Spinoza was a complex character in history but at the time of the mid 1600s, he was a heretic par excellence. What Einstein says about him is apropos for this chapter, however, because it represents what Graham was after, too. In the later stages of his life, Ben Graham was living in California and still actively researching investing methodologies, trying to find causality between underlying factors and stock returns. At this point in his life, it was not about the money anymore, but just about the quest, whose reward was sufficient in itself for the labor spent.

The next part of the process of turning Graham's recipe into a quant model he would approve of is relatively simple and straightforward. The tests we put the models through are the same ones we ran for the factors. The only major consideration is how to combine the factors into a model. We have already seen two models created from equally weighting the factors; in our case each model had six identical factors and only earnings stability was different for each. Our empirical observation of the results of those two models was that their performance was the same in a statistical sense so that we could not choose which earnings stability factor to use from these model results. In particular and importantly, the numerical values of the model's average returns were different, but they were not different enough. We could see a difference in performance in the individual earning stability factors, however, and we decided to choose the factor that Graham liked best for earnings stability, as opposed to that factor we conjured up, being the standard deviation of earnings per share, over 16 quarters.

Okay, so let's talk about factors that survive the battery of tests we put them through in the last chapter. Under normal circumstances, these tests describe the day-to-day job of many quant analysts of the type-2 variety, those whose job it is to refine the process of long-only institutional asset management. They comb through the academic literature, through the *Journal of Finance,* attend conferences, exchange information, and are always on the lookout for the next, best factor. In this vein, quants everywhere latched onto accruals and arbitraged away the effect.[1] So if accrual was indeed an alpha factor, by overuse, it could have been ultimately reduced to being a risk factor. Remember, a risk factor is a factor that, in a regression with future return (with other factors in a multivariate regression), the intercept coefficient, the alpha, is near zero. An alpha factor is a factor that, in a regression with future return, originates a positive and significant intercept term, an alpha, arising independently from any factors.

In fact, a major criticism of quants is that they use too many of the same factors and end up using risk factors rather than finding true alpha factors for their process. There is probably a grain of truth in these accusations, and August of 2007 provides some of the empirical evidence to that effect, as discussed in earlier chapters. Nevertheless, many quant analysts who report to portfolio managers who themselves were not brought up in the modeling disciplines are subjected to this job description often to their own chagrin, knowing that searching for another better factor is a waste of good time. That being the case, the fundamental factors of Graham do uphold keen economic diligence and maintain their alpha efficacy while offering provocative evidence to own the selected stocks. The Graham methodology does indeed pay royalties over the long term.

## SURVIVING FACTORS

Let us forgo the search and testing of hundreds of factors and utilize the shoulders of others who have archived the results for a wide variety of factors within profitability, valuation, cash flow, growth, capital allocation, price momentum, and exogenous variables when we begin to doubt the wisdom of Graham.[2] Then the criteria for accepting a factor, as illustrated in the last chapter, are that the top fractile outperform the bottom fractile (in our case quintile) and that the time series of return for the fractiles show relative stability.

Moreover, it is a necessary condition that the percentage of stocks and the percentage of time the top quintile outperforms either cash (i.e., offers positive return) or a benchmark is far greater than 50 percent (65 percent is nice). In addition, we need confidence in the mean returns as measured by bootstrapping, so that they are widely different between top and bottom quintiles and the benchmark. Also, we would like the IRs and ICs to be sufficient and the g-Factor to be where we want it. In our case with the Graham factors, the g-Factors were greater than one for the top quintile, but not greatly so. Lastly, the factors need to be lowly correlated with each other to reduce the impact of co-linearity, unless of course the correlation between the factors is stationary, meaning it does not change much over large ranges of time. This last requirement of low correlation also assures factor alpha diversification as well.

Table 7.1 shows the correlation matrix between factors where positive correlations are gray-scaled and negative correlations are shown in bold. This matrix was created by simply calculating the correlation between the time series of (top minus bottom) quintile returns over the 20-year time period. It is not the correlation of the factor's values themselves, but the returns of stocks selected by the 1-factor models of the factors. The top row shows that even though all spreads between top and bottom quintile are positive (except for the current ratio), the action of correlation, say, between B/P and earnings growth of –51.8 percent, means that combining both of these factors in a model will serve to lower portfolio volatility while garnering a positive differential between top and bottom fractiles. Other factor correlations like B/P and E/P are considered highly correlated, whereas the dividend-yield factor, also a value factor, is anticorrelated with those two. Size (MCap) has strong, highly positive correlation with valuation, but it is small and negative with dividend yield. Now, generally, if the correlation is bounded between –20 and 20 percent, it is interpreted as being zero. Remember that correlation is a dynamic variable in stock return time series, which means that these are not stationary values and that there is a wide variance around these average 20-year numbers through time. This means that the correlations in this table are approximates of what is a nonstationary variable and we should not read too deeply into them.

Another interesting feature involves the earnings stability factors. Notice how the earnings stability factor consisting of standard deviation of 16 quarters of EPS (Estab), has a positive correlation, albeit small with all other factors and the two Graham models, though it is insignificant with E/P. However, the two earnings stability factors between them have no correlation (numerical value of –0.1 percent), and the earnings stability factor of Graham's definition (Estab_2 = Revenue-Cost of Goods Sold – Selling General and Administration Expenses – Taxes Paid) is highly, positively

**TABLE 7.1** Correlation Matrix of Graham Factors

| | CORRELATION MATRIX | | | | | | | | | |
|---|---|---|---|---|---|---|---|---|---|---|
| | **B/P** | **E/P** | **DivYld** | **Cur Rat** | **M Cap** | **E Grw** | **E Stab** | **E Stab_2** | **Gram** | **Gram_2** |
| Top-Bot Quint. Ret. | 6.92 | 11.43 | 2.89 | −0.42 | 12.11 | 5.94 | 0.67 | 5.10 | 8.76 | 7.76 |
| B/P | | 84.2% | −60.1% | −35.6% | 71.3% | −51.8% | 25.7% | 83.4% | 89.3% | 85.1% |
| E/P | | | −68.9% | −43.9% | 58.1% | −49.6% | 3.0% | 91.1% | 81.6% | 75.3% |
| DivYld | | | | 54.4% | −14.1% | 56.9% | 14.0% | −70.3% | −39.9% | −34.4% |
| Cur Rat | | | | | 10.7% | 21.1% | 23.7% | −62.9% | −12.2% | 2.2% |
| M Cap | | | | | | −25.2% | 24.4% | 51.5% | 82.4% | 84.0% |
| E Grw | | | | | | | 16.9% | −44.7% | −33.4% | −34.6% |
| E Stab | | | | | | | | −0.1% | 32.8% | 40.8% |
| E Stab_2 | | | | | | | | | 74.2% | 66.1% |
| Graham | | | | | | | | | | 96.5% |

correlated with valuation. In addition, it is highly negatively correlated with dividend yield and current ratio, and positively correlated with size and earnings growth. Thus, Graham's earning-stability factor has a large variance of correlation across factors, which is very interesting, indeed. Overall, the combination of these factors is what Graham utilizes, so we have to accept them all as is.

Factors that have high correlation such as E/P and B/P are traditionally combined to form a superfactor in the art of alpha modeling. Since there is generally a steady, high correlation between valuation factors, we have justification for using them in a linear combination. Now, in God's equation for stock returns, all the factors would have zero correlation. One could contrive a set of factors with zero correlation, creating an orthogonal set using principal components analysis (PCA), but that is beyond the scope of this book. However, many risk models are formulated this way, and PCA is finding much application with risk vendors like APT and Axioma found in FactSet's Balanced Risk product.

In ordinary quant work, correlation tables encompass a hundred factors as users screen for a parsimonious set, first using correlation analysis; for our purposes, our surviving factors remain B/P, E/P, dividend yield, current ratio, market cap, earnings growth, and earnings stability. Also, because our two earnings stability factors have no correlation between them, we are free to include both of them in our models.

## WEIGHTING THE FACTORS

The next step in the process involves choosing weights for the factors. The easiest scientific method to employ involves regression methods to form the factor weights, betas, factor coefficients, or factor returns, whatever you would like to call them. Among risk managers and risk modelers, the term *factor returns* is prominent, but in reality they are regression coefficients when, indeed, regression is used to determine them. However, we will save that method for more advanced users later and illustrate heuristic methods at the moment.

A very simple method for choosing weights takes the top minus the bottom quintile long-term average returns for each factor, and sums them. Then, each factor's weight in the model becomes the factor's top-bottom quintile return, divided by this sum. In this way, each factor is represented in the model roughly in proportion to its contribution to its long-term return. Then, the additional art utilizes the formation of these weights for results from each scenario, creating models named from the resultant factor scenario test that formulate the weights. So for our example, we have eight factors total. Then, for each of six scenarios, we build a model for each using all eight factors. From the scenario data, we can create seven models each with a slight variation in factor weights, where Gram_All uses the whole time period of data to determine weights by subtracting the bottom quintile returns from the top. Table 7.2 shows the resultant factor weights.

Any negative top-bottom quintile returns would be given a 2.5 percent weighting before normalization (less so afterward) and kept in the model just for factor diversification purposes, as they do not add alpha (i.e., current ratio). Usually, given a quant's choices of a hundred such factors, few with this property would make it into a final model. However, Ben is not around to get permission to ignore a factor like the current ratio, which we saw adds little value, so we must include it, but we will do so cleverly. So in summary, there are seven original models, each made heuristically from the factors' responses to the different market scenarios, aptly named after that scenario that was used to manufacture the weights for that particular model.

Another way to look at these factor loadings is to put the factors into aggregated categories, as seen in Table 7.3.

Thus, in all models, the valuation category contains 40–50 percent of the weight in all models, which is exactly why Ben Graham is credited with being a value investor. Balance sheet health is a very little weight, whereas size is 25 percent and earnings is given the rest of the factor weighting. Then the models play out where only data used from each scenario is utilized to produce the weights for each model. Notice that there is a fairly wide dispersion among factor weights for each model, providing assurance that we are obtaining sufficient factor diversity in our testing.

Another method used to choose weights involves a full-factorial two-level design of experiment methodology, where we would choose a high and a low for each factor weight and run models over each permutation. So for instance, consider a three-factor model consisting of B/P, dividend yield, and Estab_2. The first factor, B/P, would acquire values of, say, 15 percent and 40 percent based purely on judgment, whereas dividend yield would take 10 and 30 percent values, and Estab_2 would take the values of 40 and 75 percent. Then, given there are three factors, we could obtain $3^2 = 9$ models with all weight combinations. It is not necessary for the weights to sum to 100 percent because these weights are really just factor multipliers. They really do not account for participation of the factor in any real meaningful way, though many consultants think they do. For our eight factors, this would offer $8^2$ permutations, equaling 64 different models to run. This is also a good method for heuristically assigning weights and is recommended when one has the time to test many models; however, for brevity's sake, we are using the simple method where weights are derived from averaged factor returns in different market scenarios.

When these models are created, we examine them just as we did with the individual factors, testing them individually and through all scenarios.

**TABLE 7.2** Model Weights for Graham Factors

Model Weights Are Therefore

| | B/P | E/P | DivYld | Cur Rat | MCap | E Grow | E Stab | E Stab_2 |
|---|---|---|---|---|---|---|---|---|
| Gram_All | 17.3% | 24.6% | 2.5% | 2.4% | 25.5% | 11.4% | 4.4% | 11.9% |
| Gram_UP | 20.5% | 22.7% | 2.3% | 2.3% | 25.8% | 8.0% | 6.6% | 11.8% |
| Gram_DN | 12.4% | 24.9% | 9.0% | 2.3% | 23.4% | 14.3% | 2.3% | 11.2% |
| Gram_GR | 17.0% | 25.7% | 5.9% | 2.4% | 23.9% | 9.8% | 2.4% | 12.9% |
| Gram_Val | 16.7% | 22.5% | 2.3% | 2.3% | 25.9% | 12.3% | 7.5% | 10.4% |
| Gram_HiVol | 18.9% | 29.1% | 1.9% | 1.9% | 25.2% | 6.5% | 1.9% | 14.7% |
| Gram_LoVol | 13.5% | 17.8% | 12.3% | 2.4% | 21.9% | 13.1% | 10.8% | 8.2% |

**TABLE 7.3** Aggregation of Factor Weights into Categories

| | Value | B.Sh.H | Size | Earnings |
|---|---|---|---|---|
| Gram_All | 44.3% | 2.4% | 25.5% | 27.7% |
| Gram_UP | 45.5% | 2.3% | 25.8% | 26.4% |
| Gram_DN | 46.4% | 2.3% | 23.4% | 27.9% |
| Gram_GR | 48.6% | 2.4% | 23.9% | 25.1% |
| Gram_Val | 41.5% | 2.3% | 25.9% | 30.3% |
| Gram_HiVol | 49.8% | 1.9% | 25.2% | 23.1% |
| Gram_LoVol | 43.6% | 2.4% | 21.9% | 32.0% |

The reader should not confuse models created *from* factor returns measured through scenarios, with testing the subsequent constructed models *through* the market scenarios.

Regarding the current ratio factor, its weight in our models is insignificant and we could ignore them, except Graham did not. However, we have a method we can employ in model construction to alleviate the lack of alpha, the lack of stock selectivity that the current ratio, a balance-sheet health measure, offers. This involves screening the S&P 1500 universe by current ratio before forming the universe of stocks to test the model with during the back test. Thus, we put a rule in the test that says, for all time, only choose stocks from the S&P 1500 that have a current ratio greater than say, 1.5. Graham preferred a current ratio greater than 2, but we want enough stocks so that when we quintile the universe we have enough for statistical significance. Using too high a current ratio trims the universe too much. In this way we are using the factor and cleansing the system of those stocks with poor balance-sheet health, just as Graham would have done.

## THE ART VERSUS SCIENCE OF MODELING

Now this section will illustrate where the art comes into the process of model building. You already saw how we were able to maintain the use of a factor that seemingly had little value in selecting stocks. Choosing stocks by sorting the current ratio offered little return over a benchmark and was not even able to bifurcate returns of top quintile versus bottom quintile stocks by this measure. Yet, by screening the universe of candidate stocks by some cutoff value of current ratio, we obtained a healthier galaxy of stocks from this universe to fish in. We can think of that process specifically as adding a margin of safety to the quant method by doing so, in line with Graham's philosophy.

In addition, we note that the margin of safety concept may never actually be experienced. For example, in the opening of Chapter 2 on risk, we discussed a parable of a bridge that withstood the weight of one car but collapsed under the second car. Assume the first car was lighter than the second car. Inherently, that was a margin of safety, yet the first car never knew it benefited from it during the process. Likewise, trimming the universe of potential investments by the current ratio eliminates unhealthy balance-sheet stocks from consideration. Consider that because so few of us monitor stocks we do not own, if unhealthy stocks eliminated through this process had their prices fall precipitously, the prudent intelligent investor may never know about it. It is only that we know it does not make economic sense most of the time (but not all the time) to have high debt, and stocks with low current ratio have low asset to liabilities ratios, making them unhealthier than comparatively valued stocks with higher ratios. Therefore, we go with the law of large numbers and try not to excavate those few stocks with low asset to liabilities ratios that might be good candidates; we exclude them all as a whole category and hide behind a margin of safety. This is the Graham philosophy at work.

The next art we will introduce to the Graham models is volatility. This choice is predicated on several pieces of information. First, we tested volatility in Chapter 4 and found it offering a lot of alpha, and second, as you will see in later chapters as we discuss SPT theory, low volatility stocks are less of a drag on long-term stock performance than high volatility stocks, and in this venue we can think of volatility as a risk factor. Thus, if we implement in the Graham process a method to steer the stock purchases toward stocks with a lower variance of return, it should aid long-term performance as well as offer a margin of safety. Especially in times like 2008, when the VIX went to exorbitant heights because of fear and contagion in the market at that time, steering toward purchasing low-volatility stocks was prudent. So, we are going to add a volatility factor defined as the six-month standard deviation of daily return to the Graham suite of factors and give it just a small weighting of roughly 10 percent in all scenario models. Except in the equally weighted model, its contribution will be identical to every other factor because all factors get the same weight by definition in this model.

The first chart, therefore, is a compilation of data from each of the Graham models, including the equally weighted model with and without the current ratio screen and with and without the volatility factor. The bar chart of Figure 7.1 demonstrates the similarity of their returns on an absolute quarterly return basis.

This chart plots average absolute quarterly returns from December 31, 1991, to December 31, 2009, for each of seven models derived from factor weights further derived from market scenarios, shown in Table 7.2, plus

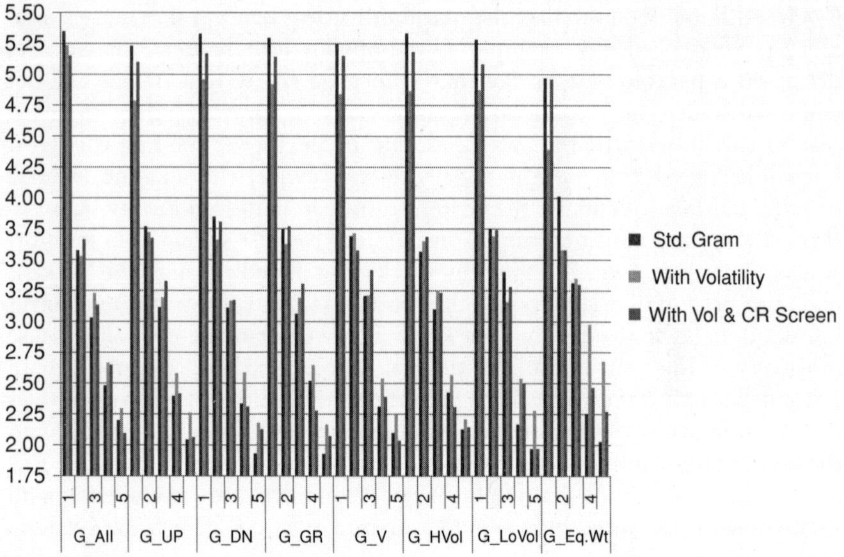


**FIGURE 7.1** Bar Charts of Graham Models

equal weight. The Std. Gram model consists of the group of models with neither the current ratio screen nor a volatility factor. This comprises the leftmost bar of all groups. Next is the set of models in which we just have the volatility factor at 10 percent weighting but without the current ratio screen. Last is the model set with both a volatility factor and the current ratio screen. The labels on the *X* axis of each model are an indicator of how the weights were constructed and does not represent average performance of any model run through any market scenario. The data in this chart are averaged model performance through all time of the study, so do not confuse the scenario naming convention with running a model through the scenario just yet.

In addition, each of five quintile performances for each model so named is shown and quite nicely, we get a monotonic decrease in performance moving from any model's top quintile to its fifth quintile, a necessary condition for any good model. From a bulk chart like this, the eye does not focus on subtle differences because, on average, their results are quite similar. However, we maintain a margin of safety because the current ratio screen is applied to the S&P 1500 universe before we form the portfolios and rank the stocks with the model, combined with the 10 percent contribution of the volatility factor, and this difference between the models is observed at the margin. We do this because we know, from Chapter 4 and SPT theory, that

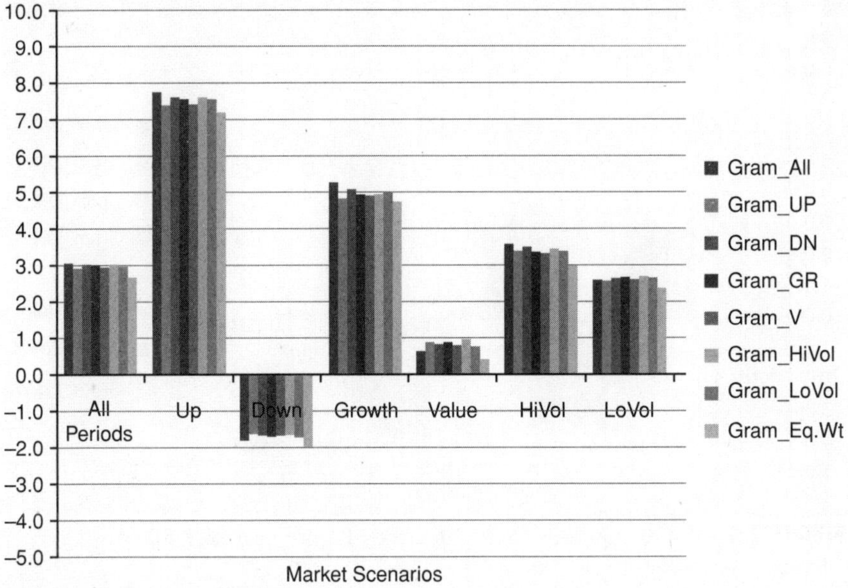


**FIGURE 7.2** Top Quintile Excess Quarterly Return over S&P 500

volatility is a drag to a stock's long-term return, and that current ratio does screen for stocks with a healthier balance sheet.

Figure 7.2 will serve to examine the average returns again for the models, but here we document the empirical results as measured through the various market scenarios. However, we only show results of the Graham model that includes both the current ratio screen and the volatility factor for brevity.

This chart displays the top quintile's quarterly excess returns over the S&P 500 for each model, in each scenario. Again, we generally do not see much difference across the models, though the Gram_All model, created by using returns measured from the underlying factors across the whole period of the study, seems to perform slightly better than the other models in almost every scenario. This is the leftmost bar of each cohort. Remember that the universe of stocks chosen to construct the models consists of the S&P 1500, whereas the benchmark is only the S&P 500. Thus, there is a smaller-cap bias to the universe than the benchmark simply because of the wider availability of market cap to invest in versus the benchmark.

In Figure 7.3, we see bottom quintile excess return over the S&P 500. Notice that the HiVol portfolio doesn't underperform the index in the top or bottom quintile? The difference between the estimation universe (S&P 1500) versus benchmark of S&P 500 explains why all models do not underperform

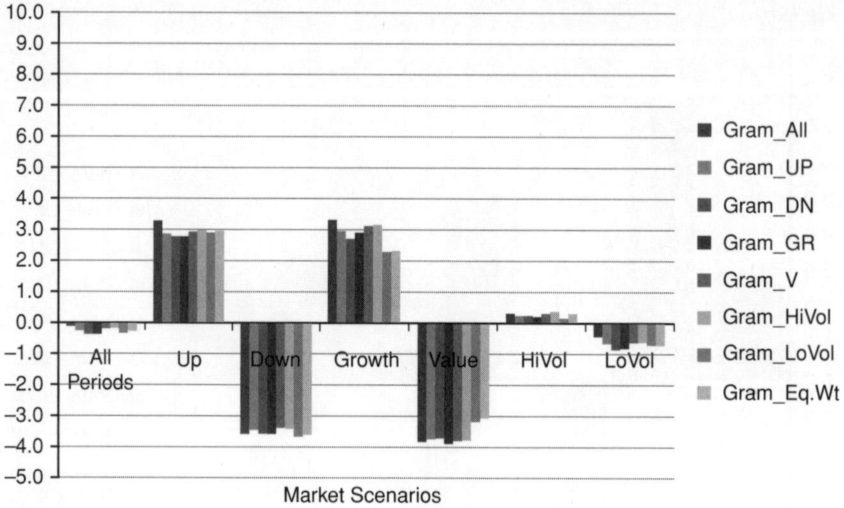


**FIGURE 7.3** Bottom Quintile Excess Quarterly Return over S&P 500

the index by a wider margin considering that the stocks are equally weighted in each quintile. Now, imagine that if you were measuring performance of a model consisting only of stocks from the benchmark, you would expect under these circumstances that the bottom quintile would underperform by a wider margin than shown here for the All Periods scenario, because the top and bottom quintile of a benchmark cannot both outperform the same benchmark.

Thus, logic dictates using a wider universe of securities in which to seek stocks to invest in than your benchmark would have, albeit assuming you have the means to screen that universe in sufficient depth. The bottom quintile excess returns over the S&P 500 bar chart is plotted on the same scale as the top quintile, offering insight as the relative magnitude of these returns.

In Figure 7.3, notice that even the bottom quintile outperforms the index in Up and Growth markets. Also, the impact of the Graham portfolios in high- and low-volatility environments demonstrates that having a bias to purchasing lower-volatility stocks in a high-volatility environment is advantageous, whereas this bias may hurt you in generally lower-volatility markets. This effect is due to the strong value bias in the Graham portfolios here and not due to the low 10 percent weighting of the volatility factor in the models. There would need to be a much more significant volatility-factor weighting to offset the impact of valuation in the model and obtain higher performance in low-volatility markets over high-volatility markets.

High-volatility markets are almost synonymous with down markets, by the way, so take note that market environments can be correlated, too.

Thus, having a low-volatility stock selection bias in 2008 was advantageous when the VIX was running high and mighty, whereas, in 2009, when the VIX collapsed, it hurt performance and did so for many money managers. To see this, we know that in 2008, the market was highly volatile and a down market, simultaneously. In addition, stocks correlated up on the downside, so they moved mainly downward together with high volatility. It was not a value environment for stocks either in 2008, because these volatile and downward-trending stocks suddenly began to price themselves into bankruptcy and valuations fell dramatically. So we would characterize 2008 as HiVol, Growth and Down, or absolutely "sucky." A horrible cross-section of extreme Black Swan and ELE events, but, nevertheless, the top quintile of the Graham models' returns would suggest they would outperform the index (on average) if those three market environments were combined. In the 2008 environment, owning low-volatility stocks was helpful because they would not have gone down as far as high-volatility stocks, because high-volatility stocks are the stocks most correlated and moving most strongly together in a downward direction. In 2009, when the VIX collapsed, stocks rebounded dramatically in March and turned on a penny, phennig, pence, and half Japanese penny; it quickly became a value environment, and an up market simultaneously, but, unfortunately, the stocks that moved higher beginning in March were only those that had fallen so far in 2008. Because this transition from HiVol, Growth, and Down to LoVol, Value, and Up occurred so very rapidly, it would have been extremely difficult for investors to reposition their portfolios and avail themselves of a renewed asset allocation. Serendipitously, we will see from the time series that the Graham top quintiles still performed admirably in the 2008–2009 time frame.

Overall, the results presented here are predicated on the underlying factors in these models, and we must keep in mind that models built with factors other than the Graham factors would behave differently than shown here. It is not often that such a strong weighting in a quant methodology is predicated on valuation, balance-sheet health, and past earnings as highly as the Graham model.

We need to consider that these charts demonstrate the broader trends of models that have similar underlying factors, even though they are weighted differently, but they do not delineate subtle differences between the models. The next series of data does allow discrimination of the models' quintiles from each other. Figure 7.4 looks at the relative performance of the models by subtracting their returns from the equally weighted model, highlighting their differences in this way. The data first has the S&P 500 index

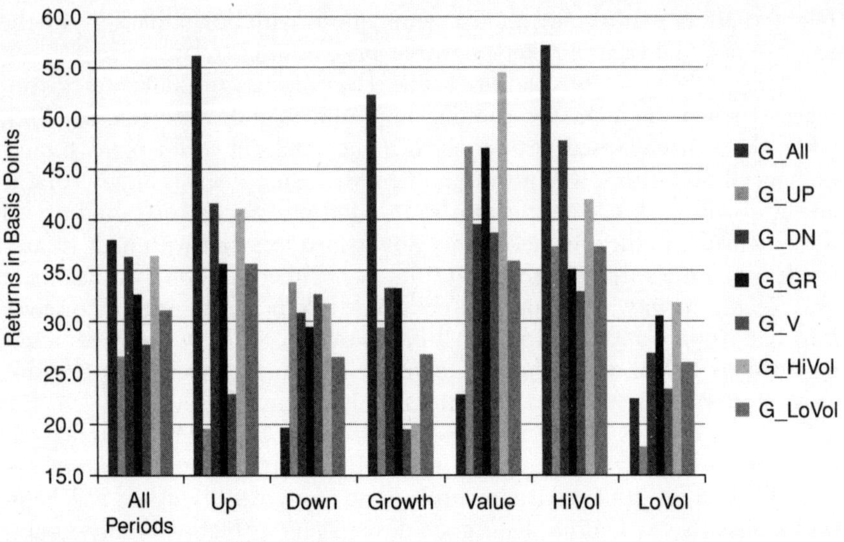


**FIGURE 7.4** Graham Relative Equal Weight Quarterly Excess Return (Top Quintile)

subtracted, to make excess returns, then the equally weighted Graham model is subtracted further from the model's quintile excess returns. This methodology is replicated across all models. This method serves to accentuate the differences between the models only. It is often quite useful to subtract large similar numbers that are trending identically, too, in order to see their differences.

The first chart, therefore, consists of the seven original models, each made heuristically from the factors' responses to the different market scenarios, aptly named after that scenario that was used to manufacture the weights for that particular model. Then, the *Y* axis (ordinate) represents the results of quarterly returns after subtracting the benchmark and the equal weighted factor model in basis points (100 basis points = 1 percent). The *X* axis (abscissa) represents the different market scenario the model was tested through. The consecutive sequence of the legend corresponds to each bar in a given scenario, running left to right. Thus, the first bar of each scenario is from the Graham model run under the full time period of the study, labeled G_All, and so on.

Figure 7.4 demonstrates that all of the models' top quintile outperform the equal weighted factor model in every environment, on average. Also, it portends to illustrate why we test through differing markets, to elucidate the effectiveness of different weighting schema. These results remind us

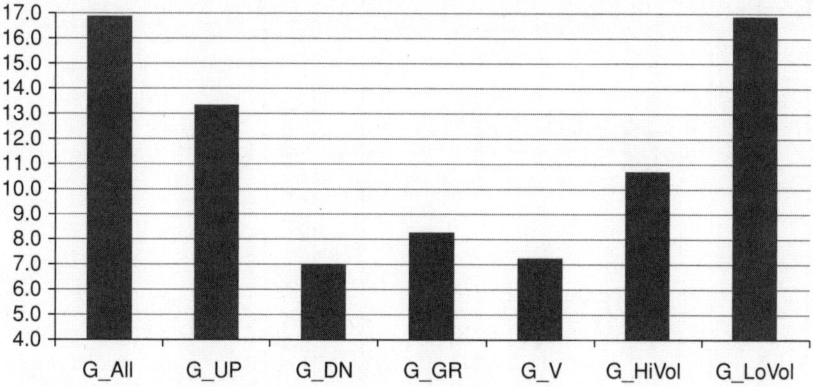


**FIGURE 7.5** Standard Deviation across Scenarios

that there is a trade-off constantly. For instance, the All Periods model has the highest returns in most markets but is the weakest performer in down markets. This would mean that in using that weighting scheme, we must be prepared to perhaps underperform in down markets relative to the other weighting models.

Next, notice the standard deviations of cross-scenario returns shown in Figure 7.5. These numbers are a simple standard deviation of each model's top quintile through all environments. The larger the number, the greater the divergence in performance in varying markets and the less stable that model would be expected to perform through time.

What we look for from this kind of data is stability. We cannot emphasize enough the importance of factor and return stability across time. In particular, we would prefer to use the model that performed the best with the least fluctuation across the different markets in an investment process. From Figure 7.5, we see that the most stable model is clearly the Graham Low-Volatility model because it varies the least among all the market scenarios we test through. However, looking at the standard deviation of return across markets and understanding the calculation, we realize that standard deviations do not include the impact of return in its mathematics. So making a choice on what model to use, we really need to examine the ratio of return to standard deviation of return. Consider that the Sharpe ratio and the information ratio are also of this ilk; that is, they have units of return over standard deviation. This of course makes them actually unitless because return and standard deviation of return are, literally, both percentages; nevertheless, that ratio is a kind of risk-adjusted-return measure. So if we chart the data and look at the ratio numbers, we have what is in Table 7.4.

**TABLE 7.4** Top and Bottom Quintile Returns Relative to the Graham Equally Weighted Portfolio

RELATIVE TO THE GRAM_EQ.WT. MODEL (bps)

**Top Quintile Average Quarterly XS Returns**

| | G_All | G_UP | G_DN | G_GR | G_V | G_HiVol | G_LoVol |
|---|---|---|---|---|---|---|---|
| All Periods | 38.21 | 26.69 | 36.42 | 32.75 | 27.84 | 36.55 | 31.30 |
| Up | 56.18 | 19.64 | 41.71 | 35.85 | 23.00 | 41.12 | 35.88 |
| Down | 19.74 | 33.93 | 30.98 | 29.56 | 32.82 | 31.86 | 26.59 |
| Growth | 52.32 | 7.77 | 33.41 | 19.51 | 17.70 | 20.01 | 26.91 |
| Value | 22.89 | 47.23 | 39.68 | 47.12 | 38.85 | 54.51 | 36.05 |
| HiVol | 57.24 | 37.45 | 47.82 | 35.26 | 33.07 | 42.09 | 37.57 |
| LoVol | 22.51 | 17.81 | 27.01 | 30.67 | 23.53 | 31.99 | 26.12 |
| Std Dev | 16.86 | 13.38 | 7.01 | 8.28 | 7.28 | 10.72 | 5.01 |
| Avg Ret | 38.44 | 27.22 | 36.72 | 32.96 | 28.12 | 36.88 | 31.49 |
| Ret / Stdev | 2.28 | 2.03 | 5.24 | 3.98 | 3.86 | 3.44 | 6.28 |

RELATIVE TO THE GRAM_EQ.WT. MODEL (bps)

**Bottom Quintile Average Quarterly XS Returns**

| | G_All | G_UP | G_DN | G_GR | G_V | G_HiVol | G_LoVol |
|---|---|---|---|---|---|---|---|
| All Periods | 16.21 | 1.96 | −9.25 | −9.58 | 7.23 | 10.16 | −6.60 |
| Up | 30.78 | −10.67 | −20.71 | −21.38 | −5.44 | 1.58 | −7.36 |
| Down | 1.23 | 14.94 | 2.54 | 2.55 | 20.25 | 18.97 | −5.82 |
| Growth | 101.15 | 64.42 | 39.63 | 57.41 | 82.11 | 83.54 | −1.89 |
| Value | −76.01 | −65.86 | −62.31 | −82.30 | −74.07 | −69.51 | −11.71 |
| HiVol | 0.84 | −4.61 | −4.17 | −9.63 | 2.57 | 8.64 | −14.24 |
| LoVol | 28.88 | 7.38 | −13.43 | −9.53 | 11.07 | 11.42 | −0.30 |
| Std Dev | 52.50 | 38.51 | 30.32 | 40.94 | 45.78 | 44.50 | 4.95 |
| Avg Ret | 14.72 | 1.08 | −9.67 | −10.35 | 6.24 | 9.26 | −6.84 |
| Ret / Stdev | 0.28 | 0.03 | −0.32 | −0.25 | 0.14 | 0.21 | −1.38 |

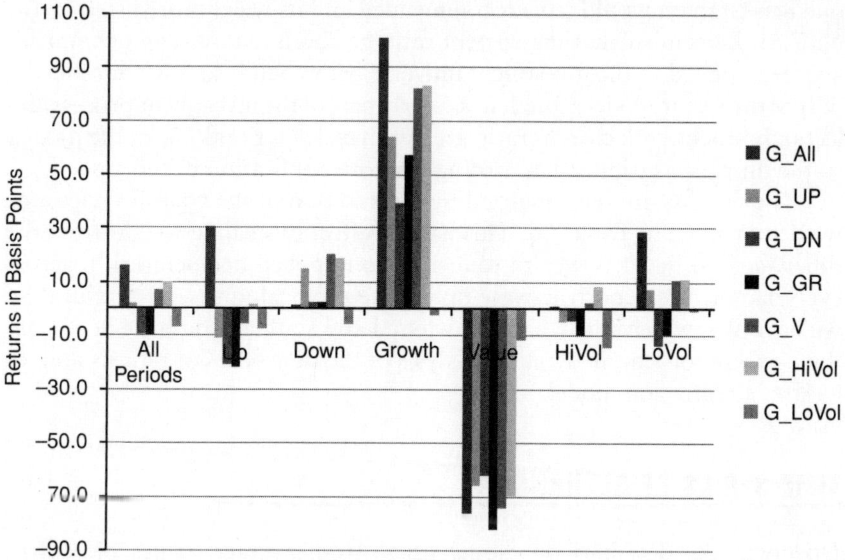


**FIGURE 7.6** Graham Relative Equally Weighted Quarterly Excess Return (Top Quintile)

Here, we tabulate the data in basis points for the returns of each model (after subtracting benchmark and the equally weighted factor model) in each environment. We do this for the top and bottom quintiles. The last three rows of each section show average return, standard deviation of return, and the ratio of the two. For the top quintile, the largest ratio is the low-volatility model, followed by the Graham down model.

For the bottom quintiles, the low-volatility model still has the highest absolute value ratio of return to standard deviation. In fact, the instability of the other models is very high as compared to the low-volatility model. This is seen dramatically in Figure 7.6 where scenarios are labeled on the abscissa and we plot the bottom quintile return. We can see that the models in the growth scenario and high-volatility period all swing widely except for the model created using low-volatility parameters (G_LoVol). Thus, for shorting stocks, we could only possibly consider bottom quintile portfolios created from the low-volatility model because the possibility of a strong positive return could happen more readily for any other model, and if short one of these stocks, we would likely suffer losses. That is what wide variance across scenarios implies.

So given the data, we could only assume the Graham low-volatility model is the only acceptable one to use in our investment process (it is the one Ben Graham would have recommended and its weights are listed in Table 7.5). Remember that the current ratio has been removed and comprises a screen applied to the investment universe beforehand, so it is not officially part of the factor model though it is clearly part of the investment process. Select only stocks with current ratio greater than 1.5 for ranking by the model, so the universe is trimmed accordingly before application of the model.

The weights are renormalized by the addition of the volatility factor as we demonstrate in Table 7.5. This has the effect of stealing weight from the other factors, but it is wealth redistribution applied democratically across every factor, used constructively unlike the political misuse of the idea. So we have $W^5$, which was what was wanted and so there you have it. We are done except for a more detailed analysis of the time series of returns and, of course, a regression model.

## TIME SERIES OF RETURNS

Do not make decisions on model usage from average values of returns over long time periods alone. Though there are measures and statistics you can and should realize from the time-series data, often there is nothing like putting a pair of eyes on the chart, which statisticians call chi by eye. Hence, the kiloword view of model performance across time is best seen in Figure 7.7, where we display a few of the model's top and bottom quintile's 12-month rolling excess return against the S&P 500 in consecutive order, beginning first with the all-period model Graham_All.

The darker area plot corresponds to the top quintile of the model, and the lighter grayscale is the bottom quintile excess return over the S&P 500. Also for all of these time-series plots, each model is aptly named from the source of its factor-weighting schema, and each is run through the whole period of the study. We are not showing scenario-based time-series graphs here. Knowing that historically, valued-oriented portfolios trailed the benchmark during the Internet bubble (1999–2000) and strongly outperformed it after the bubble, we see this behavior in the Graham model, and we would have known we made a modeling error should this not have been the result. The other models follow.

The result is similar in terms of its profile through time for the Graham UP model. This is expected, because the average values through time are similar and again, the models differ only in the relative weighting of factors, not in the actual factors, thus the similarity across time. The growth model follows and you would swear it is the same model. It is not, and the average values of return and their standard deviation demonstrate they are not. It is just a subtle difference in return profile through time and a common result

**TABLE 7.5** Final Model Weights

Final Model Weights Are Therefore

| | B/P | E/P | DivYld | 6-Mon Vol | MCap | E Grow | E Stab | E Stab_2 | TOTAL |
|---|---|---|---|---|---|---|---|---|---|
| Gram_LoVol | 13.5% | 17.8% | 12.3% | 10.0% | 21.9% | 13.1% | 10.8% | 8.2% | 107.6% |
| Normalized G_LoVol | 12.6% | 16.5% | 11.4% | 9.3% | 20.4% | 12.2% | 10.0% | 7.6% | 100.0% |

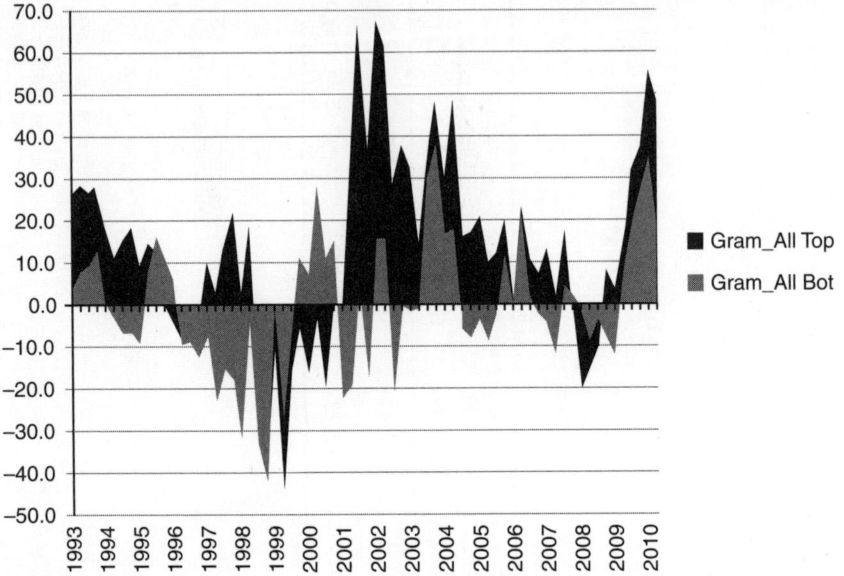


**FIGURE 7.7** 12-Month Rolling Excess Return over S&P 500 Graham All Model

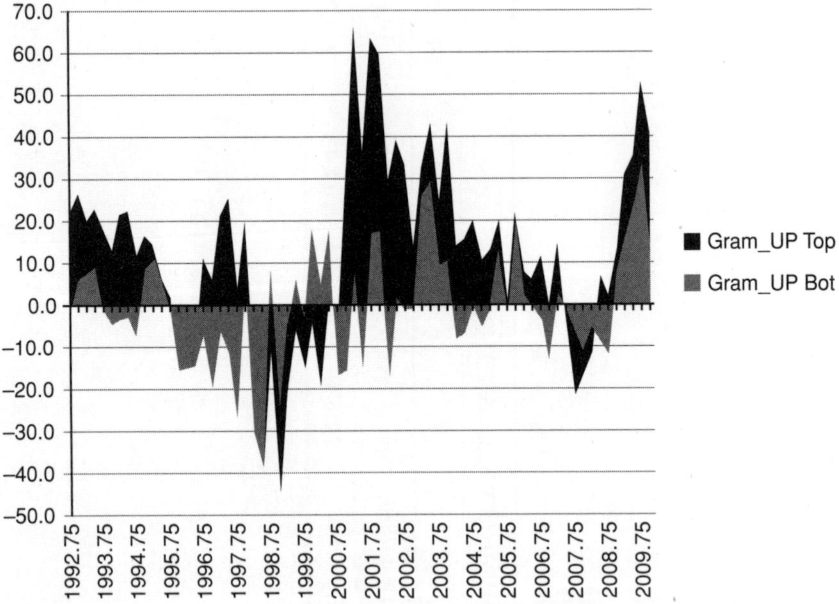


**FIGURE 7.8** 12-Month Rolling Excess Return over S&P 500 Graham Up Model

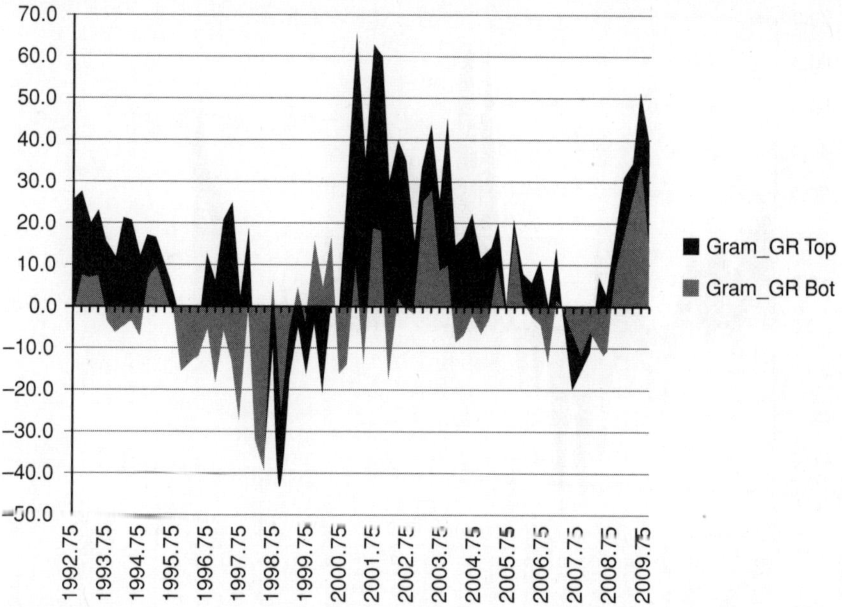


**FIGURE 7.9** 12-Month Rolling Excess Return over S&P 500 Graham Growth Model

when constructing models in this venue. The graphic display hides the level of average returns while illuminating the variance, and likewise, a chart of the average values of return hides observation of the variance through time.

What is worth so much in these time series are the clarity of occasional losses, and we should not forget that, during the Great Depression, Ben Graham lost . . . lots! This is not in stark contrast to the modern losses, either. Though it is an amusing book, Scott Patterson's *The Quants* is loaded with inaccuracies, hyperbole, and creative license en masse, but it manages to document losses among many hedge funds in 2008–2009, though these losses were far less than the Great Depression and most of the major quant hedge funds so named in the book rebounded spectacularly in 2009.[3] We mention it because you cannot be investors without experiencing losses sometimes. Graham mentioned that at times the market will just not price a security for what it is really worth, and the vagaries of the market may even move it toward greater mispricing for a while. So you should be prepared.

Last, we report the low-volatility Graham model's excess return 12-month rolling time series, and by this time, you should observe very little difference, if any, which brings us to an important point. The factor-weighting diversity is not enough to make a whole lot of difference, and this is a correct

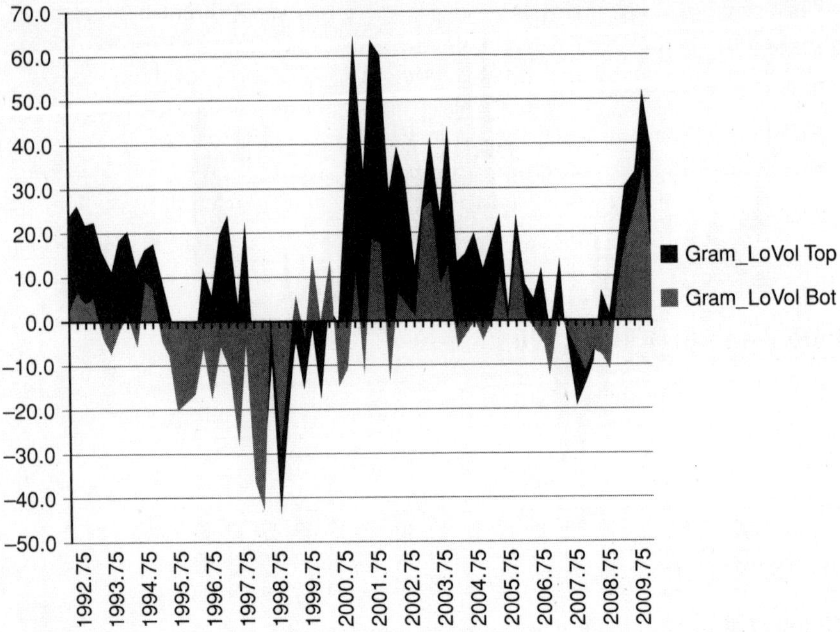


**FIGURE 7.10** 12-Month Rolling Excess Return over S&P 500 Graham LoVol Model

conclusion. Thus, most quants are not as worried about factor weightings as they are about what factors go into the model. In essence, this is what Graham did, too. He did not place a value about the relative importance of the factors; he just said that they all are important in a combined way.

Quite often until recently, many quants just took the lazy approach and equal weighted all factors. In addition, because the stocks in a given quintile are not equally weighted in a real portfolio, it is assumed that factor-weighting schemes are not ever in full influence of a portfolio so that the marginal differences in performance among different factor weightings are not ever realized in practice.

Given a constant set of factor constraints, the difference between quants who use those same factors is not too large and is a contribution to the quant meltdown of August 2007, the large amount of deleveraging due to margin calls notwithstanding. Though factor weights may be different, if everyone is using the same factors, the resultant portfolios will own many of the same stocks and the performance will be similar, but more importantly, the effect to the portfolio in different market environments will also be similar. Moreover, if we look back at the category of factor weights we showed earlier in the beginning of the chapter, valuation, balance-sheet health, size, and earnings, the weights were not so different categorically, though individual factor weights seemingly were so. Thus, the categories can be as important as the actual factors in them. Since many of the factors in a same category tend to have higher correlation among them, their individual contributions to the portfolio are nearly identical. This is an important conclusion that prudent intelligent investors must make themselves aware of, in the face of many a young or inexperienced quant's attempt to distinguish themselves from their competition by their factor-weighting schema.

## OTHER CONDITIONAL INFORMATION

The other pieces of information one must consider when choosing which model to use going forward involves the volatility, standard deviation, and Sharpe ratio. First, since much of what we are doing here is pedagogical in nature, we want to demonstrate the difference between the standard deviation of return versus the g-Factor. Figure 7.11 takes all eight models' quintiles' standard deviation of return and their concomitant g-Factors and plots them, along with the S&P 500's for reference.

We plot g-Factors on the *X*-axis and the standard deviation of 12-month return corresponding to the same model/quintile on the *Y*-axis. The S&P's g-Factor is 1 by definition, whereas the quintiles' values spread all over the graph. It is clear that for a given level of model quintile standard deviation, there can be a wide spread in g-Factor and vice versa. Thus, the correlation

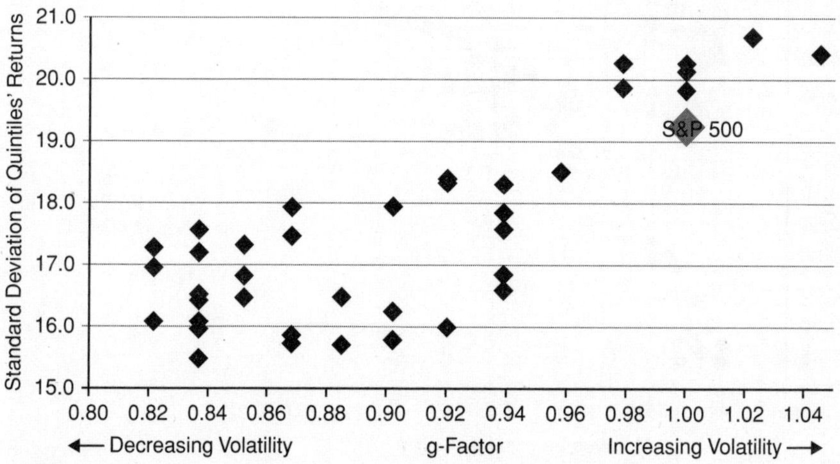


**FIGURE 7.11** Standard Deviation of Graham Models' Quintile Returns versus g-Factor

between g-Factor and standard deviation of return are not one-to-one. What is nice to know from an investor's standpoint is that most of the Graham models have less volatility than the index. However, interestingly enough, there are two model/quintile portfolios that have higher standard deviation of return than the index but are less volatile, as indicated by the g-Factor. Likewise, three portfolios have higher standard deviation of return but have the same volatility as the S&P 500. This can only be known by using the g-Factor as the recipe for volatility determination, however, because beta and the standard deviation of return miss it. Again, the g-Factor accounts for the amount of time the portfolo hangs around a given distance from its mean return, that distance being the standard deviation of the S&P 500, the reference benchmark.

Next we dramatize the differences by including the Sharpe ratio in the plot with g-Factor, beta, and standard deviation of return. The Sharpe ratio, of course, includes a measure of performance in its definition, thus we will see a correspondence with return in this plot for the Sharpe ratio but not for the other parameters. What is very unusual in Figure 7.12 is the seemingly negative relationship between beta and the g-Factor and between beta and the standard deviation of return. Now of course we do not include the *t*-Stat of the beta nor the $R^2$ of the fitted regression, so beta could be meaningless here. Nevertheless, just for comparison purposes, we put it in the graph.

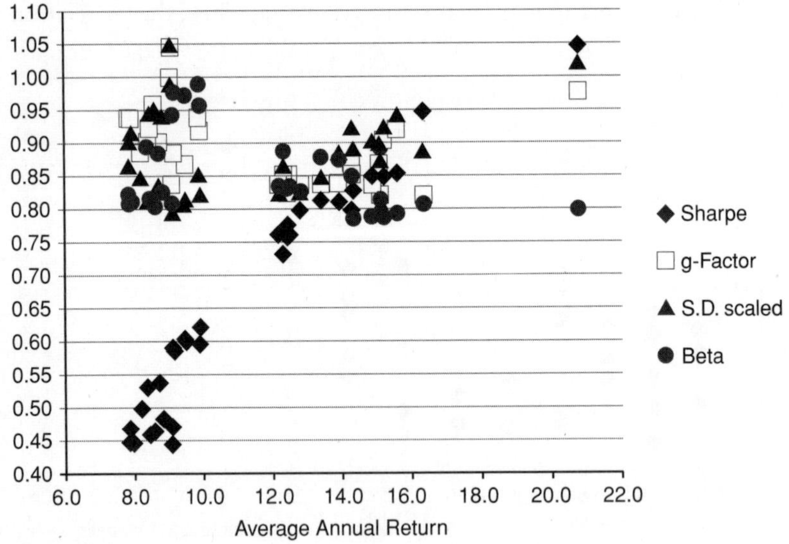


**FIGURE 7.12** Statistics of the Graham Portfolios

If you look carefully, you will see that the beta tends to underestimate the volatility of the portfolios by exhibiting low values ($0.8 < \text{beta} < 0.9$ thereabouts), while the g-Factor hovers at a higher value. The average beta is 0.84 whereas the average g-Factor is 0.91. The correlation between g-Factor and beta here is –27 percent, whereas the correlation between g-Factor and the standard deviation of return is 82 percent. The standard deviation has been scaled to fit on the plot (S.D. scaled).

We produce the following data for the models more generally, reporting quarterly statistics. However, we call your attention to beta and the g-Factor in Table 7.6.

In Table 7.6, one will notice that betas increase as we move from quintile 1 to 5, while g-Factors increase from quintile 2 to 5. Quintile 1 is unique in its g-Factor. Likewise, the $R^2$ for beta is outright poor for quintile 1, rendering its usefulness as a statistical parameter quite weak there as demonstrated by the beta *t*-Stats as well. This is a discrepancy only explained by the distribution of returns within the top quintiles. They are sufficiently broader than the other quintiles, and are equivalent to the index, thus the "1" g-Factor value, meaning that the top quintile are about as volatile as their underlying benchmarks. These data are for the models run through the whole period of the back test and not for any specific scenario, by the way, so the statistics of beta, g-Factor, and Sharpe are holistic.

## THE FINAL MODEL

For the final model, we will settle on the weights given by the Graham low-volatility model. Using a model like this does not involve forecasting returns. These multifactor models are inaccurately called alpha models, when they are actually ranking models. If these models could be used as forecasting tools, they have the implicit ability to decide when to invest, as well as what to buy. Ben Graham sometimes valued the market too richly to invest and kept some assets in cash. The use of a model like the one here offers no historical valuation comparison among stocks, though intrinsically the valuation factors do offer cross-sectional comparisons. Nor does it take into consideration the decision tree information Graham used based on high-quality AAA corporate-bond yields as a measure of relative valuation of stocks versus bonds. Hence, intelligent investors must go outside the model to make that evaluation. When the decision has been made about whether the valuations in the market are right on an absolute valuation basis versus bond yields, then the full force of the model's ranking of stocks can be brought to bear on the investment universe under consideration.

**TABLE 7.6** Beta Statistics Compared to g-Factor

| | Beta | | | | | *T*-Stat Beta | | | | | $R^2$ for Beta | | | | | g-Factor | | | | |
|---|---|---|---|---|---|---|---|---|---|---|---|---|---|---|---|---|---|---|---|---|
| Model | 1 | 2 | 3 | 4 | 5 | 1 | 2 | 3 | 4 | 5 | 1 | 2 | 3 | 4 | 5 | 1 | 2 | 3 | 4 | 5 |
| G_All | 0.82 | 0.83 | 0.85 | 0.89 | 0.99 | 8.8 | 10.3 | 12.5 | 14.4 | 15.4 | 0.52 | 0.60 | 0.69 | 0.74 | 0.77 | 1.02 | 0.87 | 0.85 | 0.94 | 1.05 |
| G_UP | 0.81 | 0.79 | 0.79 | 0.83 | 0.97 | 9.0 | 9.4 | 11.5 | 13.4 | 17.3 | 0.53 | 0.55 | 0.65 | 0.72 | 0.81 | 1.00 | 0.87 | 0.82 | 0.87 | 0.92 |
| G_DN | 0.82 | 0.80 | 0.79 | 0.84 | 0.94 | 9.0 | 9.6 | 12.1 | 13.0 | 18.2 | 0.53 | 0.57 | 0.67 | 0.70 | 0.82 | 1.00 | 0.92 | 0.85 | 0.84 | 0.94 |
| G_GR | 0.81 | 0.80 | 0.79 | 0.83 | 0.96 | 8.8 | 9.6 | 11.5 | 13.0 | 17.5 | 0.52 | 0.57 | 0.65 | 0.71 | 0.81 | 1.00 | 0.90 | 0.84 | 0.92 | 0.94 |
| G_V | 0.81 | 0.79 | 0.79 | 0.82 | 0.98 | 8.9 | 9.5 | 11.4 | 13.1 | 17.8 | 0.53 | 0.56 | 0.64 | 0.71 | 0.82 | 1.00 | 0.84 | 0.84 | 0.88 | 0.96 |
| G_HiVol | 0.80 | 0.80 | 0.79 | 0.83 | 0.97 | 8.7 | 9.7 | 11.3 | 13.2 | 17.3 | 0.52 | 0.57 | 0.64 | 0.71 | 0.81 | 0.98 | 0.85 | 0.84 | 0.87 | 0.94 |
| G_LoVol | 0.83 | 0.79 | 0.81 | 0.87 | 0.89 | 9.2 | 9.8 | 12.1 | 14.0 | 17.3 | 0.54 | 0.58 | 0.67 | 0.73 | 0.81 | 1.00 | 0.82 | 0.84 | 0.90 | 0.94 |
| G_Eq.Wt | 0.82 | 0.80 | 0.81 | 0.88 | 0.88 | 9.2 | 10.1 | 12.4 | 14.0 | 17.0 | 0.55 | 0.59 | 0.68 | 0.73 | 0.80 | 0.98 | 0.82 | 0.84 | 0.90 | 0.88 |

**TABLE 7.7** Hit Rates of Top and Bottom Quintile

**Hit Rates Top Quintile**

| | G_All | G_UP | G_DN | G_GR | G_V | G_HiVol | G_LoVol | G_Eq.Wt |
|---|---|---|---|---|---|---|---|---|
| All Periods | 61.6% | 61.6% | 63.0% | 61.6% | 61.6% | 61.6% | 63.0% | 58.9% |
| Up | 73.0% | 75.7% | 78.4% | 75.7% | 75.7% | 75.7% | 78.4% | 75.7% |
| Down | 50.0% | 47.2% | 47.2% | 47.2% | 47.2% | 47.2% | 47.2% | 41.7% |
| Growth | 60.5% | 60.5% | 63.2% | 60.5% | 60.5% | 60.5% | 63.2% | 57.9% |
| Value | 62.9% | 62.9% | 62.9% | 62.9% | 62.9% | 62.9% | 62.9% | 60.0% |
| HiVol | 57.6% | 57.6% | 57.6% | 57.6% | 57.6% | 57.6% | 57.6% | 57.6% |
| LoVol | 65.0% | 65.0% | 67.5% | 65.0% | 65.0% | 65.0% | 67.5% | 60.0% |

**Hit Rates Bottom Quintile**

| | G_All | G_UP | G_DN | G_GR | G_V | G_HiVol | G_LoVol | G_Eq.Wt |
|---|---|---|---|---|---|---|---|---|
| All Periods | 42.5% | 39.7% | 37.0% | 39.7% | 38.4% | 42.5% | 39.7% | 39.7% |
| Up | 54.1% | 48.6% | 43.2% | 45.9% | 45.9% | 54.1% | 48.6% | 48.6% |
| Down | 30.6% | 30.6% | 30.6% | 33.3% | 30.6% | 30.6% | 30.6% | 30.6% |
| Growth | 52.6% | 44.7% | 44.7% | 47.4% | 44.7% | 50.0% | 44.7% | 47.4% |
| Value | 31.4% | 34.3% | 28.6% | 31.4% | 31.4% | 34.3% | 34.3% | 31.4% |
| HiVol | 36.4% | 36.4% | 36.4% | 36.4% | 36.4% | 36.4% | 36.4% | 36.4% |
| LoVol | 47.5% | 42.5% | 37.5% | 42.5% | 40.0% | 47.5% | 42.5% | 42.5% |

Now, in conclusion, we tabulate the hit rates through time for the models in each market scenario in Table 7.7. These hit rates tabulate the percentage of time the top and bottom quintiles outperformed their benchmark. We highlight in gray those quintiles where the hit rates are greater than 62.5 percent of the time for the top quintile, and for the bottom quintile, those whose hit rates outperform the index 37.5 percent of the time. These would be the times where the models shine, so to speak. Interestingly, though the average returns for the models in the low-volatility environment underperformed the high-volatility environment, the hit rates in the table suggest that the low-volatility models actually won more often against the benchmark, even though, on average, their performance was not as strong through the high-volatility environment. The hit-rate charts represent the number of periods that the model beat the benchmark, and they are usually interpreted as probability tables, not to be confused with a formal prediction of performance. But be aware that the returns through time making up the financial time series, when examined to see how often they beat their benchmarks, are just the frequency count of model performance. If model persistence were true, we would extrapolate this performance going forward in real world out-of-sample markets. Nevertheless, the top quintile numbers stack up quite well in terms of their frequency response to performance.

So the low-volatility model (G_LoVol) is seen to have pretty significant performance in terms of its stability through time and its hit rate through time as measured by the numbers. From the hit-rate table, the down environment offers a challenge to the Graham portfolios because the top quintile loses more than it wins as measured by hit rate, as we saw in bar charts of top quintile performance (as shown in Figures 7.2 and 7.4). That is a challenge for Graham's methodology and, indeed, in the market meltdown of 1929, Mr. Graham had losses. Likewise, in the time-series presentation we showed earlier, the Internet bubble and 2008 were indeed challenges for the Graham methodology. The comfort might be that though there are losses in the market, Graham's margin of safety mechanisms do allow for lower drawdowns then the average investor might incur.

## OTHER METHODS OF MEASURING PERFORMANCE: ATTRIBUTION ANALYSIS VIA BRINSON AND RISK DECOMPOSITION

There are other independent methods for validating the results of a model involving what is known as Brinson attribution. This method uses the daily holdings of portfolios, collected over time, and measures the performance using the daily prices obtained from reputable sources, namely, the exchanges like NYSE or NASDAQ, and is an active-weight differentiator. In this fashion, Brinson performance attribution allows for the grouping of stocks into cohorts separated into fractiles of each group. FactSet has an excellent portfolio attribution module, making this kind of analysis quite routine. For instance, all the stocks can be grouped into a single sector or industry and the performance measured through time for each cohort. This is the simplest example. However, the stocks could just as easily be fractiled into market capitalization buckets and performance evaluated as a function of market cap size or valuation or earnings growth; in fact, the segregating of stocks by some grouping is limited only by one's imagination. Then, the attribution proceeds to illustrate where returns or losses in the portfolio came from: from the group or from stock selection. For instance, an investor could have made money relative to some benchmark based on underweighting a sector in the benchmark that performs poorly while simultaneously losing money from some other sector, because, while an investor overweighted a winning sector, the chosen stocks in the portfolio just did not perform as well as the stocks in the benchmark did for that sector. However, this is based on active weights, that is, the difference between weights of the portfolio minus the index. Nevertheless, we can use this methodology to examine the returns of the top quintile of the model over the last 20 years versus the bottom quintile of the model. In addition, this performance measure allows for an independent validation of the spread in performance between the top and bottom quintiles. This is a necessary step in obtaining confidence and trust in an investment process, that there be an alternative method for confirming the portfolio's returns in a back test, and that is why we do it here in FactSet.

Since the active weights of a portfolio are simply the difference between the portfolio's weights and the benchmark weights, there is no way to attribute the performance to the underlying co-varying risks in the portfolio via this methodology. It is simply a linear relationship between stock individual performance and the underlying grouping. However, referring back to Chapter 2 on risk, we could also examine the attribution another way, this being active risk-based performance analysis in which we decompose the excess returns into their active-risk exposure sources. If we could group by risk exposure, using factors from a covariance-based risk model, we would be able to attribute how much gain or loss was due to a particular risk in the portfolio. Each performance attribution measure has different emphasis, however, and the Brinson active-weight methodology is older and more tried by investment managers, whereas risk-based attribution is newer and has not been as warmly embraced by practitioners as of yet simply because not every investor has or uses a risk model. The former method, though, suffers from the drawback of accidentally selecting a report grouping irrelevant to the investment process or more specifically the portfolio construction process. However, when performed together, any inconsistent results can be immediately observed and acted upon readily.

We use Brinson analysis to chart the performance of top and bottom quintiles of the Graham low-volatility model where our groups are FactSet sectors. The data can be seen in Table 7.8, first for the top quintile.

The first three columns are for the quintile 1 portfolio and show the average weight of the portfolio in each of the FactSet sectors, followed by the total return over the period (December 31, 1989, to December 31, 2009), followed by the sector contribution to return. Then, we show the same three columns for the Russell 1000 (R1K), a large-cap benchmark, a little broader than the S&P 500 but very highly correlated to it. The active-weight column is the difference between the quintile 1 average weight and the benchmark's average weight for the same sector. Notice how quintile 1 had a large overweighting relative to the benchmark in Finance (11.5 percent), whereas it had underweighting by −7.0 percent in Health Technology. Notice also how the Graham quintile clobbered the index over this time period overall. Nice...

The last four columns are very interesting and constitute the Brinson analysis. They are the performance attribution for sector allocation, stock selection, their interaction, and finally the total attribution effect. In this light, the top quintile of the Graham model is a real outperformer over time, beating the R1K by a whopping 9,000+ percent over 20 years, albeit with a very large tracking error (the standard deviation of excess return) of 34.4 percent, even with an average annualized excess return of 25 percent (which is amazing), whereas the information ratio (excess return divided by the standard deviation of excess return) is 0.74. The sectors of Energy Minerals and Finance accounted for the largest outperformance. Therefore, we would conclude that the Graham method chose excellent stocks in those sectors. We have commented several times that Graham honed his investment skills when the U.S. economy and the majority of publicly available stocks was in IME (Industrials, Materials, and Energy) and it is comforting to see that the largest return of the Graham model's top quintile is from Energy Minerals sector (cumulative return of 1,709 percent), validating his recipe for those sectors.

Table 7.9 illustrates the differences between the raw Graham model output of the top and bottom quintile versus their mean-variance optimized portfolio counterparts. In simple terms, optimized portfolios utilize the full weight of the Markowitz methodology and result in portfolios supposedly maximizing return expectations while minimizing risk. Thus inputs are alphas forecasts from a model like Graham's and an estimate of risks from some risk model.

**TABLE 7.8** Standard Brinson Attribution Analysis

| | QUINT_1 | | | Russell 1000 | | | | Attribution Analysis | | | |
|---|---|---|---|---|---|---|---|---|---|---|---|
| Economic Sector | Port. Average Weight | Port. Total Return | Port. Contrib. To Return | Bench. Average Weight | Bench. Total Return | Bench. Contrib. To Return | Active Weight | Allocation Effect | Selection Effect | Interaction Effect | Total Effect |
| **Total** | **100.00** | **9,433** | **9,433** | **100.00** | **403.87** | **403.87** | | **2,052** | **5,009** | **1,968** | **9,029** |
| Commercial Services | 1.75 | 2726 | 178.04 | 0.97 | 155.12 | 3.04 | 0.78 | 89.37 | 146.65 | 132.53 | 368.54 |
| Communications | 3.80 | 1410 | 235.91 | 6.06 | 120.86 | 17.92 | −2.26 | 194.46 | 73.46 | 115.60 | 383.52 |
| Consumer Durables | 3.32 | 1114 | 282.79 | 2.58 | 112.32 | 10.49 | 0.74 | 155.67 | 329.16 | −10.25 | 474.57 |
| Consumer Non-Durables | 3.80 | 3056 | 248.07 | 8.49 | 752.66 | 54.78 | −4.69 | −68.58 | 28.85 | 148.96 | 109.23 |
| Consumer Services | 4.94 | 500 | 269.20 | 5.12 | 237.28 | 11.70 | −0.18 | 203.93 | 142.18 | 98.54 | 444.65 |
| Distribution Services | 1.21 | 1704 | 95.52 | 0.69 | 339.41 | 1.93 | 0.52 | 87.19 | 109.01 | 116.64 | 312.84 |
| Electronic Technology | 5.55 | 10098 | 1076.33 | 9.72 | 617.30 | 38.72 | −4.17 | 151.73 | 318.10 | 250.74 | 720.58 |
| Energy Minerals | 5.29 | 1017602 | 1672.22 | 6.89 | 768.42 | 23.37 | −1.60 | 132.62 | 1959.33 | −382.20 | 1709.75 |
| Finance | 28.58 | 1823 | 2445.62 | 17.00 | 402.31 | 66.50 | 11.58 | 272.85 | 455.48 | 341.91 | 1070.24 |
| Health Services | 2.76 | 6700 | 278.63 | 1.63 | 527.99 | 6.11 | 1.14 | 131.10 | 143.97 | 135.85 | 410.92 |
| Health Technology | 3.52 | 5326 | 308.34 | 10.52 | 691.69 | 52.82 | −7.00 | −61.74 | 219.93 | 51.58 | 209.77 |
| Industrial Services | 2.59 | 2028 | 110.77 | 1.67 | 126.62 | −0.91 | 0.92 | 102.54 | 120.15 | 106.58 | 329.28 |
| Miscellaneous | 0.25 | 23 | 1.02 | 0.00 | −94.01 | −0.06 | 0.25 | 92.06 | 0.00 | 0.00 | 92.06 |
| Non-Energy Minerals | 2.64 | 660 | 84.31 | 1.10 | 245.76 | 2.18 | 1.54 | 44.67 | 113.76 | 106.58 | 265.02 |
| Process Industries | 3.98 | 1824 | 352.46 | 3.51 | 368.75 | 15.05 | 0.47 | 116.80 | 130.19 | 131.46 | 378.45 |
| Producer Manufacturing | 4.20 | 2521 | 342.57 | 6.65 | 466.14 | 23.08 | −2.45 | 126.46 | 94.52 | 66.07 | 287.06 |
| Retail Trade | 5.09 | 1071 | 316.96 | 5.59 | 486.32 | 25.10 | −0.50 | 50.96 | 59.01 | 185.35 | 295.32 |
| Technology Services | 2.02 | 777 | 139.50 | 5.68 | 610.72 | 20.81 | −3.66 | 72.98 | 189.56 | 27.21 | 289.74 |
| Transportation | 2.82 | 4061 | 340.99 | 1.53 | 407.90 | 5.83 | 1.29 | 73.87 | 190.18 | 179.64 | 443.69 |
| Utilities | 9.61 | 1072 | 653.72 | 4.62 | 382.38 | 19.40 | 4.99 | 108.79 | 185.66 | 165.31 | 459.76 |

**TABLE 7.9** Excess Return of Final Graham Model versus S&P 500

| Year | Quint_1 | Q1_Opt | Quint_5 | Q5_Opt |
|---|---|---|---|---|
| 1990 | −4.33 | −2.99 | −5.07 | 4.59 |
| 1991 | 16.51 | −1.41 | 56.30 | 5.98 |
| 1992 | 14.92 | 3.79 | 15.18 | 4.07 |
| 1993 | 11.73 | 6.93 | 1.84 | 4.65 |
| 1994 | 3.40 | −2.67 | 2.88 | 3.77 |
| 1995 | 6.69 | −1.59 | 10.03 | 2.61 |
| 1996 | 1.30 | −3.06 | −10.77 | 2.96 |
| 1997 | 45.26 | −2.96 | −24.48 | 4.91 |
| 1998 | 141.90 | −8.43 | −5.05 | −1.11 |
| 1999 | −11.01 | −14.11 | 64.60 | 2.87 |
| 2000 | 36.60 | 12.20 | −43.06 | 2.38 |
| 2001 | 42.72 | 6.32 | −0.97 | −3.41 |
| 2002 | 17.06 | 1.64 | −18.40 | 0.55 |
| 2003 | 37.02 | 1.48 | 44.26 | 0.26 |
| 2004 | 14.23 | 4.13 | −2.27 | −1.81 |
| 2005 | 6.59 | 8.42 | −5.20 | −0.94 |
| 2006 | 2.42 | 3.59 | −8.24 | 1.78 |
| 2007 | −14.87 | −4.37 | −2.77 | 0.40 |
| 2008 | 1.95 | −0.04 | −11.28 | 1.39 |
| 2009 | 57.85 | 6.24 | 32.36 | −0.14 |
| TOTAL | 9047.38 | 80.13 | −56.27 | 175.93 |
| Ann XS | 25.33 | 2.99 | −4.05 | 5.21 |
| TE | 34.42 | 6.14 | 26.64 | 2.53 |
| IR | 0.74 | 0.49 | −0.15 | 2.06 |

In Chapter 9 we will discuss portfolio optimization in greater detail and will revisit this chart. However, portfolio optimization is one of the very first methods utilized in risk management after the adage "Do not put all your eggs in one basket." Think of it in this context, as a way of minimizing variance of a portfolio while maximizing alpha. In the meantime, we chart the excess returns for quintile 1 and quintile 5 in columns two and four for each year of the simulation. Columns three and five represent the excess returns over the S&P 500 index from the top and bottom quintiles, optimized within FactSet's software. These results represent a simple optimization where the maximum FactSet sector active weights are bounded by +/–5 percent of the benchmark's, and the maximum absolute position size is 3 percent by weight of the portfolio. Moreover, the portfolios are rebalanced each quarter with a limit of 15 percent turnover maximum (15 percent of the weight of the portfolio could be sold and 15 percent purchased). The buy universe was completely restricted to the top or bottom quintile of stocks, respectively, but the optimizer did not choose to own all of the top or bottom quintile stocks in the mean-variance optimized portfolios either. Also, all stocks within the quintile were given the same alpha, meaning the optimizers' only criteria for choosing to buy or sell a stock was based on its risk only. We used the Northfield U.S. Fundamental Equity risk model in FactSet to estimate the risks of the stocks in the top and bottom quintiles.

Now, the observation from Table 7.9 is that the average value of the top quintile is quite high, while the standard deviation of return is also high: 25.3 and 34.4 percent, respectively. However, the simple portfolio-optimized return of the top quintile of an annualized 2.9 percent—we will call it 3 percent—came with a tracking error of twice that: 6.1 percent with an IR of roughly one half. Thus, although the optimization process certainly cut down the risk, from a TE of 34.4 to 6.14, the concomitant return also fell by a large amount, from 25.3 to 3 percent. Therefore, although the risk reduction was a factor of 5.6, it came with a return reduction by a factor of 8.4, implying, in this case, that the portfolio optimization was misspecified, meaning that the constraints were most probably too tight. This tends to be a consistent error in applying portfolio optimization to a very good alpha-generating process, which is why fundamental managers tend to refuse using optimization algorithms in their investment process. Of course, that is if their investment process is any good. Quite often, the fundamental manager is overly optimistic about their process.

The bottom quintile shown in column four and its optimized portfolio of column five is very interesting. In this case, the optimization actually rescued some alpha from the bottom quintile, exactly what portfolio optimization is supposed to do. It tends to increase return and lower risk for a bad investment process. We lowered the risk of quintile 5 from a wide 26.6 tracking error to 2.5 while raising returns from −4 to +5 percent. This is a huge improvement and tends to support the hypothesis that if you have a broken investment process or are not good at picking stocks, then it might be useful to optimize your portfolio with a "mean-variance" optimizer, à la Markowitz.

In either case, with a good investment process like the top quintile or a bad process like the bottom quintile, portfolio mean-variance optimization pulls the portfolio toward the benchmark in terms of performance and in terms of its risks. Thus, the excess return and risk will both be reduced for a great investment process and returns improved and risk reduced for a bad investment process. As we say, a picture is the kiloword view, and nothing expresses this as well as Figure 7.13. Here we show a bar chart for the four columns of the data from Table 7.9. The left is the top quintile, followed by

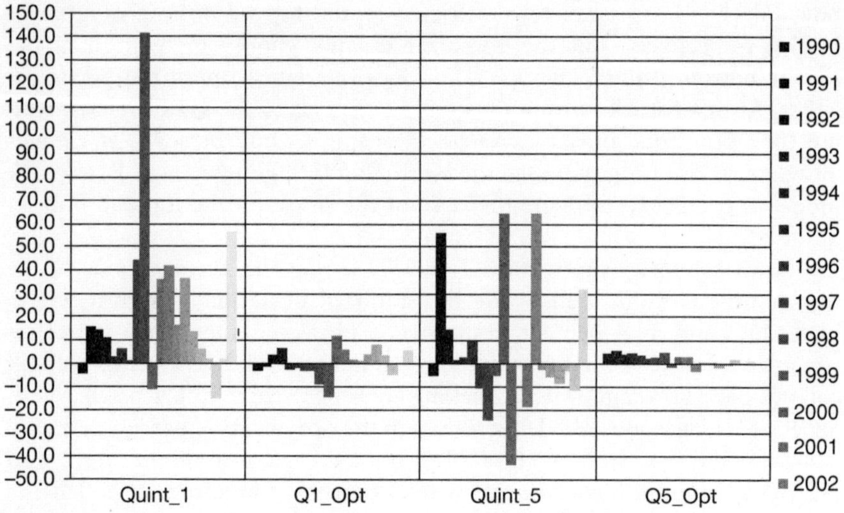


**FIGURE 7.13** Annualized Excess Return over the S&P 500 from Table 7.9 Data

the optimized top quintile; the bottom quintile is followed by the optimized bottom quintile of stocks, for the 20-year back-test period.

The reason for the huge tracking errors of the raw top and bottom quintile portfolios is easily observed (Quint_1 and Quint_5) from the dispersion of the data (variation of bar heights). The two optimized portfolios show a largely damped risk as measured by tracking error and as illustrated by the low dispersion of returns per year. This is because optimized portfolio returns will always be closer to the benchmark than either the top or bottom quintile unoptimized or raw portfolios. Specifically, the bottom quintile, Quint_5, even had some good years relative to the S&P 500 benchmark as 1991, 1999, and 2003 had 56.3, 64.6, and 44.26 percent returns over the benchmark. These were years value investing was on its head. Of course, over the 20-year time frame, it lost to the benchmark. Meanwhile, the optimized bottom quintile, Q5_Opt, shows consecutive small but positive returns relative to the benchmark from inception to about 2000, and it had only benchmark-like returns thereafter.

As we observe from the data in the Brinson attribution shown earlier, the active weight of finance had a huge contribution to the total returns of the top quintile (Quint_1). In the optimized portfolio (Q1_Opt), this concentration is disallowed, and ownership of securities is distributed more evenly across the FactSet sectors. Unfortunately, when one forces the Graham model to be used picking stocks across the whole universe of choices, across all

**TABLE 7.10** Absolute Returns

| | **Absolute Return** | | | | |
|---|---|---|---|---|---|
| Year | Quint_1 | Q1_Opt | Quint_5 | Q5_Opt | S&P 500 |
| 1990 | −7.51 | −6.17 | −8.24 | **1.42** | −3.18 |
| 1991 | **47.04** | **29.12** | **86.83** | **36.51** | **30.53** |
| 1992 | **22.59** | **11.46** | **22.85** | **11.74** | **7.67** |
| 1993 | **21.73** | **16.93** | **11.84** | **14.65** | **10.00** |
| 1994 | **4.71** | −1.36 | **4.19** | **5.07** | **1.30** |
| 1995 | **44.22** | **35.93** | **47.55** | **40.13** | **37.53** |
| 1996 | **24.43** | **20.07** | **12.36** | **26.09** | **23.13** |
| 1997 | **78.55** | **30.33** | **8.82** | **38.20** | **33.29** |
| 1998 | **170.64** | **20.31** | **23.70** | **27.64** | **28.75** |
| 1999 | **10.02** | **6.93** | **85.64** | **23.91** | **21.04** |
| 2000 | **27.49** | **3.09** | −52.16 | −6.73 | −9.11 |
| 2001 | **30.86** | −5.54 | −12.84 | −15.27 | −11.86 |
| 2002 | −5.02 | −20.44 | −40.48 | −21.53 | −22.08 |
| 2003 | **65.60** | **30.14** | **72.92** | **28.93** | **28.66** |
| 2004 | **25.15** | **15.06** | **8.65** | **9.11** | **10.93** |
| 2005 | **11.50** | **13.34** | −0.29 | **3.98** | **4.91** |
| 2006 | **18.23** | **19.40** | **7.57** | **17.59** | **15.81** |
| 2007 | −9.33 | **1.17** | **2.78** | **5.95** | **5.55** |
| 2008 | −35.05 | −37.04 | −48.28 | −35.61 | −37.00 |
| 2009 | **84.33** | **32.72** | **58.84** | **26.34** | **26.48** |
| Total | 9432.96 | 465.72 | 329.31 | 561.51 | 385.58 |
| **Ann Ret** | 25.59 | 9.05 | 7.56 | 9.91 | 8.22 |
| **Std Dev** | 44.08 | 18.71 | 39.85 | 20.45 | 19.74 |

sectors at one time, it does not necessarily pick better stocks than those stocks in the benchmark, and optimization with sector constraints does just that. Thus, we see some underperformance relative to the S&P 500 in years 1994 through 1998 for the optimized quintile 1 portfolio. However, though Graham (personified through his model here) underperformed the index in those years, it does not mean those were negative absolute return years. We show the absolute returns in Table 7.10 and one can see that the optimized portfolio had only five negative return years out of 20, whereas the benchmark also had five negative return years out of 20. Figures for years of positive absolute returns appear in bold type for ease of viewing.

Really, the most important takeaway involves the raw returns of Quint_1, the actual choices of investment from the Graham model alone, left unfettered by any formal mean-variance risk reduction application of optimization or unwise portfolio constraints. Those returns are simulated, of course, and are without any transaction costs, so they are not indicative of any future performance and, we conclude, do not prove anything (in a mathematical sense), but they do serve to suggest the wisdom of Graham's investment methodology.

## REGRESSION OF THE GRAHAM FACTORS WITH FORWARD RETURNS

We have yet to show any results from regressing the factors against forward returns versus the S&P 500 returns though we spoke at length about it in earlier chapters. We'll now visit a regression-based model and show comparative results versus the Graham heuristically constructed models. First, the data from all the Graham models was downloaded from the FactSet database for all the factors, the Graham models, and the returns of the stocks over the time period of the model, December 31, 1989, to December 31, 2009. However, returns for the dependent variable in the regression were six-months future returns. The independent variables, the factors, were chosen for the beginning date of the future return measurement. So if the date was December 30, 2000, for instance, the factors were as of that date, whereas the corresponding return used in the regression was from July 31, 2000, to January 31, 2001, thus utilizing a one-month lag. This makes the analysis more conservative, though I was using point-in-time data. The regression method chosen was a panel regression, which means that all data was stacked up, allowing a single regression both in time and in cross-section to be performed. There were 40 six-month nonoverlapping time periods, resulting in a regression matrix of 52,000 rows of data across eight columns representing the factors, which seems large but really is not at all by modern quant applications. The model regressed was shown in Chapter 4 under the Graham Formula section with the addition of six month volatility.

Table 7.11 shows the results from the regression. The top row lists the correlation of the models' returns with forward six-month returns. Across the top of this table are the quintiles' data from all models starting with the regression model on the left, followed by the Graham_All model's results, and moving across from left to right, concluding in the far right showing the Graham Equal Weighted model (Gram Eq. Wt.). All statistics and multivariate regression were performed in TIBCO Spotfire S+ statistical analysis software but could easily be done in R.

These numbers in the rows marked by the quintiles are averaged six-month return numbers with no overlapping time periods so they do not compare with previous results shown earlier. The regression statistics are

**TABLE 7.11** Regression Statistics and Performance

| | Correlation with Excess Return over S&P 500 –> | | | | | | | | |
|---|---|---|---|---|---|---|---|---|---|
| | 11.23% | 4.68% | 5.49% | 5.49% | 5.50% | 5.48% | 5.56% | 5.47% | 5.49% |
| Quint | Regression Model | Gram All | Gram Up | Gram Dn | Gram Growth | Gram Value | Gram HiVol | Gram LoVol | Gram Eq.Wt. |
| 5 | −2.42 | −0.35 | −0.10 | −0.07 | −0.08 | −0.07 | −0.12 | −0.06 | −0.19 |
| 4 | 1.37 | 1.97 | 1.20 | 1.20 | 1.20 | 1.20 | 1.20 | 1.20 | 1.20 |
| 3 | 2.91 | 3.38 | 1.23 | 1.21 | 1.22 | 1.22 | 1.26 | 1.23 | 1.06 |
| 2 | 4.07 | 4.27 | 4.02 | 4.04 | 4.05 | 4.00 | 4.04 | 3.96 | 3.85 |
| 1 | 5.63 | 5.06 | 5.98 | 6.01 | 5.99 | 6.01 | 5.97 | 6.03 | 6.17 |

Coefficients & Statistics

| | Value | Std. Err | t val | Pr(>\|t\|) | | Correl w/XS Ret |
|---|---|---|---|---|---|---|
| Intcpt | 17.786 | 0.8581 | 20.7276 | 0.0000 | | |
| FA0 | – 0.2736 | 0.0720 | −3.7984 | 0.0001 | B/P | −4.8% |
| FA1 | – 0.7013 | 0.0764 | −9.1739 | 0.0000 | E/P | −8.9% |
| FA2 | – 0.7567 | 0.0862 | −8.7786 | 0.0000 | Div | −1.8% |
| FA3 | – 0.1862 | 0.0613 | −3.0393 | 0.0024 | EGrowth | −3.5% |
| FA4 | 0.1883 | 0.0656 | 2.8685 | 0.0041 | E Stab | 3.8% |
| FA5 | – 0.3303 | 0.0663 | −4.9844 | 0.0000 | E Stab2 | −5.9% |
| FA6 | – 1.7426 | 0.0786 | −22.1600 | 0.0000 | Volatility | −11.1% |
| MCap | – 0.5789 | 0.0482 | −12.0136 | 0.0000 | Mar Cap | 4.1% |

Residual standard error: 21.43 on 52483 degrees of freedom
Multiple R-Squared: 0.01865 Adjusted R-squared: 0.0185
F-statistic: 124.7 on 8 and 52483 degrees of freedom, the p-value is 0

shown immediately below and to the left of Table 7.11. We have the intercept term that has a value of 17.786, followed by the factors labeled FA0-FA6 and the MCap or size factor. These labels' definitions, along with the corresponding factors' correlation with excess return versus the S&P 500, are shown to the immediate right. The Value for the factors' columns are the regression coefficients for the factors and have nothing at all to do with stock valuation; it is just the level of the regression coefficient, the beta.

Notice from Table 7.11 that the betas are mostly negative values except FA4, which is the earnings stability factor, and the Market Capitalization factor. Also notice that these signs correspond to those signs of correlation with excess return values. This is a common result that the beta has the sign of the correlation, but not always, because this is a multivariate regression, not a univariate one. In the latter case, regression coefficients always have the same sign as the correlation coefficient.

The next column of the regression statistics is the standard error of the regression, followed by the *t*-stat and the *p*-value. The standard error is the standard deviation of the residuals spoken about in earlier chapters. From the *t*-statistic, we see that each factor is relevant. Typically *t*-stats of greater than 2 (or less than −2) are interpreted as being significant. These values are greater (or lesser) than this value. At the bottom of the regression are the $R^2$ and adjusted $R^2$ for the regression, and note that these are not large numbers; as we've stated, financial-statement data just doesn't have that strong a relation with stock return.

We did not perform a step-wise regression, adding and deleting factors looking for the combination that would give us the best regression as measured by $R^2$, simply because the Graham method uses all of them and he is not around to ask his permission to delete any. The volatility factor has the highest weighting, by the way, and what we mean by weighting is just the size of the regression coefficient with a *t*-statistic on the order of the intercept's value (but opposite sign) indicating just how strong a factor it is. One can consider the order of the factors by the absolute size of the *t*-statistic (column t val) to get an appreciation of the relative magnitude of importance to return or explanatory power of model variance. Thus, Volatility, intercept, market cap (i.e., size), E/P, Div Yld, E Stab 2, B/P, EGrowth, and finally E Stab mark the order of importance in the regression model.

We call attention to the small values of the correlation coefficients for the model's ranks with the forward excess return over the S&P 500, on the very top row of the chart, along with the factor correlations with excess return on the column to the right of the statistics. This goes to illustrate a major criticism I have with business school curricula because among almost all MBAs met, few come away with an appreciation for just how poorly typical financial-statement data really predict return. The correlation over 20 years with 50,000 stocks factors is not very strong. This is also evident in the

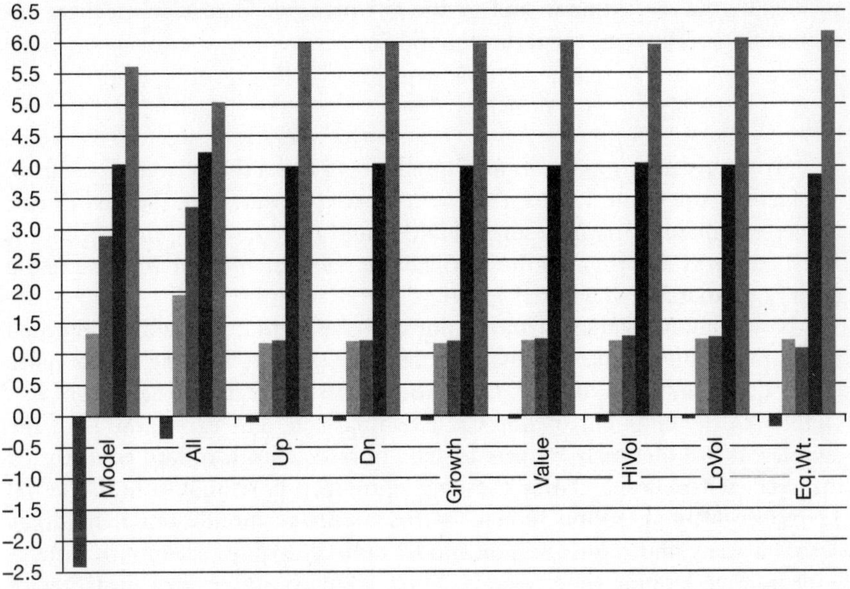


**FIGURE 7.14** All Quintiles Performance

low $R^2$ values for the whole multivariate regression where $R^2$ values of just 1.8 percent are obtained, in which taking their square root results in model correlations of ~13 percent. This means the regressed Graham model is a weak model. However, it is stronger than any of the heuristically obtained models, as evidenced by its correlation with excess return of 11.23 percent. How much better the regression model is than the heuristically created models can be easily observed in the kiloword view in Figure 7.14.

See the regression Graham model's quintiles on the far left of Figure 7.14, and each model is shown thereafter. These are for average returns across the 40 nonoverlapping six-month excess return versus the S&P 500. Remember that the universe is the S&P 1500. The nice monotonic behavior of the regressed model, along with its higher quintile 1 minus quintile 5 difference demonstrates it is better than the heuristically created models. Again, these data are measured across all time and not by market scenario. Obviously we could produce a lot more data on the regression model such as hit rates, confidence intervals on means, standard deviations of returns, IRs, ICs, Sharpe ratios, and more, but we will not for brevity's sake. The prudent investor will examine those supporting statistics before committing money to a quantitative investment strategy, however.

Alas, the regression model does not involve running a portfolio optimization on the results either; those are raw return statistics from quintiles formed by the regression model's ranking of stocks. That is, when there are regression coefficients, form the equation:

$$\text{Rank} = \beta_1 * f_1 + \beta_2 * f_2 + \beta_3 * f_3 + \cdots + \beta_7 * f_7 + \beta_8 * f_8$$

From this equation, now multiply the beta times the current exposures, the factor values, and rank each stock. Having all stocks in the investment universe ranked, sort them into quintiles and buy the top quintile; hold it for six months and then do the whole experiment again. The results are the returns tabulated in Table 7.14.

Now, there is one important point we have to add. You will be tempted to examine the charts, graphs, and time series plots looking to compare their outputs in terms of scale, level, and return figures from the start of this chapter to the end. This is not a fair comparison. The early graphs of the chapter utilize quarterly returns formed into 12-month rolling returns, for instance, whereas the charts showing optimized portfolios contain actual 12-month holding-period returns of the month-to-month actual holdings across a year, and the regression model table illustrates six-month returns with nonoverlapping time periods. Thus, we used a variety of measures of performance to illustrate a requirement of quantitative techniques and that is to measure performance a multitude of ways to ensure validity of the underlying model.

For Table 7.8 and any figure or chart thereafter, we took the individual securities out of the top and bottom quintile low-volatility Graham model and aligned them with formation dates, then input them as complete portfolios to FactSet. In this way, the FactSet attribution system saw them as something completely new to the attribution module, and let it measure the returns from the equal weighted quintiled portfolios based on the holdings as of the formation date. Thus, we used a completely separate methodology to measure the returns of the raw holdings through time, from that which was used to rank the stocks based on the weighted factors in the Graham model shown in data previous to Table 7.8. This leads to a conversation we will now have in the next chapter on building portfolios from models. In Chapter 8 we discuss real-world implications of model implementation to an investment process.

CHAPTER 8

# Building Portfolios from Models

*A few things could now be added concerning a certain very subtle spirit pervading gross bodies and lying hidden in them; by its force and actions, the particles of bodies attract one another at very small distances and cohere when they become contiguous; and electrical bodies act at great distances, repelling as well as attracting neighboring corpuscles; and light is emitted, reflected, refracted, inflected and heats bodies; and all sensation is excited, and the limbs of animals move at command of the will, namely by the vibrations of this spirit being propagated through the solid fibers of the nerves from the external organs of the sense to the brain and from the brain into the muscles. But these things cannot be explained by a few words; furthermore, there is not a sufficient number of experiments to determine and demonstrate accurately the laws governing the actions of the spirit.*

—Isaac Newton, *The Principia*[1]

So far we have made significant progress in creating a model from the Ben Graham recipe with factors derived from his writings and borrowed from the historical legacy he left us. Nevertheless, the methods discussed in this book are truly modern in that they borrow from recent academic discoveries and utilize the portfolio manager's perspective on model building for the distinct purpose of ranking securities for purchase in a portfolio. As Newton says, there are not a sufficient number of experiments to determine and demonstrate accurately the laws governing the actions of the markets. Therefore, you have to have some faith that the models and results presented here are a mere sample of a much greater distribution of outcomes that could occur. Though these numerical experiments (i.e., back tests) do not prove Graham's recipe for success is *the* recipe, they do suggest Graham's set of factors is a wiser selection of criteria for stock selection than most would offer.

In addition, a method like Graham's brings the relevance of experience while investing in turbulent times, as an investor struggles to find solace in her investment process when stress is widely found in the markets. Those times test the will and objectivity of even the most stoic quantitative asset managers, because, unlike most professions, the daily liquidity of the market changes every day, and how you, as an investment manager, are performing relative to peers and benchmark is displayed for all to see. Such immediate personal performance feedback occurs in almost no other profession, other than sports competition, perhaps, but athletes do not compete 260 days a year.

Consider, too, that the independent investor's own wealth is on the line, pure and simple. For money managers, income may be on the line but only for the truly successful money managers who are further along in their careers is wealth ever really on the line. Nevertheless, the reason we pursue the knowledge of Graham's method is because of his historic investment performance record. Moreover, the character and charm of the man, as revealed in his writings and stories from those who knew him, have created a paladin that we tend to pay homage to. Unfortunately, he honed his investment prowess in a day when the industrial, materials, and energy (IME) industries dominated the U.S. economy. Though these industries have a far smaller representation in the United States today, they are still strong in emerging economies such as those found in Asia (economies that look much like the U.S. economy following WWII), which makes Graham's method apropos for modern-day investing in that region. For example, IME currently reigns supreme in China, the world's leading exporter, as the United States was in the 1950s. This takes nothing away from Graham, as intelligent as he was, because, if he was an active investor today, his recipe for success would probably include some other pertinent factors we should include or consider in the wake of our current economy being dominated by financial companies and the service-based sector.

Alas, we have not his persona in this epoch and era to lean on for advice. Thus, as we begin our discussion of formulating portfolios from the underlying models, we need to consider that the heavy emphasis of the factors Graham chose were predicated on the kinds of companies he was investing in, and these were mostly IME companies. So, when we begin to use our model, applying it in a universe of approximately 2,000 companies in the United States and in global portfolios, there are adjustments to the Graham process we need to be mindful of, simply because the assets of the majority of firms today are not hard, tangible buildings, machinery, factories, tools, equipment, and their larder.

## THE DEMING WAY: BENCHMARKING YOUR PORTFOLIO

William Deming, a contemporary of Ben Graham, is the father of what we call Total Quality Management. Deming made his mark with Ford Motor Company in the 1950s where his impact on teaching in Japan came to the forefront.[2] In the years following the war, Deming spent two years teaching statistical quality control to Japanese engineers and executives. Later, while investigating why Americans preferred U.S.-made autos with Japanese-made transmissions, it came to Ford's attention that though both the United States and Japan were building transmissions within the same specifications, the Japanese tolerance ranges were narrower. The result, of course, was fewer defects in the Japanese-made versions.

Will Deming's first degrees were in math and physics. Statistics, which comes naturally to those trained in such hard science, is a natural application of the tools math and physics provide, so when Deming moved out of the research laboratory at Bell Labs, having been a student of Walter Shewhart, he first started rewriting Shewhart's Rube-Goldberg applications of statistical quality control. He found he had a knack for taking difficult topics and phrasing them in everyman language. Deming became famous for engineering error-reduction methods that reduced customer complaints, increased satisfaction, and lowered recalls, all of which subsequently increased profitability in a company. Ultimately, Deming's methods and philosophy evolved to initiate the Six Sigma revolution used in worldwide manufacturing, aiming for the reduction of defects to 1 in a million or six standard deviations from the mean of a normal distribution.

What is the application of Deming to investment management, you ask? It is all about reproducibility and quality control in the investment process. You see, we cannot reproduce Graham's methodologies as he practiced them. Neither can any fundamental investment process, for that matter. The analogy follows consideration of your grocery shopping habits. Imagine, if you will, the thoughts that run through your mind while shopping at Wegmans, Jewel, Dominick's, Safeway, Kroger, Food Lion, Piggly Wiggly, SUPERVALU, Aldi, Albertsons, Whole Foods, Trader Joe's, SuperTarget, Costco, Sam's Club, or Wal-Mart Supercenter. I'm pretty certain everybody in the United States has spent at least one hour in one of those stores, and the question is, to what extent can one day's shopping be reproduced some other day? Sure, you write lists, but the question is to what degree do you stick to them? This is much like fundamental investment management. The day-to-day activities of fundamental investing involve qualitative features that make reproducing an investment strategy difficult. For example, if the method led to a decision about a security to purchase a 3 percent position size, that same method practiced another time might lead to a 2 percent position. Moreover, documenting the investment decisions are so often overlooked, even many investment managers cannot recall years later why exactly they bought a stock and cannot even give good answers on why the weight of a stock in a current portfolio is often what it is.

This is why so few managers make it to an institutional platform, because if the investment consultant finds a lack of quality control in the investment process, a process that is given to a wavering variety of information capture, they will not recommend it. On the other hand, this is precisely why quantitative approaches work so well and why Ken Griffin, Peter Muller, Cliff Asness, Boaz Weinstein, Jim Simons, Robert Fernholz, Eugene Fama, and Josef Lakonishok have so many people waiting to invest with them. If these guys die tomorrow, their codified repeatable strategies will outlive them. Not necessarily so for Peter Lynch or Warren Buffett. This has more to do with quantitative strategies offering greater quality control, reproducibility, and reduction of human error due to subjectivity in the investment process.

The time has now come for the investor to put theory into practice, to test the mettle of the quant process, so to speak. The first point considers that we are making wagers under conditions that are uncertain for the most part. The Graham process is constructed by examining the more favorable responses of stocks sorted by Graham factors, leading us to treat the returns as most probable outcomes in normal environments. This is precisely why we put in place the margins of safety so expressed by Graham, to offer even more support to the probabilities we have measured and have them work in our favor. These consist of balance-sheet health via the current ratio screen on the universe of candidate stocks, the application of a heavy emphasis on valuation in the model to preclude paying too much for a security, and the addition of a volatility factor to steer us toward stocks that have less return variance. This last element is a more recent discovery and was not borrowed from Graham in any way. However (and for multiple reasons we have to ask), why is it that Graham also placed so much emphasis on historical earnings, the stability of historical earnings, and the history of dividend payments of a company? The reason has much to do with the idea of persistence, which quants purport, and in Graham's case, persistence in company records of performance, which he believed to be a leading indicator of future performance.

This persistence idea is really what the critics of quantitative methodologies hang their hat on. From Taleb to Patterson and everybody in between, they tout the nonconformance of the historical trend to persevere to the near future. Granted, quant models cannot predict the future, but extreme events, ELE events, or Black Swans are rare, and in the long run we are all dead. It is because of this truth that Graham necessarily built his reputation and performance record entirely based on that underlying ideology. The persistence of previous behavior is also why quant alpha models and risk models are believed to forecast with some accuracy, and the concept of persistence is quants' entire raison d'être. The structure of security dependence, modeled by the co-variance matrix in a risk model, is predicated on this persistence as well, in that volatility regimes stay in place for a period of time long enough to make investment decisions on. Obviously, extreme exogenous ELE events occur, increasing the mispricing among stocks, and they upset the persistence for a short period of time until fundamentals reassert themselves as the foremost cause of stock-price movements, while simultaneously restoring the correlation structure between stocks and reducing the undue correlation of strong downward trending markets. In effect, over time, reason will dominate and price near equilibrium will be reestablished, bringing stocks back to normal correlations with fundamentals. I am not saying bringing stocks back to fair pricing, but to a level of normal mispricing. This has to do with the truth about human behavior and not efficient market voodoo. But soon after a Black Swan event occurs, most often reasonableness, not necessarily rational behavior, returns to the markets.

In the meltdown of August of 2007, those quants who made no trades and kept their positions effectively lost nothing, because, by the end of August, near equilibrium was restored. This was again the case in 2008–2009. An ELE event happened because of the popping of the housing bubble combined with the use of overleverage, causing the banks to collapse. Then, fear persisted for a time (again, persistence...), driving the stock market to huge mispricing on the downside. In 2009, market participants saw this and reacted accordingly, so stocks rebounded, moving prices back toward normal mispricing. Now for those hedge funds leveraged at 30:1, there was a huge price to pay in this time period, but the cause was the overuse of leverage, not the lack of persistence in the time series of returns or volatility. ELE events are usually short-lived, and their impact in the markets is predictable even when, simultaneously, trading liquidity dries up, there is a rush to quality or hard assets, and there is an increase in correlation across the board of many different kinds of securities combined in a downward trending fashion.

On this topic we have one more thing to say; that concerns the frequency of ELE occurrences and the idea of fat-tail modeling to deal with them. Fat tails is the term given to extreme events that happen more often than given by the probability distribution of a normal curve. For extreme events to happen more often than predicted by the normal curve, the curve would have to have fat tails. We touched on this in previous chapters. Now, Nassim Taleb would have us believe that it is the disregard of fat-tail events that is the downfall of most quant models. Scott Patterson picked up on this populist idea and continued this description of ELE events being nonforecastable and implied specifically that quant David X. Li's "Gaussian copula" ruined the world in 2008. However, these two offer only the naïve story. In reality, fat-tail events are the ELE events of bubble popping, long-term capital management (LTCM) implosion, Russian currency crisis, Internet bubble, and so forth, and their occurrences give rise to an ideological argument when it comes to modeling, because in order to model ELE events, we have to determine their causes. To model regular market events, exclusive of Black Swans, we would ask the same question. What are their specific causes? In the absence of an ELE exogenous event, what is responsible for day-to-day price changes in stocks? Fortunately, we know the answer to the latter but not the former.

Given a model with fat-tails like the *t*-distribution, Cauchy, or any number of leptokurtic mathematical constructs, we would ask: What causes the tails to fatten? Is what causes fat tails, the ELE events to happen, the same cause and explanation of normal day-to-day variation in stock returns? Obviously not, or the Gaussian model would have caught and predicted their occurrence. However, if one does not know the cause of Black Swan markets, then how can one model them? That is, the shape of the distribution of returns is the result of the underlying cause of stock returns. It's not by artificially installing fat tails in a return distribution that one "automagically" accounts for the underlying mechanism responsible for ELE events.

We do know the cause of daily price variation in normal undisturbed natural markets; it is due to the fundamentals of the underlying companies and the perception in the marketplace of their worth. To add color and help you understand this, see Figure 8.1. This plot shows a graph of a Gaussian or normal distribution in light gray, a fat-tail distribution in black, and the sum of both in a dotted curve. All share a standard deviation equal to one and a mean of zero, and the area under each graph is set equal to 1. The *X*-axis is in standard deviation units so −6 implies six standard deviations from the mean. You can easily see from this graph why fat tails have that name. The further out from the mean one goes, the larger the probability the fat tails will predict some ELE event happening versus the Gaussian (normal) distribution.

Now, suppose the observed distribution of returns is the sum so that the returns due to extreme events are not separable from those due to normal events. We know from previous chapters on the distribution of returns of mutual funds that they are all leptokurtic, meaning they are more peaked

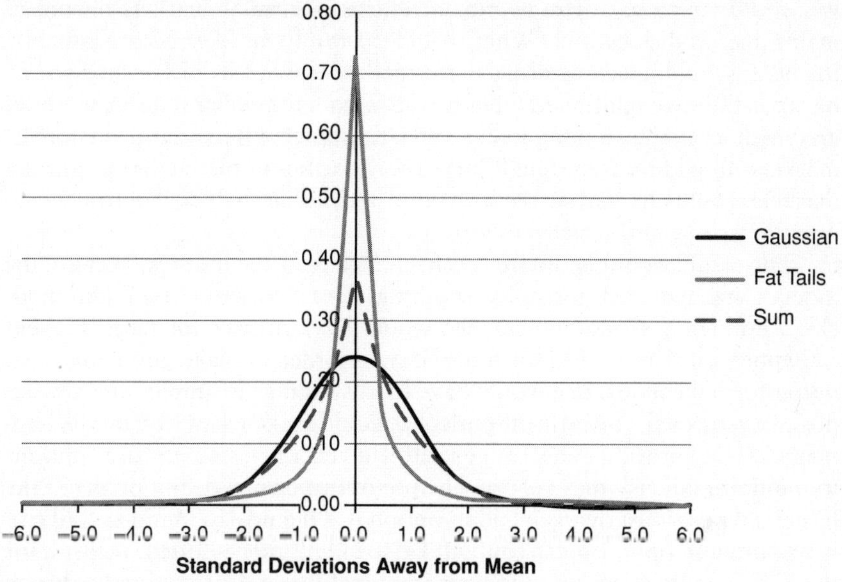


**FIGURE 8.1** Fat-Tailed, Normal, and Their Sum Distributions (Area = 1; S.D. = 1; Mean = 0)

than the normal distribution. We would say that the normal is a bad representation of the observed data, but the extreme ELE event modeled correctly by the fat tail's curve is also a bad model for the observed data near the center of the distribution, and it will poorly fit the majority of the data most of the time.

So here is the conundrum: If we use the fat-tail curve to model all returns, it will not match the day-to-day majority of returns and moves in stock prices, and volatility would be widely overstated the majority of the time. If we used the fat-tail curve to model regular events, we would expect greater return variation than we observe daily and mostly larger-than-normal variance of return than we observe. In effect, it would be like creating a scenario for the Graham models that is composed only of the time periods of ELE events. It would be like forming a time series of LTCM collapsing, Internet bubble popping, the beginning of the Iraq invasion, 9/11, and regressing returns of stocks from these periods to their causal factors formed from the previous periods.

Of course here is what the we must realize: We need a set of ELE factors and we do not know what they are. But let us say we do and we form regressions from them. Then, we would have betas to these ELE factors and we would try to use them to model returns of regular markets devoid of major market dislocations. What would the results be like? Most probably, the betas would have low levels in normal times whereas ELE events would be large. So if we multiplied them by the factors to predict returns, it would give mediocre values among stocks, obviating much differentiation in normal markets. In addition, the small but slow variation in the factors in normal markets would mix bad stocks with good and, in like fashion, confuse which quintile to long and which to short.

The result would be poorer performance than the indexes, because the indexes are managed portfolios resulting from "normal curve" like modeling. Following this argument, we would have to wait for an ELE event to happen once every 700 (or more) days in order to make any money. To outperform the index, one would have to use leverage to amplify the few but positive returns the investment portfolio would make when ELE events happen. Google knows Taleb's hedge fund, Universa Investments, uses options to minimize tail risk they report. The use of options by definition is to take leveraged positions; that is what an option is. One way to minimize tail risk is to purchase option puts; you will be spending money often, waiting for the ELE event to trigger a massive market meltdown. Unfortunately, during those 700 days between ELE events, the options would expire worthless and you would lose the benefit of buying that insurance. In other words, it is like investing in insurance policies hoping that the house fire happens, the flood comes, or your spouse dies while waiting to collect the proceeds from the event. As long as the event does not happen, the insurance premiums keep you losing steadily and continuously.

When the ELE happens, the put goes in the money and you can recoup all the money previously spent on options expiring out of the money (perhaps), taking advantage of the leverage that options provide. This is a simplification, but the few arbitrage opportunities that the market provides do not allow one to hedge severe downside risk without it costing money. The question is, does the money made during the ELE event make up for all the tiny losses accrued insuring against it? If the market really is a no-arbitrage environment, then the insurance is priced accordingly and the gains from ELE are only offset by the insurance premiums. I spend money on homeowner's insurance, life insurance, car insurance, all of which exist to protect me from ELE events. But I do not buy them for an investment but with an understanding that I will pay to avoid the loss. Does the price of any of these downside loss-prevention strategies pay off should the ELE event occur? No, it doesn't. Arbitrage opportunities inhibit the payoff from being larger than the benefits accrued to opportunities within the skinny tail. Likewise, put options are priced accordingly, and most option traders are sellers of options rather than buyers of them for this reason.

For a real-world example, consider buying a "65 Sept 18 put" on the SPY, which is the Standard & Poor's Depository Receipts (SPDR) ETF of the S&P 500 index trading on July 16 at 106.71. Assume the VIX is at 25, a relatively high volatility level, meaning that, over the next 30 days, the index could move 25 percent of 106.71 up or down. At the Fidelity web site, I find the cost of this put with a strike at 65 expiring on September 18, on the day of July 17 is 11 cents/share or $11 per option contract (for 100 shares of underlying). To purchase this we need capital of 100 × 106.71 or roughly $10,000. The probability of the SPY moving to the $65 strike price, the breakeven point, using the VIX as a proxy for the standard deviation of return of the SPY means it is a 1.66 sigma event. However, of course, it could just as easily move up rather than down, so we must multiply this number by 2 so it is a 3.2 sigma event. The normal curve says the SPDR price falling to $65 is a 1 out of 1,460 chance event, whereas the fat tails offers odds of 1 out of 77. Thus, we have, at the highest odds, a 1 in 77 chance of breaking even in this example, but if we use the sum of the normal and fat tails, we have on average, say, about a 1 in 500 chance of breaking even. Are you willing to wager a bet on odds of 1 to 500? Thus, the investment strategy of counting on ELE events means one must be prepared for long periods of time of losing money by buying insurance and, of course, playing with leverage.

Of course, most option traders have sophisticated P/L curves to view, which can more realistically demonstrate the P/L in a probabilistic calculation as a function of time, and we do not attempt to reproduce the whole multitude of outcomes of straddles, collars, and spreads. Additionally, as the time to expiration falls, and as the price of SPY falls, the put option gains in value and you could sell it. But option strategies in general are not the subject of this book so we will defer to experts on that subject.

Likewise, we cannot use the normal curve to model the fat tails. To do so, we would form a time series of LTCM collapsing, Internet bubble popping, the beginning of the Iraq invasion, September 11, and regressing returns of stocks from these periods to financial-statement data formed from the previous periods. We would find that the betas are nonsense, that their associated *t*-stats are weak and tiny, that the model would recommend we buy highly valued stocks with low earnings growth, and other associated anti-intuitive behaviors. In essence, from a statistical standpoint the fundamental factors would not have significance and, in addition, they would be backward in regard to common sense. This is because ordinary financial-statement data do not explain returns during ELE events. Most of the Black Swan market dislocations have macroeconomic bases and investor confidence issues as their culprit. But so many of the kinds of behavioral science that could model returns in fat-tail markets have little analytical or measurable qualities that can be defined by an equation. Toward the end of Chapter 10, we examine the future quant perspective and, perhaps, categorical research techniques and artificial intelligence can serve as the factors for future fat-tail type models. However, for now, to criticize quant modelers for not accounting for fat tails is like criticizing railroad engineers in 1867 for not inventing the airplane; the technology just is not there yet.

As previously stated, using factors that have higher correlation with return from normal quiet periods devoid of ELE events to model major market dislocations is a waste of time. They do not work. So the question turns to the sum curve: Is it possible to fashion some sum curve and average the effects of fat tails with normal markets? The answer is no, because they are, in effect, two underlying mechanisms involved in the observed returns, one given by each curve. The alternative is to imagine that the curve modeling extreme events, the fat-tail events, do not really impact things in normal markets, so we are saying the mechanisms that are the cause of extreme events are not on until we get way out on the curve. Figure 8.2 explains this analogy. The *X*-axis is standard deviations from the mean again. The *Y*-axis is the probability of an event happening at a given standard deviation from the average.

In this graph we plot the probability of extreme events happening out in the tails. The 95 percent confidence interval (CI) for the normal approximation occurs at 1.67 standard deviation units. Here, we start at the 99 percent

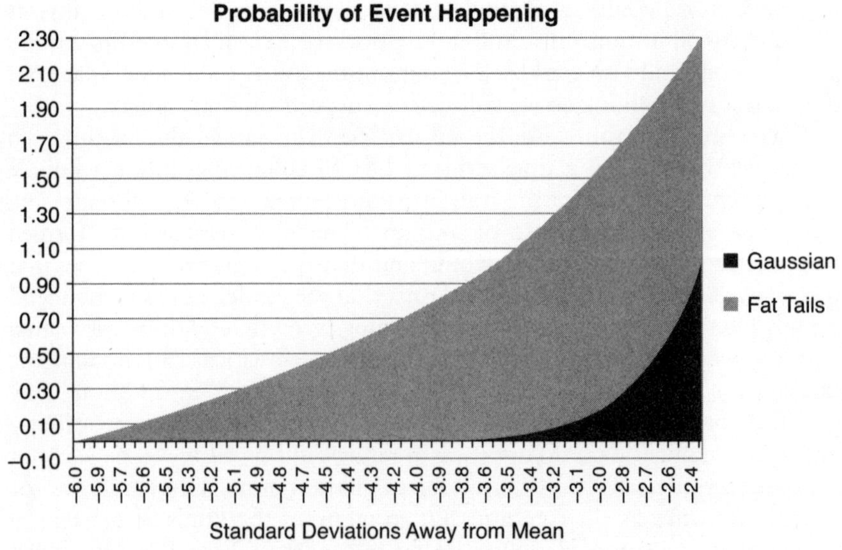


**FIGURE 8.2** Close-Up of the Left-Hand Side of Figure 8.1

CI for the normal curve and show the relative probability of events happening at increasing standard deviations from the mean. Thus, at 3.6 standard deviations, the probability of having an event given by whatever causes the fat tail is 1 percent, whereas for the normal approximation, at 3.6 standard deviations, the probability is 0.018 percent or 1 in 5,555, versus 1 in 100 for the fat tails. The probability of an event happening at six sigma is 1 out of 274,308,558 for the normal curve, whereas for the fat tail it is 1 out of 680. The sum curve is between these two extremes.

If we model market returns when they are nearer the center of the distribution, using financial-statement data and covariance matrices in risk models created from these factors, we are well and good, alive and kicking. Then, if we were to model the ELE events that occur, using extreme value models with full asymmetric copula fitting, we would also be able bodied and punching. This separation of the two environments falls under the subject of regime switching in the literature and is a topic of much research. Having lived through massive increases in computing power and evolution of finance theory able-bodied, I'm confident this methodology will grow to have serious impact in modeling stressful environments. You should pay attention to this separation-of-variables technique, and I'm sure you will hear more about it in the future. In summary, I am not saying this particular fat tail is the right one for modeling extreme events. We are only showing it to firm up your understanding of the discussion. To model the fat tail, you need to know the underlying physics or market mechanisms that cause ELE, but the math needed to deal with it has already been invented. In fact, the curves shown here are for independent events, but if we are talking about co-occurring events, then covariance matrices are involved and beyond them are copulas, which are all existing mathematical and statistical constructs providing infrastructure to model fat tails. Because we do not have the understanding of the underlying mechanisms to date to provide guidelines on exactly which fat tail, covariance, or copula to use, we are left with modeling for ordinary market environments mostly. This means relying on the persistence of their normal behavior, investing with Graham's margin of safety, and using no leverage. It's the analog of wearing seat belts though we know they only protect us in regular collisions, not from the extreme rarer event of a head-on collision with a 50-ton tractor-trailer.

One last item to be mentioned is that when ELE events happen, the whole correlation structure between assets changes, and it's this marked change in correlation between securities that is the major differentiator of ELE and Black Swan events from regular markets using a fat-tail model doesn't by itself incorporate the quick change in correlation structure, obviating some of its usefulness in modeling risk anyway.

In Graham's mind, a healthy history of regular earnings combined with a return to shareholders of some of these earnings was standing ground. That is, if it has been a consistent part of a company's record, it is likely to continue for a while. This is also the exact mentality quants have in model design. By examining the history of a model's performance and asking whether the return to the shareholder has been consistent, reliable, and stable, it creates standing ground for future investment return expectations, just as Graham believed. This standing ground offers a boundary from harm to the portfolio and corresponds to the first rule of investing: Do not lose any money.

The boundary-from-harm principle to the investor essentially means to purposefully underestimate the earnings potential of a firm so as to mitigate the necessity of accurately determining those future earnings. The application therewith of the Graham factors, in a quantitatively derived portfolio, does just this.

Now, Graham made a special point to describe that a very real risk comes from placing too much assurance in valuation alone. Just because you bought a security for a relative value far below a firm's peers or the market multiples is not a sufficient enough condition to be smug or secure when you are sleeping that you own that stock. In particular, Graham suggests bigger errors occur when these purchases are made at inopportune times in the market, especially when the firm is of low quality and when business conditions are favorable. So, for example, in 2006 perhaps buying some Real Estate Investment Trusts (REITs) that were more highly leveraged and at valuation multiples slightly below their peers would not have been a good idea. In fact, when business conditions are favorable (i.e., when the VIX for instance is quite subdued), that is the time when you must be on guard the most, because the risk to the company's earnings is high should business conditions change. Therefore, the margin-of-safety concept, requiring the observation of a moat around a business, involves an awareness of business conditions, of the overall economy, and of the market environment you are in, besides just a blind application of the Graham formulas. This is why comparing the business-earnings multiple versus AAA-rated corporate bonds is so important as a hedge and much better than spending money buying puts. In particular, the acceptable P/E should be related to the reciprocal of twice the current average high-quality AAA-bond yield. If the current AAA average yield is 6 percent, then the most P/E you would accept is 1/(2*.06) or 8.3. If it is 8 percent, the highest P/E acceptable would be 1/(2*.08) or 6.25. This hedge has to do with the yield spread acting as a kind of front-running indicator of the market's ebullient status while being a proxy for the measure of business environment, something an option does not do well.

Thus, it is fair to say that in low-volatility markets, fear and its contagion are nonexistent, and risk-seeking investors dominate the trading, defining the skinny-tail environment. In these good business environments, IPOs are abundant, as are mergers and acquisitions. In the recent past, leveraged buyouts also would occur regularly, and credit was easy to come by in stable markets. These are the times when the prudent investor must be most on guard, because what appears to be a buy may really be a risky asset. In such environments, when common stock of questionable companies (aka Internet stocks in 1999) are floated for unrealistic valuation multiples and earnings projections beyond reason occur, investors must specifically question their investment process if the nominated investment opportunities from the Graham model appear a bit too glamorous. That questioning must give an answer that satisfies the definition of persistent behavior for dividend payments and stable earnings over years, including imperfect investment periods. This is why we measure performance through market scenarios and why investment professionals look at extreme events, stress tests, and conditional value-at-risk measures, so that they employ boundary-from-harm principles and, in many ways, garner a look into what the fat tail might look like.

So, what is the benchmark portfolio and how does this have anything to do with limiting harm to an investment portfolio? Deming would point us to the benchmark portfolio. It is the Japanese transmission, made with precision, made with a reproducible recipe to high tolerance. It is the bogey; it is the target investors have in mind to construe a solution to match or surpass in performance. In Graham's investment process, the bogey was to produce a return above inflation and above the long-term average yield of U.S. Treasuries. Being conservative with an investment portfolio should accomplish two objectives: (1) protection from outsized risks, and (2) a handsome return when compounded over long periods of time. The idea of a benchmark as a bogey rather than cash is up to the investor, of course, but when purchasing stocks for equity investors, the passive but managed index is the better mirror.

It is easy to get drawn into risky investments when your goal is to produce substantial absolute returns. It is similar to sitting at a blackjack table in Vegas and doubling down when outsized losses occur, assuming you are not using the Kelly criterion.[3] The urge to make up losses can be overwhelming. If a coach told a Little League baseball player to get the ball over the outfielders and hit home runs every time he stepped up to bat, he would probably strike out more often than if he had been told to aim for ground balls headed toward the pitcher. In other words, setting realistic goals needs to be the number-two priority when it comes to investing, after the number-one priority of not losing any money, and much of what I hear at cocktail party investment conversation centers usually around home runs. Why do adults play this way?

The concept of a benchmark portfolio also addresses the psychology of the typical investor that involves keeping up with the Joneses. The topic of investing arises often in myriad social settings, especially cocktail parties. It is not uncommon to hear discussion of how much so-and-so's portfolio has beaten the S&P 500 or how much it beat another partygoer's portfolio. All measurements are relative to some benchmark. This is certainly true in sports because all the stats that make up baseball, golf, racing, and so forth all revolve around this concept of comparative stricture. Because this apparently is human nature, it is only natural to have a bogey in our minds to measure performance against. The only discussion left to have is that about a fair comparison. We mentioned in earlier chapters that, occasionally, Morningstar misspecifies the benchmark for a mutual fund. That is, it may be a large-cap value or large-cap growth mandate, and Morningstar will compare results to the S&P 500 or the Russell 1000 indexes. This is an unrealistic comparison for the simple reason that those two benchmarks are core benchmarks, having both value and growth stocks in them, obviating their usefulness as a value or growth comparator. Value and growth stocks have some slipperiness to their definition, but certainly a value-oriented fund, when characterized by the valuation metrics of P/S, P/B, P/E, and P/CashFlow, will have these values on average much lower than that of these two benchmarks. Likewise, growth measures will be higher on a growth mandate than these two indexes. These differences are significant enough that the long-term performance between value, growth, core, and quality are indeed separable and so should the benchmark you choose to compare your portfolio to. What this all boils down to is a recommendation to take the time to determine the correct benchmark in which to compare returns.

Often the benchmark has much to say about the universe of candidate stocks in which to run the Graham process through. For instance, comparing a small-cap core mandate to the Russell 1000 or the S&P 500 is also benchmark misspecification because there are no small-cap stocks in the S&P 500 and only a small fraction in the Russell 1000 (using typical small-cap definitions). Thus, the Russell 2000 (R2K) is a better benchmark for a small-cap core mandate and offers many potential buy candidates within the bench for the investor, but the investor still has to be aware of style. Most of these popular benchmarks allow for an easy universe specification, because investors can obtain their constituents and their fundamental and pricing information readily from a plethora of sources.

In general, the following list shows examples of what will work as decent benchmarks for their appropriate mandates. We also include some basic market capitalization limits for many mandates' prescription:

| | |
|---|---|
| Small-Cap Value: | Russell 2000 Value index; \$100M–\$2B |
| Small-Cap Growth: | Russell 2000 Growth index; \$100M–\$2B |
| Small-Cap Core: | Russell 2000 index or S&P 600; \$100M–\$4B |
| Large-Cap Value: | Russell 1000 Value; \$8B–NoLimit |
| LargeCap Growth: | Russell 1000 Growth; \$8B–NoLimit |
| Large-Cap Core: | Russell 1000 or S&P 500; \$8B–NoLimit |
| Emerging Markets: | EEM or MSF or Vanguard VLO |
| EAFE: | MSCI or Vanguard |
| Global: | MSCI ACWI; \$8B–NoLimit |

Just as you should know your enemies, you should know your benchmark, too. This means investors should regularly decompose the chosen benchmark into its subordinate sectors, industries, and their weightings. This is an important but seldom done chore, and these weightings are worth remembering or recording because, as stocks move over time, the relative weightings change. Though Graham was an absolute return investor (and was not taken to make investment decisions predicated on movements in the index), he had strong familiarity with the major benchmarks of his day, simply because they are relevant to understand the major components of the economy and of the available investment opportunity set their constituents provide.

## PORTFOLIO CONSTRUCTION ISSUES

Given you have a model, turning the Graham methodology into a working portfolio mostly involves simple constraints. These are the set of passive boundary-from-harm principles that you need to consider in the investment process and offers more than just diversification. Remember that there are two kinds of risk: One is stock specific and is diversifiable and the other is market risk that is not diversifiable. We had mentioned that many people thought that because they had good asset allocation they should not have suffered losses during the credit crisis of 2008–2009 or during the technology bubble of 1999–2000. Well, now we know better; diversification does not protect us from nondiversifiable risks. The risks due to poor performance can be mitigated by using Graham's margin-of-safety principles but will never be mitigated entirely. This is the job of the stock selection model and quantitative process.

If we tabulate investors' choices, it is about security selection and weighting. The objective for the Graham model is to choose the securities for investment. The job of the risk model is to choose the weights and influence the securities we should invest in. For instance, would you ever buy a security not for its alpha but purely for its risk reduction contribution to the portfolio? For example, suppose the Graham model said to buy just two securities, and they were both technology stocks. Would you then buy a third stock, say Exxon, just because you want to limit your exposure to a single industry? Risk modeling offers that kind of perspective to the portfolio in a tractable way.

In addition, other answers we need to build the portfolio involve portfolio turnover; number of securities; position size limits; industry, sector, and country exposure limits at our disposal. So, without using an optimizer, we have to choose these manually because they are not automated inputs to software. What kinds of information should go into the portfolio construction decision making then? These are:

1. Any noncompromising biases the investor has should come out first. For instance, social investing preferences are a good example. Will you buy tobacco companies or how do you feel about owning Las Vegas Sands casino? This will impact the choice of estimation universe for investing. Then be mindful of these considerations when choosing your benchmark.
2. Do you have any industry preferences? I happen to like energy companies and have always owned a couple.
3. How many companies can you pay attention to, in your portfolio? Thirty, sixty, one hundred? Your position size limit will be based on this number, especially if you equally weight your stocks. Of course, the amount of money you will invest also has an impact on the number of securities you can own. Typically, if you cannot buy $1,000 worth of a stock, you should not own it. Moreover, what is the minimum position size you will entertain?
4. Without any other good reason, equally weight your stocks if you do not use an optimizer.
5. Graham suggests either a three-year holding period or a 50 percent return; whichever comes first should set your horizon for holding a security. This will impact your expected portfolio turnover. About 30 percent turnover a year is a good number. Much more than this and you will be deviating from the Graham methodology most probably.
6. U.S. centric, international, or both? The next chapter on investing opportunities will help you focus your answer to this question. If yes to international, than how much per country?

7. The source of the data you will use to run your Graham model through. This is dependent upon which broker you use, and we will cover some of that superficially in the next section. The good news is, this is not 1976. Investors have rich in-depth online electronic capabilities these days from a variety of sources and in 2025, you'll have all data at your fingertips, or voice recognition system.
8. The broker or trading platform you would use to execute your investment decisions.

## USING AN ONLINE BROKER: FIDELITY, E*TRADE, TD AMERITRADE, SCHWAB, INTERACTIVE BROKERS, AND TRADESTATION

So where can you build a Graham model? What do online brokers offer in the way of programming easy-to-use stock screens with back testing capabilities to produce the Graham methodology? For starters, if you can subscribe to FactSet, you should. At this writing there is no better total system available anywhere, in my estimation. To use an online broker, you will need access to their screening tools through an existing account. *Barron's* is a good source for broker ratings. Every March, they run brokerage ratings for online broker-dealers (B/D's). They rate brokers on a variety of topics including costs, ease of use, ease of trade, depth of research, back testing capabilities, and so forth. *Barron's* of March 15, 2010, listed the top five ranked online brokers to be: thinkorswim, MB Trading, Interactive Brokers, TradeStation, and OptionsXpress. TD Ameritrade owns thinkorswim and they offer a complete package for back testing trading strategies. However, the objective of their package definitely seems to cater to day-traders rather than long-term investors like us.

Fidelity is the quintessential online broker for prudent longer-term investors. Though they have a stock screener in their online system, complete with a variety of classifications and categories to screen for, disappointingly, there are no valuation parameters. Yes, that is right, you cannot screen on P/B, P/S, P/CF, or P/E in Fidelity at this writing. Without that ability, Fidelity cannot offer help in creating a Graham screen or program a model within its system for Graham, as valuation is 40 percent of the model. However, Fidelity has great customer service, option accounting, and a well-rounded, easy-to-use interface.

E*Trade demands that you open an account before you are allowed to play with their stock-screening environment. However, it appears that all is there to allow ease in programming the Graham factors into a professional-level screen. In addition, they have technical categories allowing momentum factors to be included. If I ever made a speculative trade in my life, it was buying E*Trade at $13 just before the Internet bubble popped and selling my measly 300 shares for $56. I caution you, however, it easily could have gone the other way. Luckily for E*Trade, Ken Griffin's Citadel Investment Group bought a stake when it was revealed E*Trade had subprime exposure in its banking department or it would not be online now.

Schwab also has a complete package in terms of allowing the user to program models for back testing into their system; however, they require opening an account before full access is granted. What they offer above and beyond, however, is access to Greg Forsythe's Equity Ratings. He is Schwab's lead quant, and Schwab creates models predicated on many factors similar to Graham. As an account holder there, you can get access to their rankings and methodology. Perhaps his group can be tapped for consultation on your own model, too.

The best capabilities for the purposes that match our objectives in making the Graham methodology automated involves TradeStation. TradeStation is very seductive. They have complete demos showing how to program trading back tests predicated on bid-ask spreads, daily volume, and closing prices. In addition, they have a complete set of financial statement factors from the balance sheet, income statement, and cash-flow statement. They cover 18 years of history for U.S. markets and the Graham method could be programmed with ease and back tested using their software. Also, when you have it typed into their system, it can be run daily to keep you abreast of the latest stocks passing the criteria. The temptation in running a Graham model daily, however, is to trade, which is what any B/D wants you to do for it's how they make their money. Don't be seduced. It's very hard to resist the temptation to do something with your portfolio. This is one of the character traits you'll have to cultivate as a Graham-style investor.

Interactive Brokers was another disappointment in this regard. It is really funny because, when I first developed and launched a hedge fund for a firm I worked for years ago, the managing partner of the firm mandated using Bear Stearns as the prime broker to clear trades. However, I recommended Interactive Brokers and he was afraid they would not have the capital to back up their services should the market dislocate. Now, Bear Sterns is gone for exactly the reasons he feared, and Interactive Brokers is healthy and survives—the exact opposite of his forecasts. He was a fundamental investor, but he should have listened to this quant. Nevertheless, Interactive Brokers does not appear to have stock-screening capabilities and will not work as a good broker for the Graham method unless you can run a model somewhere else and make trades through Interactive Brokers. They do have a reputation for good trade execution and low cost.

All these brokers offer easy portfolio monitoring of your position with P/L reporting continuously. What is new with many of these online brokers, however, is the availability of their Open Application Programming Interfaces, or API as they are regularly termed.

API allows the enterprising investor with programming skills to actually write their own models for trading and investing and then have it "automagically" mesh with the broker's trading system. E*Trade was the first online broker to allow this application, followed by MB Trading. TD Ameritrade has over 20 developing partners writing applications, or apps, as they are called, that plug into their trading systems. CoolTrade has an automated trading software app that plugs directly into E*Trade, allowing customization with the users' own methods or techniques for trading and investing. Considering that it is quite expensive to attempt to negotiate your own deal with any big trading wirehouse or dealing with an exchange directly, these custom apps allow for a much cheaper interface direct to the trading floor through your broker.

One novel development comes from Lightspeed Financial. They offer market access tools and a software kit called Black Box, which allows algorithmic trading for U.S. equities set up much like an Integrated Development Environment (IDE), as you get with C++ programming. Just be careful you are not the reason the next flash-crash happens.

## WORKING WITH A PROFESSIONAL INVESTMENT MANAGEMENT SYSTEM: BLOOMBERG, CLARIFI, AND FACTSET

For those unencumbered by mortgages and car payments, there are more sophisticated software systems out there. These are the professional investment management systems that Ben Graham wished he had had. We will start with the mayor of New York City as of today's date. Michael Bloomberg is a rich man besides being the mayor of New York City, and his company, Bloomberg, is a media "minpire" (as opposed to empire) to the data-providing landscape. Bloomberg's initial foray was of a very different variety then ClariFI, a newcomer and FactSet's business model. Previously, Bloomberg was a machine. It was a piece of hardware that sat on the trading desk providing information content of all sorts and on all kinds of securities. It was revolutionary in its day. The drawback, of course, was that it had a very difficult interface. It made Rube Goldberg machines look as simple as an eating utensil, say a fork, in comparison. It had a whole fleet of archaic mnemonics the user needed to type into its own proprietary keyboard. But the data was there. Users eventually got hooked on the system simply because what they lacked in a user interface they more than made up for in data. Lots of it in all kinds of markets.

Now Bloomberg is trying to create a system that has some of the functionality of a FactSet or its weaker sister ClariFI. I do not doubt they will develop something powerful as their history demonstrates a lot of innovation. That is the kind of persistent business behavior Graham looks for. To describe where Bloomberg is going is to describe ClariFI, which we will cover next.

ClariFI is owned by Standard & Poors, which owns CapitalIQ, and CapitalIQ sits within the organization between S&P and ClariFI, which uses its data. Compustat is a long-term securities database of a global nature started and run by Standard & Poors and has been available for purchase by them for a long time. They purchased CapitalIQ, which started a database mostly of foreign and international firms because they were doing a better job archiving foreign-firm accounting and financial-statement data than was Compustat. ClariFI can work with either's data but is a platform designed for data management at the data level, security level, and portfolio level. In addition, it offers factor back testing and has a wonderful database of precanned factors from all the areas of interest to investors. Valuation, growth, profitability, earnings, cash flow, capital allocation, price momentum, and other technicals are all preformed, and you just select them with your mouse from a library. They are all very transparent, too, so you can easily see how their factors are constructed and, of course, you can design your own. If you are familiar with MATLAB's Simulink system used for simulation of dynamic structural evaluation, ClariFI is similar in that it allows for point-and-drag construction of multifactor models. Very state-of-the-art, slick, and easy to use. One can easily construct a model, back test it, and perform a wide variety of statistics on it with an emphasis on ease of use. They also do consulting and will help clients to design new methods and work toward uncovering new investment anomalies that will differentiate them in the marketplace. You can also perform portfolio optimization with their software.

FactSet is still the best-of-breed for equity investors, in my opinion. However, their client base is mostly the institutional user. Of course, the same is mostly true for Bloomberg and ClariFI, also. However, FactSet made their mark initially for two reasons: (1) their customer support is second to none. In fact, their customer support is so good, the nearest competitor among any product is in fifth place! This emphasis is at the core of the firm's culture and comes from the top down, beginning with its CEO, Phil Hadley. For a while, FactSet had strong first-mover advantage in its product suite because there just was nobody else that had such a wide variety of data so easily available with a GUI that you can use right out of the box without any manual or instruction. It is widely suspected that FactSet had a lot to do with Bloomberg moving away from its proprietary keyboards and monitors because ease of use always wins in the long run.

FactSet has everything ClariFI and CapitalIQ have, and then some. It has its own data, but unlike almost any other product in this marketplace, FactSet is a data integrator, so you can purchase Computstat data through the system. They also recently launched their own database, called FactSet Fundamentals, and are building other proprietary products. They have many modules, starting with real-time portfolio and market intraday tick pricing. It looks like a trading screen turning red for losses and green for up movements across global indexes and multi-asset classes. They have a company explorer module, which CapitalIQ has, allowing the user to drill down right to the audited financial statement to see where the numbers come from on a company.

They have risk models and optimizers from Barra, Northfield, Axioma, APT, and their own, and users can easily plug and chug risk models from each vendor into each optimizer. In addition, if the user is archiving their portfolio's holdings each night on the system, it is very easy to fetch the portfolios to load them into these optimizers, do a run, and output the run for trading. They also allow you to back test an optimization strategy over time. And of course you can use their alpha testing platform to create alpha or risk models, back test them, and easily port the output directly to an optimizer for back testing. This is how we did portfolio optimization back tests of the Graham models in Chapter 7. They have an "automagic" covariance matrix-making function, too, for risk-model construction. They do not have a pre-canned library of factors, however, and it is a bit more difficult to go into their financial-statement databases to build up a model, but everything you need is there to do it with. FactSet is a very menu-driven system, so they are behind the times a bit as compared to ClariFI's slick windowing environment, but that will change as they're trying to hire almost an engineer a day as I write this book.

FactSet's greatest strength comes from their portfolio attribution module, which is why the majority of their customers buy FactSet. Portfolio attribution comes in two flavors: the Brinson method and risk decomposition. When a client's portfolio is uploaded to their secure servers, the time series of data collection can be performed daily, and over-time real performance attribution can be performed. In this mode, grouping of securities—both equities and fixed income—can be done by just about any category your imagination can conceive of. Industries, factors, duration, ratings, you name it—you can group and fractile your portfolio. Relative attribution against a benchmark was actually hard work before FactSet had its PA module, and now it has been reduced to about as much labor as opening your refrigerator.

FactSet is designed for the fundamental and quant investor, as is ClariFI, but only if it is bundled with CapitalIQ. Bloomberg, on the other hand, is really only for fundamental investors at this stage. All three of these vendors allow portfolio uploading each evening so that the time series of the portfolios can be collected and held in their system for further development, analysis, and monitoring. I wish they would offer a retail version or allow a version to be sold through brokers so that if you opened an account with a broker you could also get to use FactSet. Hey, Fidelity, are you interested?

It is very difficult to summarize or tabulate all the pros and cons of so many of these online brokers simply because whatever you write down will change in a month. Seriously, the speed with which the online brokers innovate is blinding. You are better off reviewing the comparisons that come out in *Barron's* every March when details of the most major considerations are tabulated.

In this chapter, we covered the major concerns investors should have in turning the Graham model into a portfolio they would actually hold. It is a necessary prerequisite to have a security-specific model before buying a portfolio of stocks, but given only one model, many investors would still implement it very differently. Also, the Graham model is not necessarily an asset-allocation description either. Investors would form the asset-allocation strategy before using the Graham model to decide exactly what they would buy. Graham does not say too much about the asset allocation, but spends much of his time detailing what investors need to know and do to purchase a stock that is underpriced by the market. It is left to the investor to decide how to implement the purchases.

CHAPTER 9

# Barguments: The Antidementia Bacterium

*It is only in the quantum theory that Newton's differential method becomes inadequate, and indeed strict causality fails us. But the last word has not yet been said. May the spirit of Newton's method give us the power to restore unison between physical reality and the profoundest characteristic of Newton's teaching—strict causality.*

—Albert Einstein[1]

Strict causality maintains that, for every action, there is a predictable reaction. If we know all the forces acting on an agent, we can predict, through Newton's laws, that agent's position in space and time. However, quantum theory implies that we are forever incapable of giving both position and velocity with precision, thus there is a dichotomy and struggle inside science to find some pleasing solution to both perspectives. In the world of science, this still stands as a "bargument" (those disagreements that prevail when you've had too much to drink) in some circles, and it is exaggerated more so when chemists are involved, for then the –OH appendage highlights the disagreements substantially more than it ought.

When quants attend happy hour, the conversation soon breaks into barguments, too, when –OH is running recklessly through their bodies. However, hashing these disagreements out leads to a consensus on major issues relevant to modeling and theory. To begin, we will start discussing asset allocation, which is one of but not the highest contributor to investment performance in contrast to the famous, or should we say infamous, paper(s) by Brinson, Hood, and Beebower.[2] Asset allocation is about choosing the distribution of securities investors should own and diversifying them from a top-down perspective given the investment goals and risk tolerances they have. It is about the overall investment strategy. Beebower et al.'s paper has been idolized by the proponents of index and ETF management who are dyed-in-the-wool efficient market proponents.[3] Unfortunately, the work from Beebower et al., though analyzed correctly, given the pension data they had at the time, is much too broad to have bearing on an individual investor's portfolio. For instance, the typical pension owns assets in fixed income, U.S. equities both large cap and small, international equities, emerging market equities, some alternative assets, real estate, private equity, and timber or land holdings. In this regard, considering the multiple asset classes and types of assets involved, their methodology and conclusions are probably correct, which is that the vast majority of total portfolio return is due to the asset-allocation strategy. In reality, asset allocation, in this sense, is different from a more granular account of funds that are in the same mandate and asset class, have roughly the same number of stocks, similar market capitalization, and are in the same markets (U.S. vs. international) versus those found in the typical middle-class investor's IRA, 401(k), or teacher's 403(b) plan. In those plans, individual investors have choices among different asset classes like long-term bonds, U.S. Treasuries, emerging markets, and small-cap growth. So the differences between securities in a given asset class are typically much smaller than the differences between asset classes overall. This is the idea on which we address asset allocation in this chapter.

Thus, choosing a percentage allocation between fixed income and private equity is not the same as choosing between consumer discretionary and consumer staples all within large-cap U.S. equities. In the usage of Beebower et al., the discussion is really about tactical asset allocation, where an investor adjusts allocation based on their estimation of the future markets on a global colossal scale. Here, we refer to the idea of distributing dollars in a portfolio across equities in a given asset class and market with a goal of lowering the variance of the overall portfolio by removing cross-correlation among stocks in the portfolio.

## THE COLOSSAL NONFAILURE OF ASSET ALLOCATION

It has been widely reported that asset allocation failed the investor during the 2007–2009 credit debacle and liquidity freeze, and that large losses across investors' portfolio ensued, as if asset allocation led to a gasket-blowing event for some reason. This is due to a basically misunderstood but widely reported error of what diversification is and does.

There are two main categories of risk: market risk and security risk, also called systemic and idiosyncratic risk. Proper asset allocation and diversification results in minimizing idiosyncratic risk because only this kind of risk is diversifiable. An investor obtains market risk just by being in the market. The only way to remove this kind of risk is to get completely out of the market; it is not diversifiable or removable any other way. Thus, in the credit crisis, when all stocks correlated highly as they do in down markets, the VIX increased and concomitantly the total risk composed of market and security-specific risk changed their contribution percentages, so that market risk increased and security-specific risk, which is diversifiable, decreased. However, the asset allocation did its job by mitigating the security-specific idiosyncratic risk. The fact that this part of the total risk was much smaller due to the increased correlation between stocks, resulting in the level of market risk increasing, has nothing to do with the principles of asset allocation.

In fact, the idiosyncratic risk part of total risk could have been completely mitigated, leaving the portfolio fully exposed to market risk alone. In this situation, the portfolio would move in the direction of the market, downward. However, the asset allocation piece did its job. It removed the risk of correlation between stocks so that when one is up the other is down, and vice versa (using a two-stock portfolio for an example), leaving the detrimental part of the risk in the portfolio to that of market risk and where it went, so it dragged the portfolio. Asset allocation did not fail; it is this misunderstanding that asset allocation lowers all risk that is erroneous. So investors must be sure to understand what diversification does when applying it. It does not remove market risk, and in some market theories, namely, stochastic portfolio theory, portfolio variance can even be a good thing, depending on how the investor constructs the portfolio, as we shall later see.

Historically, in traditional money management the portfolio manager would allocate dollars where they found the process for picking stocks at the bottom-up level most advantageous. For instance, value managers would stick to where they are finding value. They may indeed end up with industry concentration. Of course, they clearly have value concentration, too. Likewise, a growth manager, besides having a "growthy" concentration, might also have a concentration heavily represented by technology companies. This defines the era that Ben Graham grew up in, the era in which he sharpened his investing acumen and depicted how he allocated his dollars to investments. However, this presents some difficulty when trying to offer a feature in the portfolio that will lower estimated risk involving true diversification. In Graham's mind, owning 30 companies was about right, but he did not pay as much mind to whether they all might be correlated in their return series. This is because he did not think about price movements occurring between stocks as a source of risk. Graham defined risk only at the company level for the most part and deemed a company failing as the only kind of risk other than interest rate and inflation risk.

In traditional money management, the investor typically would choose the position weights in a more ad-hoc fashion for the securities in the portfolio. Typically, the position weights were proportional to the output of their investment process, which was bottom-up fundamental, offering their qualitative assessment of expected return, so stocks with the highest return potential received the highest weight in the portfolio. In this regard, little thought was given to co-occurring or covariance risk, and just the passive risk constraints (such as maximum weight or maximum industry exposure) were involved in limiting the exposure to a given security.

To offer evidence of this effect, consider Warren Buffett's description of successful money managers of the Graham taxonomy. In a talk in 1984 at Columbia University commemorating the 50th anniversary of Graham and Dodd's book, *Security Analysis*, Buffett says the successful money manager buys a stock because he is getting more for his money than he is paying. He is not looking at quarterly earnings projections, or next year's earnings; he is not thinking about which day of the week it is; he does not care what Wall Street investment research says; he is not interested in price momentum, earnings momentum, trading volume, or anything else. He is simply asking, "What is the business worth?" With that statement, the reader should know that Graham put 25 percent of his assets in a single security, GEICO, in 1948. The definition of risk should, therefore, define the asset allocation. Graham was beholden to his definition, and that is what led to this seemingly overly large single position. He simply did not see much risk in owning GEICO at the time and never considered covariance between securities as risks in his portfolio.

Unfortunately, even small positions can carry outsized risks that are usually missed in fundamental asset management processes because there are not concrete fundamentals that relate expected return to risk on an individual security basis for the analyst to discover. This kind of risk arises from the co-varying risk due to owning multiple securities in a portfolio. To offer a much deeper description of these risks, we need to review econophysics and differentiate between differing systems.

## THE STOCK MARKET AS A CLASS OF SYSTEMS

There are ways of denoting the market in terms of their physical behaviors. These call the stock market deterministic, random, chaotic, complex, or a complicated system. Deterministic systems are systems that follow an exact describable and reproducible process. They are usually modeled easily by an analytical equation that describes their behavior. The throw of a baseball follows a known trajectory given easily by Newton's second law,

$F = ma$. As long as the ball is let go at the same angle, same revolution, and same speed, it will travel to the target with exactly the same trajectory each time. Random systems, so highly regarded by Nassim Taleb that one would think he invented the concept, are just that: completely unpredictable. If they are truly random, there is no equation to model their movement and they are not described by any known mathematics[4] except, perhaps, under stochastic calculus approximations. Not if they're truly random. Chaotic systems are somewhere in between, not completely deterministic and not completely random, very much like the weather. These are systems that are usually highly nonlinear and are very, very sensitive to their initial conditions. This is the butterfly effect at its worst, so to speak. To the uneducated observer of a chaotic system, however, it can appear random. Even in modern weather forecasting, which uses models that utilize full-blown numerical solutions to nested simultaneous Navier-Stokes differential equations on a supercomputer, the equations are commonly run over and over in an iterative fashion, each time changing the initial conditions slightly to observe the time evolution of the weather. The distribution of weather outcomes at a given time, then, allows confidence interval gauging of what the weather forecast will be like. Weather is a great analogy to a complex chaotic system.

To see an analogy of chaos in action, think of a person throwing 100 darts at a dartboard, one at a time. The probability of two throws with two darts, striking the board exactly at the same spot is very, very small. However, the probability of this person getting all 100 darts to land anywhere on the dartboard is pretty high. The dartboard acts as an attractor for the trajectory, to use the language of chaos theorists. This illustrates chaos—the dart thrower cannot always get the dart on the same identical path as in a deterministic system but he or she can get all the darts moving or trending in the same general direction or concentrated in an area.[5] Chaotic systems often do indeed demonstrate this kind of trending, but do not repeat the past exactly. They are noted by giving similar paths, so they do not repeat the past, but they do offer somewhat consistent trends, often repetitively. For you engineer, physicist, and mathematician readers out there, I know that dart throwing isn't a real chaotic system; it's actually deterministic but it serves as an example for a teaching moment.

Specifically, chaotic attractors are described by high sensitivity to initial conditions, like the dartboard analogy; any little nuance of the dart-throwers fingers changes the trajectory of the dart. In real chaotic systems, these subtle initial condition changes can be amplified, leading to exponential differences in outcomes and making prediction highly difficult. In contrast, if the stock market was a simple deterministic system, small changes to the current environment would not lead to a large change in a forecasted result. This is a proper criticism of quantitative techniques, even when putting the

Graham method into a model, in that it is a linear model, implying we can predict returns way, way out into the future, when, in reality, the forecast period accuracy falls dramatically the further out in the future we go. The uncertainty of chaotic systems like the stock market is closer to practical experience and is one reason why Graham stated he could not predict the market direction or when it would actually recognize that undervalued stocks are indeed undervalued. Though he probably did not know the mathematical reasons for his beliefs necessarily, he sure had good instincts.

Now there is a distinction between complex, complicated, and deterministic systems. Complicated systems are marked by all known outcomes, logically connected to many events in a cascaded sort of way. In fact, complicated systems are just many interconnected deterministic systems whereas complex systems are very different. Complicated systems are subject to reduction whereas complex systems are not. Complex systems have outcomes that are not all known; thus they are inherently more difficult to understand, interpret, and design around. Complex systems are chaotic in nature. The weather is a complex system. Calling the markets complicated rather than complex has profound ramifications, because the stock market is much like the weather and is a complex chaotic system, as has been demonstrated consistently.[6] Unfortunately, quantitative methods truly only work well for complicated systems and only work some of the time for complex systems.

Chaos analysis tells us that market prices are partially random with a trend component. Later we shall see that this corresponds to what is known as an Ito process. The amount of the trend component varies from market to market and from time frame to time frame. Short-term patterns and repetitive short-term cycles with predictive value are not too common. There are numerous analyses of the stock market that supply ample evidence of its chaotic behavior.[7] Specifically, the market time series has cycles, nonperiodic (meaning cyclical) in nature with lifetimes of around 40 to 48 months. It has also been documented that the market becomes more and more unpredictable during periods of time longer than this. Investing in stocks for four years or more constitutes growth coming from relationships to GDP and other economic variables that are intrinsically hazardous to guess their future values. The consequence of this is that investors incur more risk in the market than is implied by a standard normal distribution (i.e., because of fat tails) for returns with short investment horizons, while incurring increasingly less risk for medium-term horizon investment holding periods. This explains why investors needs a specific time horizon or holding period in mind when investing in the stock market, because, as we have known all along thanks to Ben Graham, it is more predictable over longer time periods (but not too long) as expected for phenomena that display semideterministic behavior. This difference in market behavior and volatility between the long and short term affects how we should analyze markets, and the tools we use depend upon our investment time horizon. Ben Graham recommended a three-year holding period or 50 percent profit, whichever comes first, before liquidation as his rule of thumb. He believed that opportunity costs eat away return beyond a three-year holding period.

Studies show that for periods no greater than 48 months, representative of the maximum typical mutual fund's holding period of 6 to 36 months, the market has an attractor, economic in character, with a correlation dimension of between three and four. The correlation dimension is used to differentiate between deterministic systems and random systems where dimensionality is a measure of system complexity. Interpreting this correlation dimension, therefore, means that there are only about three to four variables (at any one time) that control the nonlinear behavior of the markets. These analyses were noneconomically oriented investigations[8] and use concepts and practices from physics and yet their conclusion, that some small set of variables influentially control the market, is identical to the Fama-French and APT[9] analysis that concludes three or four factors explain most of the returns. Well, what do you know—physics and economics join hands on a topic! I remind you that there are seven Graham factors, but several are related, like valuation for instance, reducing the set more toward the three to four predicted by the correlation dimension.

Investors can exploit the longer-term trend component of market price action to obtain a statistical edge, if the variance of return is not too large (more on this later). This is precisely what trend-following systems do. It explains why good trend-following systems traded in diversified market portfolios tend to make money year after year whereas day-traders invariably lose in the long term. To be a successful speculator, you must put yourself in the same position as the house in casino gambling. On every bet the house has a statistical edge. Although the house may lose in the short term, the more gamblers bet, the more the house will eventually win. If you trade with an approach that has a statistical edge and if you follow your approach rigorously, like the casino you will win over the long term. The long term is where the house makes money; they can afford to lose in the short term up to some preset limit, which is really just minimizing the left tail of the return distribution. This is what good quantitative investment strategies do; they make lots of tiny little bets predicated on good long-term trending signals coming from economically important variables, availing themselves of the law of large numbers. Risk management overlays then set the limit of acceptable losses and try to minimize the left tail.

Now to summarize, a far better description of the stock market occurs when one correctly categorizes the stock market as a chaotic and complex system. This is what has been missing from the academic business school curriculums and still is not getting enough attention from financial engineering courses. The typical MBA graduate still comes away with a perspective of the stock market as independent collections of pieces of corporations. Though this is almost true, in that stocks are proxies of fractional ownership of corporations, the interaction of stocks, when encompassed as a portfolio or in an index, takes on a behavior accurately described by the mathematics of chaos theory and its subsets. The ramification of this understanding lends itself to a far better management of risk when considering the impact of the aggregation of securities.

Enter quantitative asset management at this point. One of the things that quants do well, besides understanding and applying risk management more comprehensively than fundamental managers, involves helping decide the size of the portfolio positions. This is a direct outcome of the quant process and in the most evolved firms comes about through a process called portfolio optimization, to be discussed more thoroughly later. It puts quantitative and reproducible arms around asset allocation and makes it more science than art.

George Soros's new paradigm on market reflexivity is particularly relevant to this discussion. George writes, "First I contend that financial markets never reflect the underlying reality accurately, they distort it in some way or another and those distortions find expression in market prices. Second those distortions can find ways to affect the fundamentals that market prices are supposed to reflect."[10] Surely he does not believe in efficient markets obviously either. Oddly enough, when positioning market prices in terms of nonlinear dynamical systems, (i.e., chaotic) George's new paradigm must arise because it is essential that studying the system disturbs the system itself. If many people in a market use that knowledge to optimize a trading or investing strategy, then the expectation is that the prices will alter their behavior accordingly to diminish the arbitrage source of anomalous return. For example, if everybody invested solely by selecting stocks based on valuation, then the undervalued mispricing would close entirely and value-weighted indexes would suddenly be the cap-weighted indexes. Soros is correct that market prices in a complex system are sensitive to small changes in the environment, and it is not always clear how they will respond to feedback. This interference by an observer to the phenomenon in its behavior is customary in physics (i.e., what is known as the uncertainty principle), but it has not been made much of in large systems, let alone financial markets before. Nevertheless, it is a consequence of the nonlinear process underlying the movement of market prices.

This feedback disturbance of the markets described and predicted by classifying the stock market as a complex chaotic system and separately, intuitively derived by Soros, leads to what has been understood and discovered under separate research by econometricians in that prices are described well by the generalized autoregressive conditional heteroskedasticity (GARCH) model. In the early chapters, we showed how poorly a normal distribution describes returns and offered a simple Frechet distribution as an alternative, though it was never meant for the Frechet to be the idealized function to describe returns in this context. Rather, it was easy to compute and offered an example of a better fit than normal to the data. However, the GARCH model generates data with fatter tails than the normal distribution and with higher kurtosis. It is a very good fit to the basic return distribution. Moreover, in concert with chaotic classification of the stock market and George Soros, it implies serial dependence on past values, meaning that feedback is implicit in the GARCH mathematical construction, though that concept is in contradiction to some elements of stochastic portfolio theory (SPT) we shall discuss later, but it does match the empirical results.

Moreover, volatility or the variance of return is persistent and has high autocorrelation, which means it is semipredictable. That is, the volatility of the market is more predictable than is the return and gives rise to the concept of volatility regimes in the academic literature. Feedback, being part and parcel of nonlinear chaotic systems, can be illustrated just by watching the price of some stock getting too high so that self-regulating forces bring the price back to some lower level. Implicit here, however, is that the price changes direction, not that it falls to some equilibrium level, and this direction change is often coined reversal or regression to the mean, though, strictly speaking, it is more properly called antipersistence.

One often hears people in finance and asset managers speak of regression to the mean or mean reversion when discussing stock valuation or bond spreads. Unfortunately, in congruence with chaos theory, the notion of stock returns is more accurately termed antipersistent, meaning that there really is no mean to return to, but that, after moving in one direction, the process will soon revert. Additionally, one can readily decipher stock returns as changing direction more easily than one can say where it will revert to. Calling the bottom of a stock price is much harder than simply saying it will revert direction from its current direction. This latter description more readily characterizes stock price movements more accurately than does calling it a mean-reverting process. This may be esoteric, but the underlying philosophy is very sound: Investors do not and cannot know the actual average value of any given stock. What is the average book value? What are the average earnings? Investors can compute a number, but is it the equilibrium value? Is it the fair market value? No one knows for sure. These are much harder questions for which the answers cannot be known, so calling stock prices antipersistent is more correct and comes about both from characterizing the stock market as chaotic and reflexive.

The reflexivity concept was also known by Graham. To pull a Ripley moment (believe it or not), Graham said, "All my experience goes to show that most investment advisors take their opinions and measures of stock values from stock prices. In the stock market, value standards don't determine prices; prices determine value standards." Graham is often thought of as an absolutist for saying this, but when asked if new economic conditions justify higher valuation multiples, he said that the central value might be raised but that nobody has any clear idea of just how they're to be determined, and the fluctuations around these levels will be done with excesses on the upside and extreme pessimism on the downside. He is simply saying that valuations are fuzzy. His intuition about value is right, as is Mr. Soros, as there is no real absolute value or mean value for a stock price to return to from lofty levels because whatever the correct average multiple is, perceptions from investors will move that value around. This feedback mechanism is precisely Soros's reflexivity concept so that price and valuation interact rather than valuation being wholly dependent upon price. All that can be ascertained is that when a price reaches supremely high levels (and you will know it when you see it), it will revert, antipersistence will dominate, and the price will eventually trend lower. This is the mispricing correction mechanism and works for the investor's benefit on undervalued stocks and to their detriment for overvalued stocks.

Exactly where (or when) an overvalued stock will bottom out is not able to be known. Thus, Graham's margin-of-safety concept exists similar to an engineer's in her structural designs (the overbuilt concept) so that the enterprising investor's purchased price of a stock would be set well below an estimate of intrinsic value so that the price paid is not dependent upon ever-increasing future earnings. Hence, the absolute intrinsic value and thus, a stock's absolute B/P multiple, may not be knowable, but the range of probable values is more probably so, as is the range of impact sites on the dartboard from thrown darts. So in Graham's mind, asset values twice liabilities, sizeable working capital, and a good history of stable earnings, along with very low earnings and book multiples, assures that one underestimates the intrinsic value enough to offset the impact of the true valuation being perturbed by market participants, because as soon as you believe you know the intrinsic value, it will move. The enterprising Graham-style investor would not have purchased it near that observed value, but having achieved an appropriate but not fully determined margin of safety," the investor will have bought at a severely discounted purchase price.

This is akin to buying a 2006 BMW Z4 M, which can be found on the market in October of 2010 for between $24,000 and $26,500, and depending on condition, for $16,000. If you can purchase the average car for this low value, you wouldn't be so worried if the real value is $24,000 or $26,000, would you? The enterprising Graham investor is trying to do the same for some stock.

For us, the empirical observations of investment experts such as Soros and Graham, when meshed with a theory that exculpates these observations, bring us tremendous satisfaction and completion. It is not surprising that it takes a multidisciplinary approach to interpret market dynamics correctly and explain what is considered a "cluster-mate" to most finance academics. Hopefully, financial engineering curriculums being taught from people of diverse academic and differing disciplines will someday eschew outdated interpretations that are not worth teaching. What business schools continue to get wrong in my view is that, unlike engineering and science, they do not let experiment lead the theory, but professors continue to postulate and then look for observations to support their theory. In this way, finance professors back themselves into corners with their worldview and do not accept feedback from practitioners, who function as the experimenters (using the analogy from science disciplines) in this realm. To believe in the efficient market worldview, arbitrage free market equilibrium, and pure random walk stock prices, given the tremendous experience contrary to these perspectives of Graham, Buffett, Dreman, Soros, Lynch, Rodriguez, Simons, Griffin, and Fernholz, and a host of others embroiled in a role of accolades, is wholly foolish and might be downright impoverishing. It may be that investing in stocks does not give the average investor a better chance than outperforming an index fund, but that only may mean that it is hard work to do so; it does not prove the finance academics' current prevailing viewpoints. Proof here is, of course, hard to come by, but at least chaos theory correctly predicts the role of accolades' observations, which any scientist will tell you is what a good theory does.

Lastly, and importantly, a useful analogy can be used from science concerning the behavior of single molecules, versus their behavior collectively. For instance, gas molecules follow a random walk, and yet their bulk properties are predictable when measured in an aggregated fashion, but not at the individual molecular level. Likewise the aggregation of a collection of stocks in an index or portfolio may have directional characteristics that have semipredictable behavior that is not so easily ascertained for individual stocks. It is this effect, similar to thermodynamic properties, that leads investors to have confidence in quant models, predicated on the laws of large numbers and methodologies of determining trends and patterns. This analogy ties in nicely with the next section dealing with stochastic portfolio theory (SPT), which borrows equations from physics. In particular, there is an equation in physics that allows us to solve deterministically for the time evolution of a distribution of particles diffusing through a sieve, for instance; it is named the Fokker-Planck equation. It is a differential equation but it has a drift term and it has a diffusion term. The latter term can be described as a noise component and we can write the terms down mathematically as variance or covariance terms just as in an equity-risk model. When that represents a random process, then we suddenly have an equation to describe the time evolution of a stock price, and it lends itself to solution and application as the cornerstone of stochastic portfolio theory.

## STOCHASTIC PORTFOLIO THEORY: AN INTRODUCTION

The stochastic portfolio theory (SPT) is not well covered in business school, and so it will be discussed in everyman's language here. SPT is a competing theory to modern portfolio theory (i.e., standard mean-variance, CAPM, and Fama-French methodologies), which holds the place of capital market explanations in academia. Though most economists in academia have strong math backgrounds, they are not usually multidisciplinary in their approach to problems, thus they have mostly missed the opportunity to opine about this unique perspective offered by Robert Fernholz and others.[11] Specialty schools in finance and financial engineering curricula cover this topic, and Robert Merton, Fischer Black, and Myron Scholes all derived their famous equations beginning with SPT. In addition, risk managers from back-office insurance companies also think in terms of SPT, rather than MPT, and have at their collective disposal the full arm of sophisticated nonlinear security association measures like the *t*-copula and its applications. However, the front-office portfolio managers and investment consultants hired by pension funds are mostly ignorant of SPT and how much better its application is to describing returns than is MPT.

This theory had its beginnings in physics (Fokker-Planck-like equations) and made its way into finance by way of Mandelbrot, who looked at scaling in finance.[12] In general, he found that scaling found in nature is similar to prices in the markets. An easy-to-understand analogy follows measuring coastlines.

Fractals in their easiest manifestation follow the similarity one obtains from measuring the raggedness of a coastline from various altitudes. Imagine looking at the coast of North Carolina or any rocky jagged coastline from a map scaled so that 1 inch equals a half mile. Imagine using a drafting compass or a pair of dividers to mark off distances on the map covering two points on the coast, say 9 miles apart as the crow flies. On this map with a compass set at one-half inch (one-quarter mile step size), there would be a minimum of 36 compass steps taken if the coastline were straight. But measuring the coastline distance between the two points with bays, inlets, peninsulas, and such, it could be more like 125 compass steps to mark the 9-mile crow-flies distance—meaning a compass distance of $125 \times {}^1/_4$ miles or 31.25 miles could be measured. Next, examine a map of the same area where 1 inch equals a mile so that a one-half-inch divider distance step size equals a one-half mile. The same experiment would yield 18 steps if the coastline were straight, but of course it is not, so it takes 44 compass steps, consisting of 22 miles to measure the distance. A third map has a scale now where 1 inch equals 2 miles. The half-inch divider consists of a 1-mile step size on this map. Again, the 9-mile crow-flies distance is 9 steps, but it takes 16 steps to mark off this distance, amounting to a divider distance of 16 miles. The last map has a scale where 1 inch equals 5 miles, so that a half-inch divider distance equals a 2.5-mile step size. We would expect to get, maybe, 4 steps, resulting in 10 miles.

Why, with one map, would you measure 31.25 miles and another map of differing scale would you measure 10 miles, each measuring the same distance between two points with as-the-crow-flies distance of 9 miles? This is the result of fractals, so that the higher magnification one looks at something, the more ragged it becomes. Even a flat tabletop is not flat at the microscopic level but exhibits scaling. Consider that as the scale in this example went from 1:1/2; 1:1, 1:2, and finally 1:5, the distances traveled via the measured pair of dividers went from 31.25; 31.25*sqrt(1/2) ~ 22 miles; 31.25*sqrt(1/4) ~ 16 miles, and finally 31.25*sqrt(1/10) ~ 10 miles for 125, 44, 16, and 4 steps, respectively. Now this is purely a hypothetical example, but is where fractals and scaling first found their application, in geography and topography. It is clear that, as magnification decreased, the measured distance decreased proportionally as the square root of two times the inverted map scale, as seen in the following equation:

$$\text{Measured Distance} \sim \text{Sqrt}(1/(2^*\text{Map Scale}))$$

The beginning of SPT, then, makes use of this kind of behavior and says that stock prices scale accordingly, in particular the standard deviation of return scales as the square root of time. For instance, the average standard deviation in stock price over one day is roughly 22 percent of the average standard deviation over one month (sqrt(1/21) ~ 0.22), and the average standard deviation over one day is about 6 percent of the price change over one year (sqrt(1/255) ~ 0.06) for the number of trading days in a month is roughly 21, and the number of trading days in a year is roughly 255. In addition, approximately the average return over a day is 1/5 that of the average return over a week, 1/21 that of a month, 1/63 that of a quarter and 1/255 that of a year. Table 9.1 shows the calculated numbers for standard deviation and average return measured for the S&P 500 and Exxon (XOM)

**TABLE 9.1** Standard Deviation and Average Return for the S&P 500 and Exxon (XOM): June 1990–June 2010

| S&P 500<br>X (# Trade Days) | Daily<br>1 | Weekly<br>5 | Monthly<br>21 | Qtrly<br>63 | Yearly<br>255 |
|---|---|---|---|---|---|
| Sqrt (1/X) | | 44.7% | 21.8% | 12.6% | 6.3% |
| Stdev Ratios | | 54.0% | 25.3% | 14.6% | 6.2% |
| Stdev Ret | 1.179 | 2.185 | 4.665 | 8.055 | 18.933 |
| Num Days | | 3.9 | 20.7 | 66.0 | 278.2 |
| Avg Ret | 0.037 | 0.144 | 0.761 | 2.426 | 10.229 |
| **XOM**<br>**X (# Trade Days)** | **Daily**<br>**1** | **Weekly**<br>**5** | **Monthly**<br>**21** | **Qtrly**<br>**63** | **Yearly**<br>**255** |
| Sqrt (1/X) | | 44.7% | 21.8% | 12.6% | 6.3% |
| Stdev Ratios | | 58.1% | 30.6% | 20.2% | 9.6% |
| Stdev Ret | 1.565 | 2.693 | 5.114 | 7.741 | 16.363 |
| Num Days | | 3.7 | 18.6 | 55.8 | 235.3 |
| Avg Ret | 0.044 | 0.165 | 0.824 | 2.470 | 10.419 |

over the last 20 years' daily values from June 1990 to June 2010, as obtained from FactSet.

The number of trading days is the first row of each, followed by the square root of 1/5, 1/21, 1/63, and 1/255 in the second row for the index and XOM. Then, the ratio of the daily standard deviation to the weekly, followed by the daily over monthly standard deviation, daily over quarterly, and so forth are shown as the third row. Notice how those numbers almost match the sqrt(1/X) numbers? Then the bottom row of each group shows the average daily, weekly, monthly, quarterly, and yearly returns, where the row above that is simply the ratio of the average return of weekly, monthly, quarterly, and yearly values, divided by the average return of the daily value. For instance, for XOM this ratio approximates the number of trading days 5 versus 3.7; 21 versus 18.6; 63 versus 55.8; and finally 255 versus 235.6, so that, given the daily return long-term average, the weekly, monthly, quarterly, and yearly average returns can easily be estimated by taking the daily value and multiplying it by the number of trading days. A similar trend exists for the S&P 500. Thus, scaling really exists in stock prices, following square root of time for standard deviation and proportional to time (i.e., the number of trading days) for average return as observed empirically in just these two examples.

Now, as we know, stock prices are not continuous functions. That is, they have discontinuous jumps and can even have infinite variance over certain time scales. The discontinuity in the prices of stocks can easily be observed from the Google Finance web site (www.google.com/finance). If you visit this web site, type in several tickers and just look at the three days' price history. One can quite easily observe that the start of each day's price is disconnected quite often from the previous day's close.

We tend to think of prices as smooth continuous functions, but in reality they are not. One purchase at the ask need not be the same price as the next trade and, in fact, intraday tick information has to be discontinuous by definition, because prices are nonexistent without somebody buying and trading a security with agreed-upon prices. The analogy is the price of a quart of apples at a farmer's market. There is not some apple price floating around; it is whatever you and the farmer agree on for transaction purposes. This means that stock prices are not continuous functions but a collection of single data points separated by time, and each spot has no rules about what its next value will be. This complicates matters when trying to deal with stock price data from a mathematical perspective. In stochastic theory, one thinks of stock prices as having no memory of past values, so that the next trade price is clearly only a function of its current value of its last trade price. Then, one says that stock prices follow what is known as a Markov random walk process (or Brownian motion as it is known to the physicist reader). Now, at this point in expressing SPT theory, we would still believe in the efficient market theory so that there are no arbitrage opportunities. To put this in perspective, consider the farmer's market analogy again. No arbitrage means you cannot buy these apples at this stand for $1.20, and then walk over somewhere and sell them for $1.25. Why is that? Because the shoppers have all walked around and are aware of all the apple stands' prices so they will reject buying from you for $1.25 when they know they can get them 10 steps away for $1.20. So goes the analogy of the stock market.

Under no-arbitrage rules, stocks are not mispriced and momentum cannot possibly produce anomalous returns. The concept especially applies for a Markov process that says that tomorrow's stock price cannot possibly be a function of yesterday's value, which is the opposite of what price momentum strategies hold dear. Nevertheless, this approximation is held in stochastic portfolio theory to allow the math to work, similar to the way, under MPT, the Gaussian return distribution is assumed to make the math easy. Generally, the math is never easy in stochastic theory but nevertheless it is easier than it would be otherwise if we make the no-arbitrage and no-price-memory assumption.

Now, because stock prices have discontinuities, standard calculus cannot be used. At these discontinuities and inflection points, the underlying price function is not differentiable, that is, there can be no tangent line drawn at the discontinuity. Hence, the field of stochastic calculus was invented to deal with such issues and was used in physics to handle such equations as the Fokker-Planck, the diffusion, or heat equation, and anywhere there was a phenomenon involving Brownian motion of particles with a random noisy character to their trajectory. This description says you can only integrate or differentiate the data up to the last available point in existence. A weird concept, but it has its usefulness. Then, we can say that stock prices follow a Wiener process, because of the scaling we demonstrated stock prices to have earlier. Thus, the change in stock price over some time interval is related to some constant proportional to time and another constant proportional to the square root of time. Then the stock price $s$ is modeled by a simple equation of the form:

$$\text{Ito equation}: \Delta s = a\Delta t + b\varepsilon(\Delta t)^{1/2}$$

This is the Ito equation where $a$ in this equation is coined a drift term with variance $b^2$. Now, this equation has broad application in finance, but mostly in fixed-income modeling for yield curve (interest rate sensitivities), credit risk, and derivatives. Robert Merton used this equation to begin his derivation of credit risk and bond default probability of a company by characterizing the company's stock price as a call option on its underlying balance-sheet assets, which is now the cornerstone of bond-rating agency Moody's default-rate calculations for corporate bonds.[13] Merton utilized the Black-Scholes equation to price these options, using the option-pricing equation previously derived by Fischer Black and Myron Scholes, again starting from the Ito equation. Google knows if you search using the keywords "Merton Model" or "Black-Scholes," you will find this equation in academic papers and more sophisticated versions a googleplex number of times, so it is common (we exaggerate intentionally). However, if you ask typical MBAs if they have ever heard of the Ito equation, you will hear, "nada, nein, no, nyet," and so forth. In their defense, however, Ben Graham and Warren Buffett also would not be familiar with it. However, they can be forgiven, perhaps, because they preceded its published usefulness. There can be no excuse for the ignorance of today's MBA graduates, in our view, however, but we blame the professors rather than the students.

Now, remember that under chaos-theory analysis, we learned that market prices have a trend component with partially random behavior overlaid. This is manifested mathematically in the Ito equation with the $a$ term being the trend component and the $b$ term the partially random term, similar to the drift and diffusion term of the Fokker-Planck equation. Thus, one way to think about a stock's price is to say that a stock's arithmetic return over some short time interval (its one-period return) is a drift rate multiplied by the time interval, plus a random disturbance proportional to the square root of the short-time interval. This allows us to say some interesting things about our momentum factor of Chapter 4 and a new reversal factor, and it plays right into our knowledge about stock price scaling we have reviewed with the S&P 500 index and Exxon. In these examples, the standard deviation scaled as the square root of time and average arithmetic return scaled as time. In this equation, the average returns are the first term on the right of the equal sign, and the second term models the standard deviation contribution, the disturbance term. Thus, *a* in this equation is expected return and *b* is standard deviation of return, each with its appropriate scaling of time.

Now, consider the competition between these two terms in the equation and ask: Which one dominates? If the first term dominates, that is, $a\Delta t \gg b\varepsilon(\Delta t)^{1/2}$, then the drift term, the expected return term, is much stronger than the second term, the variance term. This means that stock-price momentum can work because the expected return drift will result in a much larger contribution to the price s with every small change in time, then the standard deviation term will contribute to return.

The expected return or drift term, then, would be all you need to make money in the stock market since the first term in the equation overwhelms the second, so an alpha model or Graham model should work well under these conditions since they stand to predict return. Also, another way for the first term to dominate is, perhaps, if a particular stock exists whose standard deviation scaling is much less than square root, say fifth root like $b\varepsilon(\Delta t)^{1/5}$. Then, momentum is really going to work well for these stocks, and again, getting a good estimate of expected return through your alpha model (i.e., Graham model) will allow minting of money employing a momentum strategy!

Now, consider the alternative, for instance, if the second term, the variance term, dominates, so that $a\Delta t \ll b\varepsilon(\Delta t)^{1/2}$, then contrarian or reversal strategies will work really well. In this case, for stocks in this condition, just bet against their current direction and you are sure to make money counting on the antipersistent behavior of stocks to work for you. For some small time step, the stock price movement will be huge, but it will not tend toward some expected return term like the drift, but will move wildly in the opposite direction. Likewise, if the standard deviation scaling for a stock is less then square root, perhaps proportional directly to time, then this second term will dominate the stock price and you will mint money again in a contrarian strategy.

As we said earlier, a Markov process in Ito formalism is not arbitrageable and the square root of scaling is what keeps us all honest with regard to making money under momentum or contrarian strategies. Consider that given $a$ and $\varepsilon \times b$ of the same order of magnitude, the two terms in the Ito equation would be about the same size. Then, neither term could dominate the price $s$, and neither price momentum nor contrarian strategies could work because they would be opposing each other with equal magnitude.

There are, indeed, times when both momentum and contrarian (reversal) strategies do work (not simultaneously for the same stock, obviously), because markets are not truly efficient. This is true particularly when the standard deviation of return scales less than square root for a persistent period of time so that momentum works, and other periods of time when the standard deviation of prices scale more highly so that reversal strategies work. Therefore, the pernicious nature of the scaling is allowing for the anomalous returns to be taken by these two factors. The Ito formalism does allow for modeling of stock prices quite well and offers explanations into the designs of the momentum and reversal strategies.

It is important to make the connection between this equation for a single stock with an equation for a portfolio of stocks. Under this guise, we can derive, but we will not, that the portfolio's arithmetic return process is just like the stock's, with the drift term and variance or disturbance term. The portfolio's arithmetic return is just the weighted average of its stock's arithmetic return drift rates, as you might expect. We use the terms *drift rate, arithmetic return,* and *one period return* interchangeably to be consistent with how we hear them from different speakers and in the literature. This is all under the MPT umbrella, however, and involves arithmetic returns rather than continuous returns. To make the break from MPT to SPT theory, we move to another definition of return.

One of the main contributions of using the SPT rather than MPT formalism has to do with moving from arithmetic returns (the standard one-period returns we usually think of) to a continuous form of return. The continuous return over a short time interval is the change in the logarithm of its price. Making this change in thinking is important. Consider a stock that has an equal probability of rising 30 percent or falling 25 percent in a specific period of time. Its arithmetic return average or one-period return average is then (30–25)/2 or 2.5 percent, which, although paltry, is a positive return. Now consider multiple time periods of just such a process using a coin flip for the 30 percent or −25 percent return probability for each time step.[14] Then, over time there will be an equal number of one-period returns of either 30 percent or −25 percent. In the long run, the average return will be negative, believe it or not, amounting to a negative −0.959 percent, which means the process loses money over the long term, though its one-period arithmetic average return is positive! So thinking in terms of the continuous return, we can avoid such errors in thinking an average return is a good one, when due to the variance of return, it really is not.

However, to make this transition to continuous return from arithmetic return dirties up the Ito equation a bit. So without showing the math, when we switch to continuous return, the Ito formula results in an equation that describes the drift term (the first term to the right of the equal sign) to equal the arithmetic return minus one-half its variance. This is unlike the modern portfolio theory formula, which separates return from variance, but under SPT they are related. Here, under SPT, the long-term return (drift term) is a function of the variance; it is just not stock specific expected one-period returns and is smaller than the one-period arithmetic return by half the variance. This new drift term under continuous return formalism is called the stock's growth rate.[15] Hence the really long-term return depends on the variance, too, not just the one-period return.

So consider the difference in ascertaining the expected long-term returns of two stocks, one with returns fluctuating between 30 percent and –25 percent, versus some other stock with return fluctuation between 5 percent and 0 percent return. They both have a one-period arithmetic return of 2.5 percent, but intuitively you would choose the latter stock because of its expected lower variance of return. This feature, if you will, is accommodated in computing the stock growth rate with the Ito equation under continuous return derivation. It is saying that the realized long-term growth rate of a stock is given by:

$$\text{Long-Term Stock Growth Rate} = \text{expected return} - \tfrac{1}{2}\,\text{variance}$$

so that highly volatile stocks offer a drag on performance over long periods, congruent with intuition but putting it in a quantifiable measure. In addition, remember the volatility factor of Chapter 4? We saw empirical evidence that, by sorting stocks into deciles by volatility and measuring return, the higher return over time was with the lowest fractile of volatility. This helps explains precisely why, in the cross-section of volatility, stocks with high sensitivities to idosyncratic volatility have low average returns, and this is not explained by any of the Fama-French factors.[16] Isn't quant great? Look at what it can do for you that fundamental investing cannot by itself. Ben Graham would be proud to have had this insight in mathematical form, providing a theory for the observed empirical evidence!

Then, in continuous return format and after a lot more math, we arrive at a formula for the portfolio's growth rate, which is equal to its weighted-average stock growth rates, plus another term equal to one-half the difference between the weighted-average variance of the portfolio's stocks, and the portfolio's variance. This latter difference is termed the excess growth rate. Thus, we arrive at the crux of SPT for equities, which is the portfolio's long-term growth rate, which is an important deviation from MPT using arithmetic returns where the growth rate was simply the weighted average of its individual stock's arithmetic return drift rates. The excess growth rate is defined as one-half the difference between the weighted-average variance of the portfolio's stocks and the portfolio's variance.

Now, for an individual stock, variance is a drag on the stock's long-term return as we just mentioned earlier. For a portfolio of stocks, variance can add to return, not take away from it, provided some other criteria are met. To see this, consider that the long-term return of the portfolio becomes a function of its collection of stock's variance, too, but with a slight twist. Because of the effect of diversification, the portfolio's variance is smaller than the average variance of all the stocks in the portfolio. The long-term return, then, is a function of both of these; in fact, their difference is the excess growth rate. If the collection of stocks is highly diversified so that there is little correlation between stocks, the excess growth rate becomes a larger positive number, and it adds to the long-term return of the portfolio rather than subtracts from it.

This featured excess growth rate function of SPT has several interesting ramifications that tie in nicely with a fundamental analyst's, such as Ben Graham's, perspective. To illustrate this utility, however, we must digress to discuss the typical index construction, namely, the S&P. Now, anybody can visit the Standard & Poor's web site and after enough searching, find the recipe they use to construct the indexes. In general, these indexes are not exactly composed by determining the market capitalization of the largest stocks in the United States and weighting the top 500 by their market cap because we know these indexes are contrived, making the S&P 500 a managed portfolio. Clearly, there are other issues with index construction as we visited them in earlier chapters, but it is safe to say that the weights of the stocks in the index are proportional to market capitalization. Now, when thinking about it, it is entirely feasible to justify the concept that indexes of this type of construction will tend to overweight stocks that are overpriced and underweight stocks that are underpriced. To see why this is so, consider that overvalued stocks have positive error in their estimation of value, and undervalued stocks have negative estimation error in their price. Capitalization must return to correct value over time if mispricing exists anywhere. Thus, overvalued mispricing must move stocks toward lower market capitalization over time and lower the weight of stocks in the index that fit this category. These would be the highest capitalization stocks in the index that have the highest index weight.

Likewise, undervalued stocks must increase their capitalization to return to proper valuation over time, and these are the stocks of small weight in the index. Thus, they must increase their weight in the index as their capitalization increases to return the stock to proper valuation. There can be no other way for this equilibrium to occur and for its impact to be felt in capitalization-weighted indexes. In this case, we speak of capitalization-weighted indexes of having mispricing correction drag on their performance through time.

If stocks are mispriced, that means there is a charge to their variance for this mispricing. In other words, the stock has some motivation to move its price to correct the mispricing and, consequently, there is a concomitant increase in its variance above what it would have been if it was priced correctly in the first place. This will result in an increase in the excess growth rate of the portfolio of stocks constituting the index, because, by definition, excess growth rate has weighted average stock variance in it. Thus, the return of a capitalization-weighted index tends to experience drag because of the mispricing correction and gain due to the increased excess growth rate. The trade-off between the two has considerable contribution to the index return. In particular, large-capitalization stocks tend to suffer the highest mispricings, and, therefore, mispricing drags on their performance, whereas small-cap stocks tend to enjoy mispricing correction gain, and this helps explain the size effect found in the Fama-French equation, for instance. In the index then, it should be no surprise that equally weighted indexes tend to outperform capitalization-weighted indexes. They both have about the same amount of excess growth rate, but the equally weighted index has far less mispricing correction drag on the portfolio compared to capitalization-weighted indexes. In addition, value-weighted indexes would have mispricing correction gain stronger still than equally weighted indexes.

Thus, building a portfolio consisting of low-valued stocks that simultaneously have high individual stock variance and low cross-correlation among stocks (high diversification) does wonderful things! First, it results in a portfolio that has positive mispricing correction going for it. Second, remembering that excess growth rate is the difference between half the weighted average stock variance minus portfolio variance, this number would be high, because the low cross-correlation between stocks keeps the portfolio variance much lower than the average weighted stock variance, making the difference strongly positive. Thus, this kind of portfolio would have higher excess growth rate than does its index, and adding in the mispricing correction results in an inherent continuous growth rate because these two combinations are significantly above the rate of their benchmark. This is the process used (albeit grossly simplified here) at INTECH for instance, the asset management company founded by Dr. Fernholz and Bob Garvy.

One last qualification concerns the competing drag on stock performance of high variance of return (i.e., high volatility) individual stocks and its impact on a portfolio of stocks created with high variance of return. The drag at the stock level has to be overcome by the lowering of portfolio variance due to diversification. If the portfolio is not diversified strongly enough, and if the stocks in the portfolio are not very lowly correlated, it is possible the drag on performance due to highly volatile stocks is not overcome by the diversification. This is unique to a portfolio created by trying to use SPT, and we must be conscious of it. There are ramifications for a Graham portfolio with this. Remember, in Graham's mind, the portfolio is not an optimized excess-growth-rate function portfolio. It is thought of only as a collection of independent entities. In this regard, mixing in a volatility factor to the Graham models can be useful, as we have shown in Chapter 7, to help steer the portfolio toward purchasing more low-volatility stocks.

## PORTFOLIO OPTIMIZATION: THE LAYMAN'S PERSPECTIVE

It is not wise to invoke any asset-allocation or optimization technology or method simply as a force-fed rule to offer diversification. What optimization offers is a better way to inhibit assuming diversification, but derives a solution based on solid principles, offering reproducibility, robustness, and higher quality control over the investment process. Considering the investment process is the embodiment of the investment philosophy, optimization works in-situ to help define the investment structure and is more than mere implementation methodology. We point out that optimization has roots going back much farther than Markowitz's mean-variance recognition of 1952; in fact, the steepest decent algorithm goes back to the 1940s, even before computers were widely available. This algorithm essentially is meant to find the minima (or maxima) of some multivalued real valued function, especially when the standard method of taking the analytical derivative, setting it equal to zero and solving for the roots, does not work (the freshman calculus taught method) or when the function's minimum is not solvable analytically at all. Few realize that many more equations in physics and science are insolvable than are actually solvable, and this has led to the invention of many new computational methods that rely on number crunching to offer a near solution when an analytic solution may not exist. Thus, optimization is a general term meaning to offer a method to choose the best element from some set or domain and has been around and applied in many fields, not just finance. The two major ingredients needed to use optimization in asset allocation applications are the expected return at the stock-specific level and the risk model and its subsequent covariance matrix.

In this treatise, we are not going to actually expect you to perform optimization on your Graham-created portfolio, but we need to educate you nonetheless on what optimization is all about, because, when discussing quantitative methodologies or if analyzing different quant managers, knowing something about their portfolio-construction process is necessary to give a proper evaluation. For quant firms, optimization methodologies are clearly a differentiator. First, there are commercial optimizers out there such as MSCI Barra, Northfield Information Services, Axioma, FinAnalytica, APT, and ITG. Some sell-side firms offer them as well, like Citigroup's RAAM methodology. These are usually accompanied by an easy-to-use GUI interface, and they all come with risk models and their risk model's covariance matrix. Each is different in esoteric ways, but they indeed can have significant repercussions in the ultimate portfolio created. It is not an exaggeration to say that, for the exact same inputs of expected returns (alpha scores) and even with the similar risk models, the portfolio obtained will be more than slightly different for each vendor's optimizer.

Thus, to illustrate mean-variance optimization in the general sense and to allow differences to be identified, it is important to review the basic workings. The first thing you must do is specify a function to optimize. In finance we call this the *utility* and it is in two parts looking like:

$$\text{Utility} = \text{Alpha} - RA^{*}\text{Risk}$$

This equation represents utility where alpha is the expected returns from a model (like Graham's, for instance), *RA* is a risk-aversion parameter, and risk is the market and idiosyncratic risks for the individual securities that are specified as a covariance matrix, created from your alpha model discussed in Chapter 2 on how to produce a covariance risk matrix. The goal of optimization, therefore, is to solve for the appropriate stock weights that offer a maximum in the utility function. The solution essentially gives the weights of stocks in a portfolio with a maximum expected return for the given amount of risk taken for the size of the risk-aversion parameter. The larger the *RA*, the more the amount of the covariance matrix is included in the calculation, and subsequently, the higher the risk aversion of the investor, resulting in less alpha being let in to the portfolio. If tighter tracking error to a benchmark is desired, raise *RA* very high and push the console buttons. The solution of weights in the portfolio then would be such as to create a portfolio with similar risk attributes as the benchmark. For instance, if the average exposure to some factor like P/B in the benchmark is *X*, by pushing the portfolio toward the benchmark's risk profile with a high *RA* during optimization, the second term in the utility equation becomes dominant, and the portfolio also obtains the same exposure to P/B, namely, *X*. This is also true for industry exposures.

In Chapter 7 we actually performed portfolio optimization of the Graham portfolio's top and bottom quintiles where performance results were documented in Table 7.9. In that table, the top quintile was optimized to a tight tracking error relative to where the top quintile would have been relative to the benchmark (the S&P 500). We used a fairly high *RA* in that example. Likewise, the bottom quintile was optimized this way. The overall results for the two portfolios were to pull them in toward the benchmark and make their risk characteristics more like the bench than they would be on their own. In both cases, their tracking errors were reduced dramatically while impacting performance, too: negatively for the top quintile and positively for the bottom quintile.

However, it is important to realize that there can be more than one portfolio for a given utility. Although there may be a unique numerical solution with a given alpha and risk model, that does not mean that it is *the* solution. It is an important subtlety most professional portfolio managers do not realize. Also, the differences in weights of stocks in the portfolio, or maybe a security or two out of 100 could be different but have the same utility within numerical precision. However, that would mean that the two portfolios are equivalent in terms of their alpha potential and risk exposure and that is what is important. Note that because two portfolios might have different security weights or maybe even a security or two different, it is tempting to criticize the optimization as being unstable. But that is a red herring. The real question is: Are their utilities the same? This is an important distinction.

For all you budding quants out there, do not let your portfolio managers get away with telling you they can build better portfolios than the optimized one either. Ad-hoc stock weightings are not reproducible, have no justification for what weights to set, do not take into account the co-varying risks within the portfolio, and are usually constructed so that the biggest security weight follows the biggest expected alpha.

We hear accolades from amateurs like Scott Patterson who advocates using the Kelly criterion for setting the weights of stocks in a portfolio. This method, though aptly used for gambling when setting the size of bets when playing Black Jack in Las Vegas, is out-of-context when applied in security weighting in asset allocation; the main reason is that it has no accounting of the covariance of risks that ultimately impact the return. It is best used in IID (independent and identically distributed) univariate situations as in playing cards when there is only one bet to make, not a portfolio of bets. Ed Thorp touted the Kelly criterion in *Beat the Dealer* and later in *Beat the Market,* and Scott Patterson overestimates its usefulness in managing assets discussed in his book, *The Quants.*[17] Using the criteria for weighting a security treats each security as if it is disconnected from every other, and this is not the case. If a stock goes up, its correlations will bring some other stocks with it. Its probability of winning is co-dependent on other securities and it is this association that disallows a simple Kelly criterion from being used to set stock weights. It is plausible that Jim Simons or Robert Fernholz has derived a multivariate version of the Kelly criterion, but probably they would not publish it. Intelligent long-term investors should keep away from this method of setting stock weights.

The biggest concerns with optimization involve the specification of the risk model because, usually, most quant firms outsource the risk model to the same vendor that provides the optimization software. Other important issues involve putting passive risk constraints on the portfolio, such as limiting how much country, sector, or industry active weights are allowed. Here, active weight means (portfolio weight – benchmark weight) and, thus, there are active weights for stocks, industries, sectors, countries, and so on. The other overriding concern is the size of the *RA* parameter, which is truly a fudge factor but a necessary one. It is a fudge factor in that each vendor's software does this differently enough that the numerical value of the *RA* varies from one optimizer to the next, even with identical alphas, and this has much to do with differing risk models because the actual magnitudes of the numbers is risk-model dependent. Since most investment managers provide their own alpha model and simultaneously outsource the risk model, investment managers must ultimately rescale their alphas to be on the same order of magnitude as the risk-model factors. This means that, if the alphas have numerical values of –3 to 3 percent, and the risk model provider has values of –100 to 100, this mismatch in scaling can be a problem and the *RA* could either be dialing in too much or too little of risk aversion. Therefore, the size of *RA* is usually found by trial and error, after the scaling of alphas in proportion to the size of the risk values is accomplished. Of course, the *RA* size is dependent upon how much tracking error is acceptable or targeted by the investor, too.

The utility equation often has other terms in it as well, the next most important parameter being transaction costs. In some optimizers these are strictly fudge factors, whereas in others, they involve security-specific cost curves. The transaction cost function in the utility puts in a penalty for trading a stock so that the optimizer will not make the trade unless the gain due to alpha or risk mitigation due to covariance is above the cost in trading the stock. Thus, you can think of transaction costs as a brake to the system, mitigating excess portfolio turnover and churning.

The most frequent criticism to transaction costs involves those optimizers that include it simply as fudge factor, for instance, as a simple percentage of return. Then, every stock costs the same amount to trade in the optimizer's point of view, regardless of whether it is as liquid as Exxon or some very illiquid small-cap international stock. To see why this is silly, consider a portfolio manager who, before optimization, already decided to rebalance the portfolio doing roughly 10 percent two-sided turnover. This means 5 percent of portfolio capital will be sold, and 5 percent bought in new positions or trims. Then, the actual realized transaction costs due to trading will be spent when the portfolio trades and is not dependent upon transactions costs in the utility equation. There is no actual cost savings under these conditions because the portfolio manager already decided how much turnover he is going to do, the transactions are going to happen anyway, and cost will be incurred. In addition, a change necessary to make in a position such as Exxon due to a small change in alpha will not necessarily be made because the preset transaction cost may be higher than would be incurred with Exxon, being a large-cap and a very liquid security. In reality its transaction costs are duly minimal and perhaps the trade should occur.

Likewise, some illiquid stock whose transaction costs are very high would have a cost threshold that is set too low. A trade will be made that should not be made. Thus the process of putting in a transaction-cost fudge factor, in which you average the costs of liquid and illiquid securities to arrive at the average fudge amount, will prevent adjustments in weights of those stocks most sorely in need of transaction or change in portfolio weight, namely, the least expensive cost-to-trade stocks like Exxon and the most expensive cost-to-trade stocks like small-cap stocks. This latter effect illuminates the flaw in the bargument that it is a good thing with fudge-factored transaction costs that the optimizer will not make trades predicated on small changes in stock alpha or stock risks, which have nothing to do with real transaction costs.

On the other hand, those optimizers that utilize security-specific transaction cost curves really impact the portfolio positively, because they take into account the costs of a specific trade of a specified security. For example, Investment Technology Group (ITG) has what they call the ACE curves, which are security-specific cost curves that model real costs incurred for trading, based on the volume of the trade. In this situation, the costs of trading an Exxon might be so low due to its liquidity that small changes in alpha or risk are worth trading, whereas trading in a small-cap name would require a much higher hurdle rate in alpha change or risk, above that of transactions before executing the trade. The ACE curves see that the trade is done by properly accounting for the individual trade cost.

The importance of optimization corresponds to the importance of diversification and rebalancing of the portfolio, for that is what the main concept is about. Integral to optimization is the alpha model and the risk model, as we have said numerous times. In a provider like FactSet, where the user has a choice of many risk models and many optimizers, the burden is on the investor to choose which combinations to use. It is anecdotal evidence that choosing one particular risk model and optimizer and staying with it is wisest, because there is a learning curve to using these sophisticated applications, and it takes practice to become adept at portfolio control within the optimization and rebalancing process.

There is a terrific application of optimization that is related to the practice of risk budgeting. In this process, the optimization is run iteratively in what-if scenarios that allow the calculation of the risk decomposition based on portfolio adjustments. In this way, you can create an itemized list of portfolio changes and their costs in risk terms. Now, you cannot ask any portfolio manager, "Do you budget your risks?" What are they going to say? Anything but yes is an acknowledgement that they are not exercising their fiduciary duty. However, most probably do not budget their risks simply because most would not know what risk budgeting is about. However, applying risk budgeting constraints during optimization allows us to put boundaries on the security-specific positions that are different than just standard constraint limits. For example, if an investor is only willing to take on so much risk, these examples suggest how to spend that risk:

- No individual stock position can assume more than 5 percent of total risk.
- Each allocation decision must contribute to 4 percent of total risk minimally.
- No factor exposure can be more than 6 percent of total risk.
- None of my sector allocations can be more than 20 percent of active risk.
- No country allocation can be more than 10 percent of total variance.

In these examples, the total risk could be tracking error, a relative risk measure, or absolute total portfolio variance. Of course, it could be a value-at-risk measure, too. The output of data from the optimization process allows you to create the portfolio you desire. By changing constraints and optimization settings and then examining the risk decomposition from the output, eventually you obtain the desired portfolio. Obviously, if it is automated, that is, if you can put these risk budgets into the optimizer software, it makes it easy to do this. Currently, all optimizers allow constraint settings in active weight units; for example, industry weighting must within be +/–5 percent of the benchmark. How much wiser it would be to be able to enter the constraints in percentages of total risk. Risk budgeting is gaining importance and popularity among institutional and pension fund managers, and it is probably only a matter of time before this capability is available in vendor software.

## TAX-EFFICIENT OPTIMIZATION

In institutional asset management, tax considerations are not important at all for pensions or endowment management, for instance, because the pension benefits to a pensioner are where taxes come in to play. So tax-efficient optimization is really only useful to the individual investor managing an after-tax portfolio. This is applicable in wealth management, and many bank trust departments will supply tax-efficient portfolio optimization to clients who want it. The main considerations involve the standard issues normally discussed on a per client basis, such as the client's tax status, cap gains, and income tax rates. Often this is done in consultation with the client's CPA and their tax counselor, and they mostly involve when to take capital gains. The optimization involves extra terms in the utility that include tax costs on a security-specific (and investor-specific) basis, and it is treated under optimization just like transaction costs, so that the alpha and risk have to be sufficiently high to overcome the tax ramifications of the trade or trim. In addition, when the security was purchased and its corresponding cost basis are important parameters to be discussed with the advisors and input to the optimizer. In this sense, the history of the portfolio is important, and it contrasts with the pension asset manager's optimization, where the utility is a point-in-time consideration only of alpha, risk, and transaction costs.

## SUMMARY

This chapter addressed the alternative theories that explain returns that are less known to the investment community and give reasons for why they are needed. These competing views describe the observed empirical data of security returns and the associations among securities (the correlation structure) better than the older MPT theory. Likewise, there is a whole host of literature in other fields of econometrics and statistics that is less emphasized in popular stock market culture, lore, and media attention that is far more accurate in describing financial markets. Unfortunately, whatever can by hyped in five minutes or less often steals all of the media attention.

Chaos, nonlinear behavior, stochastic portfolio theory, and portfolio optimization require a bit more focus on the details, inhibiting their promulgation through CNBC reporters. Lastly, the preponderance of inaccurate reporting and oversimplification of investment and hedge fund managers' raisons d'être is a dispersion of misinformation of the worst kind. Every time there is a market bubble bursting, there is some journalist ready to write a book misinterpreting the history of what occurred, looking for somebody to blame, and trying to boil something down to its most basic essence but getting it wrong in the broad sense. So it has been with the credit crisis of 2008, with Scott Patterson, with Nassim Taleb, and with all of Congress. Congress missed it by invoking Sarbanes-Oxley when the Enron fiasco happened, then with their lack of oversight of Fannie Mae, Freddie Mac, and with the new legislation to regulate banking. Scott Patterson, Nassim Taleb, Steven Rattner (the "car czar"), and Barney Frank oversimplify what they have no expertise on, and then they want to be accorded the title of expert in fields and industry in which they have not been good students and they have been distracted by the seduction of fame. They are intelligent and can even write well, but they have not taken the time to really understand the issues and the practice of quantitative investing and modeling; in their defense, they would argue their time is subject to the tyranny of the urgent. They all fail to see the huge contribution to the avoidance of losses that quantitative risk methods and modeling approaches have made in the insurance industry, and they offer no credit to successes of these strategies. In Chapter 2, we used the analogy of the driver of the car who successfully drives over the bridge but does not understand the exposure he was subject to and avoided. So it is with these people. They are blind to the success of risk management and spend their time pointing fingers, which is far easier to do for attention getting than rolling up your sleeves and being part of the solution.

Much of this bargument will be further discussed in the next chapter where we will discuss the causes underlying the credit crisis and housing debacle and give supporting evidence. In addition, we will paint the worldview the prudent investor should be focusing on going forward.

# CHAPTER 10

# Past and Future View

*Dear Mother, joyous news today! H.A. Lorentz telegraphed that the English expeditions have actually demonstrated the deflection of light from the sun!*

—Albert Einstein in a postcard received by Pauline Einstein, 1919

*Do not Bodies act upon Light at a distance, and by their action bend its Rays; and is not this action strongest at the least distance?*

—Isaac Newton[1]

Newton's theory of gravity would have put the bending of light at 0.87 seconds deduced from his corpuscular theory of light. Einstein's theory of gravity would have put the bending of light at twice that, at 1.74 seconds, setting the stage for a showdown between Einstein and Newton. Unfortunately, in the year 1919, to measure the deflection, you needed a total solar eclipse to occur so that you could photograph starlight, emitted from stars appearing on the very edge of the eclipse, and measure the bending of that starlight traveling alongside the very large mass of the sun, on its way to Earth. The strength of the sun's gravity would pull that light toward its center as it travels by, deflecting or bending it ever so slightly. Knowing the positions of these stars by observing them all night long and predicting their travel throughout the day, you could compute where these stars should be located at that exact time of day a photograph was taken versus where they appeared to be during the eclipse and, in so doing, compute the deflection of light.

Several days earlier, before Einstein's mother received the postcard, Albert received a telegraph from Lorentz stating, "Eddington found star displacement at the sun's edge preliminary between 9/10's second and double that. Many greetings, Lorentz." On May 29, 1919, there was to be a solar eclipse occurring along a line connecting equatorial Africa to Brazil and two British expeditions were mounted. One went to Brazil and the other to

Guinea led by Sir Author Eddington. Eddington wrote, "The present eclipse expeditions may for the first time demonstrate the weight of light and give us Newton's prediction or confirm Einstein's weird theory of non-Euclidean space; or they may lead to yet more far-reaching consequences (i.e., no deflection)."

On November 6, 1919, Dyson spoke at a meeting of the Royal Astronomical Society, saying, "After a careful study of the plates I am prepared to say that they confirm Einstein's prediction. A very definite result has been obtained, that light is deflected in accordance with Einstein's law of gravitation." Eddington spoke next, saying that both expeditions reached the same conclusion, and the empirical evidence was that the light was bent 1.98 +/– 0.30 seconds as measured in Brazil and 1.61 +/– 0.30 in Guinea.[2]

We recite this episode from history for two reasons: (1) to keep it alive, but more importantly, (2) because theory without empirical evidence to support it is an incorrect interpretation of the phenomenon under study. Though this episode occurs quite naturally in the history of the physical sciences, in the field of finance, my experience has been that people hold onto their pet theories in the face of much empirical evidence against it.

Graham and Einstein were contemporaries though Einstein was 15 years older. Graham spent 82 years on Earth, whereas Einstein spent only 76. What they had in common though was the ability to examine what happened and prognosticate why. This led both men to lead prosperous lives, though Graham could measure his in dollar terms. It is clear that Graham did not subscribe to modern portfolio theory, as any candid reader of Graham would validate. He was the Einstein standing up to Newton in his field. Why, however, the entrenched academics have not more strongly begun to accept Graham's observations of markets and use better theories like stochastic portfolio theory and many of the ideas espoused in this book to attempt to explain the empirically measured returns of securities contradicting MPT is beyond me. It can only be that it is easier to understand the mathematics of MPT than it is to understand the physics of securities markets.

The past is prologue, most would say, and the past will most certainly occur again. The future of the stock market will most certainly involve something similar from the past. Any good student of history and any successful investor knows this. The stock market advancement of 1999 and 2000, known as the Internet bubble, followed conditions similar to many manias and is unexplained by proponents of MPT. By now, every reader has heard of Alan Greenspan's irrational exuberance statement in a speech before the American Enterprise Institute on December 5, 1996. His exact phrase was, "But how do we know when irrational exuberance has unduly escalated asset values, which then become subject to unexpected and prolonged contractions as they have in Japan over the last decade?" The next day, markets took a breather and fell worldwide.

Unfortunately, market bubbles are much easier to detect afterward. Only a few people claim a method for measuring them as they develop and fewer yet can predict them. Didier Sornette, a French physicist, is one who, using methods borrowed from chaos theory, has invented methodology for doing so.[3] His methods involve examining the acceleration of growth rates of economic systems, GDP, money supply, human populations, markets, and the intertwining of productivity and labor. His models have been used to predict critical phenomena and their breakdowns in a variety of industries and events, based on what he calls "singularities." These are a general class of division points marking significant change and have also been observed by social scientists throughout human history. His claim in 2003 when his book was published was that the United States will soon enter a period of stagnation and consolidation, which could last a full decade. We have arrived! Though his claims were based on results from applying physics to measure market dynamics, the last chapter of his book seeks explanations for his prediction based on macroeconomic and fundamental reasoning. Frankly, he has been quite accurate! The future looks grim for the United States based on debt levels, both public and individual, and it is the deleveraging of our economy and people that is the steady, consistent drag on economic growth.

Sornette also claimed a bubble was developing in the Chinese stock market, too, and, most importantly, the Chinese government has taken drastic steps recently to limit the developing real estate bubble prominent in Shanghai and Beijing. A personal interview with the department director of a major foreign bank loan office told us in October 2009 that the top five purchases of real estate within the Shanghai province were state-owned enterprises (SOEs), and they are outbidding each other for the opportunity to buy real estate with the express purposes of flipping the commercial property for profit. In addition, SOEs borrowed the proceeds from state-owned banks. Thus, even SOEs are investing in land and real estate, assuredly signs of an asset bubble. Didier Sornette has been right twice now, and the investment community and academics have taken little notice, but he explains the empirical evidence and should be taken seriously.

Lately, however, the capital requirement of banks in China has increased again, and down payments are moving toward 50 percent of property values, and making purchases of second and third homes is deliberately expensive. Liar's loans and no documentation loans do not exist in China. Chinese people need a real down payment and proof of income to get a loan. Consider that the home loan-to-value ratio in China is nearly 60 percent (versus the U.S. loan-to-value of 86 percent in the United States in 2006, for instance) and China's average household total debt-to-income is 45 percent with total debt servicing at less than 15 percent of disposable income as reported in the *Economist* and *Wall Street Journal*. Thus, the increasing valuation of properties must reflect real demand for housing, which is strong in its own right, not contrived as it was in the United States. At least the Chinese government is mindful of its bubble. You have to wonder where our government was when our housing boom was going on, while our states and municipalities were enjoying the largess of a tax harvest on overappreciated real estate.

To share a personal experience about China, in the autumn of 2009 I visited Shanghai and traveled back and forth to Shanghai from Beijing and Hangzhou. During that time, I had an informal interview with a hedge fund that had showed interest in my firm. The person doing the interviewing, however, was the head of commercial banking for a large European bank, affiliated with the hedge fund management. The interview was two way, because we were doing homework for this book and looking for the woman-on-the street perspective. We were looking for information about the economy, Asia in general, and China specifically, but from an investor's point of view. I was most interested in issues about bank lending, because of Chinese government stimulus, and whether banks were lending to small, privately owned enterprises (POEs) by state-owned enterprises (SOEs), such as Bank of China, Bank of Communications, or ICBC. Meeting with this high-level bank lending officer, therefore (who was Malaysian), was very beneficial.

First, she previously worked for HSBC for 25 years. She took this new position two years ago because she wanted to get into China officially and this job was stationed in Shanghai, the future of the world, she called it. First, her clients are all businesses across China with up to $250 million (U.S. dollar equivalent) in sales (she has a staff of more than 1,000), and they represent many different industries and companies, some old technologies and some new, she said. Her bank, a publically traded entity, makes loans to many POEs. She is specifically looking to lend to companies that are focusing on green technology because the Chinese government is offering tax credits for them. She does not worry about lending to SOEs in big cities where the local municipality is the owner because they are generally business savvy enough to leave the businesses alone and do not pressure her bank on structuring the deal, whereas the opposite is true for small towns with small provincial governments. In small towns, the local provincial is more heavily involved with the state-owned enterprise, and politics abound. She could not pressure payment, for instance, from an SOE in a small town because the mayor would come to the rescue of the company, throwing political muscle at her.

Though the largest state-owned banks are, indeed, mostly lending to infrastructure projects, she declares there is a huge trickle-down effect. The construction workers have high confidence in their jobs and are saving as well as spending. Much of the currency has flowed toward those towns in the hinterland where manufacturing has been reduced due to a slowdown of the global economy. This investment has sustained jobs that would have been curtailed much more so had there not been infrastructure spending and that has kept unemployment from rising too high. In addition, our personal observation is that there was still plenty of infrastructure activity in the big eastern cities (i.e., Shanghai and Beijing), where we saw many roads under construction and repair and new buildings going up everywhere. In fact, you would often see ten skyscrapers going up simultaneously in the same several adjoining city blocks—not just one here and one there, but ten here, five there, seven there, and so forth.

Other tidbits she told us were that there is a lot of money everywhere, and although the Hong Kong Chinese come to the mainland to buy copies of things, the mainland Chinese visit HK to buy real stuff and real brands. Another trip to Hong Kong revealed Gucci, Prada, Louis Vuitton, Christian Dior, Ferragamo shoes, and countless other luxury brands all fully staffed and busy. That said, there are plenty of Western brands all across China. Notwithstanding the usual Coke, Pepsi, McDonalds, Starbucks, and KFC, there is Best Buy, J. Crew, and many other Western stores everywhere, especially auto malls. All the major automakers are there and throughout the eastern part of the country.

The lending officer also reported that small companies have been using their own cash to push growth since bank lending does not occur so easily from the big Chinese SOE banks, though money does come in from the foreign banks, like her own. However, there is a burgeoning of private equity beginning to make many investments in startups and capital-starved companies. In general, she is more than very bullish on China from where she sits. She said that her greatest concern is that the U.S. economy will become poorer still and will not recover enough to allow time for the conversion from an export-led to a consumer-led economy to take hold, which the government of China is expediting.

Though we are concentrating on the economic issues of China, other interesting observations include the following:

- The Chinese do not wait in line. Everybody cuts and nobody gets mad, whether it is for a bathroom stall, tickets for the train, or KFC.
- The cab drivers all have manual transmissions and completely grind the gears when starting from first gear. We wanted to drive the thing out of first gear for them and teach them to rev the engine a bit before lifting

the clutch. Taxis are about half the cost for a comparable distance in Chicago when you convert their currency to U.S. dollars.

- Air pollution was outrageous. Living in either Beijing or Shanghai would be difficult for the typical American, with 17 and 20 million people, respectively, going through their industrial revolution. It took the United States from 1865 to 1965 to journey through the industrial revolution; the Chinese are taking from 1990 to 2020. We did it in 100 years with less than 100 million people on average, whereas they are doing it in under 30 years with a billion plus people.
- We saw more Rolls Royces in two weeks than we have ever seen in our lives, as well as lots of BMWs, Mercedes, Chevrolets, Buicks, Audis, and VWs. In addition, the bicycles that historically have been ubiquitous in China are being replaced by electric bikes. These E-bikes will go 30 mph and last for six hours on a charge, which is truly remarkable. Some bigger bikes are powered by liquid propane gas (LPG), and the police drive the biggest bikes—Suzuki 125 cc—which are gasoline powered. Gasoline costs about the same per gallon as it does in the United States at this time.
- Crowds are everywhere. We continually saw stores that had six clerks, whereas a comparable store in the United States would have three clerks. In construction zones they would have 60 men with picks and shovels, whereas in the United States there would have been 20 men, two CATs, and four dump trucks, leading to the conclusion that labor is currently very cheap, though China has one of the fastest growth rates of income per capita, so labor costs will not stay cheap forever.
- The Chinese do not drink much wine, but the best Grand Cru Bordeaux is on any decent restaurant's menu, and recently China has become Bordeaux's largest market by volume.
- Yes, they drink tea and lots of it, but the greater surprise is the coffee. It was the best we had anywhere so far in the world, better than in Italy, Australia, and Germany.
- There were three classes of Chinese, generally: the under 30s who are very Western, the peasants still dressing like 1960s Mao communists, and the upper-class business owners and entrepreneurs.
- Few people speak any English. If you do not have a guide as we did, it is advisable to go on a tour, because when out in the city, you cannot even read street signs like you can in Europe simply because the signs are not in our alphabet. Even in the hotels, sometimes it was not easy to communicate with hotel staff and they would often have to fetch an English-speaking employee.
- Police officers are a rare quantity, and you hardly ever see them. People moved about freely, conducting their own business without any obvious

intrusion, negotiating prices freely, bartering and selling just about anything under the sun, with many Chinese owning their own businesses and shops.

After this visit, it became clear that this was not your father's Communism. We make this statement because it is an extremely important conclusion. I had the fortunate experience to travel in East Germany and Czechoslovakia back in 1987–1989 before the Berlin Wall fell. What we experienced there is nothing like what we found China to be. Those Eastern-bloc Soviet-style Communist countries experienced a lack of goods consistently (due to a failure of their entirely central plan and state-owned economy), and there were police everywhere. In fact, in East Berlin, if you congregated in a group as large as four, a policeman would walk over and break it up. The fear of the government was palpable. All restaurants and stores were greatly overstaffed in the old Soviet empire but not for the same reasons as in China where it is just because labor is cheap. In the East Bloc it was because the government told you where your job was because the government owned all businesses and had declared there would be no unemployment. China had a 9.6 percent unemployment rate in 2009, reported just about everywhere. The World Bank, WSJ, IMF, and Federal Reserve web sites tally Chinese statistics continually because there are so many eyes on China these days. In China, the economy is much more free market and people look for work similarly to the way we do in the United States. The local newspapers, though not as free as in the West, report dissension of opinion within the government and even reported a rift of two departments where in-fighting was prevalent.

Fortunately, the Chinese are supersavers and do not have the personal debt ratios that U.S. households have. Also, they do not have a society of consumers using their homes as collateral through home-equity loans to borrow to keep up their standard of living or to purchase desired goods. The Chinese culture is more frugal than the United States and involves more debt avoidance than the United States whereas Americans will mortgage their future and take on huge personal debt to satisfy their desires, the Chinese will not. Moreover, their country has reserves and is a global creditor whereas the United States is a debtor nation nowadays. Thus, the Chinese culture and trade surplus carry with it a conservative perspective on spending and glut that we in the West should be mindful of when drawing conclusions about their economy and market. Using our standards, we see many signals rendering a consensus view of a possible shaky underlying economy. While shifting our perspective toward the share size of their personal savings, the highly educated workforce, the nimbleness and readiness of their government, and the lack of too many stakeholders in their corporations, all portend a strong, resilient economy.

It is likely that there is a bubble in Chinese real estate, but it's confined to Shanghai, Beijing, and their environs, which combined only account for 5 percent of their population. In addition, the average Chinese consumer is in a much better financial condition than the average U.S. or U.K. consumer with much lower personal debt. Nevertheless, there is a speculative fervor in Asia, considering that Macau's casinos made over $15 billion in 2009, compared to Las Vegas's casinos earning just over $5 billion; the Chinese are gamblers, but they budget their gambling whereas U.S. gamblers go overboard. The new Marina Bay Sands resort in Singapore is already minting money from its casinos from Asian millionaires and recently the number of Chinese millionaires has surpassed the number in the United States, meaning there's quite a bit of disposable income and wealth creation.

## WHY DID GLOBAL CONTAGION AND MELTDOWN OCCUR?

The credit crises of 2008 began in real estate mostly in ordinary conventional housing. In 2005, while living in a two-bedroom, two-bath condominium in downtown Chicago, I saw newly built or renovated apartment condominiums selling for $550,000. There was no way these properties could sustain those values, I thought, guided by nothing more than intuition. What began in 2006 was a steady increase in default of subprime mortgages. It began with speculators who bought houses at high leverage (high loan-to-value) for the express purpose of flipping the house. Mortgage brokers (of which there were over 50,000 who had absolutely no government supervision) allowed no-documentation mortgages, so no income verification was required. Also, down payments were waived and home-equity lines were established so that the first mortgage and home-equity loan, taken simultaneously, were at loan-to-value of 100 percent sometimes, with no income verification required and appraisers conspiring with mortgage brokers to give inflated values. To say nothing of ARMs, interest-rate-only mortgages, and other disastrous mortgage constructs, this cesspool of risk was common, whereas, just a few years earlier, a 30-year fixed-rate mortgage requiring a 20 percent down payment was standard. The beginning was with Greenspan, who kept interest rates too low for too long, making credit easy to obtain and desirable because its service costs were low. In addition, when any market is in a prolonged period of relative calm, participants start believing that markets will remain calm for the near future, and they start taking more risk. This occurred all over, from the homeowner to the large banks. This is how the state of the housing market evolved from 2005 forward.

In 2001, subprime mortgages accounted for only 9 percent of mortgages issued. Congress was cheerleading for an expansion of mortgage lending, instigating even the importance of lending to the inner city poor and using Fannie Mae and Freddie Mac to de facto guarantee mortgages. By 2005, subprimes had risen to 22 percent of mortgages issued and was increasing. The banks found a new way of removing their exposure to mortgages by securitization, with leverage. In 2004, the SEC removed the net capital rule for large banks, which limited their debt-to-equity ratio to 12 to 1. Later, the SEC relaxed capital adequacy rules for large broker-dealers (i.e., Bear Stearns, Merrill Lynch) allowing them also to increase leverage. Later, it would rise to 30 to 1 when Lehman Brothers collapsed. The whole edifice was built on the belief of continuing rising value of houses and real estate in general. Finally, in 2007 trading liquidity dried up as defaults rose due to declining home prices. Suddenly nobody wanted these mortgage-backed securities and the unfolding began.[4]

Additionally, the current media trends do not lay nearly enough blame in my opinion at the feet of our own government, which, with reckless abandon, rigged the markets in favor of home ownership at all costs. In so doing, the ordinary free-market behavior of the housing market was completely bypassed. For instance, by the middle of 2008 there were 27 million, out of 55 million mortgages, that were Alt-A, and out of these, a full 71 percent were accounted for by the government (combining Fannie Mae, Freddie Mac, U.S. Housing Authority, and those held by private entities but under requirements of the Community Reinvestment Act and HUD). Alt-A mortgages are characterized by borrowers with low credit scores, low down payments, and higher loan-to-value ratios. They're typically between prime and subprime mortgages. Thus, Wall Street was responsible for only 29 percent of those 27 million subprime mortgages. Examination of these numbers would put the onus squarely on the government's shoulders, but nowhere do the media or Congress accept any of this blame because it is far more popular for elected officials to blame the banks. Last, let us not forget Mr. Alan Greenspan, who ran the Federal Reserve from 1987 until 2006, for his contribution to the debacle. Specifically, from 2002 to 2006 a negative-interest-rate policy was run from the Fed. The Fed floated loans below the inflation rate as measured by CPI! Clearly, this was a direct cause of housing inflation, creating an overdemand, or, as Wall Street likes to call it, an oversold situation on mortgages. If mortgage rates had been higher, along with tighter lending underwriting, it is highly likely the housing bubble would not have occurred, or, if it did still, it might not have taken the rest of us down with it when it popped.

Freddie Mac and to a major extent Fannie Mae, two quasi-government institutions, have distorted the housing market simply because they had a government-mandated marching order to promote the national priority of increasing home ownership. But today, they have essentially nationalized the housing market. Consider that Canada, for instance, has higher home ownership than the United States, and they have nothing similar to Mac and Mae; they did not participate in the debacle of the credit crisis either. It is clear to most of the proletariat, those working and paying taxes, that just because those people who own homes are generally larger contributors to U.S. economic health, it does not mean making those with very poor credit ratings homeowners is going to pull them toward higher income, education, and public standing. What Congress got wrong in writing Mac and Mae's mission is that home ownership is an effect of good upbringing, education, and healthy work ethic; it is not the cause. Simply taking those on the bottom of the economy and overleveraging them to buy a house is not a magic pill to transform them into better economically viable citizens. Most people who own their own homes did not become productive and frugal after they bought the house. Those were the habits they had before they purchased their place that enabled them to do so, not the other way around.

In all, huge losses in real wealth vanished in a short period in the stock market and in people's home values. Additionally, large institutions went bankrupt and the U.S. government bailed out some with the TARP program. A contagion spread due to the cross-ownership of default guarantees worldwide. In mid-2010, we still feel the remnants of the meltdown. Government's stimuli worldwide have put many countries in dire straits due to excess national debt created via stimulus. It could have been worse, and, fortunately, it appears we dodged a depressionary bullet, though have settled in to a prolonged recession, the stock market's ebullience notwithstanding, as the S&P has regained most of its losses since its bottom of March 2009. The major consideration the intelligent investor must have is awareness that crises happen, they are normal and not Black Swans (more like White Swans), and one has to prepare for them when they occur. Again, laying a foundation of Graham's margin of safety, combined with a smart disciplined investing process, should allay fears of outsized drawdowns over the long term.

What is very troubling to those of us in the professional investing community are people like Steven Rattner, who served as counselor to the Secretary of the Treasury and was the first car czar. You would think he would know how the housing market collapsed and how the credit crisis got started and perpetuated, having been an investment banker and private equity guy for 26 years before serving government. But in the opinion page of the *Wall Street Journal* on June 9, 2010, titled "Wall Street Still Doesn't Get It," Mr. Rattner goes on a tirade, chiding how he was received during an oration he gave at a charitable event filled with "chest thumping hedge fund investors." First, he displays ignorance in confusing the investors of hedge funds with the actual hedge fund managers whom he meant to insult. This is egregious, first, because he does not know the difference. Second, implying that hedge fund managers are growling around, snorting, and cavorting like wolves and wolverines is silly, unprofessional, and puerile. In fact, hedge fund managers can hardly be compared to the traders on a highly competitive commodities trading floor, for instance, where being loud, brash, and pushy is precisely what is needed to get your order heard. If you ever stood in front of a street food vendor at lunchtime in Manhattan on a Wednesday, and tried to get your order in, you would understand that a personality trait encompassing a lot of timidity will keep you hungry quite a while. On a trading floor, the nontimid personality is the better employee. This is not the personality trait of Ken Griffen, George Soros, Peter Mueller, Cliff Asness, Robert Fernholz, or Jim Simons. Yes, they stand out in a crowd, might be overconfident and brassy, but they are not chest thumping, testosterone-filled World Wrestling participants. Rattner's comparison shows his ignorance and perhaps why he fit so well in the Obama administration, because despite the industry experience he claims he has, he still does not understand how the global economy works and where the creation of wealth comes from.

Nevertheless, the bone to pick with him involves his statement concerning the cause of the credit crises and housing debacle: "*I pivoted to my next point, trying to explain that the current hostility toward Wall Street on the part of the American citizenry was both deep and understandable.*" Clearly, he does not really have an understanding of feedback mechanisms. The populist deriding of the banks has everything to do with his administration pointing the blame publicly toward the banks, rather than standing up and acknowledging the government's role in initiating the crisis and perpetuating the mechanisms responsible for its ongoing debacle. It is incredible that somebody holding the position in government that he held was ignorant of the content of the previous paragraphs in this book. Wall Street was the minor player, Washington was the major player, and the fix involves responsibilities where the problem originated—on both ends of Pennsylvania Avenue.

Later, Mr. Rattner states that the current angry mood of the American public, the proletariat of the country, those who fight our wars and pay our taxes, was due to income inequality. He quoted a statistic that 30,000 Americans, that is, 0.01 percent of the country's populace, controls 6 percent of income. Naming the cause of voter discontent as income inequality is absolutely a convenient political ploy, used specifically to create voter anger and put a wedge between those people who are employees (the majority) with those who are the employers (the minority whose votes the left-leaning Democratic party does not obtain). Mr. Rattner is not a good student of history, for this is nothing new. When Karl Marx wrote the *Communist Manifesto*, 1 percent of England controlled something on the order of 93 to 97 percent of England's wealth. It has been the way of the world since Caesar. Jesus said, "The poor you will always have with you"; poverty is not entirely irradicable.

Specifically, millionaires are so plentiful, there is one in everybody's backyard. The 2010 Global Wealth Report prepared by Boston Consulting Group reported there were 11.2 million households globally that were millionaires at the end of 2009, up 14 percent from 2008, and that 83 percent of the world's households own 13 percent of the wealth, whereas the top 0.5 percent owned 21 percent of global wealth. These numbers are consistent with the history of the globe and, though mostly unknown to every man and woman, are pretty normal ratios historically. More recently, the number of millionaires in China has surpassed those in the U.S.

What Steven Rattner fails to realize is the much, much larger overall standard of living increase across the planet in the last 20 years, creating middle classes where before there were not any! On average, people live longer than ever these days. He completely underestimates the wealth creation across the globe and focuses on a statistic that has been in existence since the dawn of time. If you took two tribes of cave people, put them in the African plains 10,000 years ago where one tribe builds a fortress, starts farming, organizes hunting parties, while the other slothfully becomes dependent on the hard work of the former, you will get income inequality. It is as natural as rain. Organizing class warfare by creating divisions based on income is purely a political ploy to gain and stay in power. Nothing more. It is as radical and evil as Apartheid, which uses race as a division to garner the same ends. However, it is politically correct to deride those who, through hard work, perseverance, tenacity, and the ability to put off today's desires for a better tomorrow, obtain more wealth than another. It is jealousy, that provokes this behavior, and wealth redistribution, which is confiscation of property and an insult to hard work and humanity in general. Wealth redistribution is Communism, and we know it fails. It brings all of us down to the same level of poverty and life-style mediocrity, a far, far distant objective from allowing each of us to pursue an individual version of happiness. Steven Rattner does not get it. I pick on him because he's symptomatic of many well-meaning individuals who follow neither the lessons of history nor economics. How can we trust a "pay to play" pension consultant anyway, as the NYS attorney general continues to file charges against Rattner.

In retrospect, we need to be ready for more government regulation. Considering that the federal government has a monopoly on money supply, interest rates, and the mortgage market, its future controls will dominate communications, healthcare, banking, energy production, agriculture, transportation, education, labor, commerce, and the labels on cereal boxes and everything else that could possibly pass through our lips or we would wear on our bodies or read on the Internet. Currently, government spending amounts to about 44 percent of GDP and employs almost 10 percent of the U.S. labor market, providing almost 40 million people with food stamps and social assistance programs and another 50 million people with Social Security checks, not counting Medicare. Private companies only supply about 42 to 43 percent of total payrolls nationwide. So the fear we should have is that this trend toward central planning becomes a reality. What we need is for government to stand aside to allow free markets to function freely or else the Grecian formula will really have to be applied, and we will find ourselves increasingly underwhelming our trading partners, having little to no economic influence, and ultimately lowering our standard of living below Europe for starters and below the Chinese, Brazilians, and Indians ultimately.

## FALLOUT OF CRISES

In general, the enterprising investor should take note of several things as fallouts from the global financial crises emerge. First, there will be a major sea change in global free trade going forward. The 2010 debacle of Google's run-in with the Chinese government may be foretelling. Thus, increased protectionism will prevail in the Organisation for Economic Co-operation and Development (OECD) and developed market countries, especially if the Chinese do not allow their currency to rise. However, if the Chinese disconnect their currency from the dollar, it does mean it is possible for them to buy most of the world's commodities at steeply discounted prices, whereas the devalued developed world currencies (dollar, euro, and yen) will have to purchase commodities at higher prices. In either case, it is just a question of when the yuan will disconnect from the dollar and float higher. This will result in Western multinationals losing influence as the rise of state-owned enterprises of Asia and the Middle East, along with sovereign wealth funds, flex their muscles. Their state-capital model with full reserve backing will enable these state corporations to do things their Western multinational corporations will not be able to do.

We segue to help you understand that when a country allows or manipulates its currency to rise, it generally means that its exports suffer a bit due to the increased prices of its country's goods in the buying countries' currencies. Thus, if the yuan rises against the dollar, Wal-Mart will have to purchase goods from China at increased costs; if previously a flat-screen TV manufactured in China cost $250 to Wal-Mart, after the yuan rises, it will cost $350, and that increased cost gets passed on to the consumer. Thus, China deems the rising yuan as a loss in its export power because Wal-Mart's customers will buy less of their goods due to the increased costs. In addition, a 10 percent increase in the exchange rate (all else being equal) amounts to a GDP reduction in growth of 1 percent, according to the International Monetary Fund (IMF).

However, there is precedent for a country reducing its surplus current account balance by letting its currency rise. The IMF's latest release of the World Economic Outlook 2010 makes comparisons of China to Germany in the 1960s and Japan in the 1970s. Both were export powerhouses that felt global pressure from their trading partners to lower their trading surplus as China does today by letting its currency float freely. China, Germany, and Japan each held about a fifth of total world surplus at their heights (2008, 1967, and 1971, respectively). For Germany and Japan, lowering trade surplus was performed by stimulating domestic consumption by economic policy and by allowing their currencies to rise. In the 28 instances in which the IMF found a need for a country to lower its trade surplus over the last 50 years, what has been documented is that these countries did not export less afterward, but moved export to more expensive things (i.e., got on the innovation bandwagon to produce original goods rather than copying others' products). Also, they imported more from other countries and had increased demand from their own citizens. Moreover, they just saved less as a nation.

Therefore, the evidence shows that China has little to fear of an appreciating yuan as long as it is a controlled expansion with a resultant very minor decrease in GDP. Today's Germany and Japan status notwithstanding, China does not want to end up as it is today; both are currently suffering from negative GDP growth, which may persist for a while. Moreover, the reason we hear recent news of wage demands by Chinese workers has much to do with China coming ever nearer to the end of its surplus labor supply. Increasingly, employees are winning raises. The next chapter for China will involve higher value-added innovation and knowledge-intensive business developments. The productivity of labor, therefore, will increase as this transition intensifies. Right now, the yuan being undervalued is a drag on this transition happening faster, simply because the more China relies on export, the slower the transition to higher consumerism and to increased productivity in their economy through the higher incomes of knowledge workers that are available to spend. In essence, the low value of their currency maintains higher cost of goods imported to China and acts as a drag to consumerism growing. The yuan has to rise similar to Japan's letting the yen rise post-World War II, and this will expedite the move from an export-oriented economy to one with higher consumer spending, higher imports, and more knowledge workers earning developed-world wages.

We continue the discussion of currency, but reflecting on the position China finds itself in with regard to U.S. Treasuries in its surplus. In 1971 when Richard Nixon decoupled the dollar from gold and no longer let countries exchange or redeem their surpluses for gold, he institutionalized the policy of forcing countries to hold the U.S. dollar in their trade-balance accounts, which they then redeem for U.S Treasuries. At the time, this involved mostly Germany and Japan, as they had created an export economy (and garnered the ensuing trade surplus), because they had cheaper labor than the United States, in part due to strong U.S. labor union agreements propping up U.S. labor rates. Later, Korean, Singapore, and Asian tigers underpriced Germany's and Japan's labor rates, and today, China does, each garnering an export-based economy with their ensuing trade surpluses held in dollars (and their proxy U.S. Treasuries). The United States failed to notice that any country that has much cheaper labor will garner a manufacturing base and import jobs while creating an export economy. It is the natural trend of a lower-cost competitor. In many ways we have only ourselves to blame currently, along with labor unions, for off-shoring jobs, because we should have foreseen this happening as we had Germany, followed by Japan, followed by Korea, followed by the Asian tigers, as previous examples to observe since World War II.

In any event, after 1971, free-floating fiat currencies came into being. Generally, governments favor fiat systems because these systems give them more control to print money, expand or decrease credit, and also allow the redistribution of wealth by either inflating or deflating the value of money. Devaluing currency by price inflation is also one way to lower a nation's debts and running fiat currency allows this more easily than a commodity-based (i.e., gold) monetary system. China, of course, pegs its yuan to the dollar and it did this initially because it was prudent to do so in the early 1980s; the dollar was the most important entry into the world's most dynamic market. At that time, the United States was a creditor nation and not overly concerned about trade. It has been a very rapid and recent change, however, of the United States into a net debtor nation, and this change is the lynchpin of the dollar angst these days. First, consider that the United States is smaller in GDP than the Euro-zone, and China is now one-third its size but growing at three times the rate. If the United States is a 9 growing at a 3, and China is a 3 growing at a 9, then, if you do the math, in 20 years their economy will be as large as the U.S. economy. Yet the dollar is still the world's reserve currency since 1971, when Nixon institutionalized its reserve status. It's the go-to currency (and its proxy U.S. Treasuries) whenever there's a flight to quality and fear grips the globe. This affords the U.S. cheap borrowing rates due to this constant current demand for the dollar.

This cannot go on indefinitely because, even in the 2008–2009 credit crisis, there were mumblings from China and the Middle East (export nations running trade surpluses holding dollars and their U.S. Treasury equivalents) about moving to a basket of currencies for reserves. The Euro-zone voiced support for it is, of course, in their best interest to have demand for the euro.

However, divorcing the dollar would have immediate ramifications to these countries' surplus because falling dollar demand would devalue the dollar and it would mean they, in turn, would devalue their reserves because they cannot exchange their dollar reserves for gold anymore, à la Nixon 1971.

Here is where it gets real dirty. The de facto reserve currency being the U.S. dollar affords the United States two special interests. First, since the world essentially must buy the dollar because most global trade is conducted in dollars, it allows the United States to borrow at cheap rates, relative to other countries, since our debt is in demand. Second, the United States can print its way out of financial straits, thus it can inflate its way out of debt conveniently if it has to. Argentina, Greece, Portugal, Latvia, Spain, and Ireland are forced to acquire more stringent budgetary considerations to manufacture a solution to their debt problems, but the United States, whose debt is 94 percent of GDP at this writing, does not have to, all due to the U.S. dollar as reserve currency combined with its ability to print as many as it wants. Here is the kicker, however: It does not mean our economy is healthier than theirs; it just means we can delay paying the piper.

For instance, without the Chinese propping up the dollar by their reserve purchases, they are acting like a personal IMF to the United States, lending us money to keep us afloat. Should they migrate to other currencies for reserves, our boat will sink, and if it is done slowly, we will still sink but they will not devalue their reserves to their demise. If demand for the dollars falls slowly, the value may stay the same (low inflation), but the cost to the United States will rise because we will have to raise the interest rate of the debt to attract buyers. Considering the size of the outstanding debt, we would push ourselves into bankruptcy speedily. The fact that the Chinese keep the yuan tied to the dollar is really a moot point and simultaneously a red herring that makes good popular cover to our politicians. Beware: the United States prints money and borrows to go to the movies and eat dinner, but the prudent and fiscally responsible would rather lend money to someone inventing new technology. However, the demand for the dollar allows this charade to go on.... for awhile anyway. The takeaway here we borrow from Zachary Karabell of River Twice Research, who said:[5]

> *The ubiquity of the dollar allows Americans to believe that their country will automatically retain its rightful place as global economic leader. That's a dangerous dream, an economic opiate from which we would do well to wean ourselves. Don't confuse the demand for the dollar as a measure of strength for America.*

As soon as China and the other emerging market countries become large enough, and while simultaneously the United States and developed world economies grow slowly if not negatively, the ratio of economic power will change and the assertion of alternatives to the mighty greenback will rise. When that day comes, and it is coming, we may find ourselves searching for the Grecian formula, that is, a bailout with austerity provisions imposed on us by the IMF and in place of the Euro-zone, from today's emerging market countries. In such a day, governments may be forced to forgo their pension obligations for one, and secondly become has-been nations.

## THE RISE OF THE MULTINATIONAL STATE-OWNED ENTERPRISES

Let's return to an example that best illustrates the rise of the state-capital model, that being the OPEC oil embargo during the late 1970s. Consider that before the cartel, a Western oil company could easily just drill a well in Libya or some other middle-eastern country with nary an obstacle. After the rise of OPEC, which took pricing power away from the oil companies and essentially monopolized the market, there was a sea change of control, price, and profits from the older working model the oil companies used. To stretch this analogy, this will play out with companies now manufacturing in China. We will see the innovation shift from West to East as the armies of engineers the Chinese and Indians graduate every year soon begin to start thinking for themselves rather than just copying Western designs. Companies such as BYD Auto, which Warren Buffett owns 10 percent of, are purchasing four-year-old engine designs from Japanese auto companies to manufacture their own cars using these older designs and selling these cars in the Dominican Republic. This is going on now. It cannot be far off when they begin tinkering with and modifying these designs to innovate for themselves as they are doing in battery technology. This is already occurring in software, telecom, and technology companies throughout China. In fact, China just created the world's fastest supercomputer. We will see this wave of innovation come to compete head-on first and then overtake their Western competitors in information technology, telecom, automotive, and aviation technology, just as we saw it occur in consumer durables and textiles. Examples are found almost daily in the media. In the *Wall Street Journal* on Monday, July 21, 2010, page A13, we read that the CEOs of BASF and Siemens waged complaint in a meeting with China's premier Wen Jiabao. They claim the rules for doing business in China compel them to transfer knowledge, that is, intellectual property, in order to do business there.

The implications are major because, if a state-owned multinational has its government's focus, its Western competitor within that country is at a disadvantage. If China favors BYD, then GM is disadvantaged. The same is true for Baidu versus Yahoo. This will impact free trade like a tsunami, and Western nations will become more protective and establish trade barriers and tariffs going forward. This means that many companies will find themselves in a business model much like the defense sector is today in the United States and that high-technology companies like Microsoft, Oracle, Cisco, and Intel might not be able to sell some products in China due to competing tit-for-tat governmental regulations favoring each nation's companies.

The implications, of course, stretch overwhelmingly into natural resource companies. It is no secret that the Chinese and Indian state multinationals have gone on a buying spree around the world, purchasing whatever mining and oil assets they can. For instance, in the *Wall Street Journal* on May 3, 2010, we read that China's Hanlong Mining is investing $5 billion in Australian mines to compete with BHP Billiton, Rio Tinto, and Fortescue Metals Group Ltd. And guess who is providing the financing? China Development Bank and the Export-Import Bank of China, two state owned banks! While this was being announced, the previous week the company had just completed a $140 million acquisition of a stake in Moly Mines Limited, an Australian molybdenum miner. To our dismay, the bottom of the article says that Hanlong has said they want to use Moly Mines to become an international mining powerhouse.

Then, on Wednesday, July 21, 2010, in the *Wall Street Journal* an article entitled "Chinese Firms Snap Up Mining Assets" appears on page A11 of the World News section. They report that, in 2004, China accounted for 1 percent of all cross-border mergers and acquisitions in this industry, 7.4 percent in 2007, and a full one-third of all mergers and acquisitions in mining assets in 2009. In the last five years, they have completed deals in Canada, the United States, Brazil, Peru, the U.K., Guinea, Sierra Leone, South Africa, Zimbabwe, Mozambique, D.R. Congo, Turkey, Tajikistan, Russia, Mongolia, the Philippines, Indonesia, and Australia, and those are just the big ones. In July of 2010, the International Energy Agency also stated that China now accounts for the largest user of energy in the world, overtaking the United States. In 2009, China became the largest customer of Saudi Arabia. This growth is unprecedented. If you have been reading the *Wall Street Journal* regularly for the last five years, you would have read articles like this multiple times each week.

To continue this topic, in the May 15, 2010, weekend edition of the *Wall Street Journal*, China Investment Corporation (CIC, a state-owned enterprise) is said to enter into a joint venture with Penn West Energy Trust to develop oil-sands assets in northern Alberta Canada. This is just the latest in a series of moves that China has made in a major thrust to secure energy sources for the future. In the same paper, Nigeria and China signed an oil-refinery deal worth $23 billion. Under these terms, Nigeria's state oil company, Nigerian National Petroleum Corporation, along with a host of Chinese state-owned enterprises, would build three oil refineries with funding provided by China Export & Credit Insurance Corporation, another state-owned enterprise. Considering that the United States has not allowed construction of an oil refinery in this country for over 30 years, we need to consider that this is a major development and investors need to be aware of China and India's ongoing efforts to acquire natural resources; state-owned multinationals are the avenues to do this.

Lastly, to beat a dead horse, in the May 26, 2010, *Wall Street Journal*, we read that a California-based electric car company, CODA Automotive, plans on building a factory in Ohio to produce batteries using technology from Tianjin Lishen Battery of China. Anybody who believes that China's plans are just to continue manufacturing alone and not to enter the innovation arena has his head in a dark place. I would think the picture I am painting is becoming clear by now.

The Chinese banks themselves are also beginning their own growth strategies, outside of China. The Bank of China was the first Chinese bank to land in the United States in 1981 and has two branches in New York City. The Bank of Communications (of which HSBC owns a 19 percent stake), China Merchants Bank, Industrial & Commercial Bank of China (ICBC), and the China Construction Bank all have opened offices in Manhattan recently and are looking to make loans to U.S. multinationals like GE, to which ICBC lent $400 million over three years recently.[6] That these banks also have higher capital ratios than many developed world banks and much less exposure to toxic derivatives is well known. So China has become a creditor nation and the developed world is borrowing from these Asian-style lenders, perhaps to our own demise.

This will continue, but since these state-owned companies have no or few shareholders, have the backing of their government sanctioning these purchases, and are leaning on state-owned banks for financing, it is clear that Newmont Mining, Cliffs Natural Resources, Freeport-McMoRan, and Exxon, for starters, will have quite a challenge competing globally going forward. Moreover, Exxon can no longer "drill-baby-drill" wherever it wants to anymore, but if China National Offshore Oil Corporation (CNOOC) wants to drill in western China for instance, they will. The government will see to it with little or no environmental impact studies. In addition, the Chinese are forming tighter relationships with African governments that do not share Western multinationals' worry about human rights violations or environmental concerns.

A terrific "pro" example of this occurred during Exxon's May 26, 2010, annual meeting, where shareholders nominated the following proxy votes:

1. Special Shareholder Meetings (shareholders can call a meeting whenever they can get a quorum rather than wait for Exxon to host one).
2. Reincorporate in a shareholder-friendly state.
3. Shareholder advisory vote on executive compensation.
4. Amendment to the equal opportunity policy.
5. A new policy on water.
6. Wetlands restoration policy.
7. Report on environmental impact of oil sands.
8. Report on natural gas production: impact of fracturing on environment.
9. Report on energy technology concerning climate change and fossil fuel impact.
10. Greenhouse gas emissions goals.
11. Planning assumptions.

Would you think CNOOC has to deal with these kinds of shareholder-nominated proxies? Now, not commenting on the worth of these individual shareholder-promoted proxies, consider the amount of time and attention they require from management and their related costs. It is a huge disadvantage to be a Western multinational doing business globally compared to CNOOC and Sinopec's (SNP) responsibilities. These state-owned multinationals are not legacies of Communist central planning, either. They are very capitalistic and put profits first in their business activities, empowered and oftentimes aided by their government.

One common thread apparent every day in the media is emerging among Western-style developed economies, and that is their increasing loathing of natural-resource usage. This is demonstrated, not only by their increasing legislation to raise royalty taxes and banning offshore oil usage, for instance, but also by losing the political will to allow market forces to meet global demand in the energy sector. The real danger is that if the developed countries do not allow supply to meet demand through the use of Western multinational energy companies, China, Russia, and Brazil will. They will bridge the gap with other ideas, not necessarily free-market-based and not necessarily as environmentally conscious either, because they are willing to prioritize strategic concerns over economic returns and are open to dealing with pariah regimes. In addition, events like the BP oil spill in the Gulf of Mexico in April 2010 which drastically curtailed deep-water oil drilling for some time, as the Obama administration reacted irrationally to this situation. Unfortunately, when the United States discontinues using its own oil resources, the most likely benefactors are Russia, the Middle East, and

Venezuela, which are left to fill the void that nature abhors. Those candidate countries are the reasons U.S. politicians give for funding alternative energy methods to ease our energy dependence in the first place. And by closing down oil lease sites in the Gulf of Mexico or offshore of the Carolinas, we play right into Chavez's hands and actually put money in his pocket, which he then uses to destabilize the United States in Central America.

We should be asking the question: Is the planet better off with natural resources in the hands of publically traded and transparent companies, investing in free-market principles, subject to shareholder scrutiny, free of the risk of too much government interference? Or is it better off in the hands of multinationals run by foreign governments, opaque to their inner workings, less subject to profit motives (leading to higher investment because they do not need to maximize shareholder wealth and can accept lower return) and market forces, and beholden to national interests? For the foreseeable future, we believe that current political forces will continue to serve to cripple Western resource reserves while forcing much higher capital investment to maintain and build reserves, and that this will continue unabated. This will again serve to give ascendancy to the foreign multinationals versus their Western publically traded alternatives.

This all works to further support a very rapid gain in state-owned multinational companies' growth and resource reserves relative to their Western counterparts. Additionally, the Western multinationals have a legacy of union representation to deal with. For instance, GM had to halt automotive output at several U.S. plants because of a strike at Rico, an Indian firm that manufactures parts for GM. In France, railway strikes continue, as do British rail strikes. These Western-style unions are oftentimes joining hands across boundaries, too, but only within the developed countries. The U.K.'s Unite union, representing flight attendants, holds talks regularly with the Teamsters. The United Steelworkers held talks with Mexico's Cananea copper-mine-workers union. These confrontations between large Western-style multinationals and unions will continue to undermine their business proposition that their state-owned competitors do not have to deal with.

These interactions will involve more head-to-head competition between Western major companies and their state-owned competitors throughout the world. To maintain profitability, more and more trade will become regional. That is evident right now in Asia as countries such as Singapore, Malaysia, Indonesia, and the Philippines are trading more and more with China. This will work at first to circumvent the descendance of the Western multinationals as the state-dominated industries hand plays out, slowly at first. But their ascendancy is a given for the most part.

The United States, relative to Europe and Japan, is certainly still in a better position than most of the developed world for now. First, we can adapt more rapidly due to our economic structure. For example, our immigration policies combined with the modern networked economy means that there is a larger share of technical innovation being shared around the world from educated immigrants in the United States talking with their friends and family back home. This facilitates entrepreneurial activities, as a Chinese or Indian scientist will more likely refer interesting research and developments found here to his counterparts in those countries. Since modern technology allows cheap and reliable networking, ethnic similarities facilitate cross-border flows of information, and this is one reason why innovation is arising in the emerging markets at such a prodigious clip. A study of names on patents done by William Kerr at Harvard found that researchers cite American-based researchers of their own ethnicity 30 to 50 percent more often than expected from a random selection. This results in continued trade across borders to be more likely involving the United States than almost any other country, even if currently its impact is more import oriented. The fact that the United States is still responsible for the innovation does result in aiding our GDP.

However, we must be clear that the United States is losing competitiveness. In the latest world competitiveness report by IMD, a Lausanne, Switzerland, business school, the United States had dropped to third position from its usual and quite comfortable number-one position. Singapore has risen to the top, followed by Hong Kong; anyone traveling to those two city-states can smell the dynamics in the air! The bloc consisting of Asia, Africa, and India is growing trade among those countries at an astounding rate. For instance, 56 percent of China's exports were to emerging countries last year, whereas, just a couple of years ago, 80 percent went to the United States and Europe, though some of this is due to the developed world's pullback from the global crisis rather than increased trade with the emerging markets.

An article supporting the loss in United States competitiveness appeared in the Friday, July 2, 2010, the *Wall Street Journal*, which mentioned remarks GE's CEO Jeffrey Immelt made at a private dinner in Rome for Italian business leaders, expressing great dismay at links between the U.S. government's failure to support business and its additional failure to consider the growing disadvantage U.S. multinationals are having with exports. Moreover, he complained about China developing its own technology to compete with U.S. exporters, even expressing anger about Chinese "sucking" technology out of the West, again supporting the idea that the Chinese are becoming innovators rather than just maintaining their position as the lowest-cost provider.

Japan does not seem to have an economic plan. It has a government that cannot get out of its way and a declining population that is getting older, which will begin to overconsume their medical system in addition to having the world's highest debt to GDP ratio. The only thing going for them is their citizens own most of their debt, unlike the United States. Europe is suffering from way too much socialization that is crippling its ability to put funds toward economic development as its population ages and state pensions and medical care overconsume their federal budgets. Still, the United States has much too much debt owed to the world, and as we continue to avoid facing reality concerning these debts, our own growth has no choice but to remain stultified while Asia, minus Japan, plays catchup, and catch up they will. Brazil offers much hope for the Americas, provided it does not fall prey to the anti-capitalistic tirades of their northern neighbor Venezuela. With its massive resources in energy that have recently emerged, Brazil will be in a strong position to negotiate trade to their advantage. Their state-owned multinational company, Petrobras, is the exemplary enterprise of overt multinationalism south of the equator. It is unlikely that Brazil will subsume to Chavez's propaganda, given their GDP growth rate of 8.4 percent versus Venezuela's of –5.8 percent (first quarter 2010 annualized), for they seem to have an understanding of business needs, but it is difficult to be certain about the longer-term outcome.

Colombia is once again growing its oil production and will soon rival Mexico and Venezuela, now that the FARC has been reduced considerably. There's much reason to be quite optimistic about Colombia, Brazil, and Chile over the long term.

What will also serve to offer a sweet hand to the state-owned enterprises is the rise of the government unions in the developed countries. For instance, an article by Steven Malanga in the *Wall Street Journal* outlines the job Andy Stern did as the president of the Service Employees International Union and the politics involved in growing the union from 700,000 to 1,100,000 members. The article offers an example of their growing clout. He states:

> *The SEIU has also been successful at bringing employers in regulated industries into alliances that lobby government for bigger subsidies and better pay at taxpayer expense. In New York, for instance, SEIU Local 1199 made labor peace with hospitals in the late 1990s by proposing that together they begin pressuring the state for increased government aid. This powerful labor-management coalition won big gains in Albany, including some $3 billion in tobacco lawsuit settlement money that the state poured into health-care subsidies, and $2.7 billion that Albany gave the hospitals to provide raises for workers in a remarkable public subsidy for supposedly private employers and employees.*

What is important here is that the growing government unions will increasingly demand pay increases and pensions independent of national GDP growth (i.e., they will barter for it, even in the face of big recessions). Unlike their private enterprise counterparts, government unions can rely on taxation to endow themselves with lucrative retirement and health benefits, offering a drag on GDP for the developed world. This again will mean investing opportunities will increasingly lean offshore for the enterprising American investor, as the tax burden for these welfare-like retirement benefits are paid for by working Americans, increasing the debt load per capita.

To emphasize the impact, there are 23 million Americans on the dole for government pensions, both active and retired, and many of these are defined benefit pensions obtained from government union contracts. In contrast, the pension payers are the taxpayers, who themselves have less and less defined benefit pensions to look forward to as the ubiquitous 401(k) has taken over. School teachers, for instance, have the defined benefit pension and the 403(b) plan, which is their 401(k) equivalent except that it allows up to 20 percent of income contribution whereas a 401(k) usually is capped at a much lower percentage. In addition, the taxpayer had the equal insult of losing a large percentage of their savings in the market meltdown of 2008 (not to mention the tech bubble of 2000), whereas the defined-benefit union pensioner need not worry about such a travesty due to the promise in a pension of a guaranteed payout. Most public-pension employees also obtain between 75 and 90 percent of their last 5 years' average wages in their pension benefit, along with lucrative health benefits. This, of course, does not consider the spiking of pay by working a lot of overtime in the last years of work, just before retirement.

Unfortunately for the taxpayer, many states are also underfunded. Eight states in particular lack funding greater than a third of liabilities. Thirteen others are less than 80 percent funded. In the current economic climate, this seriously means that it requires bravery to invest in Munis. PIMCO in particular has been underweighting Muni investments in 2010 and fears default solely due to pension underfunding. While we witness the "almost" sovereign default of Greece, one worries whether Illinois, California, New Jersey, Rhode Island, and Massachusetts are also in an equally bad situation.[7] It is evident that in the developed world, there is a challenge for GDP growth that just is not there for the emerging markets.

It is not a coincidence that, of the $787 billion spent in the 2009 stimulus program in the United States, $275 billion went as direct grants to the states to support public-sector employees in healthcare and education. Government was originally designed by the framers of the U.S. Constitution to serve the people, and today, the proletariat exists to support the government because in a typical work week, we do not start making money for ourselves until Wednesday morning! Trying to shrink government after it has bloomed is very much like trying to put the rose back into its petal. Unfortunately, the public-sector unions have a ruinously strong collaboration with Congress, meaning that the rose also has a rusty umbrella skeleton as well, so let's not get too optimistic about budget cuts having much to do with pension and welfare benefit reductions if there is any cutting to occur at all due to this cozy relationship.

As for Greece, Ed Yardeni says it best.[8]

> *They've had a wild party, and paid for it with credit. Public wages and pension payments absorb half of the Greek national budget. The government doesn't know exactly how many people are in the civil service, and is only now undertaking a census. Estimates have been as high as one-third of the Greeks are public employees, who are guaranteed these jobs for life by the national constitution! During the last decade, their pay doubled. They get bonuses of an extra two months' pay annually just for showing up, or not, as the case may be. Obviously, the Bond Vigilantes weren't very vigilant while all this was happening, so now the Bond Gods have shut out the Greeks from the capital markets. We are clearly witnessing the collapse of a small social welfare state. Greece's taxpayers resisted paying for the spending excesses of the national government. Of course, Greece does have a VAT, which was increased by 2 percentage points to 21 percent on March 5 by Parliament as part of an austerity program that would also cut public sector salary bonuses by 30 percent; increase taxes on fuel, tobacco and alcohol; and freeze state-funded pensions in 2010. Yesterday, the country was shut down by a third national strike since these measures were announced. The Bond Gods are not buying the Greek austerity program, nor is the EU-IMF rescue plan that requires it. Over at Pimco, Mohamed El-Erian, chief executive of the bond-investment giant, declared that the recent deal to rescue Greece won't work. His firm is clearly still anticipating a contagion effect. In his recently released May Investment Outlook PIMCO's Bill Gross slammed the credit rating agencies and observed: "S&P just this past week downgraded Spain "one notch" to AA from AA+, cautioning that they could face another downgrade if they weren't careful". Oooh—so tough! And believe it or not, Moody's and Fitch still have them as AAAs. Here's a country with 20 percent unemployment, a recent current account deficit of 10 percent, that has defaulted 13 times in the past two centuries, whose bonds are already trading at Baa levels, and whose fate is increasingly dependent on the kindness of the EU and IMF to bail them out. Some AAA!*

What is striking about Ed's comments is that maybe Portugal, Ireland, or Spain is next? It could be the United States someday if we don't restrain our spending. This is the contagion that PIMCO was expecting. This is symptomatic of European welfare states, though it is at the extreme end. Nevertheless, it shines a spotlight on why the developed world will walk around in the doldrums for a while, even if our greatest fears aren't fully realized; the gross debt, increased regulation, and huge unfunded liabilities of social security and welfare programs do not promote growth.

## THE EMERGED MARKETS

It is time we clarify the nomenclature of emerging markets a bit. The name *emerging markets* was coined by MSCI-Barra, which began the Emerging Market index. There are 22 countries that make up this index consisting of: Brazil, Chile, China, Colombia, Czech Republic, Egypt, Hungary, India, Indonesia, Israel, Korea, Malaysia, Mexico, Morocco, Peru, Philippines, Poland, Russia, South Africa, Taiwan, Thailand, and Turkey. Of these, Israel was promoted out of the Emerging Market index to the EAFE index on May 27, 2010, and it is rumored that Korea will soon be promoted to the EAFE index, too, an international developed country index, leaving us with 20 emerging-market countries. At this time we should consider that, when China's current account balance is larger than Germany's and Japan's, it no longer could be called an emerging market. For instance, the United States makes up 24.6 percent of global GDP, Japan 8.75 percent, China 8.47 percent (thus, the U.S. economy is 3 times that of China, as said earlier), Germany 5.79 percent, France 4.62 percent, UK 3.77 percent, Italy 3.66 percent, and Brazil 2.72 percent. These are followed directly by Spain, Canada, then India, Russia, Australia, Mexico, and finally S. Korea.[9] Thus, the BRIC countries (Brazil, Russia, India, China) and Korea fall within the top 12 countries sorted by GDP in the world! That's quite an accomplishment for what just 10 years ago were countries thought of as Third World. They are no longer emerging. They have *emerged!*

That is a very important distinction that most investors, especially U.S. investors, are missing. Oddly enough, supporting evidence of the growth of Asia involves Hong Kong's growth in demand for luxury goods. For instance, Hong Kong recently surpassed the United States in the secondary wine auction market. According to the May 2010 issue of *Wine Spectator*, in the first quarter 2010, total sales of the HK auction houses was $28,501,810 whereas in the U.S. auction houses it was $24,343,625. Though these are small numbers when compared to total trade volume, the wine auction market is entirely indicative of exuberant wealth. High-end wine is sold only to those with money to burn, and Bordeaux Grand Crus are the majority of sales in the wine auction markets. In addition, China now is Bordeaux's biggest overseas market by volume of wine, where Bordeaux's shipping increased a whopping 97 percent from last year on volume alone, though Bordeaux's overall worldwide demand has slowed. The data lead us to change nomenclature; we will call them EdM from now on, which stands for EmergED Markets. So, please, Mr. and Ms. prudent enterprising investor, take notice, you heard it first here! For the 22 countries in the Emerging Market index (the ETF ticker is: EEM), only Colombia, Egypt, Indonesia, Mexico, Morocco, and Peru would fit the original definition of emerging anymore, for the other 16 or so countries have arrived.

The global credit crisis that started in 2007, and appears to be wrapping up in 2010, highlights a substantial change in the history of the world. These EdM countries displayed enormous resilience during this crisis and barely had their GDP growth affected. In addition, those countries that were most affected (the developed world) and fell the farthest have not recovered as well, unlike past recessions where those that fell the farthest rebounded the most. This demonstrates an unusual change in the world order. Since these EdM countries run a surplus in trade and have newly furnished reserves due to this trade in the last decade, mostly held in U.S. dollars, they also played a vital role in attempting to rescue our banking system by direct infusion of capital into Merrill Lynch, UBS, Citigroup, and Morgan Stanley. They are the future of the world. The next economic dynasty will arise from them as the United States and Europe degrade. The Western reader should not be morose because we should not be so arrogant. It is their turn. In history, seldom has any country, nation, or race maintained hegemony for more than 200 years. It is inevitable that economic power shifts around the planet. We would be smart to ready ourselves for this truth.

## THE FUTURE QUANT

The point that quantitative methods have evolved from offers little guidance to where they are going. However, what we see as unstoppable trends involves the inclusion of data in more and more electronic media and the ramifications that has going forward. For instance, in 1975, much of the information Peter Lynch was reading was in paper form. He would spend his days reading written publications of other research analysts (those he esteemed), but more importantly from companies he had interest in—annual reports, 10-K's, 10-Q's, and their ilk. Most of the information about stocks and investing were just a step above the old ticker-tape information of stock trades. In addition, as a fundamental analyst, he would visit companies, walk around shopping malls, and enter stores. All the while he was gauging the business sense the firms have, gauging the salability of their products, and also examining their financial ratios, metrics, and valuations, asking: Is the customer base for this firm growing? Is there demand for their products? He was clearly ascertaining the risk and reward ratio of a firm in his own mind but having one common denomimator in all those activities—time. The rate-determining step in obtaining investment ideas in those days was the amount of time it took to perform the detailed analysis. This is a bottleneck that quantitative methods, with their superior information "sifting and sniffing" ways, offer as an advantage over conventional techniques. This is the reason the term "surfing the 'net" arose, because of the speed with which we can obtain the high-level perspective on today's information highways.

As we said at the beginning of the book, the rise of the central processing unit implemented in the desktop PC has revolutionized obtaining information. Although that revolution changed the office environment forever, the continued digitization of financial-statement data to the torrent it is these days will sustain and facilitate information management in the decision-making process at an ever-faster pace. It was not necessarily new techniques that enabled the quant to sift through financial data faster than conventional means, because most of the numerical methods were and are well known from many fields in math, physics, engineering, and statistics from decades ago. It was just the availability to use these methods in an iterative fashion to fetch data and process it that sped the process. The PC made today's quant a possibility. Before the PC, to do company valuation, the archiving and data collection were a large part of the overall time required to do the analysis. Today, we can obtain detailed valuation metrics from canned algorithms on 5,000 securities almost instantaneously through vendors such as FactSet.

What we foresee having impact on quant involves the ability to offer statistical logic, accuracy, and precision on categorical data. This will be the next step in processing of investment information. To date, the decisions in quant on what to buy or sell and the timing of those trades relies heavily, if not entirely, on numerical data, their relationships, associations, and applications in decision-treelike structures. However, with the digitizing of words and the ability of search engines like Google, Bing, and Yahoo!, for instance, we can categorize, count, show association, and reveal hidden patterns in contextual information.

For instance, one application involves interpreting the associations of polling information. In 2000 I had the opportunity to work with a mathematican named Robert Wood while I was employed by an asset manager. He and his brother had created a linguistic textual identifier software that could find relationships between polling outcomes. For instance, a poll of 10 questions about purchasing habits at a grocery store would identify whether, if you bought milk, you also bought cereal. If you bought fish on a Friday, were you Catholic? The poll data, from a large sample, would then be accessed via their program and methodology to find the percentages of time one variable or polling outcome was linked in some fashion to another. In this way, the associations between the categorical and textual information were easily identified. I was so taken with this that I programmed a random number generation scheme in Fortran to generate 10,000 polls of 10 questions each with pre-identified correlations between the textual responses. As a test, this was put to their program, unknown to the programmers, and within 10 minutes of CPU time on a PC back then (~1998), the correct and exact correlations were identified.

A perfect operating example of this involves a company called Ravenpack. They turn news information about companies into quantitative metrics that quants can program into their models. Essentially, they form qualitative sentiment indicators about companies, using the "tags" that are associated with news stories from Reuters, Dow Jones, and other newswires. From these tags, they then discover the hidden relationships between the words and form a master equation from these relationships that create the sentiment indicator. This is cutting edge behavioral finance in action.

These kinds of information systems are probably utilized in large hedge funds like Jim Simons's Renaissance Technologies, Ray Dalio's Bridgewater Associates, D.E. Shaw and Ken Griffin's Citadel, but since they seldom publish or give talks at conferences, we do not know for sure. Nevertheless, even a simple search for how many times the word *risk* appears in a company's annual report, then forming sorts of stock returns based on the word count, results in abnormal returns. This kind of methodology—not simple word searches but textual relationships within financial information—is the next frontier in quantitative finance applications. This is all with respect to the type 2 quant.

Innovations in financial engineering that apply to other quants in the derivatives markets and trading involve more complex topics, mostly not for consideration in this treatise, simply because we have little expertise to offer. However, most likely, the trading environment will be legislated a bit more fairly. Right now there is clearly too much front running with dark pools, false trades, and the ability of some investors to locate computers nearer and nearer to the source of trading so that they can obtain a sneak preview of the order flow before anyone else. The clarity of this illegal front-running technique will lead to an arbitrage, either through normal market channels or through legislation. The egregiousness of it has to do with the concept of stale pricing. Imagine how much money you as an investor could make if you saw all of tomorrow's prices for every stock today, and you could align your orders knowing in advance what tomorrow's prices were going to be!? This is essentially what flash traders are doing. They get a first look at all the prices, before everybody else sees them, and they can align all their orders ahead of time. They just do it with computers so it is very fast, but that, in effect, is what is happening. Is that crazy or what? It should not be legal and ultimately, it will not be.

For the innovation of the derivatives markets it is really a much harder call. The demand for derivatives is huge—much larger than the stock market and bond market combined. The notional value of swap agreements is 70 percent or more of the derivatives market and is trillions of dollars globally, though swaps are pretty plain and boring. They just allow investors and companies to trade fixed liabilities with floating liabilities or vice versa, for the most part. Options on everything that trades will continue, and probably the liquidity of these will increase as the volume of trading goes up as the world and markets globalize. Though the derivatives markets due to the role of credit default swaps (CDS) in the credit crises may slow a bit, it will rebound and continue its growth unabated. Companies really do need the derivatives market to offload and spread risk. Understand that a derivative is a high-level term but any instrument whose value is dependent on some other trading instrument is a derivative. In simple terms, an index is a derivative, as are stock options. There are stock options, bond options, options on currencies, futures, commodities, and even options on options. Options themselves have a half dozen varieties, too, and the overlaying of options in various trading strategies frequently involves complicated buying and selling of many different strikes and expirations of more than a few at any one time. The growth of these instruments will continue unabated and even flourish.

As we move further into the twenty-first century, the feet leading the global economies charge will change. The United States will slowly lose its efficaciousness in influencing the world. That influence will shift eastward. The Chinese first, followed by the Indians 10 to 20 years behind, will take up the banner and baton and the two of them will have major influence, followed by countries like Australia, Canada, and Brazil simply because they're the importers to these engines of growth. Quantitative asset management will move to take a leadership role as the ever-abundant demands of securitization and risk spreading will pervade innovation in securities markets. In applying the Graham methods to the emerged markets, therefore, the importance of paying attention to valuation is abundantly clear. There has been much money chasing those eastern flags, and the intelligent investor must be careful in applying Graham's wisdom to these foreign domiciled businesses.

In conclusion, if I was 16 today, I would plan on studying Chinese, physics, and statistics. In college I would take plenty of economics and programming courses, but my major would be physics. I would not study business. You do not learn how to think critically enough in business school. I would read the *Wall Street Journal* regularly, read all of Graham's writings twice, while attending graduate school in physics, emphasizing statistical mechanics and quantum mechanics just to learn the computational tools. I would learn how to model a variety of problems, with an eye toward error estimation in all I do. Then, I would graduate and move to Shanghai for a few years, taking a job with a global asset manager, first on the risk side, then later move to the buy side. The rest of my days would involve answering the question, "Where do I invest, how much, and what's the risk?"

As for the budding quant, Google knows now and will continue to grow in its knowledge on the subject. Be quick to learn how to teach yourself from the Internet. You do not need a formal academic education on a topic to gain expertise. Just immerse yourself in reading the subject and jump in with both feet. Never put a toe in the water, always jump in with both feet. But first and foremost, gain the mathematical tools required to delve deeply into quantitative methods you do not understand. I always told my daughter, if you can do math and read, you can do anything, as everything else comes from these two skills.

# Notes

## Preface

1. Isaac Newton, "Author's Preface to the Reader," in *The Principia* (Cambridge, UK: Trinity College, May 8, 1686).
2. Fischer Black & Myron Scholes, "The Pricing of Options and Corporate Liabilities," *Journal of Political Economy* 81, no. 3 (1973): 637–654.
3. Graham, Ben with Jason Zweig, "The Intelligent Investor Revised Edition," HarperBusiness Essentials (New York: HarperCollins, 2003).

## Introduction: The Birth of Quant

1. For a general historical review of the DOS Operating System, see Rodnay Zaks, *Programming the Z80* (New York: Sybex Inc., 1981).
2. Richard R. Lindsey and Barry Schacter, *How I Became a Quant* (Hoboken, NJ: John Wiley & Sons, 2007). Selected chapter authors came into the quant business around that time.
3. Harry M. Markowitz, "Portfolio Selection," *Journal of Finance* 7, no. 1 (1952): 77–91.
4. William F. Sharpe, "A Simplified Model for Portfolio Analysis," *Management Science* 9, no. 2 (January 1963): 277–293; and William F. Sharpe, "Capital Asset Prices: A Theory of Market Equilibrium under Conditions of Risk," *Journal of Finance* 19, no. 3 (September 1964): 425–442.
5. Ibid.
6. Eugene F. Fama and Kenneth R. French, "The Cross-Section of Expected Stock Returns," *Journal of Finance* 47 (June 1992): 427–465; Eugene F. Fama and Kenneth R. French, "Common Risk Factors in the Returns on Stocks and Bonds," *Journal of Financial Economics* 33, no. 1 (1993): 3–56.
7. Graham, Ben with Jason Zweig, "The Intelligent Investor Revised Edition," HarperBusiness Essentials (New York: HarperCollins, 2003).
8. Frank J. Fabozzi, Sergio M. Focardi, and Caroline Jonas, *Challenges in Quant Equity Management* (Washington, DC: Research Foundation of CFA Press, 2008).
9. Rishi K. Narang, *Inside the Black Box* (Hoboken, NJ: John Wiley & Sons, 2009).
10. Emanuel Derman, *My Life as a Quant* (Hoboken, NJ: John Wiley & Sons, 2004).

11. Soft dollars arise from trading commissions paid to a broker/dealer. The B/D accrues them over time by adding a small surcharge to each trade, thereby collecting monies that can later be used to purchase third-party research.
12. See "S&P U.S. Indexes Methodology," downloadable from www.standardandpoors.com.
13. W. DeBondt and R. Thaler, "Does the Stock Market Overreact?" *Journal of Finance* Vol XL, no. 3 (July 1985): 793–807; N. Jegadeesh and S. Titman, "Profitability of Momentum Strategies: An Evaluation of Alternative Explanations," *Journal of Finance* 54 (2001): 699–720; Harrison Hong, Terence Lim, and Jeremy C. Stein, "Bad News Travels Slowly: Size, Analyst Coverage, and the Profitability of Momentum Strategies," *Journal of Finance* 55 (Feb. 1, 2000): 265–295.
14. Janet Lowe, *The Rediscovered Benjamin Graham* (New York: John Wiley & Sons, 1999), 77.
15. Mohamed El-Erian, *When Markets Collide* (New York: McGraw-Hill, 2008), 73.
16. Steve Forbes, "Grantham's Big Call," Intelligent Investing Transcript of interview; *Forbes Magazine*, March 2009.

## CHAPTER 1 Desperately Seeking Alpha

1. Isaac Newton, "The Comets Are Higher than the Moon and Move in the Planetary Regions," in *The Principia* (3rd ed.), Book 3, Proposition 40, Lemma 4, Corollary 3, 1726.
2. Mike Dash, *Tulipomania* (New York: Three Rivers Press, 1999).
3. Fidelity Magellan Fund, "Principle Investment Strategies," Prospectus, May 29, 2010.
4. Excerpt from *Forbes Magazine*, June 1, 1932.

## CHAPTER 2 Risky Business

1. J. C. Maxwell, "Ether," *Encyclopedia Britannica* (9th ed.), vol 8, 1878.
2. Harry Markowitz, "Portfolio Selection," *Journal of Finance* 7, no. 1 (1952): 77–91.
3. Nassim Taleb, *The Black Swan* (New York: Random House, 2007).
4. VIX is the ticker symbol for the Chicago Board Options Exchange Volatility Index, a measure of the implied volatility of S&P 500 index options. A high value corresponds to an expected more volatile market and a low value corresponds to lower expected volatility of the S&P 500 over the next 30 days. It is often referred to as the fear index.
5. Assuming S&P 500 BarraValue and BarraGrowth are proxies for market value and growth portfolios in general.
6. Nassim Taleb, *The Black Swan* (New York: Random House, 2007).
7. Ben Graham with Jason Zweig, "The Intelligent Investor Revised Edition," HarperBusiness Essentials (New York, HarperCollins: 2003).

8. Isaac Newton, *The Principia; Mathematical Principles of Natural Philosophy*, trans. by I. Bernard Cohen and Anne Whitman (Berkeley: University of California Press, 1999).
9. Abraham Pais, *Subtle Is the Lord: The Science and View of Life of Albert Einstein* (Oxford: Oxford University Press, 2005).
10. S. T. Rachev and F. J. Fabozzi, *Fat-Tailed and Skewed Asset Return Distributions: Implications for Risk Management, Portfolio Selection, and Option Pricing* (Hoboken, NJ: John Wiley & Sons, 2005). Also Y. S. Kim, S. T. Rachev, M. L. Bianchi, and F. F. Fabozzi, "Financial Market Models with Lévy Processes and Time-Varying Volatility," *Journal of Banking & Finance* 32 (2008): 1363–1378.
11. Ben Graham, *The Commercial and Financial Chronicle*, Feb. 1, 1962.
12. W. DeBondt and R. Thaler, "Does the Stock Market Overreact?" *Jour. of Finance*, Vol XL, No. 3. July 1985; Jegadeesh, N., and Titman, S., 2001, "Profitability of momentum Strategies: An Evaluation of Alternative Explanations," *Jour. of Finance*, 54, pp. 699–720; Harrison Hong, Terence Lim, and Jeremy C. Stein, "Bad News Travels Slowly: Size, Analyst Coverage, and the Profitability of Momentum Strategies," *Jour. of Finance*, 2000, Vol 55, Feb. 1, 265–295.
13. Standard & Poor's Global Industry Classification Standard Report 2006.
14. U.S. Patent 7711617; A system and method for providing optimization of a financial portfolio using a parametric leptokurtic distribution; Rachev and Fabozzi, ibid.

## CHAPTER 3 Beta Is Not "Sharpe" Enough

1. Albert Einstein, *Emanuel Libman Anniversary Volumes*, vol. 1 (New York: International, 1932): 363.
2. Excerpt from *Barron's*, Sept. 23, 1974, Dow Jones and Company.
3. Benoit B. Mandlebrot, *Fractals and Scaling in Finance* (New York: Springer, 1997); and Edgar E. Peters, *Fractal Market Analysis* (New York: John Wiley & Sons, 1994).
4. Robert R. Trippi, ed., *Chaos & Nonlinear Dynamics in the Financial Markets* (New York: Irwin, 1995).
5. J. P. Morgan, *Risk Metrics Technical Document* (New York: Morgan Guarantee Trust Company, Risk Management Advisory, 1999).
6. Nassim Taleb, *Dynamic Hedging, Managing Vanilla and Exotic Options* (New York: John Wiley & Sons, 1997).
7. R. Douglas Martin, Director of Computational Finance University of Washington Seattle, and Stoyan Stoyanov, Head Quantitative Resarcher at FinAnalytica; private conversations and presentations at Seattle GARP Meeting December 8, 2009.
8. R. Gnanadesikan and M. B. Wilk, "Probability Plotting Methods for the Analysis of Data," *Biometrika* 55, no. 1 (1968): 1–17.
9. William H. Press, Brian P. Flannery, Saul A. Teukolsky, and William T. Vetterling, *Numerical Recipes* (New York: Cambridge University Press, 1987).

10. J. E. Freund and R. E. Walpole, *Mathematical Statistics* (Englewood Cliffs, NJ: Prentice Hall, 1980).
11. Start by setting BetaY = BetaZ so that COV(S&P,Y)/V(S&P) = COV(S&P,Z)/V(S&P) then use the equality V(X1+X2) = V(X1)+V(X2)+2COV(X1,X2) to expand out the terms.
12. Years ago I submitted a paper to a finance journal outlining how similar a Frechet distribution was to some fund returns only to have a referee declare: "I hope the author is not trying to show that the Frechet distribution is an alternative of choice for describing stock returns." This speaks to traditional academic arrogance and again reminds us that old paradigms are hard to break.
13. R. Gnanadesikan and M. B. Wilk, ibid. (1968).

## CHAPTER 4 Mr. Graham, I Give You Intelligence

1. Isaac Newton, *The Principia; Mathematical Principles of Natural* Philosophy, General Scholium; 1687, trans. by I. Bernard Cohen and Anne Whitman (Berkeley: University of California Press, 1999).
2. Benjamin Franklin quote.
3. Scott Patterson, *The Quants: How a New Breed of Math Whizzes Conquered Wall Street and Nearly Destroyed It* (New York: Crown Publishing Group, 2010).
4. Eugene F. Fama and Kenneth R. French, "The Cross-Section of Expected Stock Returns", *Journal of Finance* 47 (June), 427–465, 1992; Eugene F. Fama and Kenneth R. French. (1993). "Common Risk Factors in the Returns on Stocks and Bonds". *Journal of Financial Economics* 33 (1): 356.
5. Andrew Bary, "Loosen Up, Tightwads!" *Barron's,* Feb. 1, 2010.
6. Robert D. Arnott and Clifford S. Asness, "Surprise! Higher Dividends Equal Higher Earnings Growth," *Financial Analysts Journal* (Jan/Feb 2003): 70–87.
7. Benjamin Graham and David Dodd, *Security Analysis* (6th ed.) (New York: McGraw-Hill, 2009), Chapter 42.
8. Net asset value, book value, balance-sheet value, and tangible asset value are all synonyms for net worth, which is the total assets minus intangibles, minus all liabilities (from the quarterly or annual balance sheet) divided by outstanding number of shares
9. Mark Grinblatt, Sheridan Titman, and Russ Wermers, "Momentum Investment Strategies, Portfolio Performance, and Herding: A Study of Mutual Fund Behavior," *The American Economic Review* 85 no. 5 (Dec. 1995).
10. My young daughter and I were having a conversation about an issue neither of us knew much about, and suddenly she exclaimed, "Google knows, Dad, why don't you ask it?" So, be forewarned, to the next generation Google has all knowledge.
11. Joseph Chen and Harrison Hong, "Discussion of Momentum and Auto-Correlation Between Stocks," *The Review of Financial Studies Special* 15, no. 2 (2002): 566–573.

12. Joseph Mezrich, "Trends in Quant," Research Report; Nomura Global Equity Research, Feb. 3, 2010.
13. The SEC adopted new rules to address three issues: (1) the selective disclosure by issuers of material nonpublic information; (2) when insider trading liability arises in connection with a trader's use or knowing possession of material nonpublic information; (3) when the breach of a family or other nonbusiness relationship may give rise to liability under the misappropriation theory of insider trading. The rules are designed to promote the full and fair disclosure of information by issuers and to clarify and enhance existing prohibitions against insider trading.
14. Tibco Spotfire S+ is the newest incarnation of an old software favorite of mine, S+Plus.
15. Andrew Ang, Robert J. Hodrick, Yuhang Xing, and Xiaoyan Zhang, "The Cross-Section of Volatility and Expected Returns," *Journal of Finance* 61, no. 1 (2006): 259–299; F. M. Bandi and J. R. Russell, "Separating Microstructure Noise from Volatility," *JEL,* Feb 19, 2004; Andrew Ang, Joseph S. Chen and Yuhang Xing, "Downside Correlation and Expected Stock Returns," *JEL,* March 12, 2002.
16. Abraham Pais, *Subtle Is the Lord: The Science and View of Life of Albert Einstein* (Oxford: Oxford University Press, 2005).

## CHAPTER 5 Modeling Pitfalls and Perils

1. Ogawa, T. "Japanese Evidence for Einstein's Knowledge of the Michelson-Morley Experiment," *Japan. Stud. Hist. Sci.,* 18 (1979): 73–81.
2. Jeffrey A. Busse, "Volatility Timing in Mutual Funds: Evidence from Daily Returns," *The Review of Financial Studies,* Winter 1999, 12, no. 5: 1009–1041.
3. State Street Global Markets research report, "Regime Map," December 12, 2006.
4. Atsushi Inoue and Lutz Kilian, "In-Sample or Out-of-Sample Tests of Predictability: Which One Should We Use?" *European Central Bank Working Paper Series* 195, November 2002.
5. David E. Rapach and Mark E. Wohar, "In-Sample vs. Out-of-Sample Tests of Stock Return Predictability in the Context of Data Mining," *JEL,* February 2004.
6. Robert Freeman and Adam Koch, "Can Firm-Specific Models Predict Price Responses to Earnings News?" *JEL,* February 2006.
7. Richard Tortoriello, *Quantitative Strategies for Achieving Alpha* (New York: McGraw-Hill, 2009).
8. Richard P. Feynman, *Personal Observations on the Reliability of the Shuttle* (New York: Norton, 1988).
9. Net debt = long term debt + short term debt − cash (and cash equivalents); Enterprise value = market capitalization + total debt + minority interest + preferred stock − cash (and cash equivalents).

10. Amir E. Khandani and Andrew W. Lo, "What Happened to the Quants in August 2007? Evidence from Factors and Transactions Data," *NBER Working Paper* 14465, Nov. 2008.
11. Graham, Ben with Jason Zweig, "The Intelligent Investor Revised Edition," HarperBusiness Essentials (New York, HarperCollins, 2003).

## CHAPTER 6 Testing the Graham Crackers . . . er, Factors

1. Roger Cotes, Editor's Preface to the Second Edition of *The Principia* (Cambridge, May 12, 1713).
2. Richard Tortoriello, *Quantitative Strategies for Achieving Alpha* (New York: McGraw-Hill, 2009).

## CHAPTER 7 Building Models from Factors

1. Scott A. Richardson, Richard G. Sloan, Mark T. Soliman, and Irem Tune, "Information in Accruals about the Quality of Earnings," University of Michigan, Ann Arbor, MI, and Chicago Quantitative Alliance conference proceedings, Las Vegas, April 2010.
2. Richard Tortoriello, *Quantitative Strategies for Achieving Alpha* (New York: McGraw-Hill, 2009).
3. Scott Patterson, *The Quants: How a New Breed of Math Whizzes Conquered Wall Street and Nearly Destroyed It* (New York: Crown Business, 2010).

## CHAPTER 8 Building Portfolios from Models

1. Isaac Newton, last paragraph of the General Scholium, *The Principia* (2nd ed.), 1713.
2. Rafael Aguayo, *Dr. Deming: The American Who Taught the Japanese about Quality* (New York: Simon & Schuster, 1990).
3. Kelly criterion used for judging the size of bets in gambling; J. L. Kelly, Jr. "A New Interpretation of Information Rate," *Bell System Technical Journal* 35 (1956): 917–926.

## CHAPTER 9 Barguments: The Antidementia Bacterium

1. Albert Einstein, *Nature* 119 (1927): 467; and *Science* 65 (1927): 347.
2. Gary P. Brinson, L. Randolph Hood, and Gilbert L. Beebower, "Determinants of Portfolio Performance," *The Financial Analysts Journal* (July/August 1986); Gary P. Brinson, Brian D. Singer, and Gilbert L. Beebower, "Determinants of

Portfolio Performance II: An Update," *The Financial Analysts Journal* 47, no. 3 (1991).

3. "Dyed in the wool" was borrowed from seventeenth-century England where it meant that black wool coming from black sheep was of higher quality than white wool from white sheep being dyed black. Eventually this phrase came to mean one was born into one's beliefs as the black wool is born into its color.
4. Markov chains and other special concepts do exist to model them, but they are proxies of real random systems and model white noise more readily than true random systems with jumps and infinite variance.
5. In actuality, dart throwing is indeed given by Newton's second law and is deterministic; however, the human element disallows reproducing the same initial conditions for each and every throw so the analogy works, though it is not really a chaotic phenomenon.
6. Robert R Trippi, *Chaos and Nonlinear Dynamics in the Financial Markets; Theory, Evidence and Applications* (New York: McGraw-Hill, 1995).
7. Ibid.
8. Ibid.
9. Arbitrage pricing theory (APT), in finance, is a general theory of asset pricing and holds that the expected return of a stock can be modeled as a linear factor of various economic factors where sensitivity to changes in each factor is represented by a beta coefficient. The factors are economic, however, not financial-statement data as in Ben Graham's model.
10. George Soros, "The Crash of 2008 and What It Means," *Public Affairs* 2008.
11. Dr. Fernholz received his PhD in Mathematics from Columbia and has held various academic positions in Mathematics and Statistics at Princeton University, City University of New York, Universidad de Buenos Aires, and the University of Washington; and Robert Fernolz and Ioannis Karatzas, "Stochastic Portfolio Theory: An Overview," in *Handbook of Numerical Analysis,* vol. XV; and P. G. Ciarlet, ed., *Mathematical Modeling and Numerical Methods in Finance* (New York: Elsevier, 2009).
12. Benoit B. Mandelbrot, *Fractals and Scaling in Finance* (New York: Springer, 1997).
13. Known as the "Merton Model"; Robert C. Merton, "On the Pricing of Corporate Debt: The Risk Structure of Interest Rates," *Journal of Finance* 29(2) (May 1974).
14. We use the "coin flip" paradigm simply because we model stock prices as Markov or random walk processes here, whereas, in reality, the outcomes are not random, especially if the stock is heavily mispriced, but it serves our purpose for a teaching moment.
15. Robert Fernholz, *Stochastic Portfolio Theory* (New York: Springer-Verlag, 2002).
16. Andrew Ang, Robert Hodrick, Yuhang Xing, and Xiaoyan Zhang, "The Cross-Section of Volatility and Expected Returns," *Journal of Finance* LXI, no. 1 (February 2006).
17. Edward O. Thorp, *Beat the Dealer* (New York: Vintage Books, 1966); *Beat the Market* is out of print by the same author and Sheen T. Kassouf.

## CHAPTER 10 Past and Future View

1. Isaac Newton, *Opticks,* Query 1; 1704.
2. Abraham Pais, *Subtle Is the Lord: The Science and View of Life of Albert Einstein*, foreword by Sir Roger Penrose (Oxford: Oxford University Press, 2005): 304–305.
3. Didier Sornette, *Why Stock Markets Crash: Critical Events in Complex Financial Systems* (Princeton: Princeton University Press, 2003).
4. Laurence B. Siegel, ed., "Insights into the Global Financial Crisis," (Washington, DC: Research Foundation of CFA Institute, 2009).
5. *Wall Street Journal.* May 11, 2010, Letter to the Editor.
6. *Wall Street Journal*, June 2, 2010.
7. *Barron's*, "The $2 Trillion Hole," March 15, 2010.
8. Ed Yardeni, Client Letter, May 6, 2010.
9. IMF World Economic Outlook Database, April 2010.

# Acknowledgments

From the day we are born to the day we die, we come across many people in our lives. However, few memories of them stick with us, and even fewer come to our minds often and spontaneously. Those that do are the major influencers of who we are and what we accomplish. For these reasons, I first acknowledge my parents, John and Patricia Greiner, who always told me, "You can do whatever you want in life." It is to my wife, Veronica Bridgewaters, to whom I owe large recognition because she galvanized my determination, time and time again, and held my hand when I was swearing at the keyboard. Additionally, an adumbrated motivation kept me vigilant in my writings, and that was to leave my sweet "Nessy" a small summary of what the world came from and what it is coming to.

FactSet Research Systems made their software available to me, and most of the analysis in this book would not have been possible without the assistance of their Alpha Testing and Portfolio Analysis software. A special thanks to Richard Barrett of FactSet for his continual support and friendship. I also owe a debt to Meg Freeborn and Bill Falloon of John Wiley & Sons, who encouraged and helped me through my shortcomings in composition.

Lastly, I cannot say enough about my five older (and wiser) siblings. They have formed me more than they know, and I love them all soundly.

STEVEN P. GREINER
*Chicago, September 2010*

# About the Author

**Steven P. Greiner** was the senior quantitative strategist and portfolio manager for Allegiant Asset Management (now wholly owned by PNC Capital Advisors) where he was a member of its Investment Committee. Prior to this, he served as senior quantitative strategist for large capitalization investments at Harris Investment Management. He has over 20 years of quantitative and modeling experience beginning in the sciences, industry, and finance. Currently Greiner is the head of Risk Research for FactSet Research Systems. Greiner received his BS in mathematics and chemistry from the University of Buffalo and his MS and PhD in physical chemistry from the University of Rochester, and attained postdoctoral experience from the Free University Berlin, Department of Physics.

# Index